CW00922652

'Blind tasting is a very odd activity. C[ontrary to]
what many presuppose, it has nothing [to do with]
blindfolds. It involves tasting a wine with[out seeing]
the label and it can deliver shocking results ...'
— *Jancis Robinson MW*

Thursday February 21st 2013

The 60th Oxford & Cambridge Blind Wine-Tasting Competition

The Wines

Whites:

1. Vouvray, Clos de Bourg, Sec, Gaston Huët, 2011

2. Châteauneuf-du-Pape Blanc, Roussanne Vieilles Vignes, Beaucastel, 2011

3. Le Montrachet, Marquis de Laguiche, Joseph Drouhin, 2008

4. Egon Müller, Scharzhofberger, Auslese, 1987

5. Condrieu, Coteau du Vernon, Domaine Georges Vernay, 2010

6. Chateau Climens, Barsac, 2004

Reds:

1. Saumur – Champigny, Clos Rougeard, Les Poyeaux, 2006

2. Vosne –Romanée, 1er Cru, Aux Malconsorts, Dujac, 2006

3. Brunello di Montalcino, Riserva, Biondi-Santi, 2006

4. Chateau Haut-Brion, Pessac- Léognan, 1995

5. Vega Sicilia, Unico, 1953

6. Kongsgaard Syrah, Hudson Vineyard, 2009

60 YEARS OF THE
OXFORD & CAMBRIDGE
BLIND WINE-TASTING
COMPETITION

REDS, WHITES & VARSITY BLUES

BLIND
TASTING

HEATH

HARRY WAUGH ON BLIND TASTING

'Stubbornly, perhaps, I hold firm views about blind tastings. It is so easy to pronounce with the labels in full view, but impossible to overcome prejudice. In a blind tasting, wines may emerge whose merit might otherwise easily have been overlooked. Thus, even if one does make the occasional mistake, an anonymous tasting is worthwhile in the long run.'

…

'On this occasion, however, having requested an anonymous tasting when accepting the invitation, I found myself "hoist with my own petard", for I found that, as master of ceremonies, I had to disclose my own findings first of all!'

Thirty years after he founded the Oxford and Cambridge varsity blind wine-tasting competition, Harry Waugh wrote these words in his diary after an important tasting of a collection of 131 wines from the 1961 vintage, held in January 1982 in California.

ABOVE Tasting the 1964 vintage in the *chai* at Château Latour.

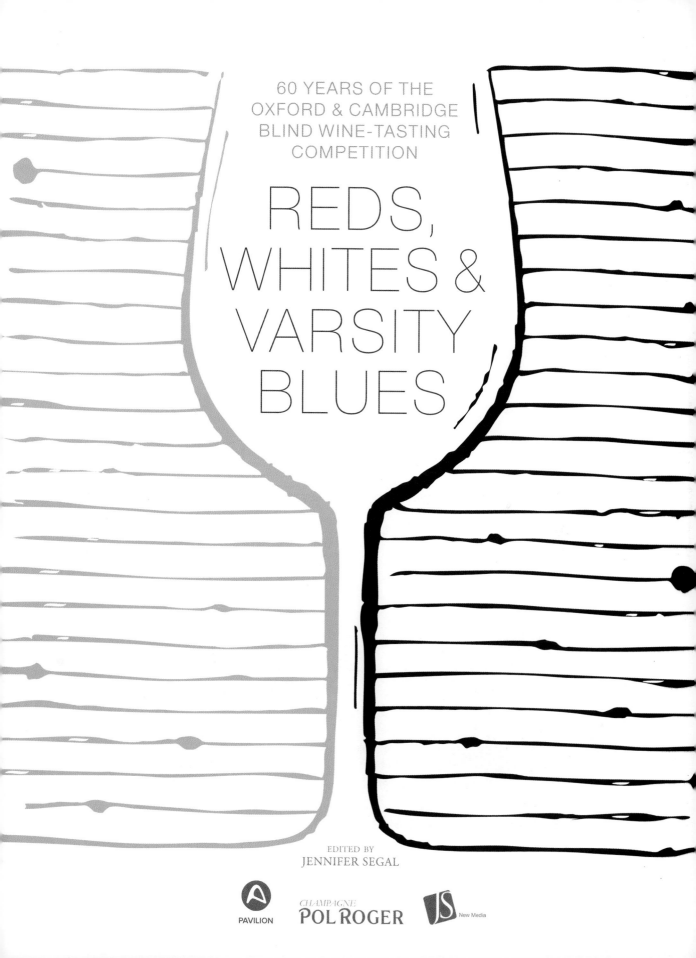

60 YEARS OF THE
OXFORD & CAMBRIDGE
BLIND WINE-TASTING
COMPETITION

REDS, WHITES & VARSITY BLUES

EDITED BY
JENNIFER SEGAL

PAVILION

CHAMPAGNE
POL ROGER

JS New Media

On behalf of the Pol-Roger family I am very pleased to be associated with this book. We established Pol Roger Ltd in the UK in 1990 and in 1992 it was a great honour to be asked to take over the sponsorship of the oldest and most famous blind wine-tasting competition. Harry Waugh was a great support to us from the start, and it was a huge privilege to be helped by him. We, the Pol Roger family and company, will do everything in our power to continue to protect and promote this esteemed heritage.

Hubert de Billy, Commercial Director of Champagne Pol Roger and a member of the fifth generation of the Pol-Roger family, Épernay, July 2013

TOP The winning Oxford team in 2000 in Pol Roger's tasting room, Épernay, France, photographed by team member Hsien Min Toh. From left to right: Chris Dark, Michael Saller, Frederika Adam, Hubert de Billy of Pol Roger, Mark Martin, Ed O'Malley, James Simpson of Pol Roger and Alex Hunt (captain). ABOVE The winning Oxford team in 1997. From left to right: Matthew Barr, David Strange, Sophie Jourdier, Andrew Comrie-Picard, Harry Waugh, Jeremy Seysses, Tim Marson and Ed Tully (captain).

CONTENTS

FOREWORD

We, at Pol Roger, are thrilled to have been able to support the genesis of *Reds, Whites & Varsity Blues: 60 Years of the Oxford & Cambridge Blind Wine-Tasting Competition*.

In the first instance, we should pay tribute to the great Harry Waugh, recently described by Michael Broadbent at a dinner at Vintners' Hall as having the 'best palate in the wine trade', for his foresight in creating this match; now the longest standing and most serious international blind-tasting competition.

The year of the first match, 1953, also marked a significant milestone in the progression towards a professional wine trade; being the first year the Master of Wine exam took place – since then many of those who competed in the match have also gone on to pass the MW. As both the MW and the Wine & Spirit Education Trust, founded in 1968, have developed away from the traditional British wine trade with a growing number of international candidates, so the varsity competition has matched these changes.

At the same time, the selection of wines in the match has become increasingly international – from the early days of predominantly classic French, with the occasional German (all, of course, sourced from the Harveys list) there is now an almost inexhaustible selection of grape varieties and countries from which the varsity match wines can be sourced. Yet those tasting continue to impress the judges with their unerring accuracy and tasting notes unencumbered with any possibility of doubt.

Pol Roger took over the sponsorship of the varsity tasting match from Harveys in 1992 and then first planned this book to mark the 50th anniversary in 2003. However, it has come to fruition only now thanks to the work of our editor, Jennifer Segal, a former member of the Oxford University Wine Circle, as well as the tremendous contributions both of previous competitors and judges.

It is our intention to hold any profits from the sale of the book in trust for both universities' blind-tasting societies: to allow them to continue their exploration of the ever-broadening world of grape varieties, countries, regions and areas.

James Simpson MW
Sales & Marketing Director, Pol Roger Ltd UK
Cambridge blind wine-tasting team member 1985 and 1986

A NOTE ON OXFORD AND CAMBRIDGE

The universities of Oxford and Cambridge are the two oldest universities in the United Kingdom. Both were founded more than 800 years ago, each an expanding consortium of what has now become more than 30 colleges and halls at each institution. Oxford is the older of the two, and the oldest university in the English-speaking world, founded c.1096. The 'Oxbridge' rivalry dates from c.1209, when Cambridge was founded by scholars seeking refuge from hostile Oxford townsmen. The most famous annual varsity contest, the Boat Race, was first held in 1829. The word 'varsity' in this instance was originally a shortened form of 'university', and in Britain refers specifically to Oxford and Cambridge.

Academic terms at the universities run from the end of September or the beginning of October to June or July. At Oxford, they are called Michaelmas, Hilary and Trinity; at Cambridge, Michaelmas, Lent and Easter (also known as Exam, or summer, term). In post-nominals, Oxford University is commonly abbreviated as Oxon., from the Latin *Universitas Oxoniensis*, while Cambridge University is shortened to Cantab, an abbreviated form of *Cantabrigiensis* (from *Cantabrigia*, the Latinized form of Cambridge), often disparagingly shortened to 'Tabs' by Oxford rivals. Although not (yet!) formally recognized by the Blues committees at either university as an official varsity sport, the annual blind wine-tasting match, founded in 1953, certainly has the same legacy, challenge, standards and spirit as 'official' varsity events.

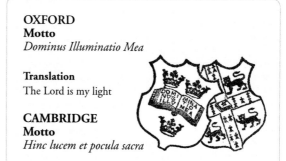

OXFORD
Motto
Dominus Illuminatio Mea

Translation
The Lord is my light

CAMBRIDGE
Motto
Hinc lucem et pocula sacra

Translation
Literal: From here, light and sacred draughts
Non-literal: From this place, we gain enlightenment and precious knowledge

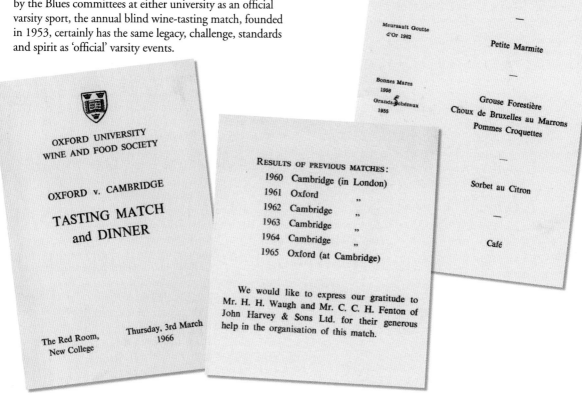

OXFORD UNIVERSITY
WINE AND FOOD SOCIETY

OXFORD v. CAMBRIDGE

TASTING MATCH
and DINNER

The Red Room,   Thursday, 3rd March
New College   1966

RESULTS OF PREVIOUS MATCHES:
1960 Cambridge (in London)
1961 Oxford   „
1962 Cambridge   „
1963 Cambridge   „
1964 Cambridge   „
1965 Oxford (at Cambridge)

We would like to express our gratitude to Mr. H. H. Waugh and Mr. C. C. H. Fenton of John Harvey & Sons Ltd. for their generous help in the organisation of this match.

Menu

Bristol Dry,
bottled 1949

Crevettes Cardinal
—

Meursault Goutte
d'Or 1962

Petite Marmite
—

Bonnes Mares
1958
Grands-Échézaux
1955

Grouse Forestière
Choux de Bruxelles au Marrons
Pommes Croquettes
—

Sorbet au Citron
—

Café

FACING PAGE ABOVE (Left) the view of King's College, Cambridge from the Backs; (right) the Bridge of Sighs over the River Cam at St John's College, Cambridge.
FACING PAGE BELOW The Oxford University Wine Circle heading into the Trinity term 1999 drinks party at Christ Church.

An appreciation of HARRY WAUGH
by ROBERT M PARKER Jr

I feel very privileged to write a short essay about the late Harry Waugh. In my early years in wine, primarily the late 1960s and the decade of the 1970s, Harry Waugh played a significant role in my formation and growing enthusiasm for fine wine. At the time, Harry was like a full-force gale, writing several volumes of his remarkably fresh, no-nonsense and down-to-earth *Wine Diary*. Secondly, his numerous lecture tours in the United States were the perfect foil for a young generation of baby boomers just discovering wine. I was fortunate to have a chance to digest thoroughly, not once, but multiple times, his candid writings on wine.

I remember attending numerous events he hosted, either in conjunction with what was then the leading organization for wine promotion in the United States, Les Amis du Vin, or as a guest of local collectors and major retailers. Moreover, his exceptionally warm and inviting personality was obvious immediately. It was clear to his many admirers that Waugh was an extremely polite, gracious and generous person who never hesitated to share his experiences, or take the time to explain his love of wine and answer what were undoubtedly elementary questions about it.

Early in my career as a wine critic, after launching *The Wine Advocate*, I was invited to London for a blind tasting of 1975 Bordeaux with most of the leading British wine writers. I was seated next to Michael Broadbent [who was working with Christie's at the time], with Harry Waugh and Clive Coates [a wine buyer and later a wine writer] directly behind me. This was the first time I had met Mr Broadbent and Mr Coates. I was welcomed generously by Harry Waugh, whom I had previously met. I remember Michael Broadbent telling me that while

Harry came to these tastings, he had been involved in a serious accident, hitting his forehead on the dashboard of a car. Consequently, he had lost much of his sense of smell. That scary story caused me subsequently to find a disability-insurance carrier that would insure my senses of smell and taste.

As fate would have it, we all guessed what we thought the wines were (they were primarily Bordeaux first growths and some of the other prestigious châteaux). I remember Harry claiming that he identified Château Latour just on texture, since he could not smell. As it turned out, he guessed more wines correctly than either myself, Michael Broadbent or Clive Coates. I thought it was a remarkable tour de force that by texture and weight alone, he was able to pinpoint so many of the top châteaux. His abilities and performance on that cold, damp, dreary London day left an indelible impression on me.

Afterwards, I was invited to his home for a meal. Listening to Harry was essentially like being in front of both a fountain of youth and optimism. While he was nearly 80 years old at the time, he was still talking about laying away additional releases of the newest vintage ports. I was deeply impressed by the amazing *joie de vivre* of this extraordinary man, and my lunch *chez* Waugh remains one of my life's enduring memories.

In closing, let me say that in all of my years writing about wine, Harry Waugh symbolizes more than anyone I have ever met (1) the essence of wine connoisseurship, (2) an unbridled enthusiasm for the subject, and (3) an unquestionable desire to share his remarkable knowledge and love of this fascinating beverage with as many people as he could. And how he succeeded!

RIGHT: Harry Waugh at Château Latour in 1964.

ABOVE Harry Waugh as a young boy dressed as Bacchus.

HARRY WAUGH
A brief biography

Harry Waugh was born in June 1904, and first entered the wine trade in 1934, at age 30, with Block, Grey & Block, the firm in which HRH the Duchess of Cornwall's father, Major Bruce Middleton Hope Shand, was a partner. It was a different era of great names and family firms, many of which simply don't exist any longer. Harry joined the Welsh Guards during World War II ('as every decent person did,' says his widow, Prue), and it was while in service to his country that he was assigned one night to guard Prime Minister Winston Churchill, a well-known devotee of Pol Roger Champagne. Impressed by Harry's knowledge of wine, Churchill invited him for dinner, and gave him a cigar, which Harry then kept in a box; for years thereafter he often took it out and showed it to people (at Block, Grey & Block Harry had initially worked with cigars before his remarkable palate for wine was quickly recognized). After the war, Harry Waugh joined John Harvey & Sons of Bristol, where he developed the firm's fine-wine business and retained a directorship of Château Latour. Much of Harveys' business then was Sherry and Port, but Harry had a special interest in Bordeaux. He went to Bordeaux and Burgundy to visit growers and winemakers when nobody else did – except, perhaps, for Harveys' historic and rival merchant, Averys of Bristol.

Harveys had always supplied Port and Sherry to the colleges of Oxford and Cambridge, and by 1950, after being asked to look after the colleges for Harveys, Harry was well ensconced and did a very good trade. He started to spend more time at Oxford when its chapter of André Simon's Wine and Food Society (WFS) was launched

in 1951, just before its Cambridge counterpart. Going around the colleges, which he very much enjoyed, he made many friends, including dons Jack Plumb (Christ's, Cambridge), Neil McKendrick (Caius, Cambridge), and Felix Markham (Hertford, Oxford) as he sold wine – particularly red Bordeaux – to them all. Happily, sales grew and grew. In those days, students and fellows would have dined in college most nights, and they dined very well, too. At the time, the Oxford and Cambridge colleges, along with the livery companies of the City of London and the London gentlemen's clubs, were the three significant groups of customers to which Harry would have been able to sell proper, serious wine.

During his visits to Oxford, Harry met an undergraduate called David P d'Ambrumenil (New), a young wine enthusiast and president of the newly formed Oxford University Wine and Food Society. David suggested one day that it might be interesting to start a wine-tasting competition with Cambridge and he asked for Harry's help. He approached friends in Cambridge, but unfortunately the WFS did not yet feature in their lives. It took about a year to set things in motion. Enthusiastic as Harry himself was, there was no precedent upon which to draw. Rules had to be created. There were inevitably mistakes, but through trial and error a blind wine-tasting competition began to take form.

Over the years, and after his retirement from Harveys in 1966, Harry held significant consultancies, including with the QE2, The Ritz Hotel, Mark's Club, Annabel's and Jacksons of Piccadilly. He was a member of The Saintsbury Club and Brook's, associated with the Brotherhood of the Knights of the Vine, and founded the English chapters of Les Compagnons du Beaujolais, the Bordeaux Club and the Zinfandel Club, before his well-received foray into the United States earned him the nickname 'the man with the million-dollar palate'. In 1966, he published his first book, *Bacchus on the Wing*, on his experiences in the wine trade. This was followed by *The Changing Face of Wine* in 1968, *Pick of the Bunch* in 1970, *Winetaster's Choice* in 1973, and ten volumes of his infamous *Wine Diary* from 1972 through to 1987.

Harry Waugh became a father (of twins) for the first time at the age of 70; his son, Jamie, now works with the wine department at Fortnum & Mason; his daughter, Harriet, is a wine writer and editor, formerly with *Decanter* magazine. He was blessed with a long life (many speculate it was the wine), and for his 90th birthday at a dinner at Vintners' Hall, guests 'were each bidden to bring a bottle' as 'having lived so long, he might have drunk his own cellar dry'.

He was decorated by the French government with the Mérite Agricole in 1984 and Chevalier de l'Ordre du Mérite National in 1989, the same year he was made an honorary Master of Wine, and appointed MBE in 1994. A grand old man of the English wine trade, Harry Waugh died in November 2001, aged 97.

An interview with PRUE WAUGH

'The Oxford and Cambridge colleges were commercial customers. From the 1950s Harry sold them first- and second-growth clarets and Burgundy, some of which Harveys bottled in Bristol. Bottling in England was Harry's bugbear. Every bottling varied, and there were dock strikes and other hazards in bringing wine over from France.

'Because Harry was older and had already made his career in the wine trade, he didn't do the Master of Wine exam, first introduced in 1953. He didn't have to do the blind wine-tasting competition, but Harry was a natural tutor, and he enjoyed it. Harveys was the training ground for the wine trade in the 1950s, '60s, and into the '70s. In particular, the 1950s was an exceptional generation – they'd all done national service and seen some of the world before university, and were a fairly wealthy generation.

'Ronald Avery was one of the first celebrity wine merchants, and as master of his ship, he could do exactly as he wanted. Harry was one, too, but he had to do what he was told under Harveys. Averys was a competitor and that was the tricky thing about it. They were both angling to buy Pétrus at the same time. Nobody's quite sure who bought it first, but they were both on the scene for the great 1947 vintage, including the Cheval Blanc which was the absolute It.

Harry's early life

'Harry's mother was poor when his father died on a train coming back from Hungary to Italy, where they were based. Harry was only about four at the time and they had to up sticks and return to England. His mother had three sons to educate and she sold the Chippendale chairs to do so. But when Harry was about 15, he had to leave: there were no more chairs.

'He went off with the Eastern Telegraph Company for three years, passing through Marseilles (he was so young that French girls embarrassed him) before they went to the Gulf. Then he worked for the Wills family of Bristol as a private secretary, and he did everything they did. He hunted and shot, and, of course, there was wine and travelling. But then it was the Depression and it was awful.

11 Downing Street to 27 Pall Mall

'When Harry joined Harveys after the war, they had a terribly cramped office in St James's Square before they moved to 27 Pall Mall. I was his humble secretary from 1965–66, but only for the one year, because when Harveys was bought out by Showerings, Harry had to take early retirement. I was living then at 11 Downing Street, and cooking supper for the Callaghans (Jim Callaghan was then Chancellor of the Exchequer), who weren't my party at all. My cousin, one of these intellectual socialists, said, "Mrs Callaghan gets very tired and she needs some assistance in the evening." So I got a lovely room up in the eaves there and I would stroll across the park to Pall Mall. They had all the silver in the cupboard and someone to clean it, but they never used it. And they had kitchen staff, but there were

> 'What was fun for Harry was that he had all these glamorous customers. People like Vivien Leigh and the Duchess of Kent.'

odd things; Mr Callaghan came home late always, because they used to work into the middle of the night, and would eat chips and Twiglets. It was quite funny.

'Harveys was enchanting, like going into the Holy of Holies, with wine all over the shop. What was fun for Harry was that he had all these glamorous customers. People like Vivien Leigh and the Duchess of Kent. Vivien Leigh stunned most men with her green eyes. It was old money in those days – it was very different. People were beginning not to have so much, but Harry could always find a wine that was good to taste that wasn't much money, and would wisely point out a Cru Bourgeois, which wasn't smart at all, or a white Burgundy that had been declassified because there was restriction on how much they could produce.

Château Latour

'After Harveys, Harry wasn't allowed to contact anybody in the UK for three years. He was at a pivotal point, and was asked to do an auction job at Christie's, but was beginning to feel he could do other things. So he suggested Michael Broadbent, who had worked in Harveys' branches up north, and who was particularly good at marketing, and he fitted Christie's beautifully. Harry had been export director and had been to America to sell Harveys Bristol Cream in the first stirrings of wine being made in California after Prohibition. So his idea was to go to California. That started his consultancy, and he gave tastings; being a director of Latour since 1962 helped immensely. Tastings in California were serious, and attended by paying customers, with a professional set-up with little baskets with wine glasses, and the most amazing meals. Americans can do everything.

ABOVE Harry and Prue with twins Jamie and Harriet at Bern's Steak House, Tampa, Florida in the early 1980s.

ABOVE Harry Waugh (centre) with Hugh Johnson (left) and Michael Broadbent (right) at the André Simon Centenary celebration at The Savoy in 1977.

'After the war, Bordeaux was desolate. There were disastrous harvests. When I first started going to Bordeaux, our noses were pressed to the windows at Latour watching the rain – they didn't know how to counteract the rot. We sometimes had a present from Latour, but were never given first or second growths; if you wanted it, you had to buy it. So Harry was buying 1975 or 1976 Margaux, and he educated the children with wine you wouldn't want to drink. When we'd come back from Bordeaux after a fortnight of drinking Latour every day, we'd joke, "Oh, how boring."'

Waugh family connection

'Auberon Waugh, a wine writer and novelist, was a distant cousin. He wrote for the *Spectator*, was highly intellectual and a fairly heavy drinker. Harry met his father, Evelyn; let's say he was (one of Harry's words for wine) "interesting". Post-war, Harry was taken into Whites, and there at the bar was Evelyn Waugh, nestling a bottle of Champagne with no one to share it. Harry was introduced and Evelyn said, "I hope you're not trying to claim relationship." But Alec, Evelyn's elder brother, was a member of The Saintsbury Club, so when Harry became a member, he met Alec, who said, "Hello, cousin," which he was: they all came from the same place in Scotland. Harry's branch went into racing and the other went down to Somerset … There must've been something of the palate in the Waugh genes; Harry's first introduction to wine had been his grandmother's wonderful vintage Port from the 1890s, but as a boy he didn't yet appreciate it.

Odette Pol-Roger

'I met Odette Pol-Roger at the International Wine & Spirit Competition. Odette, a Wallace sister and great friend of Winston Churchill, was president of the IWSC in 1984; Harry had been president in 1981. Harry, like Churchill, liked Pol Roger. He also knew one of the other Wallace sisters, who was married to a man in Bordeaux. The three sisters were famous, famous, famous. Harry knew all those people pretty well.

Waugh wedding

'The marriage idea was under wraps for ages. I was thinking, "Well, how long is *this* going to go on?" But Harry got in on time. I'd left Harveys and went on a trip to Greece; when I came back I had one or two invitations to drinkies in his flat. The third time I was invited, it was dinner, and after that … The only trouble was in those days it wasn't quite proper to be going out with your secretary, so he didn't want to admit it. It was tough because I was determined not to be mistress material. We got married in 1970. No little Harrys were produced to start with; then they came in two – Jamie and Harriet – so that was wonderful.

Puttin' on the Ritz

'The Ritz was one of the great hotels in those days. Michael Duffell was MD when Harry went in and said: "Clear out all the wines and start again." I don't think he even allowed Mouton Cadet; it all had to come in on merit. He got the staff tasting blind. We had the time of our lives when we went for various occasions. Harry loved going to The Ritz as he and Duffell were working up to something. Harry was also consulting for Annabel's, and the *QE2*. We all went to New York and back on the *QE2* when it was Harry's wine list that was featured.

Epilogue

'Harry was an extraordinary man. He'd had a hard life up until Harveys, and at Harveys it wasn't all sweetness and light; he had problems with the directors, who were hard-nosed money people. He had to find his own way, and he became quite well known in his circle. After 1970, the Oxbridge competition didn't feature in our lives until Pol Roger took over sponsorship in 1992 and invited him.'

Jamie Waugh on his father:
'He was unassuming and would never boast. With vocabulary he was keen to keep it simple – "This is quite good wine" – without loads of adjectives. "It's all about three," he'd say. "Good body, good structure, good fruit." And a nice nose. I don't know how he would describe a wine he didn't like. He would be very polite; he had good facial expressions.'

1985 OXFORD VERSUS CAMBRIDGE WINE-TASTING MATCH

by HARRY WAUGH

ABOVE Harry Waugh (right) presents the Harveys Cup to Lucas Taylor of the winning Oxford team in 1985. John Harvey looks on.

Early this year as guest judge of honour, I was invited to preside at the 32nd annual Oxford versus Cambridge Wine-Tasting Match, sponsored by Harveys of Bristol and organized for members of the Oxford and Cambridge Wine and Food Societies.

It was a somewhat poignant occasion for me because I had founded this competition in 1953, when I was a director at Harveys. Actually it was first envisaged in 1952, but at that time there was no Wine and Food Society in Cambridge; it had to wait until the following year. I felt it would be fun to do as well as useful to encourage the younger generation, and naturally the idea was received with enthusiasm.

The teams still consist of six undergraduates from each university, all of whom take the exercise extremely seriously. In 1960, Harveys presented a handsome silver cup on which the annual result is engraved.

In the early days, this was entirely a male preserve, but now young women also play their part – and sometimes with consummate success. It is interesting to note that quite a number of the competitors have subsequently become prominent members of the English wine trade.

I can mention three names that will be familiar to American wine enthusiasts: John Avery, John Harvey and David Peppercorn. Both John Avery and John Harvey are great-grandsons of the founders of their family businesses, two famous Bristol firms which date back to the 18th century.

After all these years of experience, there is by now a definite set of rules, but starting from scratch, as it were, I remember it was by no means easy to set out the guidelines. Much had to be learned through trial and error, but the guidelines were established by the time I handed over to my successor some six years later.

I am sure similar competitions must take place between universities in the United States, and it would be interesting to learn how they are handled. However, as there may be other enthusiasts around who would like to do something similar, this is what happened on March 6, 1985, at the Oxford and Cambridge University Club on Pall Mall in London.

The match was divided into two sessions; the first for the white wine and after a short interval, a second for the red. The maximum number of marks for white wine was 88 with 94 for red, making a possible total of 182 for each individual. Recent matches have been organized by John Harvey (already mentioned) and he acts as arbitrator for the judges, two senior members from each university and another judge this year was Michael Broadbent.

Naturally the selection of the wines has to be altered each year, but those for this event were: 1. Codorníu Grand Corday Brut, Méthode Champenoise; 2. Pirrot 1976 Champagne (Harveys' own brand); 3. Touraine Sauvignon 1983; 4. Sancerre 1983, Paul Prieur et Fils, Verdigny; 5. Chardonnay di St Michele 1982, R Zeni; 6. Montagny, Château de Daveney 1982, Moillard; 7. Auxey-Duresses, Côte de Beaune 1983, Dupont Fahn; 8. Beaune Teurons, Côte de Beaune 1978, Chanson Père et Fils; 9. Merlot, Grave del Friuli DOC 1982, E. Collavini; 10. Château Coufran 1982, Haut-Médoc; 11. Châteauneuf du Pape 1980, Domaine de Mont Redon; 12. Crozes-Hermitage Rouge 1982, Moillard.

To give an example of what happens, this year's results for the red wine have been included. The system of marking is shown, namely 1 for the correct country of origin; 3 for the main viticultural region; 4 for the subdistrict, if any; 2 for the village or commune; 3 for the predominant grape variety, and 3 for the correct vintage.

SCORE SHEET

At this year's competition Oxford scored a total of 190 points for white wine, with Cambridge at 175, but the latter pulled up strongly over the red-wine result, scoring 188 to Oxford's 175. It is extraordinary how close the results have been through the years, and this year's event was no exception, with Cambridge scoring 363 marks and Oxford 365. This makes Oxford six up in the overall series.

There is a prize for the highest individual score and for each member of the winning team as well as a booby prize for the lowest – in this case an annual subscription to *Decanter* magazine. Although obviously very serious, the competition makes a delightful occasion.

The maximum possible marks for each team was 1092, and if the reader thinks the scores should have been better, all I can suggest is that he should submit himself to a similar test and see how he gets on! In fact, as the years have gone by, these undergraduates have produced some astonishing results, especially since, unlike some of us in the wine business, they have untrained palates.

(AN EXCERPT FROM *FRIENDS OF WINE*, THE MAGAZINE OF THE AMERICAN SOCIETY OF LES AMIS DU VIN, APRIL–MAY 1986)

HARVEYS OF BRISTOL
An early history

The city of Bristol has a long-standing wine tradition, and its wealth and prosperity have been linked with wine and the sea since the 11th century, when the port began to develop with the arrival of huge quantities of wine from France. At one point there were so many wine vaults under the streets that, for many years, wheeled vehicles were prohibited and only sledges pulled by dogs were allowed in order not to disturb the commercial stock.

John Harvey & Sons of Bristol

In 1796, a Bristol man called William Perry bought a house in Denmark Street, on the site of a 13th-century Augustinian monastery, and began using the monks' cellars to sell Sherry and Port. He then took on a partner, Thomas Urch.

Two sea captains, father and son, both called Thomas Harvey, were also based in Bristol. In a mid-Atlantic gale, the father, his wife, and all hands were drowned, but young Thomas Harvey survived to marry Thomas Urch's sister. Their second son, John Harvey, having a strong respect and fear of the sea from tales of his grandparents' fate, remained ashore, and in 1822 joined his uncle in the Denmark Street business. In 1871, John Harvey & Sons became the trading name of John Harvey, with his sons, John II and Edward. They began regular trips abroad to visit wine-growers, to establish relationships first-hand and ensure the quality of supply for which Harveys had become known.

Harveys' most famous product received its name when John Harvey II toured a lady around the cellars and asked her to taste first Bristol Milk, then a fine oloroso Sherry. 'If that be milk, then this is cream,' she said. Harveys Bristol Cream became a proprietary brand in 1882. Two years later, the firm had its first export order to Mombasa, followed by its first delivery of wines to the United States, and in 1895 John Harvey & Sons was granted a royal warrant as the

'The value of the firm's total wine exports was more than that of all other British wine shippers combined.'

supplier of fine wine to Queen Victoria. John Harvey II, the first company chairman, died in 1900. On his death, flags flew at half mast throughout Bristol.

John II's brother, Edward, then presided as chairman until his death in 1910, when his nephew, John (known as Russell), took over. John 'Russell' Harvey III was an innovator, and with advertising, expanded brand awareness. A progressive man, he eschewed the traditional straw hat worn in the cellars, while his more conservatively attired brother, Eddy, who became chairman in 1919, made it his personal emblem. Eddy Harvey brought in mechanical bottling and automatic labelling machines, increasing the firm's ability for mass production rather than being reliant on hand-cut corks and bottling. Business modernized and expanded.

John St Clair Harvey (IV) became chairman in 1938, and the prestige and fame of Harveys' products grew until he left to serve in World War II; Eddy remained as active director. Bristol was blitzed in 1940 and '41, and when

ON THE NEW WHITCHURCH COMPOUND
(from the *Illustrated Bristol News*, 1961)

'A quarter of the area is a Duty Paid Warehouse, the other three-quarters a Bonded Warehouse under the close supervision of HM Customs & Excise. Adjoining a contemporary new office block, the wine warehouse and bottling plant now in operation is the most modern in the world. Air-conditioned throughout, the temperature is always kept a few degrees either way of the ideal 50°F. In the cask store a maximum of 540 casks tower in six rows to within a few inches of the ceiling: 400 butts of Sherry (108 gallons), 50 pipes of Port (116 gallons), with the remainder Madeira, and spirits. The sight is impressive, and so is the aroma! From the cask store the fork-lift trucks move the casks to the huge, glass-lined tanks – ten 5,500-gallon tanks, twenty 2,200-gallon tanks. From the storage tanks through glass pipes the valuable liquid runs to a filter, then tested by expert tasters and on into the production line. Ninety bottles a minute is the bottling rate – the highest in the world for a quality product. All the bottling processes are automatic, and the capsuling machines from California are the first of their kind in Europe.'

he arrived to work one morning, Eddy found the Harveys' premises completely demolished, including the house, warehouse, irreplaceable wines and its recorded history of the previous 150 years – all of it in total ruin, but for the cellars. The London office was also bombed, moved, and bombed again. Nonetheless, Eddy Harvey moved into temporary quarters and carried on.

George Edward McWatters, great-grandson of the original John Harvey, returned from service, and in 1956 became company chairman. By this time bottling lines had reached capacity, so to raise funds for expansion, Harveys became a public company in 1958. According to the *Illustrated Bristol News* of 1961: 'Such was the firm's reputation that the 800,000 shares offered were oversubscribed 55 times – nearly £26 million and allotment had to be by ballot.' Shares rose steadily. The new Whitchurch compound, opened in1960, had a production capacity of 500,000-dozen bottles of fortified wine a year, and 50,000 dozen of table wines. In the binned wine store, 200,000-dozen bottles could be stored in 'cellars above ground': a three-storey steel structure, serviced by smooth-running trolleys on ball-bearings – similar to the sledges that existed in the Bristol of old to avoid jostling the wines.

By 1961 the company had 69 agents worldwide and was exporting to 114 individual markets; Harveys also provided 30 per cent of all Sherry imported by the United States. At the time, the value of the firm's total wine exports was more than that of all other British wine shippers combined.

To supply demand, in Jerez, Spain, Harveys had access to nearly 47,000 butts of Sherry, and built what was then the world's largest Sherry *bodega*. Harveys' sherries were made exclusively from Palomino grapes from estate vineyards in Jerez Superior, and Harveys Bristol Cream

LEFT John Harvey V presents a decorated Dresden porcelain bottle of Harveys Bristol Cream to Welsh rugby player Philip Davies in the Denmark Street Cellars, Bristol, 1980.

was a proprietary blend of four Sherry styles (fino, amontillado, oloroso and Pedro Ximénez) and more than 50 different *soleras* with an average age of eight years at bottling. Further north, in Oporto, Portugal, Harveys had strong links with Cockburn Smithes, an old Port company. Its table wines came from the most famous wine districts of France, Germany and Italy. New depots opened in London and Manchester in 1959, followed by Birmingham and Glasgow in 1961.

Medieval cellars in Bristol housed Harveys Wine Museum, where tours (£8 in 1961) covered the history of Bristol's long links with the wine trade, along with a collection of wine vessels, 18th-century drinking glasses, corkscrews, silverware and Bristol blue glass, and were followed by a Sherry, wine or Port tasting. (In 2012, the cellars became a Sherry, wine and cocktail lounge.)

In 1962, Harveys' sales soared from £5.9 to £9.3 million. In July, the *Western Daily Press* noted the opening of the £70,000 Harvey restaurant in Bristol, with a 1,000-item wine list that claimed to rob New York's 21 Club of its record of having the world's longest wine list. That month, Harveys also assumed control of Château Latour, whose production was about 100,000 bottles a year. The 1952 vintage was coming to market, and at £2 a bottle it was the most expensive Bordeaux red Harveys sold.

John Harvey & Sons had come a long way since 1796, when the company motto was a phrase used by the wife of the first John Harvey, when her children won prizes at school: 'That, and better, will do.'

ABOVE Created in the late 18th century, Bristol blue glass became famous for its quality and beauty. In the late 19th century, Harveys began to sell its Bristol Cream Sherry in bottles of Bristol blue.

CAMBRIDGE UNIVERSITY

THE FIRST MEETING

The first Meeting of the Cambridge University Wine and Food Society was held on Wednesday, 5 December 1951, at 11.30 a.m. in the Gallery of the Hall of Christ's College, and there was a competition with three prizes in connection with it.

Members were invited to taste three groups, of four wines each, from bottles fully labelled. They were then asked to identify the same wines in decanters. Finally they were asked to name a single white wine as a 'Joker'.

The wines were as follows:

Group A: *Red Wines*
> Pommard Supérieur 1947.
> Château Gruaud Larose 1947.
> Château Gazin 1947.
> Cape Hermitage.

Group B: *White Wines*
> Pouilly-Fuissé.
> Graves.
> Sauternes.
> Hans Christof Liebfraumilch.

Group C: *Sherries*
> 'Dry Fly.'
> Amontillado.
> Oloroso—'A Christmas Carol'.
> 'Landrost'—South African.

'Joker': White Hermitage.

The Wines and Prizes were given by Dolamore Ltd., Matthew and Son Ltd., J. F. Miller and Sons Ltd., and Lewis Turnbull and Co. Ltd.

The *Prizewinners* were as follows:

B. P. Levitt of Corpus Christi College (1st). He had twelve correct answers and received a Magnum of Champagne.

J. R. Ross of Trinity College (2nd). He had eleven correct answers and received a bottle of Champagne.

M. Holt of Downing College (3rd). He had ten correct answers and received a half-bottle of Champagne.

This first venture was extremely successful and the Society is now well and truly started in the University.

THE SECOND MEETING

The second Meeting of the Society was held in Dr. Eden's Room, Trinity Hall, on Wednesday, 23 January 1952. It had been planned to provide Members from different Colleges who had joined the recently formed Cambridge University Wine and Food Society an occasion to meet under pleasant as well as original conditions.

The Meeting took the form of an Eighteenth-century Evening during which Members and their guests listened to music by Bach, Mozart and Handel, whilst sipping hot chocolate and toying with an array of curious pastries and old-fashioned biscuits.

Seven Members came to the Meeting in period dress, being preceded through the streets by a link-boy with a torch, and being waited upon in the Room by a black boy. There were churchwardens' clay pipes and several kinds of snuff available, and books of the period were also on show. Two members played backgammon at an antique board, and the whole affair was a great success.

OXFORD UNIVERSITY

INAUGURAL DINNER

The Inaugural Dinner of the Oxford University Wine and Food Society was held in the Banqueting Room of St. George's Restaurant, Oxford, on 26 January 1951, when the President of the recently formed undergraduates Society, Mr. David P. d'Ambrumenil (New College) occupied the Chair, with the Very Rev. the Vice-Chancellor (Dr. John Lowe) on his right, and Mr. André L. Simon, on his left.

The fare: Tortue verte au Xerez. Petites bouchées de Champignons Simon. Suprêmes de Sole Dieppoise. Dindonneau du Norfolk rôti à l'anglaise; Pommes noisettes persillées; Petits Pois. Croûte Diane. Ananas en surprise. Dessert. Café.

The wines: Irroy Carte d'Or 1943 (served before dinner in lieu of Cocktails). Reina Victoria, Rare Old Amontillado Dry. Bâtard Montrachet Cuvée Exceptionnelle 1945. Vosne-Romanée Les Grands Suchots 1933. Savigny Les Lavières 1926 (presented by Messrs. Avery's of Bristol). Coteaux du Layon 1933. Madeira Solera 1850 (presented by Mr. Horace Zeno, of Blandy's Madeira Ltd., Funchal). Avery's Fine Champagne Cognac 'Réserve de la Maison' 1878.

The chefs: Mr. F. Webb, of St. George's Restaurant, and Mr. Butler, of Magdalen College.

Mr. Anthony Blond, the hon. Secretary of the Society, proposed the toast of the Guests, who included besides the Vice-Chancellor, the Senior and Junior Proctors (Mr. A. B. Brown and Mr. J. Butterworth). Dr. John Lowe, who responded for the Guests, said that the Society would make a valuable contribution to the social education of the undergraduate, adding: 'But I hope it will do more than that, and that in addition to setting high standards of social behaviour, it will show what can be done to make the best of what we have.'

WINE AND FOOD

A Gastronomical Quarterly
Edited by
ANDRÉ L. SIMON
No. 75: SPRING NUMBER 1952
3s. 6d. net

WINE AND FOOD

A Gastronomical Quarterly
Edited by
ANDRÉ L. SIMON
No. 69: SPRING NUMBER 1951
3s. 6d. net

THE 1950s

Harry Waugh called the 1950s' generation 'stars in the universe'. Mainly public school educated and instilled with a sense of duty at an early age after a spell in national service, they entered a mostly male and distinctly British university life, rather older than undergraduates today. They were first exposed to wine at home or in the officers' mess, when Britain was a beer and gin nation: total UK wine consumption was just less than 3 bottles per capita per annum; and 3.9 per cent of its volume today. From the ashes of persistent rationing, an invigorated interest in wine and food, undoubtedly suppressed during WWII, re-emerged and the first Wine and Food Society branches were founded at Oxford and Cambridge. From which came the varsity blind wine-tasting competition in 1953 – the first and oldest contest of its kind. Wine education was informal and congenial. Under the dreaming spires, undergraduates drank classic wines from classic regions of France and Germany, served by storied merchants with whom they developed lifelong loyalties; and they sipped Sherry (much of it South African) with grand dons, enlivening, and possibly enlightening, tutorials.

The coronation of Queen Elizabeth II, also in 1953, marked a change in era although the Prime Minister was again Winston Churchill. Post-war reconstruction moved away from colonialism and the traditional British Empire, into the Iron Curtain and the escalation of the Cold War. Watson and Crick discovered DNA. The polio vaccine, and Sputnik I, were launched. 1953 also happened to be an excellent vintage across most of Europe, with top wines that have lived, and improved, well beyond their 50th birthday. The young blind tasters of the 1950s and their peers went on to become the British Establishment of the second half of the 20th century – holding distinguished offices in business, finance, law, diplomacy, politics and royal service. And a number of them joined the wine trade. They share, through their own words, a way of life and a world of wine – golden, affordable and bygone.

Cambridge		Oxford	
David Brewster	Julian Jeffs	John Albert	Dominick Jones
Michael Cottrell	Tom King	Nigel Althaus	Ian Lowe
Peter Cousin	Bryan Levitt	Nicholas Assheton	Robin Majdalany
R Adrian Cowell	James Long	Richard Bowes	Robin Hoyer Millar
Malcolm Davidson	R Keith Middlemas	Digby Brindle-Wood-Williams	David Peake
Charles de Selincourt	Tim Miller	John Cooper	Timothy Sainsbury
Frédéric Delouche	Alan Munro	David d'Ambrumenil	Jean-Henri Schyler-Schroder
Robin Don (MW)	David Peppercorn (MW)	Robert Dickinson	
Julian Grenfell	Roger Richardson	Ewen Fergusson	
George A (Tony) Hepworth	Alan Volkert	Robin Herbert	
Jonathan Janson	John Wheeler	Simon Hornby	

FACING PAGE The Wine and Food Society's first events at Oxford (January 26, 1951) and Cambridge (December 5, 1951) were recorded in the society's journal, *Wine and Food*.

ABOVE David Peppercorn at Cambridge in the 1950s.

'I was introduced to the Oxford president by
Harry Waugh, who was then Harveys' Oxford
representative, and Geoffrey Walker, who was
Harveys' man for Cambridge. And they said,
"We think it would be a jolly good idea to do
a contest between Oxford and Cambridge, you
know. What do you two think about it?"
And we said, "Sounds a very nice idea."'

An interview with DAVID PEPPERCORN MW

TRINITY COLLEGE, CAMBRIDGE, m.1951

*David Peppercorn, a wine writer, consultant and lecturer and a distinguished MW since 1962, has
rather a lot of books in his sitting room, among worldly collectables protected by two porcelain fireplace
Pekingese, and a nearby kitchen crowded with dusty and noteworthy empty bottles, e.g. Pétrus 1945:
the extraordinary end of World War II Right Bank vintage that first brought the wine to the attention
of buyers internationally. He shares his London home and under-the-road cellar with his wife, Serena
Sutcliffe, also a wine writer and an MW (the second woman ever to achieve the qualification, in 1976),
who is head of Sotheby's International Wine Department and a former varsity blind wine-tasting
competition judge.*

'I was a wine person first, before becoming a writer.
When I was at Cambridge, I toyed with going into the
law, and I spent my last year reading law. But when the
crunch came, I decided to go into wine, because wine had
always been there as a possibility as my father was a wine
merchant, owning Osborne & Son. And he always used
to say, "Do you want to come into the business?" And
I always used to say, "I don't know." All I knew was that
I wanted to go to Cambridge.

ABOVE A 1900 bottling of
Château Margaux.

'The Cambridge University
Wine and Food Society
(CUWFS) was started
by third-year people at
Cambridge at the end of the
Michaelmas term in 1951. The
leading spirit was a Yorkshire
man called Tony Hepworth
(Trinity). He was the secretary
and he ran it. At the end
of that year, we modified
the structure of the society.
Whereas at Oxford, they called
the head of the society the
president, at Cambridge, they created the position of cellarer
because they thought that was a good title for a wine and
food society. I became the cellarer in September 1952, and
I remained the cellarer throughout the next three scholastic
years. The society at Cambridge was originally affiliated with
the Wine and Food Society founded by André Simon and
A J A Symons. I remember having meetings with, and visits
from, the wonderful André Simon. When I was the cellarer,
the secretary was Roger Richardson (Christ's). We used to
have breakfast meetings, and Roger was very good at cooking
scrambled eggs over a gas ring. He used a bain-marie: you
have a saucepan with water in it, the thing with the eggs fits
into the top of it, and you scramble the eggs over the steam.

'It was that term, in autumn 1952, when the *négociant*
Jules Lebégue had its great industry tasting, and there was
an invitation from Harveys of Bristol to go as a guest.
Lebégue had an extraordinary tasting of the first half-
century of Château Margaux going back to the famous
1900 vintage – and wonderful wines of the 1920s, and
not such good wines of the 1930s. And then we had
lunch. I was introduced to the Oxford president by Harry
Waugh, who was then Harveys' Oxford representative, and
Geoffrey Walker, who was Harveys' man for Cambridge.

And they said, "We think it would be a jolly good idea to do a contest between Oxford and Cambridge, you know. What do you two think about it?" And we said, "Sounds a very nice idea." This was the year following the launch of the CUWFS at Cambridge. And then the thing was fixed up that we would have this contest in January 1953.

'It was all a bit chaotic to start, in somebody's private house in London. I remember the great drama was that the Oxford president suddenly developed a serious nosebleed, and was obviously trying to stop it, as people do. Oxford still won, but we worked out that the scoring system was deficient, and could produce rogue results. You were asked a series of questions. The first were geographical: if it came from France, if it came from Bordeaux or Burgundy. That was the first rather shambolic tasting in January 1953. What with stinking colds and nosebleeds, we said, "This is not a good time to have a competition tasting, and we'll have it closer to

when we're going down at Easter in Lent term." So that's when they've had it ever since: at the end of February, beginning of March.

'Harveys was the sponsor, and it was Harry Waugh's idea. Geoffrey Walker was the person I'd met originally at Cambridge, before this Lebégue tasting. Geoffrey Walker went on to join Mentzendorff, the Bollinger agent, and became in his era the royal cellarer, a position now held by Simon Berry of Berry Bros. & Rudd. We used to get a Harveys wine list and have a look and see what sort of wines they might put on the exam, and then we'd have tastings off the Harveys' list to sort of get our act together. After the debacle of the first match, we were determined to win the next time – and we did. In my last two years in the team, 1954 and 1955, Cambridge won.

'After the Lebégue tasting, which we would not normally have gone to as undergraduates, we sat with Geoffrey Walker and Harry Waugh and discussed

ROBIN DON MW
Trinity College, Cambridge, m.1952

'I competed in the tasting match against Oxford in 1954 and 1955, and if my existing record says I did also in 1953, it's probably right, except my recollection is that Cambridge won all the matches in which I participated! In my last two years, I was secretary of the Cambridge University Wine and Food Society, under the auspices of which the competition was arranged, and so I was involved in providing logistics of the match with Harry Waugh. The cellarer at that time, and fellow member of the tasting team, was my old friend David Peppercorn. Even at the age of 22, I was fascinated by the art of matching wine and food – and it is a hobby I have pursued over the last 60 years with great enthusiasm. However, I have seldom had a more perfect gastronomic dinner than at Emmanuel College in 1955. Those were the days. And the finest wines did not cost a king's ransom.

'As things turned out, I was spotted as a suitable recruit for Harveys by Harry Waugh. My wife and I

were married a month after I left Cambridge (we have now chalked up 58 years) and I dutifully took a steady job offer: after two miserable years in banking, during which time Harry Waugh asked me to join Harveys about every six months, I finally succumbed and spent eight years in the company, which proved an excellent learning ground for the wine trade. The first two years were spent in the London office with Harry Waugh. I passed my MW in 1965.'

THE CAMBRIDGE UNIVERSITY WINE AND FOOD SOCIETY DINNER
Emmanuel College, March 1, 1955

Hors d'oeuvre Chaud *Champagne Ayala 1945*

Tortue Claire *El Cid Sherry*

Homard Thermidor
Le Montrachet Marquis de Laguiche 1950

Noix de Vaux Doria
Château Malescot St-Exupéry Margaux 1948

Sorbet au Citron

Poulet Sauté Chasseur
Château Latour Pauillac 1934
Petits Pois à la Française
Endive braisé
Pommes Nouvelles

Barquette Eureka

Ananas Royale *VdP d'Hauterive*

Café *Calvet Grande Champagne Cognac 1906*

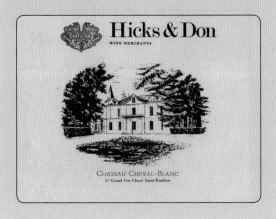

Hicks & Don
WINE MERCHANTS

CHÂTEAU CHEVAL-BLANC
1er Grand Cru Classé Saint-Émilion

the idea of the competition. I don't know if the idea was a way of procuring people for the trade from both universities. The Harveys people might well have thought it was a good way of finding people – in fact, quite a number of people then did join the wine trade, either directly from university or soon afterwards.

'I was not the only person up at Cambridge who came from a wine-trade background; several of my contemporaries had fathers in the wine trade. David Gummer's (Christ's) father was the head of Dolomore, which was big then with the universities. Dolomore had a shop in Oxford and a shop in Cambridge, and the head office was in London, in Portman Square on Baker Street. It was quite an important firm in

Jonathan Janson
Trinity College, Cambridge
'I took part in the first blind wine-tasting competition for Cambridge against Oxford in 1953, but my assistance in the tasting was largely drinking the wine!'

those days, but has disappeared since then.

'I recruited James Long (Magdalene), who joined our company and then went into Morgan Furze. And there was a dynamic, able man called Tim Miller (Trinity Hall), now unfortunately dead – he died very suddenly in his forties – who had a very successful career. He started off working at Harveys, then he went to Trust Houses Group, which wasn't very big in those days. Robin Don was destined for banking; he went into the bank but decided he was bored with that, and he then joined Harveys and became a Master of Wine (MW). Another person who went into the wine trade because he had a family business was David Rutherford. David Rutherford was a member of the CUWFS, but he certainly didn't take part in the competition.

'Bubbles can burst easily, and you can lose a reputation calling claret Burgundy. Blind-tasting is a whimsy.'

DAVID RUTHERFORD
Trinity College, Cambridge, m.1951

David Rutherford was destined for the wine trade as the sixth generation in his father's firm Rutherford Osborne & Perkin. An early member of the newly launched Cambridge University Wine and Food Society, he remembers being surprised at one of its inaugural events when wine merchant Allan Sichel, at a tasting of clarets, decanted over a torch. Not being chosen for the first varsity blind wine-tasting team was a relief, as David held firm to the benefits of keeping well under the parapet. 'Bubbles can burst easily, and you can lose a reputation calling claret Burgundy,' he said. 'Blind tasting is a whimsy.' He remembers his father doing just such a thing, but then also spotting ten wines right the next day. Rutherford Osborne & Perkin was founded in 1814 in Madeira, after the family, self-proclaimed 'sheep-stealers from the border of Scotland', stole women and sheep and escaped as *personae non gratae* to 'harder liquors' after the 1745 Jacobite rebellion.

Historic moments of Rutherford Osborne & Perkin. TOP A J B Rutherford (left) with Señor Osborne of Duff Gordon Sherry and Charlton Heston at the London premiere of *El Cid*, 1961. CENTRE André Simon (left) and A J B Rutherford (right). BELOW The firm's new home in Dean Street, London, 1970.

'There was certainly a channel there, and Harveys was involved in the early days of the MW exam. Harveys was very interested in education, and it was one of the firms that were a source of giving people very good training; a lot of the early MWs came through and had been trained at Harveys.

'The first MW exam also took place in 1953. And, of course, this was all to do with the structure of the wine trade, because the wine trade had thus far been extremely family, so-to-speak. When the MW started, it was a joint project between the Vintners' Company and the Wine and Spirit Trade Association.

'We used to buy our wines from Harveys' shop in London. A number of us lived in London, so it was easy for us to bring stuff up – although in general the Cambridge people always claimed they spent much less time in London than Oxford people did, because Cambridge, in those days, seemed much more remote. The actual journey was more difficult and even the train took longer.

Dons

'In those days if you had a university society or club you had to have a don as senior treasurer to ensure that the finances were not mismanaged – and he'd act as your sponsor. We were very lucky in that we had Professor Jack Plumb, who later became master of Christ's College. Plumb was great; he was an historian and I used to go to his lectures, and he was very generous to us. I remember having dinner with him in his rooms on several occasions, and on one particular occasion with one of the first television chefs, whose son was an undergraduate. The chef had a little beard, and had given us a cooking demonstration on Swiss fondue [see right], and we entertained him to lunch afterwards. And Jack Plumb very generously provided us with a bottle of something like Haut-Brion 1906, as you do. Everyone was impressed with it; our guest was *very* impressed. We didn't see pre-First World War wines all that often, and it was pretty good.

'And Denis Mack Smith I knew well. He started a wine circle in Peterhouse, and was instrumental in buying wine for the Peterhouse cellar. After I went down he invited me to do a tasting for them. I remember his wine circle well; these were much more intimate affairs. Soon afterwards an old member of the college, William Stone (1857–1958), died. He'd lived all his life into his 90s in Albany, Piccadilly, and every time a set of rooms fell vacant he bought them. By the time he died he owned about half of Albany, which he then left to the college. They were worth a great deal of money, and a book was written about him called *The Squire of Piccadilly*.

'Denis Mack Smith then became a fellow at All Souls at Oxford. I used to see him from time to time; he had a good sense of humour, and he's an Italian historian. I can't say I have read all the books that I own, but I have read his book on Mussolini, and I had a very nasty moment with it. My wife and I had taken a short winter holiday in Grenada, and hadn't realized that there was a quasi-Marxist regime in Grenada that was cosying up not only to Cuba, but more sinisterly to North Korea. We arrived on the island and found there was a deserted American Medical School and hardly anybody staying in the hotels. We met another English couple staying in another hotel, and they had the same experience – just a handful of people – and then we saw all these North Koreans around. And of course, this was just before Reagan's American invasion in 1983. But I had his book with me when I was in the tin-pot airport there – a small hut, literally; you had to fly to Barbados to catch the big plane home to London – and the chap at passport control said, "What is that book?" He had seen the name Mussolini, which rang the wrong bells for him. And so I said, "It's a good book to read because it tells you what a frightful, frightful person he was." So I diffused that situation.

'There was a time Denis brought out a bottle of 1945 Latour; he was very encouraging with people who were into wine, and would share it, enjoy it with them. Hence he invited me, after I'd gone down, to do a tasting for his circle. Everyone sat around; it was a biggish room, but people were sitting around on the floor because there weren't enough chairs. It was a very good evening.'

SWISS FONDUE

A Meeting of the Society at which Mr. Philip Harben prepared a Swiss Fondue, on Monday, 20 October, at noon in D.1a, Pembroke College.

Mr. Philip Harben, who is well known in connection with Television, had an interested gathering of sixty-five members and guests when he visited Cambridge, to show the Society how to prepare a Swiss Fondue.

He used the following ingredients:

7 lb. of Grated Gruyère Cheese.
2 bottles of Alsatian White Wine.
1 gill of Kirsch.
2 oz. of Cornflour.
1 Head of Garlic.

The Wine and Cheese were placed in a large pan over a fast hotplate, and when warmed up, the Kirsch, Cornflower and Garlic were added. The latter was well chopped up. When the mixture was sufficiently warmed it became of a pleasant texture, and was sampled by those present in the traditional manner.

Mr. Harben spoke briefly on the subject of Fondues, and recommended members to try the two Alsatian wines provided with it by Messrs. Dolamore: Le Moulin Blanc, Riesling, 1949, and Le Cerf d'Or, Gewurztraminer, 1949. The combination was unanimously pronounced excellent.

ABOVE How to make Swiss fondue, *Wine and Food*, No. 76, Winter 1952.

JACK PLUMB
Christ's College, Cambridge

Sir John Harold Plumb, FBA, known as 'Jack', was a hugely influential historian. From a working-class background, he took his first degree at the University of Leicester after failing to gain a place at Cambridge, but by 1934 he had been uniquely accepted for doctorate supervision by G M Trevelyan, one of the last historians of the Whig tradition. By 1946, he was a fellow and tutor of Christ's College – as well as its wine steward. He was a prolific writer on 18th-century history, including a biography of British statesman Sir Robert Walpole (1956 and 1960), and his enduring classic, *The Pelican History of England in the 18th Century* (1950) (only eventually surpassed by the work of his own pupil, Roy Porter). Plumb established himself as one of the few English historians to reach a wider public with *The American Experience* (1989) – so much so that on his death the Union flag was flown from the US Senate by request of the President and a unanimous vote in Congress. A brilliant tutor, Plumb nurtured future historians Norman Stone, Niall Ferguson, Linda Colley and Simon Schama. He had a complex, ebullient personality with a reputation for rudeness. He was a bon viveur – his Vincennes and Sèvres porcelain were said to be superior to that in the Fitzwilliam Museum, and his cellar spectacular. He was a co-founder, with Harry Waugh and Allan Sichel (of Château Palmer), of the Bordeaux Club in 1949, and an active senior member of the Cambridge University Wine and Food Society. Plumb became master of Christ's College in 1978 and was knighted in 1982. He died, aged 90, in October 1991.

ABOVE Christ's College, Cambridge, in the 1950s.

ABOVE The Old Court, Peterhouse, 1950.

DENIS MACK SMITH
Peterhouse, Cambridge
All Souls College, Oxford

Denis Mack Smith, CBE, FBA, FRSL, was a history fellow and tutor at Peterhouse, from 1947 to 1962, where he held his own wine circle and was responsible for buying wine for the college cellar. During World War II, he worked in the Cabinet Office, but he is best known for his books on Italian history from the Risorgimento onwards, especially studies of Benito Mussolini; Camillo Benso, Conte di Cavour; and Giuseppe Garibaldi.

Like Sir John Plumb, he was one of the wine-loving, entertaining dons who marked the golden age of Cambridge's history faculty in the 1950s and '60s. From 1962 to 1987 Denis Mack Smith was a senior research fellow, thereafter emeritus fellow, at All Souls College, Oxford, a college famous for having the best wine cellar in England, apart from that of the Queen. He is also an honorary fellow of Wolfson College, Oxford and was named Grand Official of the Order of Merit of the Italian Republic in 1996. One of his most respected works is *Modern Italy: A Political History* (1997).

ABOVE All Souls College, 1951.

An interview with SIR EWEN FERGUSSON GCMG, GCVO

ORIEL COLLEGE, OXFORD, m.1951

'At my christening in Singapore, I was given a teaspoon of Champagne and instead of spitting it out I licked it up and smiled happily.'

A distinguished former diplomat, Sir Ewen Fergusson was noted for his legendary wine cellar while serving as British Ambassador to France in Paris (1987–92). Among his many achievements, he played rugby for Oxford and Scotland, achieving five caps. In his own words 'a crashing wine bore', he is a past treasurer of The Saintsbury Club.

LEFT Sir Ewen Fergusson, 1993.

'The great thing about being an ambassador is that you do a certain amount of entertaining, and if you're sensible you are friends with people who make wine. Anthony Berry was a grand old man – a real gentleman wine merchant. And Harry Waugh was a tremendous enthusiast for encouraging the young. I'm not saying you don't find them nowadays, but the wine trade in its heyday was different.

'By the time my mother was born in Liverpool the family had retired from the wine and spirit shop business, but obviously there's some wine component in my genes; at my christening in Singapore, I was given a teaspoon of Champagne and instead of spitting it out I licked it up and smiled happily. I was already interested in wine at junior school in Australia, and I'd go round after my parents had friends in, sipping up the Sherry. My parents offered wines of some distinction, but after the war it took time for wine drinking to come back; the good wines from before the war had all been drunk out. In 1945, just before we left Australia, they were given a bottle of Chateau Tahbilk, one of the best white wines from the oldest family winery in Victoria, and they allowed me a glass on-board the ship. Then in my late teens my father took me out to dinner with business contacts of his at The Ritz, and I was handed the wine list and told to choose the wine. We had a 1934 Château Margaux.

'Oriel College wanted me to come up straight away, when normally people did national service first. My history tutor at Rugby School was an Oriel man, and I had a scholarship – although I'd wanted to go to Magdalen because of the glamour. Before I went up to Oxford, I spent the summer months in France in Tours. The family I stayed with was keen on the local wines, and I remember bringing up to Oxford, heavy in my suitcase, six bottles of 1947 Bourgueil. So that was a start, but it was difficult to combine wine tasting with rugby football training. On about my 19th birthday we went to Cardiff to play, and on the way back we stopped before Chepstow. All the other hearty chaps were swigging back great pints of beer. Having had my summer in France, I ordered half a bottle of Burgundy from the wine waiter. You could feel the eyes on me: *who is this fellow?*

'The Oxford University Wine and Food Society (OUWFS) had tastings and a dinner, but there was no competitive aspect; there wasn't such a thing as a blind-tasting competitor – it wasn't heard of. Then, suddenly, out of the blue, came the idea that there should be a match between Oxford and Cambridge. What would one be awarded? A claret?

'I became secretary, then president, of the OUWFS, and one would organize a dinner to coincide with the wine merchants' tastings, who would then be invited in the hope of getting some really nice wine at a cut price. I wrote to

'All the other hearty chaps were swigging back great pints of beer. Having had my summer in France, I ordered half a bottle of Burgundy from the wine waiter. You could feel the eyes on me: *who is this fellow?*'

TOP Ewen Fergusson (top) in white and scrum cap for Scotland v New Zealand February 13, 1954; ABOVE Barbarians' Squad 1954 Easter Tour of Wales (third row, sixth from left).

'At Number 10, the French Prime Minister, Rocard, took a huge pleasure in the Margaux 1983, and towards the end of lunch mellowed visibly. He said, "Madam Prime Minister, I bet you that within 20 years Europe will be a federal state." She looked at him and said, "It'll take a thousand years." He said, "Ah, but I see you accept the principle." That's an example of wine's beneficent effect.'

Matthew Gloag in Perth, who produced Famous Grouse, then called Old Grouse, and they said they would be glad to let me have some 1933 Burgundy for a dinner. So it was all very informal, and amateur. In the contest there were ten wines, and the standard was such that if you guessed the area for each of the wines – Bordeaux, Burgundy, north Italian – you would have been the champion. It's now taken tremendously seriously; people mug up on it and they're almost Masters of Wine before they go into the competition. It wasn't like that at all.

'Having finished playing rugby football at Easter, with the Barbarian tour of Wales, I did have to open a book or two in order to get a degree. My tutor said to me, "Ewen, you can play games, you can have a social life and you can work, but you can't do all three and hope to get a decent degree." I did all three and I got a not-too-bad degree. You know, that was my life at Oxford.

'I have five caps for Scotland; I played against the All Blacks for Oxford and for Scotland, and against England, France, Wales and Ireland. Against Cardiff, there was Rex Willis and Cliff Morgan. Later, when I was in Paris [as ambassador], the committees of the teams would come and I would give them graduated entertainments. The Scottish committee got a black tie dinner with wives. The English got lunch. The Welsh committee got drinks, and there was difficulty over the Irish because it was important to persuade the French that I was at least as much an ambassador to the Irish side as the Irish ambassador.

After Oxford

'After Oxford, my own national service was fascinating because there were just three of us who were university graduates. One was absolutely cheek by jowl with people from parts of society one had no direct practical experience of: people from the shop floor of steel mills in the North East; barrow boys from the East End. I found that an enthralling experience. My battalion was in Germany and the colonel said, "We brought you here, Fergusson, because you're an ex-international rugby footballer and we're desperately short of a heavyweight for the boxing team." So for six months or more I boxed. I hated it – it wasn't my sport at all – but we ended up winning the army regimental cup. I was beaten in the final of the Rhine army cup because my opponent had quite a lot of experience in boxing.

'I came out of the army in October 1956, when the Suez Crisis was at its height. I arrived in the Foreign Office and they said, "What the hell are you doing? Who wants to come to the Foreign Office? It's an absolute horrendous disaster that the Prime Minister has landed us in. Go away." I said, "But I need some money," and the chap looked at me as if to say, "Well, people who come into the Foreign Office don't need the money." So I was then put into the Africa Department to help out.

Wine and my life

'Wine has been a leitmotif of my life. In 1993, when I'd come back to London and was working in Coutts, I was asked if I would take over the chairmanship of the Government Wine Advisory Committee, which I did for 11 years. I was also chairman of The Savoy from 1994 until it was bought by the Blackstone Group in 1998.

'Government hospitality normally decided what to drink at Number 10. I went to lunch there one day, and there was Margaret Thatcher and Charles Powell, her private secretary, and me on one side of the table. On the other side were Michel Rocard, the French Prime Minister, and Elizabeth Guigou, a European expert and French minister. Rocard took a huge pleasure in the Margaux 1983, and towards the end of lunch mellowed visibly. He said, "Madam Prime Minister, I bet you that within 20 years Europe will be a federal state." She looked at him and said, "It'll take a thousand years." He said, "Ah, but I see you accept the principle." That's an example of wine's beneficent effect.

'When the Queen came to Paris in 1992, the principal claret offered for dinner by the President at The Elysée was a Latour 1978. For the return banquet at the embassy, we then gave Mitterrand a Latour 1964. The ambassador offered wines from his personal cellar. There was no such thing as a government cellar in the embassy in Paris; you gave what you bought when you became ambassador. As the price of wine had gone skyrocketing, it became progressively more difficult for ambassadors to give exceptional wine. But I had, of course, already accumulated a certain cellar, and some 80 cases came with me to Paris in the summer of 1987. So I was able to give people things to drink that I thought the ambassador should be able to offer.'

A LIFETIME OF TASTING AND BLIND TASTING WINE
by SIR EWEN FERGUSSON

'Various generations have produced adages such as "If you want to guess the wine, the best bet is to tip the butler," or "There's no substitute for sneaking a look at the label," or "It helps to know what is in your host's cellar." My own enthusiasm has survived innumerable failures and humiliations.'

'Very few of the millions of wine drinkers in the world know much about the wine that they drink. If they are wine-growers, they may recognize every aspect of their own wine, but they will mostly be ignorant about wines from other regions. Being French, for example, is no guarantee of expertise in New World wines.

'English-speakers are likely to have their own copies of masterworks by such learned authors as Michael Broadbent, Robert Parker and Hugh Johnson, and may well subscribe to wine magazines – of greater or lesser popular appeal. They can learn to smell and taste and look at what they drink; they enjoy guessing what unknown liquid is put in front of them and some, who have space and inclination, can lay down wine so that they can drink what they have chosen when "it is ready to drink" (by no means an exact science).

'Guessing right is always difficult. Much of my life has included friendship with people in the wine trade. Various generations have produced adages such as 'If you want to guess the wine, the best bet is to tip the butler," or "There's no substitute for sneaking a look at the label," or "It helps to know what is in your host's cellar." My own enthusiasm has survived innumerable failures and humiliations. When I was up at Oxford, I was asked to dinner by Michael Maclagan, noted historian and wine-lover, who took an interest in the Oxford University Wine and Food Society (OUWFS). On the day of the dinner, I had a filthy cold and nearly pulled out. I arrived at Mr Maclagan's house; the door was open but there was no sign of him. I crept in; on the left was the dining room with two decanters and the empty bottles beside them: 1947 Château La Gaffelière and 1943 Clos Fourtet. I retreated to the front door where my fellow guest had just arrived. We rang the doorbell loudly. Mr Maclagan appeared. In due course we went into the dining room and dinner started. We were asked to guess the wines. Unable to taste anything because of my cold, I nevertheless confidently asserted that they were the 1947 La Gaffelière and 1943 Clos Fourtet. Alas, I got them in the wrong order ...

'Members of the OUWFS were regularly invited to the wine tastings offered to senior common rooms by a range of distinguished wine merchants. That was where I met Otto Loeb, founder of O W Loeb & Co, at a tasting in Trinity Old Bursary, where he was showing not just the Rhine and Mosel wines for which he was famous, but five Bâtard-Montrachets. He asked me for my opinion. Fortunately, my callow views coincided with his. It was the start of a long and, for me, very fruitful friendship, generally but especially in wine-tasting terms (Lafites from the 1870s and Trockenbeerenauslesen from Maximin Grünhaus, to give the flavour of what he was ready to offer).

'I also got to know, by the same route, Harry Waugh, then running the wine side of Harveys – not, I think, the sherries that kept Harveys prosperous.

MARCH 5ᵗ 1954

University Vintages

AT the Oxford and Cambridge Club yesterday afternoon I watched a wine-tasting encounter between teams of six from each University.

Oxford was captained by Ewen Fergusson, a Rugger Blue and triple international cap. David Peppercorn led Cambridge.

There were 10 wines to be tasted. For guessing a type correctly there were five marks.

The vintage earned two and the district, commune and actual name, one each. There was a bonus of three marks for each completely correct answer.

Cambridge beat Oxford by 200 points to 156. Mr. Jack Harvey,

chairman of the firm which organised the tasting, said they should be rewarded not with Blues, but with Clarets.

DAILY TELEGRAPH

He was famous for his knowledge of claret but also of the Burgundy region. He introduced, to a market that recognized no more than the name Beaujolais, the names of Morgon, Chiroubles, Chénas, Juliénas, Brouilly and the other delicious products of the Gamay grape. He was also a master-chooser of young men to join him in the firm (he floated on me the notion of going to work there, but grudgingly allowed that entry into the Foreign Service offered a permissible alternative to becoming a wine merchant). Harveys became my wine merchant as soon as I had anything to spend on wine, my first purchase through Harry, in 1957, being five cases each of modest Cru Bourgeois wines – 1953 Château Dutruch Grand Poujeaux and 1953 Château La Grace Dieu, for around £6 a case (of 12 bottles). A few years later in 1964, Harry wrote to me to say that 1961 was likely to be an exceptional year, though expensive, and that he had taken the liberty of reserving a selection of wine for me: magnums and bottles of Château Palmer – this at £30 a case (!) – Cos d'Estournel, Figeac and so on. I still have a magnum of the more slowly maturing Cos and am saving it for my 80th birthday next year.

'The first tasting match was a casual affair, with no thought of prior preparation. The marking gave five points out of ten to the broad classification (Bordeaux, Burgundy, Rhine, etc). If any competitor had been able to identify the ten wines even at that level correctly, he would have got half marks and would have won quite easily. No one did. We were not serious students of wine, just drinkers who enjoyed quality (Quantity? Of course not). Perhaps Cambridge was different: they won the second tasting.

'Pleasure in wine tasting followed me around the world. When I was in Ethiopia in the early 1960s, I organized a couple of blind tastings for diplomatic friends: one from my own small cellar (shipped to Addis Ababa by Harveys) and one when I asked my guests to bring a bottle from their own stock, carefully concealed from prying eyes. The genial French ambassador failed to identify his own bottle.

'At the embassy in Paris, many years later, to encourage the interest in my staff, I had a tasting of English wines. It was enjoyable – I used on occasion to serve English wines to my official embassy guests – but it was disillusioning to find that, in terms of quality/price, they did not stand up to the Aligoté that was served at the supper after the tasting. I next had a vertical tasting of Les Forts de Latour (English-owned at the time), with a simultaneous horizontal tasting of 1970s. The Forts de Latour came out well.

'I asked my guests to bring a bottle from their own stock, carefully concealed from prying eyes. The genial French ambassador failed to identify his own bottle.'

And I had a Champagne tasting. The three favourites were Roederer, Bollinger and – wait for it – Pol Roger.

The embassy had an association with Pol Roger going back to Winston Churchill's visits after the war. He became very friendly with one of the three beautiful Wallace sisters, Odette Pol-Roger. Cuvée Winston Churchill dates from this warm relationship, and Pol Roger became the staple Champagne for the ambassador's hospitality. Odette was a friend of successive ambassadors – her family, too. For the most glamorous occasions, like the visit in 1988 of the Prince and Princess of Wales and the state visit of the Queen in 1992, Mme Pol Roger offered us the chance of serving Cuvée Winston Churchill of appropriate age, and joined us to enjoy the company and the wine, at the respective banquets served at the embassy.

'After five-and-a-half years, I left Paris and started a series of new activities. I was asked, early in 1993, if I would take over as the chairman of the Government Wine Committee, set up in the early 1920s to advise Government Hospitality on wine purchases. The chairman was always an experienced ex-diplomat; there were four members from the wine trade, all Masters of Wine, who gave their services free. The role of the committee, which met roughly four times a year, was to advise on new purchase and then, in due course, to taste wines in the substantial stock held in the cellars of Lancaster House, to assess when they were ready to drink and could be released for consumption. Government Hospitality controlled the purse-strings, i.e. how much should be bought and what wines should be served on the occasion of which foreign visit. The quality of wine provided for ministers to entertain their foreign guests was very high and well known by reputation in the diplomatic world. Of course, as wine prices at the top level have escalated, it has become a matter of careful choice to ensure that quality is maintained.

'My link with wine tasting did not end when I retired as chairman in 2004, as I was asked to be treasurer of a club that I had joined many years before: The Saintsbury Club, founded in the early 1930s by André Simon to do honour to Professor George Saintsbury. Since, on entry, new members are asked to give a gift of wine, repeated at intervals thereafter, the cellar has come to have an impressive stock – in quality if not in quantity. There are two dinners a year, and this not only keeps the stocks from getting too big but offers an opportunity for members to taste an exceptional range of wine.'

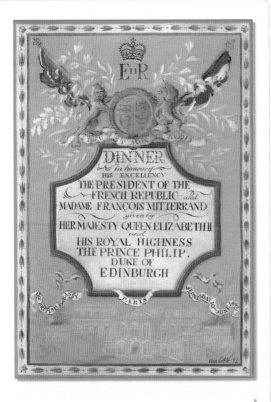

Menu

Saumon d'Écosse en Belle Vue
Salade de Concombres
~
Contre-Filet Rôti à l'Anglaise
Sauce Raifort
Pommes et Carottes Nouvelles
Petit Pois à la Française
~
Salade
Fromages
~
Soufflé Glacé aux Cerises

Les Vins

Chiddingstone Pinot 1989
Château Latour 1964 (magnums)
Pol Roger ~ Cuvée Sir Winston Churchill 1985

ABOVE Banquet given by HM the Queen for President
Mitterand in Paris, 1992. The claret was a gift from
David Orr at Château Latour and the Champagne was
a gift from Odette Pol-Roger. The menu was designed
by Alec Cobbe.

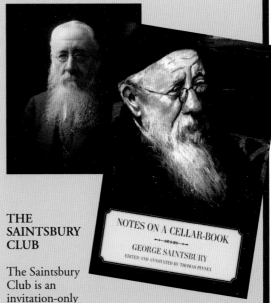

NOTES ON A CELLAR-BOOK
GEORGE SAINTSBURY
EDITED AND ANNOTATED BY THOMAS PINNEY

THE SAINTSBURY CLUB

The Saintsbury Club is an invitation-only meeting of literary-minded oenophiles. It was founded by André Simon in 1931, when he arranged a dinner in honour of George Saintsbury (1845–1933), professor of literature at the University of Edinburgh (knowledgeable about both French and English literature), when he was on his deathbed. Since its first publication in 1920, Saintsbury's classic *Notes on a Cellar-Book* has remained one of the greatest tributes to drink in the literature of wine. It is a collection of tasting notes, menus and robust opinions, along with anecdotes and recollections of wines and spirits consumed by Saintsbury – 'from the heights of Romanée-Conti to the simple pleasures of beer, flip and mum'. Professor Saintsbury was also a journalist, reviewer, critic and editor.

The Saintsbury Club is made up of 25 members of the wine trade, and a further 25 members who come under the rubric of 'men of letters'. Only one or two new members are elected each year, and to date there are no women members. Membership was capped at 50 people, because an Imperial bottle, the equivalent of eight regular bottles of wine, would serve one glass each for 50 people. It is a lifelong membership, with retirement only upon death, infirmity or resignation, and members are expected to contribute to the cellar.

The club's current cellarer is Anthony Sykes, who is also the current master of the Vintners' Company which celebrated its 650th anniversary in 2013, and its archivist is Oscar Wilde's grandson, Merlin Holland. Former blind wine taster Sir Ewen Fergusson, who became a member in 1979 when he was only 47 (considered quite young by the standard age of membership), was treasurer until recently. Other members have included Harry Waugh, Auberon Waugh, John Avery MW, Michael Broadbent MW and John Harvey.

An interview with
ROGER RICHARDSON

CHRIST'S COLLEGE, CAMBRIDGE, m.1952

'David Peppercorn was, and is, a dignified person, but I can remember him throwing buns at other people under the table during the lunch.'

Following Rugby School, national service and Cambridge, Roger Richardson joined his family's furniture-manufacturing firm, Beaver & Tapley. He is a past master and trustee liveryman of the Worshipful Company of Furniture Makers and a trustee of the Woodland Heritage.

LEFT Christ's College matriculation photograph, 1952. Roger Richardson is top row, third from the left.

'I competed in 1954 and '55. Prior to Cambridge, my father, who was a member of the Wine Society, was always on the search for the ultimate, undiscovered cheap wine – unrealized yet for how good it was – so we drank quantities of Yugoslav Sylvaner.

'David Peppercorn was the cellarer – the boss, so to speak. I was his secretary and I became cellarer of the Cambridge University Wine and Food Society (CUWFS) during my last year. We organized tastings by writing to merchants. It was pure blackmail because they knew we were likely to go on in our lives to be drinkers of wine, and if they refused, their name would be mud among that circle of people. About once a term there was a dinner or a lunch. Once we chartered a restaurant car from British Railways and had a CUWFS lunch on the journey from Cambridge to London; there was about enough time to have lunch as it took just over an hour.

'In the summer, we organized a Pimm's tasting and an outdoor lunch. We all got fairly well lubricated. David Peppercorn was, and is, a dignified person, but I can remember him throwing buns at other people

under the table during the lunch. Jack Plumb, at Christ's College, looked after us – presumably to see that we behaved and didn't get into debt. He was professor of history and had a most fantastic cellar.

'Tutoring was entirely through merchants. So when Loeb came, he would say, "This is Mosel, Pfalz, Nahe – and these are the differences." Harry Waugh gave us a number of tastings. He was very affable, and good-looking. We also had a tasting with Ronald Avery. We didn't know much about the geography; we learned about villages in Burgundy and communes in Bordeaux by reading Harveys' wine list. You scored marks for the vintage, whether it was Burgundy or Bordeaux, for the village or commune, and for the château. Consequently, if a number of us could get the château right we would score an enormous number of points. We'd therefore look at Harveys' list extensively to see which wines, particularly in Bordeaux, had run through for the past few years: Calon-Ségur was consistently in each of the lists. So the instruction to the team was to guess Burgundy or Bordeaux, the vintage, and the village … but in the end if you aren't sure, put down Calon-Ségur, St-Estèphe. I put down Calon-Ségur, and it was indeed one of the wines. The whole team scored highly, and we won handsomely. We revealed in the end – glasses having loosened our tongues – to the Oxford team how we'd done it, employing strategy. And they said, "Typical bloody University of the Fens – Technical College of the Fens." I don't think we awarded a top taster then, though there would've been many contenders for bottom taster.

'We were older than current undergraduates. Most of us had done national service before university, and by the time I left Cambridge I was 24. Some of us used to

A RESTAURANT CAR LUNCHEON

For this Meeting a special Restaurant Car was attached to the 12.15 train from Cambridge to London on Wednesday, 17 February 1954.

The Fare: Grapefruit or Crème Portugaise. Fillets of Sole Mornay. Roast Chicken; Brussels Sprouts; Rissole or Boiled Potatoes. Coupe Jacques or Cheese, Celery and Biscuits. Coffee.

ABOVE A Restaurant Car Luncheon, *Wine and Food*, No. 81, Spring 1954.

smoke in those days. I gave up smoking for the match with the result of all the wines tasting completely different to what I'd been used to. I don't think Italian wines were over the horizon yet. Sherry, of course, was, and French and German wines, with the exclusion of Alsace; I can't remember ever having an Alsace wine.

'Prior to Cambridge, I was at Rugby School. Ewen Fergusson was in the same house, and Tom King (Emmanuel) was a few years behind in a different house, but wine was strictly forbidden there. When my parents came down we went out, but I rather doubt we had wine at a meal; we would have had cider. Wine was not such a big thing as it is now; there were no pubs where you could get a glass of wine. It was beer or cider.

'I had an uncle who also went to Christ's, and I was lucky to get into the college because if you mentioned you'd had family there, the admissions tutor would ask the difficult question, "Why are you thinking of coming to Christ's?" And the answer you're meant to have given him was because they do well at rugby football. I said, "My uncle was here," and apparently, I didn't know it at the time, he was rabidly anti-patrimony, and that could've been the kiss of death. Today I wouldn't have had a chance of getting in with the qualifications I had: my A-level results, so-to-speak. I read natural sciences for two years, and then history for the last year. I'd had two years of completely forgetting about school in the navy; I never caught up with what the physics lectures were about – and mathematics was teaching differential equations. It was quite unenjoyable floundering. History was a level playing field because you were given a special subject, and it was very enjoyable.

'I didn't lay wine down until I was married and had a house of my own. The house had an air-raid shelter, and racking it up meant there was room for 300 bottles. There was a little cupboard in this air-raid shelter full of gas masks, and I threw them away; those World War II gas masks are now worth a fortune! For a number of years I went to auctions, and I bought a case of Sauvignon de Touraine at a Christie's auction for a very low price. After it was duly delivered I tasted it and it was oxidized. So I took a chilled bottle back to Christie's and said to Michael Broadbent, "Taste this and tell me if I'm right in thinking it's so bad it's refundable." He uncorked it and said, "I agree it's oxidized, but it's not undrinkable. Just treat it as" – it's a wonderful expression – "a summer glug."

'There's a joke I heard only the other day: a girl was sitting having a glass of wine out in the garden with her husband, watching the sunset, and she said, "You know, I don't know what I would do without you." And he said, "Oh darling, that's absolutely wonderful." And she said, "I was talking to my glass."'

CLARET FOR LAYING DOWN—continued			
1948 VINTAGE			
Château Bottled			
	District	Per Bottle	Per ½-Bottle
Château Cheval Blanc	St. Emilion	19/-	—
1945 VINTAGE			
Bottled in England			
Château La Croix de Gay ..	Pomerol	—	8/-
Château Gazin	Pomerol	15/6	—
Château Bottled			
Château La Dominique	St. Emilion	17/-	—
Château Gruaud Larose	St. Julien	18/-	9/6
Château Beychevelle	St. Julien	18/-	9/6

Harvesting in the Bordeaux district

Page Twenty-five

ABOVE Roger Richardson and the Cambridge team studied the Harveys Autumn 1953 list in preparation for the 1954 varsity blind wine-tasting match – which they duly won.

A contribution by
JULIAN JEFFS QC

DOWNING COLLEGE, CAMBRIDGE, m.1952

Julian Jeffs read natural sciences at Cambridge, but took a poor degree after spending most of his time enjoying life and drinking wine. He then became a barrister but always continued his interest in wine, writing and editing a number of wine books.

'It seems a long time ago. David Peppercorn, a friend and a fellow member of the Cambridge University Wine and Food Society, dropped in and told me that he had a cold and might not be able to taste wine against Oxford, so would I do it? My father had a fine cellar and had brought me up on the bottle. He also had a good library of wine books, and by the time I went up to Cambridge I had read most of them, but had not yet started to learn the nuances of flavour and, to my shame, had not tried to remember the subtle differences between wines of one district and another in Bordeaux, Burgundy, the Rhine and the Mosel, or those between the various vintages, though I had plenty of opportunity to do so at home. So when I went to the first tasting competition I think I came bottom but one. Although we knew the wines were to come from Harveys we had not studied their list nor had any preliminary tastings. We were thoroughly unprofessional.

'We went to London by train and then to Sir Roderick Jones's magnificent house in Hyde Park Gate. We did not meet him or his wife, Enid Bagnold, but one of their sons was on the Oxford team and was our host. The tasting took place around a vast marble table. Harveys was well represented and Jack Harvey gave me a piece of advice I have always followed since: "Taste the reds before the whites." Oxford won, and I cannot remember the rest of the day.

'I went down to read for the Bar but I got a job in advertising to pay off some of my debts and worked under an old journalist who taught me a lot. Then I applied myself to my law books, but in February I wondered why I was reading them surrounded by snow when there were sunny places in the world, so I put them in a suitcase and went off to Spain by train, stopping at Alicante. I had taken the precaution of getting my father's wine merchant to give me letters of introduction to his suppliers in Jerez. I went from Alicante to Cádiz in a tramp steamer by way of Melilla and Ceuta. When I reached Jerez in an ancient bus I fell completely in love with the place at first sight, even though it was raining cats and dogs.

ABOVE Sherry – the drink of dons. The most popular brand then was Findlater's Dry Fly. *Wine and Food*, No. 84, Winter 1954.

One of my hosts was the late and much-loved head of Williams & Humbert, Guy Williams ("Don Guido"). When I told him I loved the place but had to go back to England because my money was running out, he offered me a job and I was there for eight months, learning all I could about Sherry. I read all the books about it I could lay my hands on in English and in Spanish and found none of them complete and accurate, so I set about writing my own. This was in 1956. In 1958 I was called to the Bar and took some time off to finish my book, *Sherry*, which was published in 1961, by which time I was a pupil in the chambers where I stayed until I retired 30 years later. It is now in its fifth edition.'

RIGHT Sherry Tasting, *Wine and Food*, No. 76, Winter 1952.

SHERRY TASTING
A Tasting of Sherries given by Harveys on Wednesday, 29 October at 5.30 p.m. in the Trinity Junior Parlour.
Eleven Sherries were shown to members in the following order: Fino; Manzanilla; South African Pale Medium Dry; Fanfare—medium rich wine; Reina Victoria—light Amontillado; Club Amontillado; Amoroso; Anita—brown; Sunburn—rich, medium brown; Falanda—golden; Bristol Milk—Oloroso.
All the Sherries were of moderate price, to suit the undergraduate, and were well appreciated by forty-nine members and three guests. The meeting was honoured by the presence of Messrs. Geoffrey Walker, and Henry Warr, of Harveys.

THE WINE AND FOOD SOCIETY

'The object of the society is to bring together and serve all who believe that a right understanding of good food and wine is an essential part of personal contentment and health and that an intelligent approach to the pleasures and problems of the table offers far greater rewards than the mere satisfaction of appetite.' *André Simon*

The Wine and Food Society was founded in London by André Simon in 1933. In January 1934, a society banquet for nearly 400 people was held at The Savoy, launching what would later become the International Wine & Food Society (IWFS), then the world's only society of gastronomic enthusiasts not associated commercially with the wine and food trade. In the 1930s, anything that smacked of extravagance was distinctly unfashionable, and Simon, considered an eccentric by some, rose to the occasion. His philosophy suited an era of austerity, and has continued to appeal since: he urged high culinary standards while deploring waste. His position was one of moderation and simplification. Although brought up in a period of long, elaborate meals, he eschewed overly complex dishes, preferring a restrained sequence of wines to accompany a limited number of courses. He took his apéritifs (Champagne if at all possible) without hors d'oeuvres. A proper dinner, he insisted, should begin with soup, with the fish to follow requiring only basic preparation. He served lesser wines first, reserving mature, noble ones for the main course and cheese; Sauternes with dessert, and Cognac – or more often, Port – afterwards. He adapted simpler fare with facility; it was always quality, not quantity, that mattered.

Simon was known for his skilled diction, witty conversation and entertaining stories, delivered with a disarmingly engaging French accent. In 1934, he travelled to the United States, where he founded branches in a number of cities including New York, Boston, Chicago, San Francisco and Los Angeles. The US was followed by trips to Australia and South Africa, and the network grew. Simon founded and edited the society's journal, *Wine and Food*, which kept the organization unified during the war. By 1947, there were 1,500 members worldwide. Today the IWFS has over 6,000 members across 131 branches based in 31 countries.

ABOVE André Simon CBE, Légion d'Honneur, painted by Sir James Gunn RA.

NOTABLE PAST HONORARY PRESIDENTS

1933–1970 André Simon
1981–1982 Harry Yoxall OBE
1984–1991 Michael Broadbent MW
2002–2008 Hugh Johnson OBE
2008–2012 F John Avery MW

EDITORIAL

When the Wine and Food Society was founded, in 1933, there were over two million men, women and children living, or rather barely existing, 'on the dole'. Whether unemployment, the dole and maybe World War II might have been avoided had proper steps been taken then to meet the Hitlerite menace, is not for us to say, but to champion the art of good living at a time of such acute depression was considered by many a challenge, and by others an insult. We begged to differ. We claimed that there never was greater need than in the gravest hours of economic crisis to remind each other that best always is best, and that it is of the utmost importance not to lose sight of, and the desire for, whatever is best, whether it happens to be within our reach or not. Then came the war, and truth suffered a complete eclipse: to deceive the enemy became our duty, not merely the enemy in the field, but the potential enemy in our midst. Truth was banned. Again we begged to differ. We claimed that farm butter will always be better than margarine, shell eggs better than powdered eggs, fresh fish better than tinned snoek. When the war came to an end, planned mediocrity, not peace and plenty, was regarded as the best that we could possibly hope for, and we have been expected ever since to be grateful for austerity. Of course, we accept it, not gratefully but as cheerfully as we can, clinging to the hope that there are better times to come. We fully realize that these better times are not just round the corner, but we have sufficient common sense and honesty not to pretend that colourable imitations are 'just as good', and that we never wish for anything better. It is to guard against the very real danger of becoming used to and satisfied with lower standards of taste, quality and values that the Wine and Food Society exists. In spite of wars and rumours of war, we refuse to accept mediocrity and austerity as inevitable, still less, of course, as being desirable.

ABOVE Editorial written by André Simon, *Wine and Food*, No. 69, Spring 1951.

ANDRÉ SIMON by HUGH JOHNSON

KINGS COLLEGE, CAMBRIDGE, m.1957

André Louis Simon (1877–1970) was the charismatic leader of the English wine trade for the first half of the 20th century, and the grand old man of literate connoisseurship for a further 20 years. In 66 years of authorship, he wrote 104 books. For 33 years he was one of London's leading Champagne shippers; for another 33 years active president of the Wine and Food Society (WFS). Although he lived in England from the age of 25, he always remained a French citizen. He was both Officier de la Légion d'Honneur and holder of the Order of the British Empire.

André Simon was born in Paris in St-Germain-des-Prés, between the Brasserie Lipp and Les Deux Magots (the street has since been demolished), the second of five sons of a landscape painter who died of sunstroke in Egypt while the boys were still youths. From the first, young André's ambition was to be a journalist. At the age of 17 he was sent to Southampton to learn English and met Edith Symons, whose ambition was to live in France. They married in 1902 and remained happy together for 63 years. Simon was a man of judgement, single-mindedness and devotion all his life. He was also a man of powerful charm – the very model of his own description of the perfect Champagne shipper, who 'must be a good mixer rather than a good salesman; neither a teetotaller nor a boozer, but able to drink Champagne every day without letting it become a bore or a craving'.

He became a Champagne shipper, the London agent of the leading house of Pommery, through his father's friendship with the Polignac family. It gave him a base in the centre of the City's wine trade, at 24 Mark Lane, for 30 years. From it he not only sold Champagne; he soon made his voice heard as journalist, scholar, and teacher.

Within four years of his installation in London he was writing his first book, *The History of the Champagne Trade in England*, in instalments for the *Wine Trade Review*. A S Gardiner, its editor, can be credited with forming Simon's English prose style: unmistakably charming, stately, and faintly whimsical all at once. He spoke English as he wrote it: with a fondness for imagery, even for little parables, but with an ineradicable French accent that was as much a part of his persona as his burly frame and curly hair.

His first history was rapidly followed by a remarkable sequel: *The History of the Wine Trade in England from Roman Times to the End of the 17th Century*, in three volumes in 1906, '07, and '09, the best and most original of his total of over 100 books. None, let alone a young man working in a language not his own, had read, thought and written so deeply on the subject before. It singled him out at once as a natural spokesman for wine: a role he pursued with maximum energy, combining with friends to found the Wine Trade Club in 1908, where for six years he organized tastings and gave technical lectures of a kind not seen before – the forerunner by 45 years of the Institute of Masters of Wine. In 1919 he published *Bibliotheca Vinaria*, a catalogue of the books he had collected for the club. It ran to 340 pages.

World War I ended this busy and congenial life, full of dinners, lectures, book-collecting and amateur theatricals. Before war was declared Simon was in France as a volunteer, serving the full four years in the French artillery, where as *un homme de lettres* he was made regimental postman before being moved on to liaison with the British in Flanders and on the Somme. It was in Flanders that the irrepressible scribbler wrote his bestseller, *Laurie's Elementary Russian Grammar*, printed in huge numbers by the War Office in the pious hope of teaching Tommy, the British soldier, Russian.

In 1919, Simon bought the two homes he was to occupy for the rest of his life: 6 Evelyn Mansions, near Westminster Cathedral (where he attended mass daily), and Little Hedgecourt, a cottage with 28 acres beside a lake at Felbridge in Surrey. Gardening these acres, making a cricket pitch and an open-air theatre, and enlarging the cottage into a rambling country house for his family of five children were interspersed with travels all over Africa and South America to sell Pommery, until suddenly, in 1933, caught in the violent fluctuations of the franc-pound exchange rate when Britain came off the gold standard, he could no longer pay for his Champagne stocks, and Pommery, without compunction, ended its 33-year association with him.

Simon began a second life at 55: that of spokesman for wine and food in harmonious association. Already, with friends, he had founded The Saintsbury Club in memory of the crusty old author of *Notes on a Cellar-Book*. With A J A Symons [no relation to Edith] he founded the Wine and Food Society (now the International Wine & Food Society). Its first (Alsace) lunch at the Café Royal in London in the midst of the Depression caused a sensation, but its assured success came from the ending of Prohibition in the United States. Sponsored by the French government, Simon travelled repeatedly to America, founding its first society branch in Boston in December 1934.

Meanwhile, while working briefly for advertising agency Mather & Crowther, he conceived the idea of *A Concise Encyclopedia of Gastronomy,* to be published in instalments. It sold an unprecedented 100,000 copies. Research, writing and editing (and finding paper to print) the encyclopedia and the society's quarterly magazine occupied him throughout World War II. His daughter Jeanne and her family moved into Little Hedgecourt for the war and thereafter. His son André was a wine merchant. His two other daughters and a son all retired from the world into religious communities.

Simon was a better teacher than a businessman. He was repeatedly helped out of difficulties by adoring friends. Thus the National Magazine Company gave him an office in 1941, to be followed by the publisher George Rainbird. In 1962, his friend Harry Yoxall suggested that, at 85, daily responsibility for the society and its magazine was too burdensome, and bought the title from him for Condé Nast Publications. But in his nineties, Simon was still exceptional company at dinner and gave little picnics for friends beside his lake. His final book, *In the Twilight,* written in his last winter, 1969, recast the memoirs he had published *By Request* in 1957. On what would have been his 100th birthday, February 28, 1977, 400 guests at The Savoy Hotel in London drank to his memory with the claret he had left for the occasion: Château Latour 1945.

FROM *THE OXFORD COMPANION TO WINE.*

WORKING WITH ANDRÉ

Hugh Johnson recalls his apprenticeship with the founder of The Wine and Food Society.

'I was 22 when we first met; André was only 84. His name was already a legend to me, as I had joined the Cambridge University Wine and Food Society as an undergraduate. His presidential presence loomed behind our activities. And active we were: London's finest wine merchants made regular visits to indoctrinate their future customers.

'Nor were we raised on a strict diet of the classics. In 1959 we had our introduction to the wines of California – remarkably avant-garde in those days. California was already my El Dorado; I had spent the summer there, aged 18, and I knew I would be going back.

'In 1961 I was a very junior hack at Condé Nast Publications when I was sent to interview the great André Simon in his office in Grosvenor Gardens. I remember my first impression clearly. He sat with his back to the window, the sunlight making a halo of his curly white hair. His hand was huge; his accent as studied as Maurice Chevalier's; his figures of speech and choice of phrases deliciously oblique. He was fond, whether speaking or writing, of parables. I can't remember by what parable he let me know that I could be useful to him.

'André had been carrying the society on his broad shoulders for a long time. During the Depression he had achieved miracles of morale-boosting gastronomy, holding dinners at the Café Royal, which showed how good "fare", as he called it, need not be expensive. Through his friendship with Oliver Simon of the Curwen Press, a high-quality printer hidden down in Plaistow near the docks, he had even found paper to keep his quarterly, *Wine and Food,* going throughout the war.

'At 84 he was looking cautiously around, I suspect, for the means to assure that his society survived him. He also had wanderlust: he wanted to see the world rather than sit in an office. One of the means of release in sight was

Condé Nast, whose chairman, Harry Yoxall, had started the English edition of *Vogue* and was a discriminating lover of Burgundy. I never heard them discussing me, but I am sure Yoxall must have said, "I'll let you have young Johnson" – or words to that effect.

'André had started his career in what used to be called Grub Street during his French military service, aged 20, as subeditor of the *Revue de l'Artillerie.* Did he perhaps see in this fresh-faced Englishman an echo of his own start? Or even a means of revenge? Whatever he thought, I found my duties as a copywriter on *Vogue,* and subsequently *House & Garden,* too, increasingly steered towards wine, and specifically the Wine and Food Society. I wish I could find my diary for 1962. The '63 one is pretty laconic, but increasingly includes meetings with André and lunches with Madeleine Heard, the society's formidably matronly secretary, often at Verrey's, a robustly old-school French restaurant at Oxford Circus.

'My copy of the Winter 1962 edition of *Wine and Food* reveals (I scribbled all over it) my deeper involvement. In the Spring 1963 edition I am named as editor, André as editor-in-chief and Harry Yoxall as consultant. It was the first to have illustrations (they were line engravings I scrounged where I could). And it included its first article by Elizabeth David, whom, my diary reminds me, I took to lunch at the United University Club in Pall Mall (whatever did she make of that?) on André's 86th birthday on February 28.

'That was quite a day. In the afternoon I went to *The Sunday Times* to see another famously formidable lady, Ernestine Carter, to begin my stint as the wine man on that paper (on the fashion pages). And in the evening it was André's birthday dinner at The Savoy, where the menu was *consommé riche au fumet des pommes*

ABOVE Hugh Johnson (aged 24) working with André Simon (aged 86) in the office of the Wine and Food Society, 1963.

d'amour; paillettes dorées au Chester; quenelle de saumon Neptune; suprême de volaille favorite (pommes amandines; brocoli Milanaise); parfait glacé prâliné Savoy; le gâteau anniversaire' café. And the wines: La Riva Fino, Wiltinger Klosterberg 1959, Château Ducru-Beaucaillou 1952, Pol Roger White Foil, Bisquit Dubouché VSOP. What a history of change there is in that wine list: Sherry, hock, claret, Champagne… it sounds like the 19th century. And I suppose it was.

'My diary, alas, only gives me glimpses of that year. I can tell you what I gave my father for his birthday (stogies). I went to Bristol to see Harry Waugh, and Bordeaux to do a story on the châteaux for *House & Garden* – and met the Marquis de Lur Saluces, the old-school grandee of Château d'Yquem. In September I went to New York (I was writing for American *Vogue*) and met yet another formidable lady, and André's sparring partner for many years, Jeanne Owen. There were, shall I say, political difficulties between the New York chapter of the society and headquarters. I wish I could say that my visit did anything to reduce them.

'Suddenly, on November 18, 1963, my diary notes "made Gen Sec of W&F Soc". The entry for November 20 goes some way towards explaining the suddenness, or at least the date: "André S. to Australia, Canberra, Waterloo, 3.30". That for November 22 has a totally different resonance: "President Kennedy assassinated".

'At this point, at least for a while, I wrote almost daily entries. They record a life among the fleshpots I can scarcely believe was mine. André had just moved the society's office from Grosvenor Gardens, where he was the tenant of the Rev Marcus Morris and his National Magazine Company, to the offices of another well-wisher, George Rainbird, at 2 Hyde Park Place. Rainbird was a successful publisher; his books incorporated colour photography in ways that changed international co-edition publishing. Two Hyde Park Place overlooks the park, a few doors down from Marble Arch: a dignified and leafy setting, and only ten minutes walk from the Connaught Hotel, which began to play a surprisingly large part in my life.

'André has often been described as having a peasant's instincts. He certainly knew how many postage stamps there were in the desk drawer. He counted them on each morning's visit to the office; he remembered each letter coming in and going out. How to reconcile this with my diary entries: "lunch: Quaglino's", "lunch: Ivy", "dinner: Mirabelle", "lunch: Trader Vic's", and frequently, "lunch or dinner: Connaught" is a bit of a puzzle. At the age of 24 I was signing the bill at places I now visit at intervals of years. But then I was learning a rather odd kind of trade.

'Before he disappeared to Australia, André gave me some basic training in how to negotiate with a banqueting manager. They are not lessons you could apply today, when there are waiting lists at every restaurant you would want to go to. One lesson I vividly remember applied to a magnificent room at a hotel I will not name. A canny organizing secretary was well advised to sit in a strategic seat to keep an eye on proceedings in a mirror. The mirror reflected the doorway behind the service screen, where waiters bring bottles in, and sometimes take them out…

'André was away four months, travelling on from Australia to New Zealand, and home by sea. We had a Christmas dinner at The Ivy two weeks after he left, then dinners at Martinez, a Spanish restaurant famous for its tiled patio, (we drank a 1933 Rioja and an 1830 oloroso Sherry); at Quaglino's, at Trader Vic's – my special favourite – with Paul Masson's new 'varietal' wines, and a Hungarian dinner at the Law Society, an odd arrangement in retrospect, but an exciting introduction to the beauty of Tokay.

'The happy pattern continued on André's return in March 1964. By this time, *Wine and Food* was becoming more ambitious. We were publishing Philippe de Rothschild's poetry, translated by Christopher Fry: a sad goodbye to the bars of Les Halles as the market heart of Paris was demolished; more Elizabeth David and the first work of Alan Davidson, then a diplomat in North Africa, on Mediterranean fish; Evelyn Waugh on Champagne; a gourmet gardening series, even short stories – and of course, André's epic account of what he ate and drank and with whom in the Antipodes.

"Memorable Meals" was still our equivalent of *Queen* magazine's "Jennifer's Diary": the spiritual heart of the magazine, the place where hospitality, generosity and occasionally plain vulgar ostentation were chronicled – although one meal (and not the least memorable) consisted of bread and margarine and cocoa on the deck of a warship about to land troops in Italy. My most memorable meal at the time (the competition was stiff) was a lunch at André's home, Little Hedgecourt in Sussex. He invited Elizabeth David and Jim Beard, America's food guru, a genial giant with a figure like Humpty Dumpty and just as much hair. I collected Jim at his hotel in my Mini. I don't remember how we got him in and out of it, but I do remember his laughter. Lunch was in André's much-loved garden (gardening, after books, was his off-duty passion) and an example of his creed of simplicity, not always observed in the society's banquets. We ate a roast chicken and drank Château Lafite.

'To André, the acts of writing and editing were almost sacred. He loved printer's ink, as he said, almost as much as wine, and would take rare books from the shelves of his amazing library in Evelyn Mansions to caress them with his huge hands. One day he showed me his one page of a Gutenberg Bible, the first European printing, which lived in a leather folio. The jet-black precision of the impression was almost startling, its perfection strangely moving. "Printing was perfect at the start," André said. "It has never been better than this."

'Back from Australia and New Zealand he was working on *The Wines, Vineyards and Vignerons of Australia*, published in 1966: an incredibly far-sighted project, when Australian wines beyond the Invalid Port variety were still unknown in Britain. He instigated the

100-guinea (£105) André Simon Award for the literature of gastronomy in February 1965, at the Fanmaker's Hall, and awarded it to Cyril Ray for *The Compleat Imbiber* Number 7. Then he set off for a tour of South Africa: "11.20, Waterloo. ALS to Pretoria Castle".

'My life was also changing. I was writing more for American magazines; I had met my future wife, Judy Grinling (at vintage time 1964, at Château Loudenne in the Médoc); and I was aiming to write a book. To my future father-in-law's alarm I proposed to his daughter and resigned my job at Condé Nast – which meant the editorship of *Wine and Food* – in the same month.

'I continued to work on the society's affairs, organizing dinners, but André and Harry Yoxall had already lined up my two successors: John Hoare as general secretary and Julian Jeffs as editor. My diary records little let-up in the browsing and sluicing: visits to Claridge's, Le Caprice, the Ecu de France, Wolfe's (the mould-breaking restaurant started by David Wolfe) continue. So do tastings at shipper's offices, hotels and livery halls. And, I'm happy to see, almost daily riding from livery stables in Hyde Park. Would my liver have stood the strain without that? How did André's?

'I stepped down officially from the society's affairs on June 21, 1965, when Judy wrote in my diary, "André to lunch. What shall we give him?" I wish I had recorded the answer, but I suspect it was Judy's favourite, *poulet à l'estragon*. I was signed up to write my first book, *Wine*, and we set off together to do the research all over Europe. The total immersion it entailed kept me away from the society, though not from occasional lunches and dinners with André. When our first daughter, Lucy, was born, and duly taken to Little Hedgecourt for inspection, André gave her a basket of pullet's eggs: one for each week of her just-beginning life.

'And there was a working sequel, too. In 1967, André confessed he dreaded the coming winter. His sight was too poor to read any more; just as bad, he could no longer see the food on his plate. I suggested he look for local help with a dictaphone and a typist to dictate a fresh batch of memoirs. (His first, *By Request*, came out when he was only 80). A week or two later I called to ask about progress. "I can't manage the newfangled machine," he said. "But hallelujah! I find I can still type on my old machine." It certainly was old: a stand-up model from the 1920s. And it had a problem: when the carriage came to the end of the line the bell didn't ring. I asked to see the already plump manuscript, only to find that the last word or two of each line had been typed on the roller rather than the paper.

'But the memoirs were marvellous – much better, in my view, than *By Request*. His memory, though spasmodic, was in overdrive. He asked me to help with what came out, in 1969, as *In the Twilight*, printed by the Curwen Press with the fine paper and binding that George Rainbird had promised – and André so richly deserved.'

An interview with
THE RT HON SIR TIMOTHY SAINSBURY

WORCESTER COLLEGE, OXFORD, m.1953

After Oxford, Sir Timothy Sainsbury joined his family firm, J Sainsbury's – the first to put wine on supermarket shelves – which had been founded by his great-grandparents, John James Sainsbury and Mary Ann Staples, with a grocery at Drury Lane in 1869. There he held a place on the board, modernizing counter-service shops into self-service, before he stepped down to pursue his career in politics, becoming a member of Parliament and Minister for Trade & Industry.

'At the end of the 1954 match Harry Waugh was so worried about the Oxford team's poor score that he said unless we did better … it wouldn't be worth going on.'

'There were very few women at Oxford at that time – only five women's colleges, and we counted ourselves lucky because there were only two at Cambridge. Oxford also had much better communications with London, and the Marlborough Secretarial School was a source of ladies and dates for our parties. St Hilda's did admit ladies who were "prepared to use lipstick", but on the whole most of the colleges thoroughly disapproved of women who were interested in parties, so for those of us who were interested in upmarket girlfriends it was difficult.

'When I think of the three girls I took out in Oxford days, one was from London. She played cello with the National Youth Orchestra and then eventually married the master of Hertford College, who, sadly, was killed in a car crash. Her son was a friend of our youngest daughter at Cambridge later, so it's funny how those things go around. Then I took out a girl whose father wrote travel books and they lived in north Oxford. And a girl who was at St Hilda's and we're still great friends.

'When I went up to Oxford in autumn 1953, there was still food rationing, and most of us had done national service, so we were older. I had been in the army, nearly half the time in Germany, where I'd had wine every evening in the mess. In Germany then, wine was inexpensive and good value. I competed in 1954, but I didn't do very well; I distinguished the Bordeaux from the Burgundy, but I called the Burgundy Bordeaux and the Bordeaux Burgundy, and so my score was very poor. At the end of the 1954 match Harry Waugh was so worried about the Oxford team's poor score that he said unless we did better he felt we weren't taking it seriously and that it wouldn't be worth going on. In 1955, when I

captained the blind wine-tasting team, we did quite a lot better, but Cambridge still won relatively easily. At the time, Harry Waugh seemed a grand, distinguished figure, and I was slightly in awe of him. By all accounts he was happy to share his knowledge with enthusiasts. He was a man who believed that we all ought to be appreciating, understanding and enjoying wine.

'Our team was drawn from the Oxford University Wine and Food Society (OUWFS). I had provenance. My mother's family, Adams, were wine merchants. Adams & Sons joined up with Grierson and became Grierson Oldham & Adams, but disappeared 25 years ago when it was taken over by Holt's. The company used to ship its own Port; the notable vintage Port shipped was 1966 and I've still got a few bottles. They also imported their own Sherry (I always had Sherry in my room at Worcester College in Oxford), and they shipped their own Champagne, which was called Lemont. It was called Lemont because my grandfather, my mother's father, was called Leonard and his brother was called Montgomery. The company was a major supplier to the House of Lords.

Sturgeon success

'My great coup as chairman of the OUWFS was to have a sturgeon feast during Lent. Sturgeon, traditionally if landed in England, belonged to the Crown. You could, however, have a sturgeon feast in Lent. So we organized a sturgeon feast, promoted by Unilever and laid on by Mac Fisheries, for the society, which was a great success. Mac Fisheries was owned by Unilever, an amalgamation of Lever Brothers and Van den Bergh & Jurgens, which was a Dutch company formed when the Van den Berghs joined up with our great Dutch rival. The two companies were developers of margarine and fats, and my paternal grandmother was a Van den Bergh. In 1955, there was still a Van den Bergh on the main board of Unilever, and so we had the sturgeon feast at the Ehrsam Hotel in Oxford. When Cambridge heard about this, they were furious, because my cousin, Peter Van den Bergh, was a member of the Cambridge University Wine and

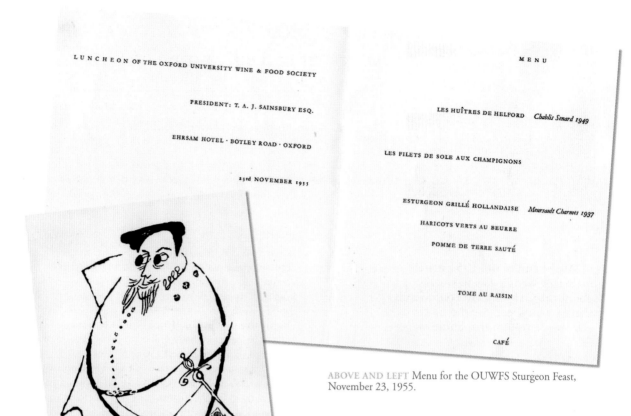

LUNCHEON OF THE OXFORD UNIVERSITY WINE & FOOD SOCIETY

PRESIDENT: T. A. J. SAINSBURY ESQ.

EHRSAM HOTEL · BOTLEY ROAD · OXFORD

23rd NOVEMBER 1955

MENU

LES HUÎTRES DE HELFORD   *Chablis Senard 1949*

LES FILETS DE SOLE AUX CHAMPIGNONS

ESTURGEON GRILLÉ HOLLANDAISE   *Meursault Charmes 1937*

HARICOTS VERTS AU BEURRE

POMME DE TERRE SAUTÉ

TOME AU RAISIN

CAFÉ

CECIL'S FAST

ABOVE AND LEFT Menu for the OUWFS Sturgeon Feast, November 23, 1955.

Food Society and they had never thought about doing one themselves.

'Under the leadership of my contemporary, Robin Don, now an MW, members of both the Oxford and Cambridge wine and food societies formed a wine-buying club. We met monthly to taste wines and to buy them.

'But again, there weren't women in the society at that time. My late uncle, Peter Adams, who was once described as the fourth best palate in the world (I often wondered who the other three were), sold me La Tâche Domaine de la Romanée-Conti 1947 or 1948, meant to be a very good vintage. And he said to me – this must have been in the early 1950s – shockingly, "Don't ever give it to a woman because they won't appreciate it." Now we realize that women on the whole have better palates than men, and at the 50th anniversary celebration of the

blind wine-tasting competition at Vintners' Hall I walked into the room and half the people there were female. Many of the wine writers now are female, and I've even got a niece in the wine business.

'At Oxford, I was an honorary vintner and cellarer of the Gridiron Club, and I was a member of the Bullingdon, which has since become notorious. We were only moderately naughty in my day; we had an annual cricket match against the Oxford City Police. It was a very jolly occasion, and I knew where I was going to field by putting my gin and tonic down. I also ran in the relays for Oxford – the first time relay was the 4 x 110; it just shows you how long ago: we were running yards not metres. I ran the second leg and there'd been a very good party at Christ Church the night before; I got to bed, I suppose, at about half past two in the morning, maybe a bit later. I must've run it rather well and we won the 4 x 110 relay. I lasted the five relays, and the last one was the 4 x 220. It was cold and wet and by then the alcohol had worn off and I was feeling terrible. Luckily, by the time I took over the relay, we were a long way behind anyhow, so it wasn't blamed on me, thank goodness.

'Socially, not many people had wine in their normal drinking in the 1950s and '60s. We drank only when we first married and we had wine at weekends; we didn't have wine every day, and we only drank at home. People didn't go out to eat that often, and the choice of restaurants was limited.

Wine in supermarkets and battle with the brewers

'I came from the Sainsbury supermarket family, and at that time Sainsbury's didn't sell wine. When I joined the firm in 1956, there was just one shop that had an off-licence, and it was a curiosity; we had bought a trading grocer who had an off-licence and somehow or other it was kept. And it was not self-service; it was counter service.

'Sainsbury's was a pioneer of getting licences: one of the first to challenge the brewers and the off-licences, which were very against the idea of supermarkets selling wine. It was a big battle, with Charrington and Truman the two dominant breweries then. Bristol was the first supermarket that got a licence to sell wine, but licensing hours applied, so you had to cover up the drinks section if it was outside licensing hours.

'The brewers felt that we were muscling in on their trade. The battle was quite tough, but it didn't last very long – three to four years – and then it became straightforward when they realized this was actually going to increase the market. They became suppliers and sold to the supermarkets. It changed the dynamic. The big change socially then was when a housewife went shopping, for example, and the drink was now in the basket with everything else, instead of the drink being bought by the man separately. Turning wine into part of the weekly household purchase was a big revolution: cauliflower, Chablis, soap.

'Sainsbury's sold Italian wine right from the beginning because my father's PA was the wine buyer for the first off-licence shop, and he had an Italian wife. Of course we did also have the dreaded Mateus Rosé, Liebfraumilch and Yugoslav Riesling. Downmarket cheap wines were early offerings. I think from early on the British were used to seeing wines other than French on the shelves.

'Another factor that greatly influenced wine drinking in Britain was the package holiday, and going abroad as opposed to just going to Blackpool. Some people, of course, went to as near an English pub abroad as they could find to drink as near as English beer as they could find, but some would also sample the local wines in France, Italy and Spain.

The politics of the day

'Politics was not frightfully exciting at that time. Rationing stopped in 1954, but when I first went up to Oxford you had your own butter ration and you took it into hall with you from your room. We were moving into the Macmillan era, and had never had it so good. Bonfire regulations were still in place but we were moving away from the post-war gloom.

'I was not involved politically at Oxford at all, but when I came down in 1956 it was a very dramatic year, what with the Suez Crisis and the Hungarian uprising, and I got involved with politics straightaway. It was a direct consequence of those dramas in the autumn of 1956, and I've been involved in politics ever since, until I retired.

ABOVE Matriculation photograph, Worcester College, Oxford, 1953. Timothy Sainsbury is in the second row, sixth from left.

Alan Clark's Rose

'I became Minister for Trade. Alan Clark had been Minister for Trade, then David Trefgarne for a year, and then when I became Minister for Trade I shared Alan Clark's diary secretary, Rose. Clark had written about her in such a personal way in his diaries, which I thought was grave. Something was said, and I thought I should challenge him to a duel on behalf of the honour of my diary secretary, but before I could have done so I realized that Rose was delighted – she was now the most famous diary secretary in Whitehall.

'One of my most memorable occasions, however, was when I went to represent the British government at the inauguration of Doña Violeta Barrios Torres de Chamorro in 1990 as the president of Nicaragua, when she beat Ortega and the Sandinistas, contrary to everybody's expectations. Ortega and his commandants were all lined up in their battle fatigues. Ortega is her cousin in some way – there have been five Ortegas and four Chamorros as presidents of Nicaragua, and there are Chamorros on the Ortega side and Ortegas on the Chamorro side: all very incestuous.

'There was a reception for representatives of countries that had been particularly supportive for her, and Britain was one, so we all lined up to shake hands. She was a motherly lady, and was the only candidate because her husband had been assassinated. I realized as I was coming towards the front of the queue that it was not just shaking hands, it was a kiss on both cheeks. When I got to the front – kiss, kiss on both cheeks – and when she realized where I'd come from I had another kiss to take back to Margaret.

Bye bye to Chardonnay

'Tragically, I began getting migraines in my sixties, triggered by Chardonnay. I used to love white Burgundies, and I virtually had to stop drinking most Champagne 20 years ago. A young blanc de blancs Champagne served at a wedding would be instant headache material for me. It's got to be mature Pinot-based Champagne and on the whole only vintage.

'Our boat is the greenest boat in the Mediterranean, as it consumes only a gallon a mile! And Pol Roger is always on board for special occasions.

CAMBRIDGE MENUS IN THE LATE 1950s
A dinner, held at St Catharine's College, Cambridge, on November 28, 1957

(before dinner) *Anjou Coteaux du Layon 1955*
(Hallgarten)

Chassagne-Montrachet 1952
(Bouchard Père et Fils, bottled in England)
(oysters or smoked salmon)

Dürkheimer Hochmess Scheurebe 1953
(Weingut Zumstein)
(red mullet)

Château Lafite-Rothschild 1950 (château-bottled)
Château Gruaud-Larose 1950 (English-bottled, Dolamore)
(guinea fowl)

Niersteiner Hipping Terrassen Auslese 1953
(Geschwister Schuh)
Niersteiner Orbel Riesling Trockenbeeren Auslese 1953
(Franz Karl Schmitt)
(fresh pineapple cream)

(cheese soufflé)

Cockburn 1935, *Bual* 1815
(dessert, coffee)

A private dinner given by David Damant at Queens' College, Cambridge, on St Eligius Day, 1958

Manzanilla
(caviar)

Haut-Brion Blanc 1955
(turbot)

Haut-Brion 1950
(mousse de jambon aux truffes)

Latour 1934
(roast grouse; mushrooms on toast)

Yquem 1949
(la meringue corbeille aux Fruits)

Schloss Johannisberger Beerenauslese Rosalack 1949
Croft 1927, *Graham* 1935

'I was in the 4th Queen's Own Hussars regiment in Germany, and our colonel was Winston Churchill, who was a great devotee of Pol Roger Champagne.'

LEFT 2nd Lt James Long (1953) and Winston Churchill (1895), both as junior officers of the 4th Queen's Own Hussars.

An interview with JAMES LONG

MAGDALENE COLLEGE, CAMBRIDGE, m.1954

James Long was at school at Charterhouse before national service with the 4th Queen's Own Hussars' regiment under Colonel-in-Chief Winston Churchill. After Cambridge, he was recruited by David Peppercorn into the wine trade, where he remained for the rest of his career.

'I became connected with wine during national service. I was in the 4th Queen's Own Hussars regiment in Germany, and our colonel was Winston Churchill, who was a great devotee of Pol Roger Champagne. I'd been to school in Germany prior to that, at a place called Schule Schloss Salem, where Prince Philip, the Duke of Edinburgh, also went to school. The school was started by its first headmaster, a famous German adventurer and educator, and founder of Outward Bound, called Kurt Hahn. Hahn was imprisoned for speaking out against the Nazis, and in 1933 fled persecution to Britain following an appeal by Prime Minister Ramsay MacDonald and founded Gordonstoun School in Scotland.

'One of the things I dealt with in the army was our mess, because we employed quite a number of German cooks and nobody other than me spoke German. Schloss Bredebeck had been a hunting lodge. It was a beautiful and well-equipped building out in the country with one of the best messes in Germany, quite famous for its food and drink. We had a lot of relatively good wine there, and our own riding school, and that's how I first began to be interested in wine. A lot of the officers in the regiment were quite well off, so we ate and drank very well.

Meeting Colonel-in-Chief Winston Churchill

'I met Churchill when I joined my regiment in 1951, and we had a regimental dinner at the Grosvenor House Hotel in London, then one of the top hotels in town. Churchill was by then again Prime Minister, and all of us young subalterns (I was only 18) were taken to meet him

and shake his hand. He sat in a corner of the room and had a pint tankard in front of him, which looked as if it contained tomato juice. I was later told that it was liberally laced with vodka. We went into dinner and sat at one of those tables with three sprigs; Churchill sat at the top.

'At dinner we had the whole range of white wine, red wine and Port. Churchill had an ice bucket in front of him with a bottle of Pol Roger Champagne in it and he drank the whole bottle for dinner. I don't know why he joined the 4th Queen's Own Hussars; they were probably the only regiment that would accept him because he was a bit of a renegade, but in fact he was fond of the regiment and always attended the dinners. We had an officers' dining club where, years later, we entertained his grandson, also called Winston Churchill, who was an MP from 1970–97. One of my jobs was organizing the retired officers' dining club cellar, and Bill Gunn MW, with Pol Roger UK, kindly used to help me source the house Pol Roger Champagne.

At Cambridge

'After national service I went up to Magdalene at Cambridge, which I didn't particularly enjoy. I'd had such a good time before that it was a bit of a comedown when it came to university life. However, one of the things that I did do was to join the Cambridge University Wine and Food Society (CUWFS). I was on the committee, and in my last year I was cellarer.

'Both at Oxford and Cambridge there were a number of dons with fine cellars. Denis Mack Smith, a Peterhouse don, was a famous historian. I read history, and so on occasion he

ABOVE Winston Churchill with Odette Pol-Roger.
RIGHT Churchill was an enthusiastic racehorse owner.
He sent Odette a telegram with the news that his
horse, Pol Roger, won the Black Prince Stakes at the
Coronation Meeting, Kempton Park in 1953.

NATIONAL SERVICE

In Britain, conscription was introduced during
World War I from 1916 to 1919, and again from 1939
to 1960. Post World War II, from 1948 onwards, it
was known as national service. The Military Service
Act of 1916 called up men aged 18 to 41, unless they
were widowed or ministers of the church. It lapsed in
peacetime, but was revived by Neville Chamberlain's
cabinet in 1939 for single men 20 to 22 years of age
due to concern over the rise of Nazi Germany. When
war broke out on September 3, 1939, the upper age
limit was extended to 41, and by 1942, women were
also included. Over 1.5 million men were recruited
and of these 1,128,000 joined the British Army, and
the rest the Royal Navy and the Royal Air Force (there
was a market in forged medical discharges and a small
number sought to avoid service by using medically
unfit men to impersonate them). By 1949 healthy men
aged 17 to 21 were conscripted to national service for
18 months to two years, including a number of blind
wine-tasting competitors of the 1950s. For many, it
was their first time away from home, and they learned
new skills and travelled at a time when many could not
otherwise have afforded to do so. It was a time of great
camaraderie, as men from disparate backgrounds were
thrown together under the discipline of basic training,
and bonds of friendship were formed.

THE 4TH QUEEN'S OWN HUSSARS

The 4th Queen's Own Hussars, named after George
III's wife Queen Charlotte, was a cavalry regiment
in the British Army that famously took part in the
Charge of the Light Brigade at the 1854 battle of
Balaclava in the Crimean War. Founded in 1685
as a single cavalry regiment in the midst of the
Monmouth Rebellion, they went on to serve with
distinction throughout the 18th and 19th centuries,
against Jacobite rebels, the French and the Afghans,
among others. Sir Winston Churchill, 'the Greatest
Hussar of them all', first became a cornet in the
4th Hussars in 1895, becoming a colonel-in-chief
in 1941, when he was Prime Minister – a rank he
retained until his death in 1965. Churchill's pay
was £150 a year, but he needed an additional £500
to live in the style of a cavalry officer. Roy Jenkins,
his biographer, describes how Churchill arrived in
India with the Hussars in October 1896, so eager to
get ashore after a 23-day voyage that he dislocated
his shoulder on the harbour steps. He played a great
deal of polo, wrote journalistic articles and sought
to be involved in any military action so that he
could distinguish himself through personal bravery.
His correspondence with his mother also reveals his
time with the Hussars in India as one of prodigious
reading and self-education.

taught me; he was a key person behind the CUWFS, and regularly produced bottles for undergraduates he felt were truly interested in wine. Donald Beves at King's was another well-known don who was rumoured (entirely incorrectly) to be the "fifth man" of the Cambridge spies, after Philby, Maclean, Burgess and Blunt. Trinity, St John's and King's had amazing cellars. Even Magdalene had a pretty good one.

'We had several tastings a term, and it was all men then. I had connections with Gilbey's, a firm I later joined, and I organized one of the first tastings of Smirnoff vodka, which was quite a merry evening. Harry Waugh, of Harveys, leveraged the CUWFS as a recruitment centre to bring people into the wine trade. Harry was loved by all and lived well into his nineties – he was a charming person, very knowledgeable and supported the society a lot, as did another marvellous merchant called Otto Loeb. Loeb was a confirmed bachelor, and had a fine company specializing in German wines. Although I'd been in Germany, I didn't actually like most German wines then. Apart from wines from specialists like Loeb, it was a sea of Liebfraumilch.

'As cellarer of the CUWFS in 1956–57, I captained the blind wine-tasting team. The match was downstairs in a basement room, and I can remember it being rather dim. I did well, and much to my surprise got the highest score. Julian Jeffs, who became a judge, and who wrote a number of books on Sherry and Spanish wines, was another competitor. And Tom King, now the Rt Hon the Lord King of Bridgwater CH and a former cabinet minister, was in the society and had a lovely old Citroën we used to drive about in. Tim Miller, sadly, died quite young; he became managing director of a company called J R Phillips, which had the agency for Cointreau and used to sponsor *The Love of Three Oranges* [Prokofiev] at Glyndebourne. I also had friends in the society at Oxford, and Ewen Fergusson and I were flown out with a few others on one occasion to one of the big producers in Champagne.

Joining the wine trade

'I went into the wine trade because of the CUWFS. I had wanted to go into the Foreign Office, but I failed the exam, so I was told by my parents that I had to get a job, and the only thing I knew anything about was wine. I was friendly with David Peppercorn, whose father had a wine business called Osborne & Son.

'Just before I was due to leave Cambridge, David's father, Jim Peppercorn, bought shares of a firm called Morgan Furze, which was then a wine merchant. It had premises in Drapers Gardens in the City, and Jim managed to move the licence from the City to the West End, just off Park Lane in Brook Street, which was a plum position. Jim wanted somebody to go in as an assistant to help an old colonel, and I was asked if I would like to do it. I was lucky – not by design but by chance – and I concentrated on supplying hotels, restaurants and nightclubs. Eventually Morgan Furze became the principal supplier of restaurants and nightclubs in London, and then was bought by Gilbey's.

'By 1974, Gilbey's had amalgamated with Justerini & Brooks and Corney & Barrow to form International Distillers & Vintners (IDV). David Peppercorn, by now a Master of Wine, who had started with his father's firm, Osborne & Son, had become chief wine buyer for the lot, but then decided to go out on his own. They were looking for a new wine buyer and David recommended me. I was the first non-MW to be a wine buyer for a very big organization, and I stayed on with IDV until 1991, when they sold Peter Dominic. At 57, I went out on my own as a consultant. I had nice consultancies in Bordeaux and Italy, and I finally retired from the wine trade in 2009.

'I remember selling Pétrus by the cask, not in bottles, in the early 1960s. But for a few exceptions like Cheval Blanc and St-Emilion, Right Bank wines like Pomerol really weren't very well-known. At one time, as a buyer, I bought nearly the most Champagne of anybody in the country. And I used to buy 50,000-plus cases of Muscadet. In the '70s it was popular, then suddenly went down. I looked after Lafite for about ten years, from 1980. During that time, I used to go and stay at Lafite. The wines that Eric Rothschild opened just for supper were absolutely incredible. I once took Eddie Penning-Rowsell[*] for a weekend there, because Eric Rothschild wanted him to come. Poor old Eddie – he was getting pretty old by then – actually wept tears over the 1953; he got completely carried away with this wine. Eddie was famously left wing, a Champagne socialist. Cyril Ray[**], who had rooms in Albany, was similar and firmly called himself a socialist; he used to have breakfast at The Ritz every day.'

[*]Edmund Penning Rowsell (1913–2002): UK journalist and wine writer.
[**]Cyril Ray (1908–91): UK author, journalist and food and wine writer.

OFFICERS AND COMMITTEE—1956-57

President
L. C. G. CLARKE, Esq.

Vice-Presidents
G. A. HEPWORTH, Esq.
D. MACK SMITH, Esq.
(Senior Treasurer)
B. C. ROBERTSON, Esq.

Cellarer
J. P. LONG (Magdalene)
20 Hertford Street

Junior Treasurer
R. G. PAYNE (Trinity Hall)
E.5 Trinity Hall

Honorary Secretary
The Hon. M. W. M. DAVIDSON (Pembroke)
18, Fitzwilliam Street

Committee Members
S. H. SWAYNE (Magdalene)
A. G. MUNRO (Clare)

FOISTER & JAGG LIMITED, CAMBRIDGE

ABOVE The CUWFS officers and committee, 1956–57.

ABOVE Tom King (front row, centre) at an Emmanuel College XII Club dinner at Cambridge, 1955–56, in a room where the Cambridge University Wine and Food Society also held many of its functions.

THE RT HON THE LORD KING OF BRIDGWATER CH
Emmanuel College, Cambridge, m.1953

Tom King was educated at Rugby School, where he played front row on the rugby team with Ewen Fergusson, prior to heading to Cambridge: 'I was certainly a member of the Cambridge University Wine and Food Society 1953–56.'

Good friends of his, the late Tim Miller, and Robin Don competed in the team for the match with Oxford – as well as James Long who recalls Tom King 'had a lovely old Citroën we used to drive about in'.

Lord King was elected MP for Bridgwater in 1970 and is a former cabinet minister under Margaret Thatcher and John Major. He was Defence Secretary from 1989 to 1992 during the Gulf War; serving under him in the Ministry of Defence was outspoken Tory MP Alan Clark. On the back benches, King was chairman of the Intelligence and Security Select Committee, which unmasked one of the longest-serving Soviet spies of the Cold War, British civil servant and KGB source Melita Norwood. He has been a life peer since 2001.

Once, in 2011, on being given a surprise present of a bottle of Pol Roger Champagne in the House of Lords, he looked askance over both shoulders – the Independent Parliamentary Standards Authority restricts gifts of hospitality that exceed £30. He needn't have worried. It was a bottle of non-vintage.

ABOVE Emmanuel College, Cambridge, 1955.

'From the moment we got to Christ Church, Robin always had a case of Bollinger under the table. He was a good friend to have.'

An interview with
THE HON NICHOLAS ASSHETON
(d.2012)

CHRIST CHURCH, OXFORD, m.1954

After Oxford, where he shared a room with fellow blind taster Robin Herbert, the late Nicholas Assheton was a stockbroker for many years. He became deputy chairman of Coutts Bank under chairman and former blind taster Sir Ewen Fergusson, before joining Her Majesty's service as treasurer and extra equerry to Queen Elizabeth the Queen Mother.

'I was quite interested in wine from an early age. The headmaster at Cothill, my first school, talked about wine and lent me George Saintsbury's *Notes on a Cellar-Book*, which I've since read often and find very enjoyable. At home, my father and grandfather didn't drink wine, really – grandfather drank beer, and my father martinis in the evening – but they did drink Port and Champagne. This was in the 1950s.

'I do remember having a taste of Taylor's 1924 as a boy, but then I had an embarrassing moment. My parents gave a cocktail party at home when I was about ten; I was handing around drinks and eats. I was very good and didn't taste any drink at all, until nearly the end, when I went into the pantry where there were some nice ladies washing up. They gave me a mixture of gin and whisky and God alone knows what else. Luckily, all the guests had gone when my head started rolling around. I felt ill and had a terrible red blood vessel in my eye, which I was terrified I would have to explain when I got back to school. I learned a lesson – but it wasn't nice getting a hangover.

'At Eton, there was a pub where boys could drink a limit of two pints of beer after rowing. Then I went in to the army and was in barracks in Windsor for national service. At Oxford, I shared a room with Robin Herbert, who I had also been to school with – from the moment we got to Christ Church, Robin always had a case of Bollinger under the table; he was a good friend to have.

'I was chairman of the Oxford University Wine and Food Society (OUWFS), and got Robin involved – who wasn't prepared to do anything naughty – and another

friend called John Cooper (New) who, sadly, died young. We chose wine merchants we knew or who were particularly highly regarded. O W Loeb was German and charming, and gave quality tastings. Harry Waugh was keener on Oxford than Cambridge, I think, because he was Harveys' man for Oxford. He was good-looking, not very tall, encouraging of the young learning about wine and the best Bordeaux man at that time. Ronald Avery was also impressive and had a high reputation.

'The Pimm's party on the playing fields was the biggest we had, and remarkable, because in those days Pimm's made No. 1, No. 2, No. 3 and No. 4, and brought down ample supplies of all four of them. Pimm's No. 3 was brandy-based, alcoholic and delicious; at good hotel bars in those days you'd get a brandy Pimm's. But we didn't mean to be clever about what we were drinking; it was all very jolly.

'Bruno Schroder (University) was the treasurer of the OUWFS. He was, and is, an eccentric man and flies his own aeroplane. Subscriptions were not more than a tuppence halfpenny, but not always easy to get; Bruno would go to the rooms of members who hadn't paid up and sit by their beds until he got the money out of them. He became a good merchant banker afterwards.

'I was in the match in 1957, and there were two clarets, one Burgundy and a Rhône, and I said it was a Rhône. That won the match because we got just one point more than Cambridge. I was very pleased with that, as was everybody – Cambridge had won the previous three years. So that was great fun.

ABOVE Tom Tower, the main gate into Christ Church, Oxford, seen from the Great Quadrangle or 'Tom Quad', 1957.

Life after Oxford

'After Oxford I went into a firm of stockbrokers my father had been in before the war. The senior partner was a great family friend and kind to me. I went straight in and I stayed for 30 years. Then Big Bang came in 1986, and everything changed and we sold the firm. Before Big Bang, you were actually using your own money, and you'd got your own clients. There was no question of people being paid exceptional amounts, because you were paid your share of the profits. In a good year, that could be quite reasonable if you were a fairly senior partner. In a bad year, it could be bloody awful. In 1974 we lost money; it all went wrong – the oil crisis and a Conservative government. Then it turned around for a long time: keep buying, keep borrowing – bonfire of the vanities. Parts of it were fun, but it was always a worry. When things go like that, you know there will be a fall.

'I went to Coutts Bank for 12 years. Ewen Fergusson was my chairman at Coutts; I was the deputy chairman. When he returned from Paris [having been our ambassador], Ewen Fergusson was given the most amazing collection of directorships. Apart from Coutts, he was chairman of The Savoy Hotel, and a trustee of various museums, but he was a diplomat, not really a businessman. The French loved him because he had a marvellous cellar, and he's extremely jolly and clever; he was a popular ambassador in France. Coutts has always had a royal connection, through to George III, then George IV sacked Coutts. The royal family came back after George IV died, and has been with Coutts ever since. The Queen is the favourite customer.

In Her Majesty's Service

'I worked for Queen Elizabeth the Queen Mother from 1997. My predecessor was not pleased – a bit dotty and very cross – and was heard to mutter, "Some little clerk from Coutts has taken my job." The story was let out at a lunch at Coutts by the Queen, and she said, "Oh dear." It was quite funny. From 1999 I became the Queen Mother's treasurer and I signed the cheques. Her cellar, though, was entirely in the hands of the steward. After she died they nearly had an attack because they found all this amazing wine next to the boiler room in Clarence House, where she had lived since 1953.

'When she was in London, which was about half the year, I saw her nearly every day, and I used to go with her to the Sandringham Flower Show in the summer. In the last year, she didn't come back to London after Christmas. She was wonderful – absolutely – and a tough Scotswoman. The last time I saw her was the Eton Beagles lawn meet at Royal Lodge. We thought it would be cancelled, but it wasn't and with a large lunch party before it. She went out wearing a thin coat. It was very cold, February, and she spent half an hour talking to the boys and the hounds. Then they moved off and she said, "Let's go and walk around the garden." So we walked around the garden for a quarter of an hour in the freezing cold. She enjoyed horse racing and talking about hunting, and was interested in musicals. She had a lot of friends, often half her age; she was very good at making friends. When she was going to a lunch in the City every now and again I would go with her; she was very easy to work for.

'Her Majesty's generation was still pre-World War I and brought up old-fashioned to some extent. No member of the royal family talks about any other member of the royal family; they are terribly close. They talk about things and events and what was in the paper that morning. The Queen Mother liked gin and Dubonnet for a cocktail before lunch; with lunch a glass of claret; in the evening a martini; and a bottle of Champagne at dinner. She was absolutely loved by everyone.

'I was taken to The Saintsbury Club once by Ewen Fergusson. He's a tremendously good provider if one goes and has dinner with him, but the club has got a lot of old people and I expect they'll have a great rush of the young to the head. I joined the Vintners' Company in 1955, one of the "Great Twelve" City of London livery companies.

'A good fun club, looking for younger members, is the Beefsteak. I'm on the committee, and Julian Jeffs is a member. It's a lunch club in an odd place off Leicester Square. It's got one big room, with a big table that takes about 30 people, and most days it fills up. It's a mixed group: quite a lot of political people, quite a lot of literary people.

On his wine cellar

'I've got one bottle left of 1982 Pichon Longueville Comtesse de Lalande – the first non-first growth awarded 100 points by Robert Parker. I know I'll end up drinking it with Ewen. And there are five bottles of Latour 1955. The oldest bottle is 1934 Latour in magnum; Robin Herbert gave it to me for our 70th birthdays.'

A NOTE FROM JACQUELINE ASSHETON

'The bank has a purple Coutts World card, like the black American Express card: the sign of somebody who is fabulously wealthy. Once we were going on a cruise with the Fergussons, and we were in Gordon Ramsay's restaurant, Plane Food, at Terminal Five. Ewen held forth two purple Coutts World cards, saying, "I was chairman and this was the deputy chairman," and the waiter was suitably impressed. Then he put the card in and the pin wouldn't work – three times! He'd mixed them up and killed Nick's card, and Ewen Fergusson had to pay for our drinks all the way around the Baltic.'

BEEFSTEAK CLUBS

The original beefsteak clubs were 18th- and 19th-century all-male dining clubs. The first one was founded in 1705 by actors celebrating the beefsteak as a symbol of the patriotic and Whig concept of liberty. Members often wore a a blue coat and buff waistcoat with brass buttons and a gridiron motif displaying the words: 'Beef and liberty.' Steak and potatoes were accompanied by Port and porter. The Sublime Society of Beefsteaks was started at the Theatre Royal, Covent Garden, in 1735. William Hogarth, Samuel Johnson and other men of the arts were members. It closed in 1867, but was revived by the famous actor manager Henry Irving, the proprietor of the Lyceum Theatre, who hosted dinners there from 1878 until his death.

Beefsteak clubs exist today at both Oxford and Cambridge. The Gridiron Club, referred to as The Grid, is a beefsteak club founded by and for Oxford undergraduates in 1884. The grilling gridiron symbol appears on the club tie and on the sign outside its current premises in The Golden Cross at Cornmarket Street. At Cambridge, Beefsteak Club initiates are treated to a lavish seven-course dinner, each dish accompanied by a bottle of wine, served in a room with tarpaulin covering every surface.

The current London Beefsteak Club was started in 1876, and moved to its premises at Irving Street, near Leicester Square, in 1895. It quickly became a place to dine after the curtain had fallen in the West End and many politicians and people of the theatre became members. Members meet for luncheon at a long table that seats 30. Anthony Lejeune, in his book *The Gentlemen's Clubs of London*, describes the open-timbered roof like a medieval hall.

ABOVE The dining room of The Beefsteak Club, London.

THE HON EDWARD ADEANE CVO
Magdalene College, Cambridge, m.1957

'I attended a good many wine tastings when I was at Cambridge, and remember Hugh Johnson (King's) and Michael Cottrell (Magdalene), later of Saccone & Speed, being stalwarts of the Cambridge tasting scene, and Peter Noble of Christopher & Co visiting on several occasions. I was a few years younger than the rest of my contemporaries, however, including blind wine taster, the Hon Malcolm Davidson (Pembroke), now Viscount Davidson. I was called up to national service but there was then an Act instituted that only those born through September 30, 1939 would continue to go – my birthday was October 4.'

President
L. C. G. CLARKE, Esq.

Vice-Presidents
G. A. HEPWORTH, Esq.
D. MACK SMITH, Esq.
(Senior Treasurer)

Cellarer
THE HON. M. W. M. DAVIDSON (Pembroke)
18 Fitzwilliam Street

Junior Treasurer
R. K. MIDDLEMAS (Pembroke)

Honorary Secretary
THE HON. J. P. F. ST. L. GRENFELL (King's)
2 St. Clement's Gardens

Committee Members
A. G. MUNRO (Clare)
A. D. HIGNETT (Magdalene)

THE CAMBRIDGE UNIVERSITY
WINE AND FOOD SOCIETY

LENT TERM 1958

Thursday, January 23rd   6 p.m.
A tasting of Clarets will be given by Averys of Bristol Ltd., in the Benson Hall, Magdalene.

Tuesday, February 4th   6 p.m.
A "Special Selection" tasting will be given by Dolamore Ltd., of Cambridge in Dr. Eden's Room in Trinity Hall.

Tuesday, February 11th   6 p.m.
A tasting of Hocks and Moselles will be given by O. W. Loeb & Co. Ltd. in the Old Library, Pembroke. No guests permitted.

Tuesday, February 18th   1.0 for 1.15 p.m.
A Luncheon will be held, details of which will be circulated later.

Tuesday, February 25th   6 p.m.
A tasting of Red Burgundies will be given by Morgan Furze & Co. in Dr. Eden's Rooms, Trinity Hall.

Friday, March 7th
The Annual Tasting Match against Oxford University.

An interview with
ROBIN HERBERT

CHRIST CHURCH, OXFORD, m.1954

'Life is all made up of who your friends are.'

Robin Herbert was at both Eton College and Christ Church, Oxford, with Nicholas Assheton, before Harvard Business School and a career in investment banking. He was president of the Royal Horticultural Society from 1984 to 1994.

'I was at Christ Church with Nick Assheton, who had been at Eton with me. I drifted into the Oxford University Wine and Food Society (OUWFS) in 1955, invited to tastings, and we were both on the team for two years. We had lunch with Harry Waugh, who I think was keen for Oxford to win, so he gave us tips without revealing the names. We lost the first year, and beat Cambridge in 1957. Nick clinched it: he spotted a Rhône wine. John Cooper was also on the team, and Timothy Sainsbury, who became an MP. I'm terribly evil about Cambridge – not plugged in to that scene at all, but James Long is a great friend, and was on the team for Cambridge in 1957.

Early years
'My parents died when I was very young – by the time I'd gone to Eton – and I had a mentor who was good on wine called William Crawshay, who was later knighted. He was a great friend of Ronald Avery. That's when I was first exposed to good claret, when Cheval Blanc, bottled by Averys, cost £1 a bottle. William Crawshay got all sorts of military crosses for work with the French Resistance. He was a larger-than-life figure, and I got on well with him, and his wife, who was a great family friend. He always had a good table of nice clarets and we used to talk about wine. Life is all made up of who your friends are.

Up at Oxford
'I used to go to Averys' tastings at Oxford. It was a natural thing to do, as I was friendly with Ronald Avery, and I started buying wine then. And when I came down in 1957, I started putting wine away. We would have lunch with Ronald in the Mauretania Restaurant – he had bought the interior fittings of the ship and plopped it down in Bristol where his offices were. André Simon was in the Sunday papers every week in my day, and the key wine merchants were Loeb, Harveys and Averys. There was always this love-hate relationship between Harveys and Averys in Bristol. Averys staff were the gentlemen and Harveys were the players: that sums it up.

'The Christ Church dons certainly enjoyed drinking claret and drank wine at high table. First growths weren't

OXFORD AND CAMBRIDGE UNIVERSITIES
THE ANNUAL WINE-TASTING MATCH

This Wine-Tasting Match was held at the Oxford and Cambridge Club, in Pall Mall, London, on Thursday, 28 February 1957. The wines, which were tasted 'blind', of course, were as follows: *Beaujolais:* Fleurie '52; *Claret:* Château L'Enclos '45; *Rhône:* Châteauneuf-du-Pape '53; *Burgundy:* Chambolle-Musigny '49; *Claret:* Château Rausan-Ségla '49, Château Léoville-Barton '50; *Bordeaux blanc:* Château La Tour Alain '53; *Hock:* Dürkheimer Hochmess Scheurebe '53; *Moselle:* Uersiger Würzgarten '55; *Burgundy:* Montrachet (Bouchard Père) '50.

Oxford won with a score of 262 to Cambridge's 246. Both teams dined together after the Tasting, but no score was kept of the tasting of four Vintage Ports served after dinner.

ABOVE The fifth annual varsity blind wine-tasting match, chronicled in *Wine and Food*, No. 94, Summer 1957, was held auspiciously on André Simon's 80th birthday, February 28, 1957. Oxford won, interrupting a three-year winning streak by Cambridge.

the domain of the aristocracy then. I was lucky to be there. I read history for the first year, then decided I wanted to go to Harvard, so I switched (to my tutor Hugh Trevor Roper's fury) to philosophy, politics and economics for the second and third year. I did courses on investment because I wanted to go into the money business.

'The university scene was interested in politics, but I went to one union debate and said, "That's not for me," and never went near it again. But there were a whole range of people there who all rushed in to make speeches at the union. People like Michael Heseltine; Rod Carnegie, who went on to great things in Australia; and Paul Channon, who became a minister in Thatcher's government and later a life peer. There were far fewer ladies at Oxford in those days – two-fifths of Christ Church is now ladies – and our social life was often in London. There was no drink-driving law, and you could get to London in an hour if you put your foot down; it was a different world. We were allowed cars because we had been in the services.

'I left in 1957 for Harvard Business School, and went to work on Wall Street as a security analyst. Then I joined a small private bank called Leopold Joseph in London, where I was involved in every known capacity from bottle-washer to chairman, including chief executive from 1964 to 2004, when we sold it. You were meant to know your way round, and to be able to tell a Graves from a Pomerol. When I joined the board of NatWest, they served Latour every day for lunch. We drank it too young, but there we are. Nick Assheton became a director of Coutts under David Money Coutts, then deputy chairman. When he retired he went to be treasurer for the Queen Mother, and he walked in her funeral procession. I was lucky enough to go to lunch with the Queen Mother a few times – martinis and Port at lunch, her staff dying to get back to their desks, but she wasn't going to move.

'My friend John Cooper, who was on the team and who died young, was living in London and working at Schroder's in the 1960s, and bought a hogshead of Pétrus. He was a clever investment man. A scholar at New College, he read PPE and got a first.

'Nowadays I know all sorts of people who buy wine with a view to selling it, which is presumably a disaster, because it means you're into a bubble and it'll burst at some stage. I've invested in all sorts of things over the years, but I've never invested in a wine business. As someone who ran a private bank for 20 years or more, I would never, ever have lent money on wine. It didn't produce any income.

'Wine tasting was a peripheral part of life. There were so many other things we were doing at Oxford at the same time. I had a horse there and was secretary of the drag hunt. A drag is when you pursue a false line, not a genuine fox; foxes pee on it and some poor man runs ahead of the hunt. It was an activity that was revived after the war.

'A feature of that era was if you went to dinner with someone or to stay with them at the weekend there was always good Port served – Taylor's or Fonseca – and Sherry as an apéritif. Champagne arrived subsequently. We bought Champagne – and the exact price I paid for Bollinger was 17 shillings, I think. It sounds quite high now. At dinner parties you'd start with cocktails and martinis, through dinner drink white Burgundy and Chablis, then claret and finish with Port. I had one friend who was deeply into German wines, Trockenbeerenauslese and Auslese, but that was unusual. We all drank Port at Oxford because you could buy good Port for less than £1 a bottle. People come out to dinner in the country now and if you offer them Port they will turn it down because everyone's got to drive home. They say it's because of the alcohol, but New World wines can be 15 or 16 per cent alcohol by volume; I think people just don't drink Port.

'I've kept in touch with a handful of contemporaries and we go back to reunions at Christ Church, and give to the college financially. I never became a vintner because I was too busy in my horticultural life. I was president of

ABOVE City gent with requisite bowler hat and umbrella.

THE CITY IN THE 1950s
by ROBIN HERBERT

'In the City in those days people went round in their bowler hats and umbrellas to the different banks to pick up liquidity, and that went into the discount market, which no longer exists – seven or eight discount houses like Union Discount, all gone now. They picked up and managed the liquidity, and paid it back when you wanted it back. They all wore a bowler hat – or top hat in many cases. You'd see them talk to the treasurer of each of the banks, collect money and talk about rates. It was competitive and dependent on personal relationships. So much of the City in those days depended on personal relationships – it was all about personal relationships. That went out the window from 1995, or perhaps from Big Bang onwards.

'When I was doing national service (aged 18 in 1952) you were told by your regiment that if you were going to London you would be expected to walk around in a suit with a bowler hat and rolled umbrella. It had to be a proper, rolled-up umbrella: not one of these things you fit in a pocket nowadays. A proper umbrella made by Brigg & Co.'

the Royal Horticultural Society from 1984 to 1994 and that brought me together with Hugh Johnson, who had a very good garden at Saling Hall. We are both on the council for the International Dendrology Society, a gang of people who go round looking at plants.

'Wine was certainly part of the experience of companionship – absolutely.'

ABOVE David Peake, Joint Master of the Christ Church & New College Beagles, in the foreground in his hunt coat and white breeches, March 1958.

An interview with
DAVID PEAKE

CHRIST CHURCH, OXFORD, m.1955

David Peake was a soldier prior to Oxford, where he was the president of the Wine and Food Society in his last year. After Oxford he pursued a career in banking. He is a founding shareholder of the Liv-ex wine exchange and chairman of the wine committee for the Goldsmiths' Company.

'The fun of being involved with the Oxford University Wine and Food Society (OUWFS) was meeting wine merchants of considerable eminence at the time: Ronald Avery of Averys, Otto Loeb of O W Loeb & Co, Dolamore and lots of others. At that stage of one's life, talking about wine with these great merchants gave an added dimension to the whole thing. Harry Waugh was a delightful man: completely unpompous and unaffected, and an enormous enthusiast with an ability to enthuse the young. The story goes that one day he was being interviewed by an over-assiduous journalist who asked, "Tell me, Mr Waugh, have you ever confused claret with Burgundy?" And he replied, "Not since lunch."

'I competed in 1957 and '58; we won the first match and lost the second; I had a cold in the second one – but one would say that, wouldn't one? I was president of the

OUWFS 1957–58, succeeding Nicholas Assheton, and prior to him it had been Timothy Sainsbury. The society had been founded with the right intentions in 1951, but had slipped into a period of people enjoying more of the drinking aspect rather than the knowledge aspect – not really interested in what lay behind it all. Timothy Sainsbury began to pull it around and put it onto the right lines: more serious – but not boringly serious. Nicholas Assheton followed, and I hope I followed on in similar lines.

'Ian Lowe (Oriel) was the secretary, and he went on to become a curator of ceramics at the Ashmolean Museum, and Bruno Schroder, the banker, was the treasurer. Bruno was an extremely efficient treasurer. The subscription then was 10 shillings a term, but rarely had the full membership paid its dues. Bruno would bicycle around to everybody before breakfast, lean over them as they were snoozing, and say, "Come on: pay up." And he got everyone fully paid up.

'I did drink wine before Oxford. I was a soldier before I went up, so I was a bit older – nearly everybody of my generation had been in national service – so one had usually had a glass or two of something by then. I was lucky: my father loved claret and vintage Port, and I was brought up from an early age with wine. It was a natural thing for me.

'The OUWFS was initially a local spin off of André Simon's Wine and Food Society. Each college had its own dining club where they would eat and drink more than they should, but the OUWFS was the only society devoted to the study of the enjoyment of wine and food. Merchants would give tastings to the dons, who were buying for the college cellars over lunch. Then kindly, most of them agreed to stay on to give a tasting to the society in the early evening – we were tagged on behind selling wines to the colleges. Tastings took place in several different colleges, but it was a university-wide society. The committee then entertained the merchant to dinner in a hotel restaurant or The Gridiron Club.

'One memorable event in particular was a lunch at the Hotel Ehrsam (which is no longer there) [see right]. The theme was oysters, and smoked salmon for those who didn't like oysters; I love oysters, and English cheeses. Timothy Sainsbury was instrumental in arranging this, because he had a family connection to Mac Fisheries, which had a branch in Oxford. Mac Fisheries provided the oysters and the smoked salmon free, and Sainsbury's provided the English cheeses free. Those were the days …

'The wine and wine-writing world has become much more lively today, and professional. When I was at Oxford there were few people writing articles about wine. People talked about it a bit, but not in the way they do now; it has become immensely high-profile. There may have been one or two lady undergraduates who attended some of our tastings, but it wasn't the same world as it is now.

Wines to buy
'In specialty wine shops you would only probably buy French wines from the classic regions, although I don't think many undergraduates, even better-off ones, were in the market for buying large amounts of wine for themselves at that time. But in college we had the buttery – a sort of bar where one could buy bottles from the college cellar at near cost. In 1955–58 the wines that were available for sale that we were drinking were 1935 clarets at £1 a bottle – it was wonderful. They weren't the Latours and Lafites, but they were very much the next rung down.

'The first vintage and wine I bought for myself to lay down was Léoville-Barton 1953: a lovely year for wine. In 1959, however, it was an incredibly hot year – so much so they were hosing down the roofs of the châteaux to keep the wine cool enough for fermentation to be completed.

OXFORD UNIVERSITY
MICHAELMAS TERM MEETING

This Meeting was held on 20 November 1957 at Ehrsam's Restaurant, Oxford, beginning with a Tasting of Oysters— Dutch, Helford River, Whitstable and Colchester, provided by Macfisheries— and ending with a Tasting of English Cheeses—Caerphilly, Cheddar, Cheshire, Blue Cheshire, Lancashire, Lancashire Sage, Leicester, Derby, Double Gloucester, White and Blue Stilton, White and Blue Wensleydale, provided by J. Sainsbury. There was a main dish in-between of Moules Marinière, with some Pommes Purée. There were three white wines served, a Chablis 1953 from Messrs. Grierson & Oldham; a Swiss Fendant 1954, Montibeux; and a 1952 Bâtard Montrachet, shipped by Messrs. Bouchard, Père & Fils.

ABOVE The Michaelmas term meeting of the OUWFS was held at Ehrsam's Restaurant, Oxford, as reported in *Wine and Food*, No. 97, Spring 1958.

That year some quite good names made wine that was not ever fully fermented; it was a tricky vintage. In the 1950s the Médoc was still the classic area of Bordeaux, the Loire was on the map, but we'd never have dreamt where in the hell Fronsac was.

1870 Lafite and a Scottish country house sale
'The oldest wine I ever bought was Lafite 1870, in magnum. It came out of the first country house sale that Michael Broadbent from Christie's organized from Glamis Castle in Scotland, where it had sat for ages in that very damp, cold cellar. Wines came up in three or four lots: the bottles were nicely labelled in the first lot – I knew the Americans would buy these, as they loved the souvenirs, and in 1971, the six magnums went for £600: £100 a magnum. I bought the third lot at £450. I shared them with friends, and kept three of them. The first magnum, which I remember drinking very well, was absolutely amazing and pre-phylloxera. I didn't dare stand it up because I didn't know how long it would last. I pulled the cork out in the cellar, and we poured it straight into the glasses because I was terrified it would vanish. It lasted for about three-quarters of an hour, then it did fade away. That first magnum was delicious.

'The second magnum I drank with friends; it was not quite so good. So I looked at the price and sold the third magnum back through Christie's for £1,000; I had bought it for £75. I asked Michael Broadbent who on earth would pay £1,000 for a magnum of wine of that age. He said, "Well, we have a standing order from a country club in Florida for any pre-phylloxera wine." It was flown out, I think. I always had the idea it was sitting in a seat on Concorde, and that it would be drunk at some great diamond wedding or similar.

'Years later, I was in Tokyo on banking business with Kleinwort Benson, and our man out there took me to dinner at a restaurant in Tokyo. The Japanese sommelier was extremely friendly and being proud of his cellar insisted on taking us down for a tour. It was not too big; there was shingle on the floor, and wine everywhere. Most of the wines were old vintages: 1945s, lying with their labels facing upwards. I looked across the floor and there, lying in the corner, was a magnum. It had a slip label – Lafite 1870 – and no other indication. I said, "Where did that come from?" And the man said, "We bought it from a country club in Florida."

'Whether it was truly my magnum I don't know, but the likelihood is that that wine went from me to Florida and ended up in a restaurant cellar in Tokyo.

LEFT A magnum of Château Lafite 1870 from Glamis Castle.

MICHAEL BROADBENT MW
TASTING NOTE: RED BORDEAUX 1870

Together with 1864 and 1865 one of the most magnificent of all the classic pre-phylloxera clarets ... Spring frosts reduced the potential crop and a bakingly hot summer escalated the sugar content, leading to an early (from 10 September) harvest of superripe, concentrated wines.

Château Lafite One of the all-time greats and, at its best, a powerhouse ... In fact, such a powerful and tannic wine that it was virtually undrinkable for half a century. Nevertheless, bottlings varied and, as always, provenance plays a part. Tasted on 18 occasions. The most magnificent were (and still can be) the Coningham-bottled magnums from Glamis Castle. Of the 48 originally binned in 1878, 41 magnums had remained undisturbed until I and a friendly wine merchant packed them up for a great sale at Christie's in 1971.

[From *Michael Broadbent's Vintage Wine*]

Madame Bollinger and old Champagne

'I never buy wine for investment purposes – the sale of that one magnum, the Lafite 1870, is the only wine I've sold in my life, except among friends and family – but I'm interested in the idea, and I was a founding shareholder of the Liv-ex wine exchange. They're very good and have created a niche and an index, but the investment side of wine never interested me. I bought wine to lay down, to drink, and then I made the same mistake as a lot of English people, which is that we tend to worship age to a point where we leave wine too long. My father was a great friend of Mme Bollinger, and whenever he was driving to the south of France he would always stop off to see her for lunch, and she'd fill the car with what she regarded as really quite old Champagne. Mme Bollinger was filling the car with 1928 Bollinger – delicious still – just after the war. He loved it, and she'd say to him, "You're mad. You like the stuff when it's gone over the top. It tastes of straw and it's ridiculous."

ABOVE Madame Lily Bollinger on her bicycle.

On wine preferences

'I enjoy wine that I was brought up on, but I can't afford to buy it now. Apart from the Lafite magnums, I've cut off certain purchases out of a sense of value. I don't like paying more than £40 a bottle for anything. I've been lucky because I bought a lot early on – at home now we're drinking 1982 Cos d'Estournel. I'm chairman of the wine-buying committee for The Goldsmiths' Company, one of the big London livery companies. We buy quite a lot of wine, but with regard to clarets it's now very much the second wines of a château, and sometimes the third.

We also look for the smaller châteaux from the less well-known regions of Bordeaux – for example in Fronsac – that are owned by the big names.

Oxford life beyond wine

'I was a master of the beagles at Oxford; I had to run around to wear off the wine I'd tasted the evening before. It was much more energetic than the drag. The drag you do on horseback chasing a bag of aniseed around. Beagles you run around – less frightening – and you chase a hare, which you never catch, so it didn't quite matter. I still keep beagles.

'I was also a member of the Bullingdon Club, which now people are terribly ashamed of and I'm not at all. I've got a lovely photograph of the Bullingdon members in my day: Robin Herbert, Nicholas Assheton – it's fading a bit. I don't hide it like the Prime Minister does. The Bullingdon went in great phases, and it went through a bad period of being banned just before we were there, with bashed up places and everything – just how the OUWFS had been through a bad patch – probably the same people involved. The wave of vandalism, I'm happy to say, did not carry on when I was involved, and we weren't banned from anywhere. We just had a good time and drank more than we should've done. We were rather a goody-goody generation, actually, funnily enough.

'If people ask, "What's your favourite vintage?" I really can't say; the 1960s were probably above all for consistent quality: 1961 was lovely, long-lasting and huge, 1962 magnificent, 1966 delicious. I bought them all. When my wife and I moved out of our family house we'd lived in for 30-odd years to one of our farmhouses, I still had quite a few wines from the '60s. I decided I wasn't going to leave them all for my son to drink, who lives there now, so we had a wonderful time finishing them up.

'The 1966s went down well; they were the Latours and Lafites, Haut-Brion and Palmer, and the other wines that I love. I don't buy them any more, because they're ridiculously priced. We were so lucky because that was before the great inflation. Prices were much, much lower obviously than they were 20 years later. It wasn't until the 1970s that the whole thing went mad, so we were able to buy wine really for what now seems to be ludicrously low prices. And dining out in London: one could take a girl out to London for a very good dinner and a bottle of wine for £5. It makes one green with envy, doesn't it?

'Those who had the luck as I did, to have parents who knew and loved wine: that was an excellent start. At home, my father's clarets were 1928s, '29s, '33s and '34s and in particular, '37 Pontet-Canet. The OUWFS provided the jumping-off point for those who did not have that start at home. It was extremely enjoyable. From the wine merchant's point of view, I often wonder whether the balance sheet worked out; in my case I suspect it has. I've bought a lot of wine in my life, and nearly always from wine merchants who I remember coming down to look after us. But I've never been a keeper of empty bottles: full ones, but never empty. I have the memories.'

THE LIV-EX WINE EXCHANGE

The Liv-ex wine exchange was started by Justin Gibbs and James Miles, both stockbrokers and friends. Miles first came across top Bordeaux wine at a lunch, where one of his friends had secured a parcel of ten cases of 1995 Lafite, and persuaded each of the lunch party to buy two cases each at £700 per case. James Miles bought four cases. A couple of years later, as the Asian crisis was unfolding in 1997–98, he sold them at £1,800 per case, and was able to buy 20 cases of more affordable names like Lynch-Bages and Haut-Bailly.

He learned about fine wine by accident. In 2000, the two friends decided to build Liv-ex, an online stock exchange for wine. Within weeks, however, the Nasdaq peaked and then proceeded to fall 78 per cent; customers and venture capitalists were in no hurry to sign up to new dotcoms. They faced challenges: they knew very little about wine and at least 12 other companies were trying to do something similar. Broadband then was too slow to support a trading exchange, but they kept going by a strong belief in their idea and business model. Since many great wines can take ten years or more to mature, and can often last 50 years, there would be plenty of opportunities to trade these wines, and the supply chain was long and fragmented.

Merchants have been speculating in wine for hundreds of years, but there was no actual market place for a market worth about £654 million per year. The exchange was built around the middlemen, who provided capital, expertise and time to both customers and suppliers. Intended as an information business, they set it up as a club of merchants paying a subscription, and commissions were billed on transactions. Data was published online. At the beginning, as the internet was slow, the two partners patiently worked the website more as a telephone exchange. Ten merchants signed up in July 2000 for the launch. Liv-ex was entirely self-funded in the first year by redundancy cheques from former employers, and they furnished their office above a pizza kitchen in south London, with cast-off furniture and equipment. It was freezing in winter, boiling in summer, and buses rumbled past the window. They wrote regularly to shareholders and were able to top up funding in 2002. Wine funds arrived in 2003, using Liv-ex data to take portfolios to market.

In 2004, they launched the Liv-ex 100 Fine Wine Index, which was described by Reuters and the *Financial Times* as the 'wine industry's leading benchmark'. Merchants use it to value their own and customers' stocks. Today, more than 60 per cent of trade is done by Liv-ex members directly on the web. Fine wine has produced an average compound return of 13 per cent over the last 20 years, beating most other asset classes. New markets such as China and Russia have come in, trebling the market to £1.9bn in the last five years. The exchange currently has 277 members in 25 countries.

OTTO W LOEB

(An interview with Chris Davey, managing director of O W Loeb & Co)

By the end of the 19th century, Otto Loeb's father, Sigmund Loeb, was an established wine broker in Trier on the Mosel in Germany, at a time when Mosel wines were valued more highly than most wines from Bordeaux. Today, O W Loeb & Co is a wholly independent and award-winning company based in London with an extensive list of German, French and New World wines.

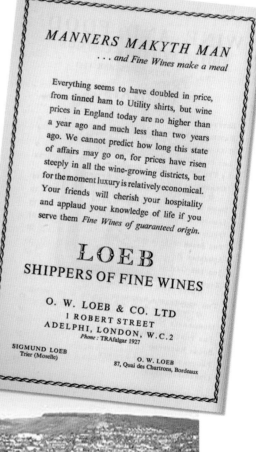

'Otto W Loeb's grandfather, Leopold, started the family wine business in 1874. His father, Sigmund, established the Loeb name on the Mosel River, and in 1903 was a founding member of the Mosel Wine Producers Association: an organization for traders rather than winemakers. As in Burgundy, few German producers sell their wine direct for export. Sigmund Loeb operated in Trier, exporting fine Mosel wines until 1995. Loebstrasse, a road that runs north from Trier up the Mosel and to the Ruwer Valley, was named after Otto's father, Sigmund, who had been a member of the town council for 30 years.

'Sigmund had a very good palate and would buy in the wines, and his son Otto would go out and sell them. Otto then came over to England from Trier to focus on export as a travelling salesman in the 1920s and early '30s; he also went to New York. The Christie family of

TOP RIGHT An advertisement for Loeb in *Wine and Food*, No. 69, Spring 1951.
ABOVE The Mosel Valley.

Glyndebourne loved his Riesling, and Otto did the list at Glyndebourne in its earliest opera seasons. He was Jewish and in 1934 fled from Nazi Germany to England, where he set up Henry Gerson Wines with his cousin of that name, before setting up O W Loeb & Co in 1938. He started importing and selling German wines, but with the onset of war few people wanted them.

'After the war, Otto remained in England to build up his business. It must have been incredibly difficult, as "Otto Wolfgang Loeb" is an unmistakable German name, and, understandably, there was little positive feeling towards Germans or German products. But I think he was just a fabulous guy and that's what made the difference. Otto Loeb was not only a great salesman, but he was an intelligent man with a sensitive palate who understood and knew wine. He was one of the first of the merchants to put on tastings at the colleges after the war, for commercial reasons, rather than educational reasons, desperately trying to flog inventory. German wine had been big at the colleges before the war, but afterwards, the public perception of its image went down. The producers were still making great wines, but there was also rubbish coming over into the UK, particularly in the 1960s. It was the colleges that kept the German wine business going when everything else was on the slide.

'Anthony Goldthorp, the son of a valued customer, then joined O W Loeb & Co and gave tastings at Oxford and Cambridge. He then became managing director as Otto started to retire. In 1961, David Dugdale, also a customer and enthusiast, joined the board. David financed and owned the company effectively from the early 1970s until 1997, and David and Anthony were responsible for expanding the Loeb list to some of the finest growers in France.

'German wines were highly regarded 100 years ago until the war, but less so today, sadly, because people don't understand them. A Berry Bros. & Rudd list from 1911 shows that the great wines of the Mosel and the Rheingau were more expensive than Lafite and Latour. In fact, the most expensive wine today is still German *en primeur*. At auction at Trier, Egon Müller or J J Prüm Trockenbeerenauslese still fetches more than Lafite or Latour *en primeur*. But because the perceived value has gone backwards, German wines are actually the best-value wines going today. A 1966 bottle from Egon Müller says O W Loeb & Co on the neck label; Loeb had such a presence in Germany then that the company's name was put on their top wines.

'O W Loeb & Co goes up to Oxford and Cambridge three times a year now, and invites everyone to Wadham at Oxford and Pembroke at Cambridge, where the long-standing, now retired wine steward for Pembroke was Peter Johnson: a lovely guy in his early 80s, a bit hunched, and a Geordie. Loeb always had a lunch after the tasting; at Oxford, it was at The Elizabeth restaurant, which is not there any longer. The company now gives a dinner every other year for Oxford and Cambridge.'

> 'It was at a tasting of Dr Loeb's that I first encountered wines from Chile which he showed in 1957 or 1958: he was remarkably far-sighted.'

IAN LOWE
Oriel College, Oxford, m.1955

'I took part in the competition in 1957. It was on joining the Oxford University Wine and Food Society (OUWFS) in 1956 that I became taken up with the generous wine tastings provided by numerous wine merchants. Nick Assheton was chairman and John Cooper was secretary, and it was John who selected me as his successor in 1957–58, when my chairman was David Peake. I don't think that I observed then at what a disadvantage I felt, coming from a beer-drinking family, finding myself among those who were habitual drinkers of claret, whose fathers had cellars on which they had been raised.

Two Cambridge friends also involved then were the Hon Edward Adeane and Charles de Selincourt (Magdalene). Another OUWFS member, who gave me a copy of P Morton Shand's seminal book, *A Book of French Wines* in 1960, recently shared a magnum of Château Fombrauge 1967 – what a treat! I have very grateful memories of my education in wine all those years ago and still drink it daily.

ABOVE The Loeb cellar in London in the early 1980s.

THE 1960s

Blind tasting in the 1960s was still an all male preserve (as Sir James Cropper aptly notes: 'we were fairly monastic'), but by all accounts they were having a good time. The tasting match had thus far taken place in Harveys' cellars, and at the turn of the decade purportedly on one occasion in White's, the oldest and most exclusive of gentlemen's clubs, with both André Simon and the Marquis (Bernard) de Lur-Saluces who owned Château Yquem in attendance (Frédéric Delouche recalled 'they added greatly to our nervousness'). But through the 1960s, the match, more often than not, was a home grown affair – held in college at Oxford and at The University Pitt Club in Cambridge. Hugh Johnson was elected to the Cambridge University Wine and Food Society committee; Simon Bingham (Lord Clanmorris) drolly recalls he 'gave a tasting at which there were eight pairs of wines labelled A–H and 1–8. All one had to do was to match up each pair. Hugh Johnson came bottom and the winner was Colin McKinnon who claimed he just put down his Army number.' Both John Harvey (Cantab) and John Avery (Oxon.), sons of the two historic rival Bristol wine merchant families, were in the tasting match in the 1960s – only narrowly missing competing against each other by a couple of years. Cambridge would sustain its lead (having won four of seven varsity matches in the 1950s), winning five of nine competitions in the 1960s. Total UK wine consumption was at just over five bottles per capita per annum.

Student life, however, was influenced by complex cultural and political trends and marked by civil unrest (the darker edges of which included the assassination of JFK and the Vietnam War; the lighter side, Neil Armstrong on the moon and the Beatles). In 1968, when Jancis Robinson arrived at St Anne's, the tasting match was ambiguously recorded as 'no contest' – shortly before a streak of anarchism culminated in the student protests in France, followed two years later by the Garden House Hotel riot in Cambridge. One might imagine undergraduate blind tasters were perhaps participating in – or fleeing from – riots that year ... or under the influence of flower power, heading to Woodstock.

Cambridge		Oxford	
Edward Adeane	Diarmid Guinness	Charles Arnold	Mark Pellew
James Butler	Norman Hammond	John Avery (MW)	Harry Turcan
Michael Cottrell	Jonathan Harris	W Lawrence Banks	Bill Turcan
R Adrian Cowell	John Harvey	Digby Brindle-Wood-Williams	Julian Wontner
James Cropper	David Hudson	Richard Fildes	David Weber
Frédéric Delouche	William Legge-Bourke	Christopher FitzGerald	Tim Noble
Tony Doggart	Jeremy Pope	Michael MacKellar	
James Dugdale	Robert Pryor	Mr Pace	
Duncan Geddes	Alan Volkert	Peter Paice	

FACING PAGE Oxford undergraduates in subfusc and gowns celebrating post exams in 1966. During exams candidates often wear a carnation in their buttonhole, white for the first exam, pink thereafter and red for the final exam.

An interview with
R ADRIAN COWELL

KING'S COLLEGE, CAMBRIDGE, m.1957

On hearing rumours of his own death, R Adrian Cowell responded with verve: 'It was fun to see that I passed away last year. If there really are obituaries, I'd be delighted to see any that you can forward to me in Hell. Or France, which is where I live.' NB: (John) Adrian Cowell, an acclaimed British documentary filmmaker who read history at St Catharine's College and was a founding member of the Cambridge University Wine and Food Society, died aged 77 in November 2011. R Adrian Cowell, a retired stockbroker, is alive and well, drinking Pol Roger Champagne in Poitou-Charentes.

'My uncle introduced me to Port when I was six. The 1908 and 1912 vintages in his cellar seemed delicious to me. Perhaps that kindled my interest in wine. At school I proposed to start a dining club, but sadly, the idea was vetoed by my housemaster. Nevertheless, I used to try some of the London restaurants with a school friend, including Le Caprice, the Café Royale and Boulestin, whereupon deliberating the prospect of another bottle, the wine waiter settled the matter with a judicious "The night is young, sirs."

'Malcolm (Lord) Davidson (Pembroke), who knew me from Westminster School, was cellarer of the Cambridge University Wine and Food Society (CUWFS) in my first year. The cellarer was chairman of the undergraduate committee, which often met without the senior members of the university who oversaw the society's affairs; new members were selected by the committee after an open tasting each year. Amusing minutes, written by the late Michael Cottrell (Magdalene) and by me, record that in 1959, I was in the tasting team with Julian (now Lord) Grenfell (King's), Alan Volkert (Clare), Michael Cottrell, Freddie Delouche (Pembroke) and Peter Cousin (Magdalene): "Mr Cowell, who spent an inordinately long time over the wines, vindicated himself with great panache by scoring far more points than anyone else." The next year (with Michael Cottrell, James Butler (Pembroke), Edward Adeane, Alan Volkert and Freddie Delouche), my own minutes record that the match was won for Cambridge "by the outstanding performance of Mr Butler and the cellarer", the latter being Michael Cottrell! I also recorded that "The heavy debts which the society inherited from Mr Grenfell's term of office should be reduced by fixing the general subscription at three guineas" (about £3.15) and that "The cellarer elected H E A Johnson a committee member."

'The Wine and Food Society (WFS) in London, founded by André Simon, was the inspiration for the CUWFS, which was listed as a branch in its quarterly magazine. In 1954 Cambridge subscribed for membership of "The Wine and Food Society", but it is not clear if the subscription was maintained. The precise relationship was vague, but I did call on the Great Man, and was given some instruction by his secretary, Madeleine Heard. This included the advice that Le Caprice was her favourite place for dinner, "But of course it's no good going there unless you know Mario" (whom I supposed to be the head waiter, and did not know). What she did not know was that I had patronized the restaurant while at school.

> 'Mr Cowell, who spent an inordinately long time over the wines, vindicated himself with great panache by scoring far more points than anyone else.'

'There were magnificent wines in the cellars of King's (where I read moral sciences tripos, parts 1 and 2) and St Catharine's, and no doubt other colleges, but undergraduates were not able to buy the finest, and the existence of these was not widely known. However, early 19th-century wines were sometimes produced by benevolent dons for CUWFS members, which was a great consolation. Senior members of the university who were on the CUWFS committee were extraordinarily generous: Dr Denis Mack Smith and Dr Denis Marrian invited the undergraduate committee to taste the first-growth clarets; Dr Sidney Smith gave early 19th-century wines; and Dr Donald Beves gave helpful comments at tastings.

'Merchants were sometimes asked to dine at The University Pitt Club, where a private room could be taken and its excellent Port consumed. Committee members lucky enough to be allotted the finer rooms in college also entertained merchants and friends. Excellent meals were to be had in the rooms of committee member Anthony Hignett in Magdalene. King's kitchens also provided

ABOVE The magnificent dining hall at King's College, Cambridge, 1955.

very good private meals for those lucky enough to have rooms in Gibbs' Building. St Catharine's was perhaps the best kitchen of all, under the watchful eye of Dr Sidney Smith.

'As honorary secretary of the CUWFS in 1959–60, I organized its functions and kept the minutes of the proceedings as brief as possible. The committee appointed the tasting team from committee members; I therefore joined the team. Michael Cottrell's minutes of the January 1959 committee meeting noted that "The first tasting of the Lent term was a competitive one ... As usual, few of those who attended were willing to submit their findings, and thus, again true to tradition, the committee established itself as the probable choice for the tasting match ..." No ladies were members of the society, so there were none on the team.

Preparing for the match

'Preparation for the match at the Oxford and Cambridge Club involved a series of late-morning practice tastings for the team, of the kinds of wines we expected might be chosen for the competition. Usually there were six white wines and six red. There was little formal instruction from the trade, but the annual programme of tastings usually involved some discussion of the wines presented by merchants to the society. Otherwise, we were self-taught and I don't recall any serious coaching or training. I do like to sniff all the wines before tasting, and to warm any cold ones in my hands before sniffing. Oxford seemed rather frivolous and superficial and not to take tasting sufficiently seriously. New World wines were not much in evidence, but I believe were sometimes used in blind tastings to confuse the competitors. There was much more interest in the fine wines of the Rhine and Mosel than today. Some believed that the best German sweet wines were preferable to the best Sauternes.

'Today's globalization and the world of billionaire bling wine collectors had not begun in the late 1950s. Instead, the British market for fine wine was held back by the weak economy and a weak currency as well as stupidly high taxation. The top rate for high incomes was around 80 per cent – higher if the income was "unearned". The skilled London wine merchants and retailers were under pressure from weak demand and high interest rates on money borrowed to finance stock. Many closed and the skills of their UK buyers and bottlers were lost. Only tax-deductible business expenses could save the day. The entertainment of clients to meals could be claimed against income tax at 80 per cent, so that those taxed as individuals, such as stockbrokers (not companies, whose tax was lower), could have a £10 lunch for £2 net. In 1960, with the Roederer at £1.40 and a light luncheon wine such as Latour 1950

ABOVE The Royalists' summer party, Cambridge 1960 – Adrian Cowell (left) and Hugh Johnson (right).

at £1.20 a bottle retail, there was still hope. What client could resist? The 1952 vintage Pol Roger was then a heady £1.75, but one might still just have managed a bottle between two.

'My elder brother was a scholar at Trinity, with rooms on Newton's staircase; he and I used to buy wine together at Restell's auction rooms. Delicious Chablis was to be had at 30 pence a bottle. And there was a bargain Chambolle-Musigny from the cellars of British Rail, which we called "Chambolle de Chemin-de-Fer".

'After two years of national service, I retired to Cambridge as a flying officer on the Royal Air Force Volunteer Reserve. Remaining in the reserve was not, however, 'voluntary'; it was compulsory. The Cold War was still raging and the Cuban missile crisis looming. I might have had to get the old uniform, which I used for gardening, rapidly cleaned and pressed.

'With taxation so absurdly high due to the burden of debt left by World War II, rescue came for a few from the generous benevolence of an American lady, Miss Keasbey, who gave money for bursaries to enable some hard-pressed parents to send their children to Oxford or Cambridge. It was her generosity that made it possible for me to buy *Meaning and Truth* by Bertrand Russell and still spare the three guineas for the CUWFS subscription.

'Had it not been for the CUWFS I might not have met Michael Cottrell, whose family owned the distinguished wine business Saccone & Speed. He was a splendid friend with a great sense of humour, as well as being a gifted wine taster. His minutes of committee meetings were written with a light touch. After we had discussed the vexed question of the long waiting list for admission to the society, he minuted that, following a tasting for prospective members, "A number were elected ... During the course of the year, deaths, lunacy, cirrhosis of the liver and differences of opinion with the governing body of the university will undoubtedly cause further vacancies and elections."'

ABOVE Tony, with top hat and in morning coat, as judge's marshal in Cambridge following his graduation with a law degree in the early 1960s.

'My fondest memory of our 1961 tastings is of the Champagne tasting in May Week, which I organized as the society's honorary secretary, and to which Pol Roger, which remains my favourite *grande marque*, generously contributed four bottles.'

An interview with
TONY DOGGART

KING'S COLLEGE, CAMBRIDGE, m.1958

After reading classics and law at Cambridge, Tony Doggart practised as a barrister before joining Robert Fleming & Co. He is now Vice-Chair for Marie Curie Cancer Care, where he set up an annual wine auction dinner as a fund-raising event (recently raising £116,000 in a single evening).

'I joined the Cambridge University Wine and Food Society (CUWFS) in 1958 through several friends at King's, including Hugh Johnson and Adrian Cowell. Leading London wine merchants were keen to display their wares to win the hearts and minds of future customers, while members of the society had a unique opportunity to become familiar with a huge range of wines. The cost of two guineas (about £2.10) a term for weekly Thursday tastings was outstanding value for money.

King of cellars
'At that time King's had no college wine society, but Donald Beves, who taught French literature at King's and had a legendary collection of glass (now bequeathed to the college), had an extensive cellar. He regularly entertained me and several other members of the society to dinner: old dessert wines, including Château d'Yquem dating back to the early 1900s, were a highlight.

'My father was also a graduate of King's and maintained a network of friendships with its dons. His position as a resident MA gave me access to the fellows' wine cellar. This had been extensively restocked in 1945, having been drunk dry by US servicemen billeted in the college during the war. Restocking included all the 1945 first-growth clarets, with the most expensive, Château Lafite, priced at 26 shillings a bottle. My parents both enjoyed wine, and encouraged me to take an interest.

When I was aged 19 we went on a tour of French vineyards with Donald Beves, who insisted on seeking out exceptional wines for dinner.

The end of national service
'The ending of national service at the time I became an undergraduate created two streams of new students. Those who had spent two years in the forces were more mature; others were exploring a new freedom from school routines for the first time. The result for the latter group was often a wasted first year spent in trial and error, often involving alcohol. I was doubly lucky in avoiding the national service birth deadline by three months, and in having had parents who encouraged sensible wine drinking and a school that already gave freedom close to that of Cambridge. Wine was a central interest. Apart from rowing in my first year, I successfully avoided other sporting activities.

RIGHT Château Lafite-Rothschild, 1945.

The 1961 competition

'As honorary secretary of the CUWFS in 1960–61, I was part of the 1961 tasting team against Oxford, captained by John Harvey, a scion of Harveys wine merchants, and aided and abetted by Hugh Johnson. The core of the team was chosen from the CUWFS by the cellarer for their experience and tasting abilities.

'Harveys of Bristol supplied wines for the tasting match at the Oxford and Cambridge Club. The firm's representative was, if my memory is unblurred by time, Tim Miller. John Harvey, as cellarer, obtained wines from Harveys for pre-match regular blind-tasting sessions. The merchants Christopher's, Hatch Mansfield and Saccone & Speed also supplied wines for tastings, and O W Loeb was most generous in bringing an exceptional range of German wines, always culminating in one or two Trockenbeerenausleses. Mainly this was driven by Otto Loeb's generosity and enthusiasm for educating young palates.

'A high point of tasting evenings was the chance to entertain the visiting wine merchant to dinner, and as secretary, I organized these dinners in my rooms at King's. The college made a special effort, even trusting us with college silver candlesticks.

Russian roulette

'In the 1960s, few New World wines were imported (or drinkable). I organized the first tasting of Russian wines (via the Russian trade delegation in Highgate). Mainly Georgian, most of the wines were undrinkable. Few of the Russian wines tasted at the event were competitive with Old World products in quality and they were not readily available in shops.

'My fondest memory of our 1961 tastings is of the Champagne tasting in May Week, which I organized as the society's honorary secretary, and to which Pol Roger, which remains my favourite *grande marque*, generously contributed four bottles. As proceedings were drawing to a close in the wine room of King's College, members of the committee were anxiously looking to see what unopened bottles might need rescuing for future consumption. A promising bottle of Pol Roger stood invitingly on the table. At that moment an arm appeared from beneath the table and perceptively grabbed the bottle for more immediate enjoyment by its owner and partner, who had taken temporary refuge beneath the table. The arm belonged to the next year's cellarer of the society.

'No women were members of the CUWFS at that time, and in the university the men-to-women ratio was nine to one. The weekly tasting was a social, networking event. Since women were still excluded, romances had to be pursued elsewhere. However, undrunk bottles of Champagne from the May Week tasting did enliven a punt trip on the slow-flowing Ouse at Hemingford Grey with my girlfriend (who is now my wife).'

ABOVE Punting at dawn on the River Cam was de rigueur after a May Ball.

An interview with
JOHN HARVEY

CLARE COLLEGE, CAMBRIDGE, m.1958

John Harvey joined his family firm, John Harvey & Sons of Bristol, in October 1961, after national service and three years at Cambridge. He is the honorary secretary of The Saintsbury Club.

LEFT Harry Waugh (left) with John Harvey (right) in the 1960s.

'I did my national service in the 9th Lancers at Detmold, Germany, for 15 months of initial training before officer training at Malvern. Germany was a nice place to be, and I organized the wine cellar for the officers' mess. The officers didn't particularly like German wine, and so we imported Harveys (why not?) among other wines, from a local distributor.

'At Cambridge, I was the cellarer of the Cambridge University Wine and Food Society (CUWFS), when Hugh Johnson, who was at King's College, was also on the committee. But when it came to the contest, I thought the first red was a claret and it was Burgundy. I got them all the wrong way round, and I came last. The 1961 tasting match was held downstairs in Harveys' cellars in London at 27 Pall Mall. Ted Hale was involved with the

'You rarely went to a tutorial at Cambridge without being offered a glass of South African or Spanish Sherry: amontillado usually, medium-dry.'

competition then. I wish I'd tasted a little better. There was no formal training in those days, but we'd go together as a team to tastings visiting wine merchants had put together; Harveys and Christopher's came, and Dolamore, which also sold to the colleges.

'Hugh Johnson didn't know yet what he was going to do; he had the idea that he wanted to do something about wine, but he didn't want to go into the trade. Only a few years later he came out with *Wine*, followed by *The World Atlas of Wine*. Michael Broadbent was also writing about wine then, while he was still at Harveys, where he ran the shops – proper Harveys wine merchant shops within the food sections of leading department stores. We had one in Manchester, and I worked in the one in Bristol for a bit. It was located next door to the fish counter and opposite the cheese counter; I threw my suit away after working there for about six months: the smell was terrible!

Fine wine at Cambridge

'Dr Sidney Smith of St Catharine's College was the senior member and president of the CUWFS. He was a remarkable man who did remarkable things – a memorable character – and he invited the committee to dinner and opened an 1870 or 1871 Lafite. It was an amazing wine. We all enjoyed it thoroughly, and I went round the following morning quite early to thank him for opening it. He said, "Well, my boy, I could teach you something else." He got the bottle, which was standing up with sediment in it and a bit of ullage, poured out some fairly clear liquid, and said, "Just taste that." It was better than it was the night before. Just think of all the wine you throw away, if you don't cook with it! Sydney was hell-bent on teaching young men in their formative years the delights of wine; he had a very deep cellar and was only too happy to open good bottles for us. And, you rarely went to a tutorial at Cambridge without being offered a glass of South African or Spanish Sherry: amontillado usually, medium-dry.

Shows slow improvement

JOHN HARVEY, fifth of that name to serve the Bristol wine firm, did somewhat better as a non-competitor in the 24th annual Oxford v Cambridge wine-tasting match at the firm's Pall Mall headquarters yesterday than he did when captaining the Cambridge team in 1960.

Oxford won yesterday by 393 points to 287 to put them two up in the series.

But Mr Harvey's 56 points still fell short of this year's individual winning total of 96 scored by Michael Plumley of Oxford and of the woman champion's 58 attained by Vicki Pritchard-Davies, also of Oxford.

It was encouraging to see that the success of Oxford's Sarah Stewart-Brown in finishing second overall last year had persuaded the university to increase female representation in the six-strong team from one to three, especially as one of the three, Rosemary Kerslake, admitted to having taken up wine-tasting only three weeks ago.

ABOVE Press clipping of the 1972 competition. The article describes it as the 24th match but in fact it was the 19th.

Otherwise, in those days generally, we were drinking what was called South African Burgundy and Algerian wine: anything we could get hold of for half a crown or whatever we had in our pockets, which wasn't much.

'I was the last of national service generation and so when in 1958 I went up to Cambridge I was already 21. In my second and third years, people who were three years younger were coming up straight from school. You didn't go to pubs outside of the college bars, unless perhaps you made an arrangement to go to the Pickerel. It was difficult to find women at Cambridge then; Girton* was a long way on a bicycle. There was Newnham, too, and a lot of scurrying around several English-teaching schools attended by lots of foreign ladies who had come over to Cambridge to learn English. I wasn't very gregarious, but I did play rugby wing and three-quarters, and I had a university team trial. My opponent got the ball and I never saw him again – he was just so much faster! – so I only played half a Blues game.

'Clare College had its own active dining club and we arranged tastings given by the same people who came up to sell wines to the colleges. We also tried to introduce ourselves to better food. There were people who had experienced French cooking and the like, but we're

*Founded 1869, Girton College, Cambridge, was Britain's first residential college for women that offered an education to degree level; it went co-educational in 1976. Newnham, founded in 1871, is still an all-female college today.

talking about a period when rationing wasn't that far away; we had all known rationing for a ten- to 15-year period, so there wasn't a great deal of luxury. A big night out was a spaghetti Bolognese, from a restaurant opposite Caius, in a little passageway called Dog Lane.

'There just wasn't a lot of money around. Since an expensive bottle of plonk cost 15 shillings, CUWFS tastings built up to maybe one or two good wines out of eight, to bring people on and keep the costs down. With the college dining club, I would go and have a long chat with the catering manager. He said, "Why don't you try teal?" I'd never heard of teal. So we had teal, and everybody said, "Oh gosh, this is rather good." Teal is a form of wild duck, very cheap at a certain time of year when there are lots of them. Nobody knew. But it was good stimulation for the caterers, too; instead of daily institutional food, they got to pull a few stops out and a recipe book.

'If we invited the don in charge of the college cellar, then we had better wine – there were all sorts of ploys – but they were generally happy to help, and to give us good wines because this was a proper reason. I used to do my tastings in a room at King's. It wasn't a great room, but I could open the windows on both sides, so we had fresh air.'

ABOVE Harveys of Bristol Sherry advertisements from the 1960s.

An interview with
SIR JAMES CROPPER KCVO

MAGDALENE COLLEGE, CAMBRIDGE, m.1959

Sir James Cropper was at Eton prior to Cambridge. He is the Lord Lieutenant of Cumbria and was the sixth chairman of his family business, James Cropper Speciality Papers, a firm that produces bespoke cases and luxury carrier bags for Champagne.

'I turned to David, and saw that the winning silver cup he'd been holding had snapped in two – it had gone into the dashboard. I said, "David, look what you've done to the cup! You've broken it!" He turned to me and said, "Look what you've done to my head! You've broken it as well!" He was streaming with blood.'

'My father had a cellar at home, and he used to buy Château Talbot. I still buy Talbot, and Cissac, and lay down wine with Corney & Barrow. I haven't been buying as much recently due to prices, but I've got enough laid down now to last my lifetime.

'When I went up to Cambridge in 1959, Adrian Cowell, who was a family friend, was already there at King's. Adrian was the honorary secretary of the Cambridge University Wine and Food Society (CUWFS), and he asked me to join. He had also introduced Hugh Johnson to wine tasting, and to the CUWFS. Adrian and Hugh had the only undergraduate rooms in the Gibbs building at King's, and when dining there with them we were told we weren't allowed to jump up and down on the floor because Michael Jaffe, a professor of fine art and art history, who became director of the Fitzwilliam Museum for many years, had rooms below with Rubens hanging on his wall. We didn't want to dislodge those.

'I was asked to take over as cellarer by Adrian, and I was in the varsity match in 1962. Jonathan Harris (Trinity) became secretary, and David Hudson (Trinity Hall) was treasurer. Robert Pryor (Trinity) and William Legge-Bourke (Magdalene) were also in the team that year. I lived at Magdalene in Thomson Lane, and trained our team by buying half-bottles of wine from Dolamore. Peter Noble, a wine merchant who ran Christopher's in Jermyn Street in London, also provided wines and helped train us.

'The team trained on hock: ordinary Spätlese, Auslese, and Trockenbeerenauslese. We also had Mosel, and white Burgundy and white Bordeaux – Chablis and Sauternes – and Sancerre from the Loire. The CUWFS was the only society of its kind at that time, and you were chosen for the team by your friends. David would host tastings in the Eden Rooms at Trinity Hall, and we occasionally had tastings in the Fitzwilliam. We were fairly monastic, as most of the colleges were men only, and we spent a lot of time in our own company. We weren't that serious about the tastings. It was rather a waste to spit the wine out, and I think we had quite a few hangovers.

CAMBRIDGE UNIVERSITY
THE MARCH MEETING
This Meeting was the occasion of a Dinner at Le Jardin Restaurant, Cambridge, on 7 March 1962.

The fare: Pâté du Patron au Cognac. Mousse de Brochet Dieppoise. Filet Mignon Chasseur au Cognac; Petits Pois au Beurre; Haricots verts sautés comme en France; Pommes Parisienne. Crêpes Simone flambées; Petits Fours. Café Moka.

The wines: Vin Blanc Cassis. Puligny-Montrachet 1955. Château Léoville-Barton 1952. Château La Fleur Petrus 1952. Château Lafaurie-Peyraguey 1937. Reserve Malmsey Solera 1830. Rouyer Guillet 1910.

ABOVE *Wine and Food*, No. 114, Summer 1962.

'The society had a dinner once a year. I organized one in Le Jardin, a new French restaurant; it was a great success with *mousse de brochet* (rooster pike) as the main dish [see image facing page].

'In the 1962 match, Harry Turcan from Oxford had the highest score of anybody, and Robert Pryor had the highest score for Cambridge. Somehow, overall we came out on top; I got one wine absolutely right: a 1949 Château d'Yquem.

Disaster strikes

'We won the 1962 match and had a good meal afterwards. I then drove home with David Hudson. At that time I had a white MG Magnette, a beautiful car with a nice interior. It was fast, and I had a reputation for driving rather fast (I once drove from Cambridge to London, before there were any motorways, in 55 minutes; it's 50 miles).

'Driving back to Cambridge, there's a famous sharp left-hand corner, called Jack's Corner, which I knew I could get around at 50 miles an hour but no faster, and I hit black ice. We slid across and over the verge, along the other side and into trees. We overturned three times and came to a rest. I was one of the first people to put Britax lap belts in my car, and they kept us in the car. When we came to a stop the headlights were still on and there was steam from the radiator. I turned to David, and saw that the winning silver cup he'd been holding had snapped in two – it had gone into the dashboard. I said, "David, look what you've done to the cup! You've broken it!" He turned to me and said, "Look what you've done to my head! You've broken it as well!" He was streaming with blood.

'The police turned up. I had a slight cut in my head. There was no breathalyzer in those days, luckily. They took us off to the police station, where they locked us up and called for a taxi. A Rolls Royce taxi turned up, which was quite unusual, and drove us back to Cambridge. The MG Magnette was a write-off. The cup was a nice silver chalice, like a communion cup, and narrow where it had snapped. I took it to Garrard, silversmiths to Her Majesty the Queen, in London to have it mended.'

ABOVE A 1960s MG Magnette.

MICHAEL BROADBENT MW
TASTING NOTE: 1949 CHÂTEAU D'YQUEM

In *Michael Broadbent's Vintage Wine*, Michael Broadbent awarded the 1949 white Bordeaux vintage five out of five stars, calling it 'a great vintage, still superb', while noting that it had been picked during the driest October on record. From over a dozen notes: 'lovely, soft, complete in the 1960s', when it featured in the 1962 varsity competition; 'rich bottle age and botrytis honey and apricots' in 1995; 'exquisitely floral, orange blossom bouquet' in 1998; and in 2000 'gorgeous (the wine not our host)'. His first tasting of Château d'Yquem, *c.*1950, is attributed to Dr Thomas Kerfoot: 'a family friend near us in Cheshire, a man of great taste', who owned a manufacturing chemist in Lancashire. 'We sat in his garden on a lovely summer evening and drank Yquem with nectarines. I'd just come out of the army and was studying architecture; I knew nothing about wine ... this was the first really great wine I'd ever tasted. I think my first sip ... must have lingered in the back of my mind, a sort of delayed spark which brought me eventually into wine.'

HARRY TURCAN
Trinity College, Oxford, m.1959

'Having won the individual cup in 1962, I was immediately offered a job by Harveys, but was advised by my father that I already drank more than was good for me. He suggested that I should look for a job elsewhere. After a decent interval I decided to follow a career at the alternative bar, the Bar. Drinking wine, we didn't venture far into the New World in those days, and the choice was between Burgundy, Bordeaux and Rhône. I was lucky enough to have drunk the exact Rhône wine with my parents only a week before it appeared in the match, so that was a useful start.

'I believe Oxford only lost the competition by the marks for a single correct identification, and recall that one of our team, who should perhaps remain nameless, changed his mind about whether one wine was a Burgundy or a claret – with disastrous consequences: he then got every one wrong. If he had stuck by his original assessment we would have won handsomely!'

'Cambridge is a very beguiling place – I met people there who have been friends for life.'

JONATHAN HARRIS
Trinity College, Cambridge, m.1960

'I went up to Trinity College, Cambridge, in 1960, after Harrow. My friend James Cropper asked me to be secretary of the Cambridge University Wine and Food Society. Justerini & Brooks (J&B) was one of the merchants that gave tutored tastings. Dick Bridgeman was a director of J&B and an old Harrovian; I used to play rackets against him, and I worked for the company in London, underneath the arch below Charing Cross, on Christmas vacations in the early 1960s, delivering wine.

'When I was at Cambridge we were still very traditional and we used to wear a suit on Sundays. And we wore gowns. I read economics and law; I enjoyed reading law, and got a probably ill-deserved 2:1. I was green, and foolish, as I only went to the lectures of my subject. Just recently I stayed in college, and I was looking at the list of lectures. It's fascinating to think one was up there and never took advantage – shocking, really.

'We enjoyed ourselves. We shot, we beagled, we punted and played games for the colleges. Most would have played real tennis. I played squash and rackets, but only because I had at Harrow. I mainly used to go up and down to London dances, and venture off to the country and back in a drafty motor car.

'There was an interesting Scottish whisky tasting. These unblended liquids were fascinating, very powerful. Some were entirely colourless, and they stayed in your nose for several days.

'After Cambridge, I was an antiquarian, a shopkeeper selling second-hand things. I still have English concave diamond-cut crystal glasses that were made in about 1770, and the quality of the cutting is quite extraordinary. The cutting of the stone develops into the bowl; it's worked out mathematically, and the jewel cutting has got to be dead on. I found them and bought them in Newcastle 40 years ago. I serve Delaforce 1960 Port in them from my father's cellar, though these were most likely not used for Port in the 18th century. Port was a much weaker drink then, hence you could have a "two- or three-bottle-a-day man", which, translated now, would kill you.

'Cambridge is a very beguiling place – I met people there who have been friends for life.'

Officers 1961-1962

PRESIDENT
Dr. Sydney Smith

VICE-PRESIDENTS
D. Mack Smith, Esq.
G. A. Hepworth, Esq.
Dr. M. G. M. Pryor

SENIOR TREASURER
Dr. D. Marrian

CELLARER
J. A. Cropper (*Magdalene*)

HONORARY SECRETARY
J. W. Harris (*Trinity*)

JUNIOR TREASURER
R. C. Pryor (*Trinity*)

COMMITTEE MEMBERS
W. N. H. Legge-Bourke (*Magdalene*)
D. P. M. Hudson (*Trinity Hall*)

ABOVE The Great Gate, Trinity College, Cambridge, in the 1960s.

ABOVE The dining hall at Magdalene College, Cambridge.

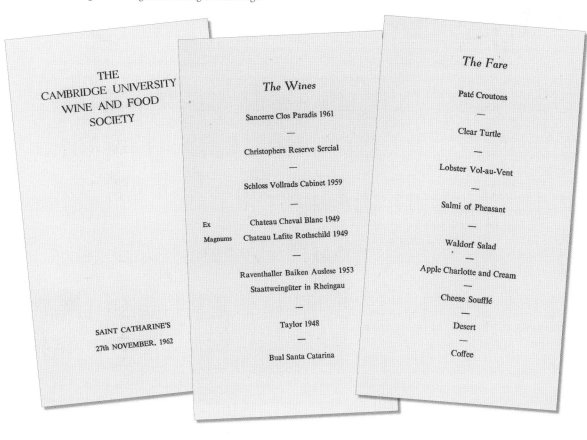

THE
CAMBRIDGE UNIVERSITY
WINE AND FOOD
SOCIETY

SAINT CATHARINE'S

27th NOVEMBER, 1962

The Wines

Sancerre Clos Paradis 1961

—

Christophers Reserve Sercial

—

Schloss Vollrads Cabinet 1959

—

Ex   Chateau Cheval Blanc 1949
Magnums   Chateau Lafite Rothschild 1949

—

Raventhaller Baiken Auslese 1953
Staattweingüter in Rheingau

—

Taylor 1948

—

Bual Santa Catarina

The Fare

Paté Croutons

—

Clear Turtle

—

Lobster Vol-au-Vent

—

Salmi of Pheasant

—

Waldorf Salad

—

Apple Charlotte and Cream

—

Cheese Soufflé

—

Desert

—

Coffee

An interview with
ROBERT PRYOR QC

TRINITY COLLEGE, CAMBRIDGE, m.1959

*Robert Pryor is a retired circuit court judge in the
West Country; he was a member of the Cambridge
University Wine and Food Society and a varsity
blind wine-tasting competitor in 1962.*

'When I went to Cambridge, the senior tutor of Trinity College was a distant cousin: a chap called Mark Pryor. I tried for a scholarship and failed. Then I went and had an interview with him for less than five minutes, working out exactly how we were related to each other, and whose grandfather was whose, and he said, "When are you coming up?" Then he said, "What are you going to read?" I said, "I'm not absolutely sure. I think I'm going to read law." He said, "Make up your mind by the end of your first term." That was my entry to Cambridge. It's quite utterly different now. I'm a classic example of the drawbridge coming up just after you've gone through.

'My admissions tutor had also said to me, "The trouble with you people who've done national service is it takes us six months to get you back to the idea of doing academic work." I was lucky enough to have become an officer at that young age. You sat in leather armchairs and people brought you whiskies. I served mostly in England, but I went out to Tripoli – pre-Gaddafi, obviously; it was King Idris in those days. I was in Tripoli for only four months. Otherwise, I was at Winchester Barracks in the Royal Green Jackets. The Green Jackets had an absolutely brilliant chef – an officer in the catering corps, which was slightly unusual – who knew what to do with army rations. On an ordinary day, you'd come into the mess for lunch and have one hot soup, one cold soup, two or three entrées, two or

'I'm a classic example of the
drawbridge coming up just after
you've gone through.'

three main courses, a pudding and cheese, as a matter of routine, and variety. I put on two stone while I was in the army.

'George A "Tony" Hepworth, who started the Cambridge University Wine and Food Society (CUWFS) in 1951, later set up a Wine and Food Society branch in Yorkshire. He organized a three-sided competition with the CUWFS, of which I was a member, and the West Riding of Yorkshire branch, against the dons, who were got together by Dr Sydney Smith of St Catharine's College. On the day, Tony Hepworth and Sydney Smith were discussing the wonderful wines they had in their cellars, and which was the best they ever tasted. They were talking endlessly about Château Latour, and Sydney trumped by saying that the best vintage was 1919; Tony, being too young, hadn't got that in his cellar. When it came to the competition, we had to identify a red in four different vintages. Having been party to their conversation, my little ears flapping, I decided it was Latour. I couldn't do it by tasting. Then I looked closely – I'd learned a few of the vintages – and one of the wines was going quite brown and was obviously old. So I put 1924, and the next one 1948, both of which came right. I had no idea what I was talking about.

'In our 1962 competition we had two clarets, two Burgundies and a Rhône, and one of the whites was a recent vintage of Château d'Yquem. I remember that because I was frightfully disappointed I didn't taste it. I merely looked at it and smelt it, and thought if I taste it it's so sweet I won't be able to taste anything else at all. We also had a white Burgundy, Mosel and hock, and perhaps an Alsace *à petit grains*: with a slight fizz. My triumph was that I got nine out of ten right; I got the Rhône wrong; I said it was Burgundy.

ABOVE Great Court, Trinity College, Cambridge in the late 1950s.

A sporting life at Cambridge

'I used to shoot on weekends in the winter when I could – usually pheasants or partridges – and at times with James Cropper, who is also a very good shot. And I did a little bit of rowing, but I wasn't very energetic at rowing. It sounds as though all I ever did was lounge about, eating and drinking, but I did do a certain amount of work.

'I was a member of The University Pitt Club, where I used to go and have lunch and play snooker in the afternoon. It was formed in the days of William Pitt the Younger, or just after, when everything was terribly political, but wasn't nearly so rumbustious as the Bullingdon Club at Oxford. I was also a member of the True Blue and The Beefsteak dining clubs at Cambridge. They both stemmed from the 18th century, and were supposed to be on opposite sides of the political spectrum, but I found myself a member of both. The Beefsteak was the Whig club, and the True Blue was for Tories.

'The headmaster of my school, Mr Curtis, had been at King's College just after World War I, when the Depression was coming, and he'd had rooms above John Maynard Keynes, the great economist who wrote *The Economic Consequences of the Peace*, the famous book about the Treaty of Versailles and the reparations imposed on Germany. Curtis was having a get-together of the King's rugby XV, and they were drinking, shouting and yelling. A porter came up and knocked on his door and said, "Mr Curtis, could you make a little less noise? The Cabinet is meeting in the room below." Several ministers had come to see John Maynard Keynes.

A pipe of proper Port

'I stayed with a godfather in the early 1960s, on the long vacation from Cambridge, and he was showing me around his cellar. There was a pipe of bottles of Port, and he was going around in a frightfully traditional manner with a bit of wood with a candlestick on the end – very old-fashioned. He held it near this bin and said, "This is Quinta do Noval 1931." Many years later, I saw a wine auction in the newspaper where a single bottle had been sold for £6,000.

'A friend of mine once had Lord Goddard to dinner, when he was Lord Chief Justice (1946–58). Goddard was a great one for his Port, and they thought they'd catch him out. They bought some Port and Lord Goddard pronounced it was very good, proper Port. They all laughed at him, and said they'd bought it at the local grocer. But later they found out that somebody's butler had been stealing Port from the cellar, and selling it to the grocer, who had been selling it on. Lord Goddard was right: it was proper Port.

Recollections of Churchill

'Bread wasn't rationed throughout the war, and then in 1945 a Labour government came in and they rationed bread. You can imagine Churchill, who'd lost the 1945 election to everybody's astonishment, having presided over the entire war which we damned well won, although it beggared us, making great speeches about the Labour Party rationing bread, the staff of life. Had the war never happened, however, and he not been given that incredible opportunity, he would've gone down as a troublesome maverick. He had an American mother, and had made a wonderful speech to Congress: "I might have been addressing you as President if …"

'One of Churchill's great speeches during the war was describing what happened at Dunkirk, which was an incredible deliverance, although a defeat. Huge numbers of troops were rescued from the beaches at Dunkirk, with the Germans edging closer; they were mostly English, some French and other nationalities. Churchill described this in his speech: "We've got 330,000 troops, and quite a lot of them have still got their rifles." It didn't sound too brilliant. But in the second half, he described the superiority of our navy and our air force. By the end of the speech, you thought it was only a matter of time before we won. It was quite extraordinary, the way he managed to instil this sense of optimism. I always think the greatest "I told you so" in history was when he said in 1940: "Hitler knows that he must defeat us in these islands or lose the war." And when we got to 1945, the war had been won, and Hitler had lost.

A cousin's secret cellar

'A cousin of mine inherited a big house when she was about 15. The previous owner had been an eccentric spinster, who lived alone in this house on an estate, and her father had been a rather bibulous Irish priest, a minister for the Church of Ireland. He drank quite heavily, and had a standing order with Corney & Barrow. When his only daughter took over, she just kept it on, because she thought that's what you did – but she didn't drink at all. My cousin's father, my uncle, went in and found this cellar absolutely stuffed with wine.'

ABOVE Winston Churchill and Odette Pol-Roger at Brighton races, June 1952.

'Those of us at Cambridge in the early 1960s viewed it
then and now as a "golden age" full of people who
went on to achieve great things.'

THE CAMBRIDGE UNIVERSITY
WINE AND FOOD SOCIETY

by JAMES DUGDALE, 2ND BARON CRATHORNE KCVO

TRINITY COLLEGE, CAMBRIDGE, m.1960

*After Cambridge Lord Crathorne joined the fine art
auctioneers, Sotheby's. Later he became involved with a hotel
group who created Cliveden, among others. At Westminster
he is Chairman of the All Party Parliamentary Arts and
Heritage Group. He became Lord Lieutenant of North
Yorkshire in 1999.*

LEFT James Dugdale with the Harveys Cup after the 1963 match.

'The Cambridge Societies' Fair, held at the Examinations
Schools and the Corn Exchange at the beginning of
each academic year in October, was a great way to work
out which interests to pursue, from well over 100 societies
ranging from the "Group for the Abolition of Hanging"
to the "Tiddlywinks Club". The Cambridge University
Wine and Food Society (CUWFS) was one of several I
decided to join; the members were congenial, like-minded
undergraduates sharing in the pleasures of the table.

'The CUWFS programme consisted of a number of
tastings organized by the secretary or cellarer, whereby
different wine merchants presented their wines to
members and the assorted dons associated with the society.
Spittoons were available, but not made much use of,
and indeed, towards the end of an unruly tasting on one
occasion, I remember that even the glasses were bypassed
by a couple of members in favour of drinking straight
from the bottle (I'm glad to say a rare occurrence)!

'On October 31, 1961, Honorary Secretary Jonathan
Harris wrote to confirm that I had been elected to the
CUWFS membership, and requested that I send my
subscription for the year of 3 guineas to R C Pryor at
Trinity College. Nine days later, on November 9, there
was a tasting of ports given by Mr Ionides of Percy Fox
& Co in The University Pitt Club [see page 77]. Percy
Fox was the sole importer of Warre & Co (the first British
Port company established in Portugal, with roots tracing
back to 1670) and the tasting included Warre's 1927 and
'55 vintages – both superb.

'The following year, as junior treasurer among the
officers for 1962–63, I recorded in my diary that we
met on October 18, 1962, at 6pm in the Blundell
Room of Sydney Sussex College, then in other venues
on November 1 and 8 at 6.30pm, and on November 27
for a dinner in St Catharine's College: eight courses with
eight wines, which included magnums of Château Lafite-
Rothschild 1949 and Taylor's 1948 Port [see page 69].

'The CUWFS driving force in 1962–63 was its
cellarer, Diarmid Guinness (St Catharine's) of the
brewing family. He was a man of great charm and we
were all surprised when on Saturday December 8, 1962,
he married Felicity Carnwath, as most of us preferred the
idea of sowing a few wild oats before taking such a step.

'Diarmid was keen to win the varsity blind-tasting
competition against Oxford and arranged a number
of tastings in his room for his team in February. He
selected wines from the Harveys of Bristol list, as Harveys
supported the society and organized the competition.
Diarmid concentrated on giving us wines typical of their
region, and we concentrated on that rather than worrying
about which château or which year.

'The excitement of the competition at the Oxford
and Cambridge Club, on Pall Mall in London, arrived
on February 25, 1963. Cambridge was represented solely
by the CUWFS committee, whose tasting talents were
varied. Oxford was far more democratic and chose its
team on blind-tasting merit. There were five whites and
five reds, and in those days all from France and Germany,
with a possible ten points for each wine, making a
possible score of 100. The categories and points value for
each category were as follows: Type of wine (5), vintage
(2), district (1), commune (1), actual name of wine (1).

'The reds were from Bordeaux, Burgundy and
the Rhône areas. The whites included were Mosel, a
hock, a Burgundy and Bordeaux. The wine that caused
the most confusion was a sweet white wine, which

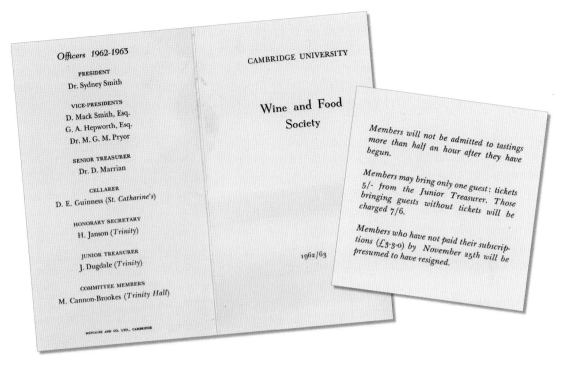

caught people out, as many plumped for a Sauternes – everyone except for me, as I put correctly that it was a Trockenbeerenauslese. Thanks in the main to Diarmid's tutoring, we won the competition and I won the individual cup.

'When I was told in my slightly inebriated state by the rather serious man from Harveys that I had the top score of 49, I wasn't quite sure whether to believe him, but when he suggested that I should consider going into the wine trade I thought it must be true! It was a thoroughly enjoyable event and we were delighted to have won, in spite of one of our team's members having hardly scored any points – with a score not reaching double figures!

'The society dinner at The University Pitt Club two weeks after the competition success was held on March 11: another delicious meal with wines selected by the president of the society, Dr Sydney Smith. His explanatory notes make it clear just how good and rare the wines were [see pages 76 and 77].

'The Château de Saché 1949 from the Azay-le-Rideau region was one of only 500 bottles that were produced that year. The Clos de Tart 1955 was particularly interesting. Apparently this vintage was a disastrous one for the producer, Mommessin: the wine went wrong in bottle and only two casks of it were shipped to England. One was bottled by Sandeman in Scotland and this was drunk at the dinner. The Quarts de Chaume 1943 was also rare, with only 270 bottles made.

RIGHT Top talent: A 1961 playbill for *Beyond the Fringe*, a surrealistic comedy revue considered ahead of its time with unapologetic and often humiliating caricatures of authority. The show was a major influence on members of the Cambridge University Footlights Dramatic Club.

Pigeons and the Pitt Club

'Many members of the CUWFS were also members of The University Pitt Club, one of many clubs which were started in the memory of William Pitt the Younger, in an elegant building with a classical portico in Jesus Lane. George was the rotund and genial major-domo who kept admirable control over the undergraduates. One of the pleasures of the Pitt Club was being able to take the pigeons I and fellow members shot in the woods

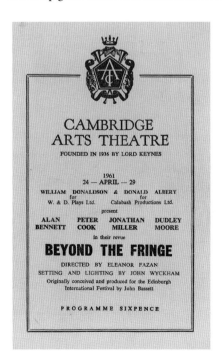

In Memoriam

Mr Philiph Gurdon
(Late MAGDALENE)

Mourning Clothes
Pitt Club 12.30 p.m.

'It is finished, blessed Jesus'
H.M. 122

A mock funeral procession, which included Prince
William of Gloucester, marching past the lodgings
yesterday of two Cambridge undergraduates who
have been sent down.
LEFT: Prince William, who is at Magdalene, taking part in
the proc

MOCK FUNERAL AT CAMBRIDGE

PRINCE WILLIAM A 'MOURNER'

DAILY TELEGRAPH REPORTER

PRINCE WILLIAM OF GLOUCESTER marched through the narrow streets of Cambridge yesterday wearing an untidy morning suit and a top hat which fell over his ears.

He was taking part, with 50 other undergraduates, in a mock funeral for two undergraduates sent down from their colleges for failing examinations.

Prince William, who is at Magdalene College, walked solemnly through the streets as a sports car bearing the two "bodies" was drawn by "mourners" in full morning dress. The undergraduates sent down are Philip Gurdon, 22, of Magdalene, and Simon Keswick, of Trinity.

SITTING IN COFFIN

Gurdon said before the procession: "Don't think we are taking being sent down lightly." He was wearing a Palm Beach shirt, pale blue slacks and a brown trilby hat. He sat in a coffin, with Keswick beside him in the car in a smoking jacket over pyjamas.

Traffic piled up behind the procession as it moved from the Pitt Club in Jesus Lane round through Market Square and back to the club, into which Gurdon was carried in his coffin for tea.

Hymns were played by two accordionists, two trumpeters and three drummers.

ABOVE James Dugdale (left) with Mark Heathcote.

belonging to the Jockey Club at Newmarket. I was able to organize this, as my father was a member. Colonel Nicol Gray of the Jockey Club was only too pleased to have his pigeon problem addressed, at least in part, by enthusiastic undergraduates, and it was quite common for a single gun to shoot 50 pigeons in an afternoon. The Jockey Club keeper, Pike, assisted with the picking up. We enjoyed a plentiful supply of pigeons' breast dinners, accompanied by good claret from the Pitt Club's excellent wine list.

'On one entry in my diary I noted shooting clay pigeons against an Oxford team. I mention this because Pol Roger, sponsor of the varsity blind wine-tasting match today, also sponsors the Lords versus Commons annual clay pigeon shoot, and the House of Lords clay pigeon shooting team, of which I am currently captain, and this year the Lords won the cup.

'One event organized by Pitt Club members made national news, when in October 1962 we staged a mock "funeral" for two members who were sent down for failing their exams. About 50 members of the Pitt Club dressed in mourning clothes paraded through Cambridge with two coffins in an open-top sports car 'pulled' by six members with Philip Gurdon and Simon Keswick on board. The reason for the national publicity was that Prince William of Gloucester was one of the top-hatted mourners. Philip had failed his engineering exams for two years running, and Simon was sent down after a year of reading economics (he subsequently became a highly successful businessman). The cortege was followed by two accordionists, two trumpeters and three drummers (of which I was one) playing suitable hymns throughout. The police helpfully organized the necessary traffic diversion.

We were following a Cambridge tradition: the previous person to be given a mock funeral was *The Sunday Times* colour supplement editor and cartoonist Mark Boxer. He was rusticated by King's College in 1953 for publishing a blasphemous article in the university publication *Granta,* which he edited.

Drumming for the Footlights

'The Footlights Dramatic Club was, and still is, famous for the extraordinary talent it has fostered. I was elected a member in 1962 because of my friendship with Hugh Macdonald, musical director of the Footlights and sometime president (now Professor Macdonald and world expert on Berlioz). Our generation included, among others, Graham Chapman, Tim Brooke-Taylor, Bill Oddie and John Cleese, whose best man I was for the first of his four marriages. *Double Take* was the first Footlights Revue to be taken to the Edinburgh Festival Fringe, in 1962. I was the drummer in Hugh's trio and on stage for the highly successful three-week run. At Cambridge I much enjoyed playing drums in jazz, dance and rock bands. I ran the Cambridge University Dance Band and played with the Band of Angels, whose leader, Mike D'Abo, later became Manfred Mann's lead singer. I still take to the skins whenever the opportunity arises.

'For those (and there were many) who were interested in going into politics, the Cambridge Union Society was a great stamping ground. The first debate every year was "This House has no confidence in Her Majesty's Government". On October 11, 1960, Colin Renfrew proposed the motion when Leon Britten was president. Both have had stellar careers and are now colleagues in the House of Lords.

Sporting times

'My games at university were croquet and real (or royal) tennis, which I was encouraged to take up by my delightful tutor, Dr Theodore Redpath, a world expert on the philosopher Wittgenstein and with whom I had many matches. It is a perfect game for those who find squash and tennis too energetic. My friend Ben Hay (Queens') was secretary and then captain of the Real Tennis Club and responsible for The Giraffes (the club team for real tennis), and included me in a number of games for the university at the bottom of the pecking order. I think my taking the trouble to buy my own racquet showed a keenness that was rewarded by a place on the team. Ben gave me the "giraffe" emblem sweater for real tennis, which I was delighted by. Our professional coach was the wonderfully colourful Brian "G&T" Church.

'I have the happiest of memories of my three years at Cambridge, where the CUWFS greatly added to the pleasure of being an undergraduate. Re-reading this, I can't quite believe how lucky we all were to have been at Cambridge at this time and how friends made then are still friends today.'

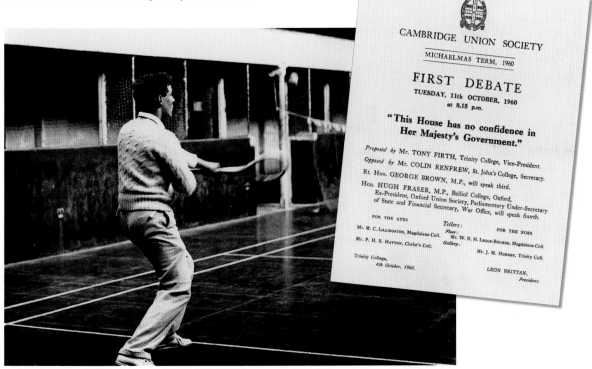

ABOVE 'Real tennis is a perfect game for those who find squash and tennis too energetic'. James Dugdale in the Green Court on Grange Road, Cambridge.

ABOVE The University Pitt Club committee, summer 1962. Back row, left to right: Diarmid Guinness, Johnny Dudley, Malcolm Innes, Nic Ullswater and James Dugdale. Front row, left to right: Simon Garmoyle, William (Bill) Legge-Bourke, Mr Burnett, Mr Wilson and Robert Pryor.

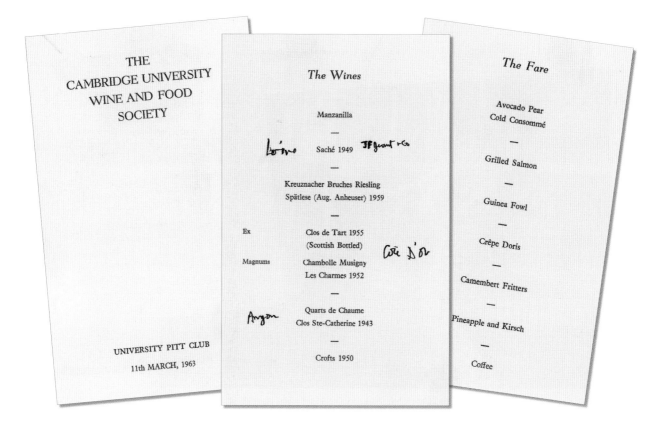

THE
CAMBRIDGE UNIVERSITY
WINE AND FOOD
SOCIETY

UNIVERSITY PITT CLUB

11th MARCH, 1963

The Wines

Manzanilla

—

Saché 1949

—

Kreuznacher Bruches Riesling
Spätlese (Aug. Anheuser) 1959

Ex   Clos de Tart 1955
                    (Scottish Bottled)
Magnums   Chambolle Musigny
                    Les Charmes 1952

Quarts de Chaume
Clos Ste-Catherine 1943

Crofts 1950

The Fare

Avocado Pear
Cold Consommé

—

Grilled Salmon

—

Guinea Fowl

—

Crêpe Doris

—

Camembert Fritters

—

Pineapple and Kirsch

—

Coffee

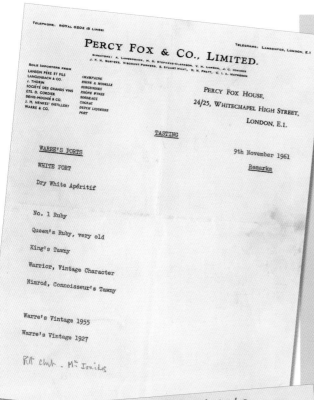

PERCY FOX & CO., LIMITED.

TELEGRAMS: LANSONFOX, LONDON, E.1

DIRECTORS: A. LANGENBACH, H. O. STEPHENS-CLARKSON, V. H. LANSON, J. C. IONIDES
J. P. H. SURTEES, VISCOUNT FURNESS, E. STUART HUNT, K. H. PRATT, C. L. A. MATHESON

SOLE IMPORTERS FROM
LANSON PÈRE ET FILS
LANGENBACH & CO.
J. THORN
SOCIÉTÉ DES GRANDS VINS
ETS. D. CORDIER
DENIS-MOUNIÉ & CO.
J. H. HENKES' DISTILLERY
WARRE & CO.

CHAMPAGNE
RHINE & MOSELLE
BURGUNDIES
RHÔNE WINES
BORDEAUX
COGNAC
DUTCH LIQUEURS
PORT

PERCY FOX HOUSE,
24/25, WHITECHAPEL HIGH STREET,
LONDON, E.1.

TASTING

WARRE'S PORTS

9th November 1961

WHITE PORT

Remarks

Dry White Apéritif

No. 1 Ruby

Queen's Ruby, very old

King's Tawny

Warrior, Vintage Character

Nimrod, Connoisseur's Tawny

Warre's Vintage 1955

Warre's Vintage 1927

Pitt Club - Mr Ionides

Pitt Club dinner 11th March 1963

Sache 1949 Region of Azay-le-Rideau
Vineyard of Alfred Arrault
Only 500 bottles are made every year

Kreuznacher Bruches
Riesling Spatlese   Region of Bad Kreuznach in the Nahe
From the Vineyard of August Anheuser

Clos de Tart   1955 was a disastrous year for the owner Momessin.
All the wine went wrong in the bottles and only
two casks were shipped to England, one being bottled in Scotland
by Sandeman.

Chambolle Musigny From the Cote D'Or and from the vineyard of
Roblot Pere et Fils.

Quarts de Chaume   Coteaux du Layon (Anjou) from the vineyard
of Charles Baumard.
Only 270 bottles of this wine were ever made

All the wines are domaine or Chateau Bottled with the
Exception of the Clos de Tart.

PP Dr Sydney Smith

THE UNIVERSITY PITT CLUB

The University Pitt Club is an all-male dining club at Cambridge established in 1835 in honour of William Pitt the Younger, a student at Pembroke College who went on to become the youngest Prime Minister, under King George III, in 1783, at the age of 24, until 1801 and then again from 1804 to 1806. Founded as an undergraduate political club, with membership for life, 'to uphold in general the (Tory) political principles for which Mr William Pitt stood', the Club's political events were combined with 'the pleasures of social intercourse at dinner, when party fervour among friends, dining in party uniform, might be warmed towards a political incandescence by the speeches to successive toasts'.

After its first few decades, the political element diminished while the social element increased, and by 1868 the Pitt Club elected members without considerations of political party. It temporarily closed in 1917, when many Cambridge men joined the forces for World War I, but by 1920, the club had 'become nearly normal again, "the only real trouble", according to the minutes, "being the horrible scarcity of whisky"'.

At first, the club met in the rooms of members, over the shop of a bookseller on Trinity Street, and over a furniture shop on Bridge Street on the corner of All Saints' Passage. Since 1864, the club's premises have been at 7a Jesus Lane. Originally designed as Victorian Turkish Baths by Sir Matthew Digby Wyatt, the building was auctioned off to its own architect for £2,700, who leased half of the building to the Pitt Club, and the other half to Orme's Billiards Rooms. Towards the end of the 19th century the club bought the entire three floors of the building. Its mid-19th century, neo-classical architecture boasts stucco porticoes, ionic columns and entablature. Since 1997 the University Pitt Club has occupied only the first floor of the clubhouse.

The club was a popular venue for CUWFS events (and on occasion, the varsity tasting match) in the 1960s. The club remains a meeting place for members and their guests to eat and drink in pleasant surroundings, and maintains reciprocal relations with the Oxford and Cambridge Club in London, and with its equivalent at Oxford, the Gridiron Club.

FACING PAGE AND LEFT The CUWFS in the early 1960s at the Pitt Club, including a menu, Port tasting and wine notes by Dr Sydney Smith.

'At one particular château ... this man was watching the arrival of a harvest he had awaited for many years, in the knowledge that he would probably never see its like again.'

LEFT Tasting Château Rieussec in the late 1980s.

TASTING THE 1961 VINTAGE BORDEAUX, IN CASK

by DAVID PEPPERCORN MW

TRINITY COLLEGE, CAMBRIDGE, m.1951

'I retain a powerful impression of driving around the St-Emilion region during the vintage in September 1961. It was very hot and we encountered complaints that supplies of ice for cooling fermenting must were running out. In those days, the standard method of cooling was to pass the must through a device resembling a milk-cooler; must went through a battery of pipes arranged horizontally, while cool water ran over the exterior of the pipes. If this was not enough, big blocks of ice wrapped in sacking were lowered into the vat.

'The incident that remains in my mind was the reception of the grapes at one particular château. Presiding was the elderly owner, in his shirtsleeves, but wearing his Sunday-best trousers and a stylish straw hat. This man was watching the arrival of a harvest he had awaited for many years, in the knowledge that he would probably never see its like again. As soon as the wine had been run off into cask, the paucity of the crop was evident. There is an old Bordeaux adage that when a crop is small, it will be smaller than expected. In fact, the message had got through before the harvest, due to severe *coulure*, and this had an immediate effect on prices, as many owners, short of money, had sold a part of their crop *sur souche*, or "on the vine". Once the crop was in vats, they realized that the proportion sold in this way had been too high, and prices doubled overnight.

To safeguard the quality and integrity of what we had bought, I subsequently had many wines château-bottled instead of shipped in barrel for bottling in England, as was common practice at that time. Comparisons between château bottlings and UK bottlings in later years showed we had been wise to be cautious.

'The problem, once samples started coming in, was to find enough wine to meet demand. By 1962, when the wines were first tasted, I was spending more and more of my time at Château Loudenne, with Jean-Paul Gardère, then working with us as a *courtier* based, unusually, in Margaux, later to become (together with Henri Martin of Château Gloria, more famously head of the Bontemps) an administrator of Château Latour. There was in addition Henry Lacoste, a specialist in Graves and Sauternes. Some tastings were in the *chais* of the respective châteaux, but many were samples sent to Loudenne.

My 1961 vintage Bordeaux tasting notes
'My surviving 40-odd notes cover only the leading châteaux, apart from a few special cases: Gloria, Ormes de Pez and Lanessan, where there were close connections. Notes for many other wines for shipment in bulk for London bottling were not preserved. No note survived for Haut-Bailly, but the sample was a one-off, not part of a general tasting, sent in by Henry

Lacoste. I knew then from reading of the reputation of the château, especially in the 19th century, but I had never seen a bottle in England, let alone tasted one. I discovered later that it was mostly to be found in Belgium – and indeed, the owner at that time was Belgian. The wine was sensational; I had already tasted Haut-Brion, La Mission and Domaine de Chevalier, so it was up against strong competition. In a January 1968 note, I compared Haut-Bailly favourably with Pape-Clément, which I had first tasted in March 1963 just before bottling. Only one *tonneau* (= four casks = 96 cases at that time, later 100) of Haut-Bailly was offered, but the price was high. I decided to bite the bullet and buy, and it proved the beginning of a long and happy relationship.

'The 1961 had a strong vintage character due to the ripeness and concentration of the wines. They were also markedly fruity, and thus enjoyable to taste young, with none of the tough tannins all too frequently found in this epoch. At Latour in April 1962, for example, I noted the colour as "almost black", with a powerful Cabernet aroma, and by March 1963, wrote "surprisingly elegant for Latour at this stage" (I have just tasted this great wine again, and it still combines strength, richness and elegance in magnificent fashion). At Lafite in June 1962, I found the 1961 "finer, with more flavour and richness than the 1959". However, by March 1963, although a "lovely wine", it was looking "rather soft and much lighter than Latour". It was to spend another year in cask prior to bottling from cask to cask, with all the bottle variation now so apparent.

'At Mouton in April 1962, I found the wine disappointing, lacking its usual "velvety quality". But by March 1963, the wine was "now very typical of 1961, powerful but not overpowering". At Margaux in April 1962, the wine had "all the finesse and charm of Margaux … with good body and fruitiness – looks like a great Margaux". I had not seen an impressive Margaux since the 1953.

'Down in the Graves at La Mission Haut-Brion, the wine seemed 'very big, full and complete, much fuller than Haut-Brion' – which was, in fact, not unusual at this early stage, as I was to discover. In March 1962, I thought Haut-Brion "very elegant with much breed and style, less full than La Mission and Chevalier". However, by October 1964, I noted that it was "very powerful and fine, certainly a great wine and one of the best 1961s". I was learning!

'I did not taste as extensively on the Right Bank; our relationship with J P Moueix did not begin until 1963, when I tasted a range of its 1962s. I did, however, taste Cheval Blanc and Pétrus 1961 in April 1962. For Cheval Blanc, I simply noted "a great wine – the *maître de chais* compared it with the 1934. Smell

ABOVE A Château Latour 1961 double magnum sold at Sotheby's June 2012 auction for £15,863.

of ripe bananas, very full and fruity". I was later to discover that the nose of ripe bananas came from the Cabernet Franc. Pétrus, I found, was a "big, elegant wine, perhaps not as outstanding as Cheval Blanc".

'One of the show-stopping wines, right from the start, was Château Palmer. In April 1962, I noted the wine was "delicious, very long and silky – it reminds me of a Pomerol". And by October 1962, I thought "the nose magnificent, the wine very full and curvaceous, a Burgundian among Médocs". Another wine that made a great impression was Léoville-Las Cases. In March 1962, I only noted that it was "fleshy and well finished", but by March 1963 I found "great richness, wonderful bouquet; already looks like a very great wine, better than Ducru or Barton, one of the very best 1961s".

'Let Château de Villegeorge serve as a final footnote. This *cru*, actually in Avensan, has vines that are entitled to both the Margaux and Moulis appellations, so it ends up as simple Haut-Médoc. It is also located in a place that is very prone to spring frosts, and suffered much damage in 1961. The resulting wine was something of a curiosity, as it was offered with compulsory château bottling: almost unheard of at this time. I thought the wine promising in October 1962, while noting "a certain toughness, but it is fruity with breed". Although, for modern tastes, it might seem a little rustic, one can still see its attractions today. We have just downed a bottle!'

An interview with
THE HON MICHAEL MACKELLAR AM

BALLIOL COLLEGE, OXFORD, m.1962

After Oxford, where he spent the summers working at Averys of Bristol, Mike MacKellar became an Australian politician and a government minister.

'I was born and raised in Australia. I did an agricultural science degree in Sydney, and then went to Balliol in 1962 and did a three-year degree in two years. I was looking at the noticeboard in the agricultural building one day and a tall, well-built chap raced up beside me to look at it, too, and it was John Avery. John was at Lincoln and did agricultural economics, and I read agricultural economics and international trade at Oxford. So we'd see each other regularly during the term, studying in the same area together.

'Balliol was founded for poor Scottish students. I qualified on two counts: I was poor and I was Scottish. The student part escaped me a bit, but I was reasonably good at a variety of sports, so they accepted me. I played cricket and rugby for Balliol, and Blues tennis, although I didn't play in a university match. John was a good skier and got a Blue for skiing. I became friendly with John, and he said, "What are you thinking of doing in the

'Ronald Avery was a most unusual man, a delightful man, and a real eccentric (as was John), to be admired and cherished.'

holidays?" I was a penniless student, and said I needed to make some money because I was putting myself through. He said, "Well, come down and stay with us, and work in the cellars with my old man."

Life with the Averys
'So I went down to Bristol and stayed with the Averys for the summers, and got on terribly well with the family. It was most extraordinary. They had this French antique that was supposed to be Marie Antoinette's bed. I was holed up in this extraordinary room with extraordinary furnishings, with bottles of priceless wines hanging around everywhere, gathering dust in the corners. Old Ronald Avery became a great mate of mine, and we got on well because we both liked cricket; he thought that Larwood and Jardine were the greatest living Englishmen because they'd beaten Bradman in Australia.

'Averys was a fairly catastrophic company, and so we tried to put a bit of organization into it, restacking wines. That first summer, the Beatles had their first big hit "Love Me Do". This was early on before there were mobs in the street, which they didn't get until they came to Australia and had a big show in Melbourne; they still show photographs of them on the balcony of the hotel where they were staying. There was a lot of that song going on

ABOVE View of the library in the Front Quad, Balliol College, 1965.

in the cellars that summer, with delightful blokes working there. I'd be off to work in the cellars, looking scruffy, and Ronald would ring up around lunchtime and say, "MacKellar, are you decent?" I'd say, "Well, reasonably so." And he'd say, "Come and have lunch with me." They had the Mauritania restaurant, and we'd have a nice lunch with excellent wines, and chat about all sorts of things: Australia and trains and cricket and wine. He introduced me to marvellous wines, and I learned a lot about French wines from him. John often wasn't there; during the summer vacations, I think, he was in France.

'Ronald Avery was a most unusual man, a delightful man, and a real eccentric (as was John), to be admired and cherished. He was mad on trains, and John was mad on trains. I remember seeing him in his laboratory, pacing. Ronald had built a world reputation for being able to choose young French white wines, and he used to blend, and mix brandies.

'My mother came out to visit me and I introduced her to John and to Ronald. My mother was an attractive woman, and Ronald liked attractive women, so they got on well. He taught me a great thing about wine, actually, with my mother. We were staying at a property they had down near the river. He said, "Mrs MacKellar, would you like a Sherry before dinner?" And she said, "I'd love one." He said, "Well, I'll just go and get you one." And he produced this priceless Sherry, which I thought was absolutely delicious. My mother tasted it, and he said to her, "What do you think of that?" And she said, "I think it's very nice, but I'd like it with a little bit of lemonade." I nearly fell through the floor with embarrassment. But this was the great lesson he taught me: he just said, "My dear, if that's how you like to drink it, that's how you should drink it." He always said, "You should drink the wine that you like, and don't let anybody tell you it's good, bad or indifferent. If you like the wine, drink the wine."

'My mother had been brought up in the city, but we came from the bush. In Australia in those days, in the country areas, we didn't drink much wine at all. People who did were known as "plonkos". People drank beer and rum; it was even difficult to get wine in a hotel. There were wine bars outside the country towns where the itinerants and the Aborigines turned up because you could get a lot of alcohol – a flagon of wine, Port and Sherry – very cheaply.

'John came out to Australia in 1965, with his father, and they had a ball. They created quite a storm because they went to the cricket and Ronald would sit up in the grandstand drinking Champagne. This was unheard of. He'd take a hamper with Champagne in it. That's when John got his real appreciation of Australian wine, as did Ronald, and they started importing Australian wine into the UK in the 1960s. They met the famous Australian winemakers at the time: the O'Sheas, the McWilliams, the Seppelts – that sort of people. They had introductions to people all around the place.

'John was involved with the Oxford University Wine and Food Society, but I wasn't. I'd been to one or two meetings, but I didn't have a lot of money at that stage. When the match came up, he said to me, "Look, why don't you come along to the tasting when we choose the team? Dad's given you a lot of expertise. Come and see how you go." So John took me along to the selection, and I got into the team. You were rated on how successfully you performed in the blind tasting. I've never been particularly good at blind tastings, but I was good enough to get into the team simply because I'd tasted a lot of wines with Ronald and John and knew a bit about it. Ronald Avery had taught me how to taste wine: aerate it, suck it through your lips. John used to taste water the same way. If he had a glass of water, he unconsciously used to taste if at though it were wine. We went down to London for the 1964 match, and we lost. It was good fun except that I was totally out of my depth.

'I hadn't met John Harvey then – he went to Cambridge – but I knew a lot about him, because the Harveys and the Averys had been competing for hundreds of years. When I came back to Australia, he was living in St Ives in 1965, and I went up to see him to introduce myself to him, as a friend of the Averys, who had said, "Harvey is living in Sydney – look him up." Subsequently his marriage broke up and we shared a flat right opposite the Sydney Opera House, and had a tremendous time.

'Harvey and I indulged in a bit of wine tasting, as you can imagine. When I got married, he was my best man. Averys was founded in about 1793, and Harveys around about the same time. There was a deal of controversy as to who really owned the title of Bristol Milk because they both produced Bristol Milk. But Harveys' Bristol Milk was more widely known internationally than Averys'.

Politics and Australian wine

'I was an agricultural extension officer, and was going to do a PhD in America, but somebody persuaded me to have a crack at politics. I moved up fairly quickly to the federal parliament in 1969, and wine played a part in my political career. I got into government in 1975, when Malcolm Fraser was Prime Minister. A cabinet minister called Tony Street and I shared the responsibility for the wine evenings in parliament. We'd get a prominent winemaker to come along to display their wines and talk to us about them. So I got a reputation as knowing a bit about wine. Malcolm Fraser and Tony Street knew a great deal about wine. Tony knew about Australian wine, whereas I knew more about European wines at this stage. But Malcolm used to say, "Right, MacKellar: what are we going to drink tonight?" If there was a state function on, I was the person to organize and choose the wines.

'The Queen and the royal family came to visit Australia a few times. The first was in late 1970, and I also had lunch with the Queen and the Duke of Edinburgh in 1980 at Yarralumla, the governor-general's residence. Charles and Diana were here at one stage as well. I chose the wine for the official dinner at Parliament House, and had a special red wine selected from South

Australia. I rang up the producer, on the advice of many, and said, "Which is the best?" And we got a special release. We also had a Clare Valley Riesling from South Australia – if you want to taste a nice Australian Riesling, get a hold of a Clare Riesling.

'I was Minister for Immigration and Ethnic Affairs, and then became Minister for Health. It was the fellow who suggested I go to Oxford in the first place who asked me when I came back, "MacKellar, have you ever thought of going into politics?" And I'd said, "No, not really." Although I'd become very interested in politics while I was in Europe because I had a real experience going through the Berlin Wall and Checkpoint Charlie. Like a lot of students in the 1950s, I felt that socialism sounded good. It read very well, but when I saw it in action it absolutely horrified me. I couldn't understand why you had to build great big electrified fences, with a light each side, and shoot people who tried to get away from it. I remember going through Checkpoint Charlie in 1963 and there were bloodstains on the wall on the East German side where they'd shot people trying to get out.

'I'd won a scholarship from Balliol to go and look at how the ancients may have got wood from Greece to Italy, and hitch-hiked around Europe for three months with a splendid girl I had gone through agriculture with. You can't do it these days, unfortunately. But then, if you were hitch-hiking around with an attractive girl, it was the way to go. We carried everything in backpacks, and slept in a tent at night, keeping to camping grounds in the cities.

'When we went to Checkpoint Charlie, we hitch-hiked into West Berlin, and the chap driving us had been a Luftwaffe pilot in World War II. He looked after

us, and told us what to do and how to get to various places. We were only in East Berlin for a couple of hours. Coming from a small relatively poor country town in New South Wales, I was used to people not having a lot of money. But there were old women sweeping the streets with rags around their feet instead of shoes, and I thought, "This is not a good thing." It had a major impact on me.

Wine as agriculture
'My job in agricultural extension was to go out among the rural communities of New South Wales and form organizations to formulate policies. We'd do things like short-term skills courses on agriculture. As Minister for Immigration and Ethnic Affairs, I saw the composition of Australia's population change quite dramatically over the years. We had people from Europe, southern Europe, Greece, Turkey, Germans, Dutch and Brits, all of them used to drinking wine. So the proportion of people who were used to having wine as a significant part of their lifestyle went up quite dramatically. As this happened, the whole of Australia became more interested in wine as well.

'Wine is an agricultural business, and it was fantastic how places were developing: the Hunter Valley in New South Wales in particular, and parts of the Barossa Valley and Clare Valley in South Australia. And subsequently, we had Western Australia zooming through with the Margaret River. I was really pleased to see this. John Avery kept coming to Australia and travelling around all these great places, saying, "Mike, you better try this wine or that one," and "This is good and that's good." He was out here just last year judging the Hobart Show; the wines in Tasmania now are very good as well. When Tyrrell's 1947 did extremely well in Paris, people noticed. It was one of the first Australian wines to do well in international competitions, but that success continued with other wines.

A matter of taste
'I'm very catholic in my tastes; I just like nice wines, but you know these fashions. There was recently a push for Australian Rieslings, because for a long while everybody was drinking far too heavily oaked Chardonnay. And New Zealand Sauvignon Blanc swept through the market. Now people are interested in Pinot Grigio and Pinot Gris. I've been pushing for the excellence of Riesling as a member of the Bendigo Wine and Food Society, through which I learned a lot about the Clare Valley, going to all the different wineries.

'I'm John Avery's son Richard's godfather, and I'm also John Harvey's son James's godfather. Richard is an actor and John was a great supporter of theatre, particularly musical theatre. It didn't strike me when he was at Oxford, but I knew about it later because he was telling me about how he invested in a number of Andrew Lloyd Webber shows very successfully. The sudden loss of John Avery [in 2012] really knocked me around.'

ABOVE Ronald Avery (right) in the Avery cellars, in the 1960s.

AVERYS OF BRISTOL
An historic wine merchant

Henry Avery was a famous 17th-century pirate who operated out of Madagascar, specializing in diamonds. A century later, his presumed descendent, Joseph Avery, joined wholesale wine and spirit importer Lax and Co in Bristol, an important port in the West Country, where Joseph's son, John, later purchased a small retail wine business and pub that was to become Averys of Bristol.

The firm can trace its roots in Bristol back to 1793, three years before the founding of rival wine merchant John Harvey & Sons of Bristol. It was an unfortunate year for the company's Bordeaux suppliers, as it marked the murder of the Girondins and the establishment of *La Terreur* in revolutionary France. The west of the UK, from Bristol to Liverpool and Glasgow, was an important route for goods coming into the country, as they didn't have to pass through the dangerous English Channel. It is no coincidence that these three cities built their wealth on the back of tobacco, slavery and alcohol imports. Early French wines had come into Bristol from Poitiers and Anjou, then Bordeaux, and there was regular trade with Spain. And Portugal had been an established source of wines for England since a formal trade agreement with Castile was signed in 1466.

John Avery purchased the historic premises at the bottom of Park Street in 1860 (documents show that wine has been stored on the site since around 1746), which he then rebuilt as the ornate Georgian-style Mauretania building, which is still there today. A reduction of excise duty on wines (not spirits) in the 1860s saw sales prosper, with the pub accounting for a significant proportion of profits. The original John Avery then died in 1882, leaving the business to his three sons: John Clarke, Edwin and Joseph. In 1919, John Avery's

'Avery's set me on the path to a long lifetime's enjoyment of wine and an absorbing semi-professional occupation.' Edmund Penning-Rowsell, former Wine Correspondent for the *Financial Times*.

grandson Ronald gave up his studies at Cambridge to continue in the family business. Ronald Avery became a wine-trade legend. In the 1920s he pioneered the practice of travelling abroad to estates to taste and choose the finest Bordeaux and Burgundy wines, when the norm was to buy from an agent in the UK. Ronald introduced great wines from St-Emilion and Pomerol, most notably the now-famous Château Pétrus.

He had the foresight to build up stocks, and in the 1930s, through a dearth of good vintages, Averys was a key distributor of 1929 claret: one of the century's great vintages. From 1923, at Averys' cellars in Bristol, Ronald also bottled fine Bordeaux and Burgundy wines to ensure their authenticity, among them Château Margaux until 1947. In 1938, he bought the fittings from the decommissioned *RMS Mauretania* for a bar and restaurant of the same name, where he entertained friends and customers. In the 1940s he was one of the first to sell wines by mail, writing personal letter to clients. Averys of Bristol had until then prospered locally, but under Ronald's leadership it became one of the finest wine merchants in the country – a serious rival to traditional merchants in St James's, London.

Ronald's son, John, inherited his pioneering spirit and in the late 1960s, long before the New World wine boom got under way, he began importing top names from Australia and New Zealand, including Penfolds Grange in 1968.

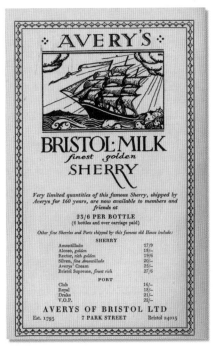

LEFT *Wine and Food*, No. 75, Spring 1952.

An appreciation of
JOHN AVERY MW (d.2012)

LINCOLN COLLEGE, OXFORD, m.1962

John Avery was one of the UK's most renowned wine merchants and played a key role in introducing New World wines into the country.

Francis John Avery was born in Bristol in 1941, into Averys of Bristol, one of the oldest family wine merchants in England. At Oxford, he read agricultural economics at Lincoln College, through which course of study he befriended fellow blind taster-cum-Australian politician Mike MacKellar. It was on visiting Mike in 1965 that John was first directly exposed to New World wines and, after subsequent trips with his legendary wine merchant father, Ronald, became responsible for the first shipment to England of Grange Hermitage, as well as wines from Tyrrell's and McWilliam's of Australia, and Matawhero of New Zealand.

As president of the Oxford University Wine and Food Society (OUWFS), John arranged magnificent functions: a blind tasting of Champagne on the Lincoln College Barge, a Pimm's party in the Worcester College gardens, and a Burgundian dinner held in hall at Lincoln which was attended by celebrity guest André Simon, who introduced each of the wines. His life-long friend Richard Henriques (Worcester) recalled that at that particular dinner: 'John had chosen lamb as the main course, but there was a hitch: the college chef had applied an ample treatment of garlic to the lamb. John dashed into the kitchens. He was in all normal situations the most tolerant of men, devoid of any prejudice, but he hated with a passion just two things: garlic and onions. He demanded that the lamb be cooked without garlic – but

that was not possible. A compromise was reached. We would taste all the wines before the lamb was served: an intermission of well over an hour.'

At Oxford he was also in the university bridge club (not his natural habitat), and on the university ski team, where he found himself surprisingly graceful. In 1965, he captained the blind wine-tasting team to victory, after an integral role in cleverly brokering an alliance with the upstart rival society, the Oxford University Wine Circle, to field conjoined talent after a deflating Cambridge three-year winning streak. In his own words:

'I was a member of the OUWFS, and president of the society (1964–65) and captain of the tasting team in 1965; we beat Cambridge that year! Jamie Pope (Trinity), later of Eldridge Pope Dorset Brewers, was captain of the Cambridge team in 1964 and 1965. In 1964 I was treasurer, Mark Pellew (Trinity) president, and Bill Turcan (Trinity) secretary; both are still customers of Averys! Charles Arnold (Trinity) was also in the team.

'As far as I remember, we never paid any dues to André Simon and so could not be considered a "paid-up branch"! André, however, recognized us, and came up for a dinner I organized, and my father, Ronald, provided some special wines. The last one was Mouton 1920 and it was "corked", which was a great disappointment! I remember apologizing to André for the corked bottle, but he brushed it off, saying, "If you go to a race meeting and have five winners and one loser, you are not disappointed."'

According to Henriques, John was most enthusiastic in his training. 'It was my task to select and pour the wine, leaving John to identify the wine,' he recalled. 'He was bold back in those days, sometimes bolder than bold; more than once he accused me of mixing up the bottles and once accused the shipper of bottling a substitute wine. Typically after every tasting training session John would arrange a lunch party, when the remainder of each bottle was enjoyed by all.

'Our final year at Oxford required us to move out of college and into accommodation. John and his tutorial partner, Richard Parker (now the Earl of Macclesfield),

ABOVE John Avery won a Blue at Oxford for skiing.

Neil Williamson (who shared legal tutorials with me) and I shared a house at 210 Woodstock Road. John, I suspect unknown to the university authorities, was the Averys rep for the county. His room was packed with cases of fine wine. Deliveries had to be made to the best restaurants, including The Elizabeth immediately opposite Christ Church – now, sadly, a Chinese restaurant. John frequently needed porterage assistance and the patron always made us most welcome.

'Post Oxford, John returned to Bristol and had by now taken to visiting Australia with some regularity. As a visiting wine expert he was reported in the press as saying that he hadn't tasted a good Australian wine yet. This was an inspired observation, because all the best wine producers were determined to remedy matters and John was soon introduced to the very best Australian wines and became very well known in the smartest Australian wine circles. John was very proud of the fact that when Ronald next visited Australia, Ronald was regularly introduced as "John Avery's father".'

Finally, according to Hugh Johnson, John Avery was: '… the wine merchant whom Geoffrey Chaucer, a vintner himself, would have taken with him to Canterbury. He was an unstoppable storyteller. Stories helped to sell wines. Without stories they are just drinks … His whole smiling, well-nourished, noisy personality was on the side of the young, the small, the striving.'

RIGHT *Sydney Morning Herald*, August 24, 1965.
BELOW RIGHT John wearing his college tie at Oxford.

A survey on our wines

The championing of Australian wines by a fellow member of the Oxford wine tasting team prompted English wine importer, Mr John Avery, to come here to try our local wines—although he has "not tasted a good one yet."

Mr Avery, export manager and son of the managing director of Avery's of Bristol, one of England's oldest wine and spirit merchants, is making a six-month survey of Australian wines.

While he was studying for his Bachelor of Agriculture degree at Oxford, Mr Avery met Mr Michael MacKellar, of Wollstonecraft, now an extension officer with the Agricultural Bureau of N.S.W., and they became fellow members of the Oxford Winetasting Team, which was, unfortunately, defeated by Cambridge.

"I've tasted very little Australian wine and that was frightful, although Australian port is good," said Mr Avery.

"Andre Simone told my father Australians do not keep wine long enough—it should be 10 years for a red. An old red is my favourite wine.

"As for hints on drinking wine, I think it's all been said before.

"But I do think there is too much snobbery about what wine to drink with what."

Mr Avery will tour vineyards in the Hunter Valley, Victoria, the Irrigation Area and South Australia.

As well as looking for Australian wines to send to England he will look at the market for imported French wines here.

"When I go back I am thinking of getting the title of export manager—we haven't got one at the moment. Now I'm just the son of the managing director."

His father, Mr Robert Avery, is a keen cricket fan and hopes to be able to combine business and pleasure by coming to Australia himself in time for the first Test.

If this is possible, Mr and Mrs Avery will arrive in Sydney in November.

Thursday January 28th

O. W. Loeb will give a tasting of Californian wines in the Old Bursars Trinity College.

~~Post Pones~~

Tuesday February 2nd

Ian MacKenzie, of MacKenzie Sherries, will give a sherry tasting accompanied by a film, in the Red Room, New Col...

Thursday February 25th

Christophers, Ltd., will give a tasting of selected French wines, in the Refectory, Christ Church.

Tuesday March 2nd

Avery and Co. will give a blind tasting in the Red Room, New College.

Thursday March 4th

Annual tasting match versus Cambridge, at Oxford, followed by dinner in king's College.

OXFORD UNIVERSITY

WINE AND FOOD

SOCIETY

DOM INVS ILLV MINA TIO MEA

HILARY 1965

COMMITTEE

Senior Member
O. P. WOOD, ESQ.

President
F. J. AVERY
Lincoln

Secretary
P. PRIDEAU-BRUNE
Christ Church

Treasurer
C. FITZGERALD
Lincoln

An interview with CHRISTOPHER FITZGERALD

LINCOLN COLLEGE, OXFORD, m.1963

*Christopher FitzGerald read classical mods and law at Oxford, before joining city law firm
Slaughter and May, where he became a partner, then joined the board of NatWest and the FSA.
He captained the Oxford team to victory in 1966 and '67.*

'Oxford had lost three years in a row against Cambridge. It was the 1964–65 academic year, and John Avery was president of the Oxford University Wine and Food Society (OUWFS), and I was treasurer. John had already been in one, if not two, teams that had lost and was frustrated. So we approached Peter Paice (St Catherine's), and another Mr Pace (Jesus), who were heading the recently established Oxford University Wine Circle. We thought we'd better make a decent show, and join forces with the rival society to broaden the pool. It was the first time the tasting team was selected from members of the Oxford University Wine Circle, in addition to members of the OUWFS; Oxford won for the next three years.

'As far as the OUWFS was concerned, the Wine Circle was very much Johnny-come-lately, but our membership at that time was limited to only 14, and there was a desire by a wider number of undergraduates to enjoy tastings and to learn about wine. The 1965 match was my first and John's last. The senior member was Oscar P Wood, a don at Christ Church, and the team, once chosen, was hosted for a blind tasting rehearsal at his house. There were no women in the club. There were women's colleges,

'John Avery took me under his wing when I arrived.'

but neither the societies nor the team were co-ed. The OUWFS met once a fortnight, but unlike the Wine Circle, which had lectures and a glass of wine, our meetings were purely tastings, and apart from talking with the presenter, there was not really any talking at all.

'Membership dues were a guinea a term (about £1.05), to subsidize the sole expenditure of entertaining the presenter to dinner at The Elizabeth after the tasting. The Elizabeth was opposite Christ Church, and about the only posh French restaurant in town. Much to the envy of everybody I knew, in my year as president I dined at The Elizabeth 12 times, which was ten times more than anybody else in their entire time at university. I had some very good dinners.

The Avery connection

'My father was in the navy, and when he came out of the navy he went to live in Somerset. He knew nothing about wine at all, but he used to go and have lunch at a hotel in Ilchester, near Yeovil. One day, Ronald Avery, John's father, was there selling his wares. Ronald always rolled up his sleeves and took the hard work direct as often as not. He fell in with my father, and my father with him, and the rest is history; my father became very interested in wine. Ronald thought this was amusing and gave him a lot of help and instruction, and sold him a fair amount as well by having him to lunch and dinner in Bristol. So from the age of about 14, I tasted really quite serious wine without knowing how serious it was.

'One day at lunch with Ronald my father mentioned that I was going up to Oxford. Ronald said, "My son is at Oxford, too. Which college is your son going to?" And my father said, "Lincoln." He said, "That's where my son is. I'll tell him to look out for him." So John Avery took me under his wing when I arrived. He was the junior common room cellarer at

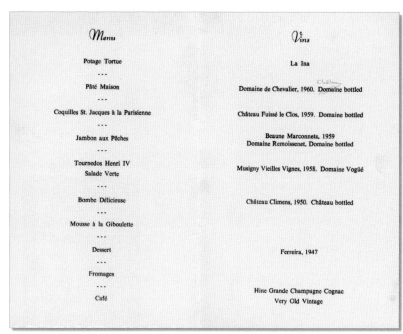

Menu	Vins
Potage Tortue	La Ina
Pâté Maison	Domaine de Chevalier, 1960. Domaine bottled
Coquilles St. Jacques à la Parisienne	Château Fuissé le Clos, 1959. Domaine bottled
Jambon aux Pêches	Beaune Marconnets, 1959 Domaine Remoissenet, Domaine bottled
Tournedos Henri IV Salade Verte	Musigny Vieilles Vignes, 1958. Domaine Vogüé
Bombe Délicieuse	Château Climens, 1950. Château bottled
Mousse à la Giboulette	
Dessert	Ferreira, 1947
Fromages	
Café	Hine Grande Champagne Cognac Very Old Vintage

ABOVE The OUWFS Annual Dinner at Merton College, May 11, 1966.

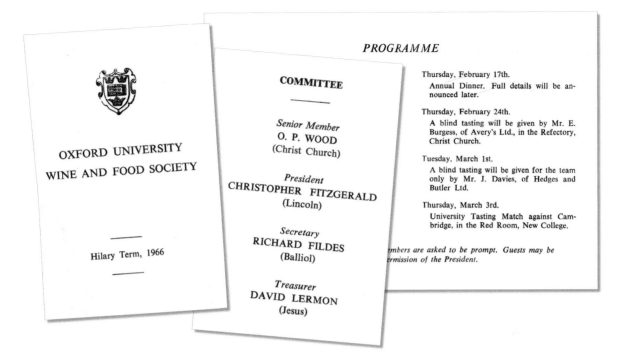

OXFORD UNIVERSITY
WINE AND FOOD SOCIETY

Hilary Term, 1966

COMMITTEE

Senior Member
O. P. WOOD
(Christ Church)

President
CHRISTOPHER FITZGERALD
(Lincoln)

Secretary
RICHARD FILDES
(Balliol)

Treasurer
DAVID LERMON
(Jesus)

PROGRAMME

Thursday, February 17th.
Annual Dinner. Full details will be announced later.

Thursday, February 24th.
A blind tasting will be given by Mr. E. Burgess, of Avery's Ltd., in the Refectory, Christ Church.

Tuesday, March 1st.
A blind tasting will be given for the team only by Mr. J. Davies, of Hedges and Butler Ltd.

Thursday, March 3rd.
University Tasting Match against Cambridge, in the Red Room, New College.

...mbers are asked to be prompt. Guests may be ...ermission of the President.

Lincoln, and got me to join the OUWFS. When he became president, I became treasurer, and when he left I became president, and took over his role at Lincoln. The president after me was Richard Fildes (Balliol), and I captained the team still under him. The tastings produced phenomenal amounts of interesting wine, and fostered a close connection with the enjoyment and appreciation of wine. A claret tasting would have 16 bottles – different communes back to back set out down a long table – and you would work your way around. The more often and regularly you tasted, the more you began to see why you liked this more than that, and also understand the reasons why this was different from that, and so on. It was an extraordinary education.

'The OUWFS was mostly undergraduates, if not all, and there was one annual dinner. One was held in Merton, and we managed to get Musigny Vieilles Vignes 1958, Domaine Vogüé. It was a festive, black-tie, eight-course affair with a wine for each course. But that was the only food to appear in the OUWFS, apart from a few dry biscuits at tastings.

'Merchants, including Harveys, Averys and O W Loeb, were generous. Michael Broadbent was still at Harveys then, just before he went to Christie's in 1966. As president, at the end of term I was responsible for arranging tastings for the following year; once I met Michael Broadbent in the Manor Hotel, Castle Combe, for lunch. He came out from Bristol, where he was still working for Harveys; I drove from Oxford. Michael Broadbent actually bothered to drive all that way, to meet some snotty undergraduate, to discuss the tasting that Harveys was going to do the following year. It amazed me – and, he paid for lunch.

'Harry Waugh came to the last competition I was in; it was the only time I ever met him, in 1967. He was a grand old man and slightly small. Dolamore had a shop in Paddington, and Freddy Price was a great supporter, and is a South African wine expert nowadays. Hedges & Butler was still around. German wines were represented by old man Hallgarten, who came to Oxford himself, and by Deinhard and Loeb. One of the German merchants told me how to tell the difference between a hock and a Mosel by the colour of the bottle: Mosel is green whereas Hock is brown. He said, "All you've got to remember is MG," and I never forgot that. I suppose they all saw the students as the market of the future.

'The senior common room cellars were the best at Oxford, but we didn't often have access to these. We had a perfectly respectable cellar at Lincoln, and our senior common room cellar had very fine stuff in it; certainly in those days, far too much Port went down. Veuve Clicquot came and gave a tasting on a barge on the Isis, and Pimm's gave a garden party. It was riotously dangerous because it was on the college sports ground in the pavilion, and we didn't limit the number of people. Waiters in white jacket solemnly prepared glasses of all six flavours to taste – a lot of people never got past No. 1.

'People were drinking Bordeaux, Burgundy and German wines, and restaurant lists were the same. You wouldn't go to a restaurant and drink Italian or Spanish wine. In the mid-1960s, neither made very good wine anyway, and certainly not that undergraduates could afford: the top levels of Barolo and so on. It was Left Bank Bordeaux. Pomerol was mostly going to Belgium, although Averys would've started to bottle and sell Pomerol by that time.

'I tasted first growths with my father and Ronald Avery, but they wouldn't have appeared in our fortnightly tastings. And I went to a tasting of 1962 Bordeaux when they didn't even call it *en primeur*. Impossible to fathom, they were so inky black – how anyone was supposed to know what they would be like in ten years' time, I don't know. My father used to smoke between courses because he said it cleared his palate, but nobody thought about smoking or not at that stage.

'The competition was held in college at Oxford, and at Cambridge in a university club. We switched between the universities; in my time it was never in London. Again, wines in the match were from France and Germany, and France was only Bordeaux and Burgundy, maybe Alsace, but that would've been to catch you out, because you would expect it to be German. There was no mark given for identifying a grape type because it was obvious, or should've been. You got marks for identifying the region, the commune, château and vintage. My personal great achievement was getting a Clos de Vougeot exactly right, including the year, which scored an enormous number of points. The match was in the evening, followed by a good dinner in the relevant college.

'I attended the 50th anniversary reunion in 2003. The varsity match was beforehand, and we had an amusing competition for those who wished to take part afterwards. I was staggered by what they were having to taste and be able to identify: Australia, New Zealand, Romania. Oxford won both that year, I'm pleased to say.

'In the 1960s, apart from John Avery, who came from the trade, no one in the team was headed in that direction; it was much more amateur. But it was a good time, and a social opportunity to meet with friends, and friends of friends, in the company of a wine merchant, and to learn a bit about wine. And the tasting match was a challenge once a year to sharpen your wits – and your palate.

A more innocent age

'At Oxford, we were frightfully conservative at that time. There were a few rebellious souls, certainly from 1963 onwards. The Summer of Love was 1967, student protests in Paris 1968, and Woodstock 1969, but I had gone down by then. I don't remember the use of drugs, but once I went to a party at a friend's house in north Oxford, and in my innocence said, "What on earth is that smell?" Somebody had to take me aside to say that someone was smoking pot. There would have been a radical ten per cent, but most wore corduroy trousers, jackets and duffel coats. Things started to change in the end of the 1960s, and dramatically by the early 1970s, but I would characterize the 1960s as not much different to the 1950s.

'I played rugby for Lincoln, and captained the college team one year. The only time I rowed was in the Summer VIIIs rugby races. We managed to keep a good Saturday fixture list. Weekdays we played against other colleges, but on Saturdays we played the second or third teams of some

of the London clubs, like Harlequins A, by combining with Brasenose next door in a team called the Blinkers, surprise, surprise. Lincoln was a relatively small college, with about 250 undergraduates and 60 graduates; now it has doubled in size, with 300 undergraduates and 300 graduates, and half the intake is made up of women.

'I keep an interest in wine. I bought a distinguished vintage bottle of Clos la Coutale, a Malbec-Merlot blend from Cahors, when I was still at Oxford, from a corner shop in Paddington. I couldn't believe it: I paid 10 shillings! And before I went to Hong Kong I paid a visit with my father to the Bartons in Bordeaux and bought a case of 1978 Léoville-Barton. Beyond that, I wasn't in a position to buy anything until post-1982, as I was in Hong Kong, and unaware of the beginnings of the *en primeur* market. The first vintage I bought *en primeur* was 1985, and by then I was living in Kensington, around the corner from Haynes, Hanson & Clark, and I knew Anthony Hanson quite well, so I bought Burgundy from him. My cellar has never been bigger than about 50–60 cases. I buy now from my good friends at Lea & Sandeman.

The accidental guest

'My connection with John Avery paid off in various ways over the years. He rose through the ranks at the Vintners' Company, and eventually became master. They always had big lunches after committee meetings and were quite often expected to bring a guest. John could be shambolic: a lovely man, but he'd often forget whether he had invited anybody to something or had never got round to it. He phoned me one day and said, "I don't suppose you're free for lunch tomorrow?" And I said, "As it happens I am." I had a fantastic time. I said, "Look, John, I have no pride in these matters. If you've forgotten, or somebody has dropped out, just ring me. I can always say I'm busy and can't come." After that I went as his guest a number of times, on a day's notice, including to The Saintsbury Club and the only time I've been to Vintners' Hall. Steven Spurrier and Edward Demery, Royal Cellarar, were on the other side of the table. It was very entertaining.'

EN PRIMEUR

Also known as wine futures, *en primeur* refers to the process of buying wines, typically abroad, before they are bottled and released onto the market. Wines are purchased exclusive of duty and VAT ('in bond') and then usually shipped two to three years after the vintage. The wines most commonly offered *en primeur* are from Bordeaux, Burgundy, the Rhône Valley and Port, although other wine regions are adopting the practice. Once they have landed in the country of purchase, the customer chooses to store them in a bonded warehouse or have them delivered. The taxes become payable only once the wine is withdrawn from a bonded warehouse.

THE ELIZABETH

The Elizabeth restaurant, at 82 St Aldate's, was a popular place for the OUWFS to entertain visiting wine merchants in the 1950s, '60s, and '70s. In 1951, still in the era of rationing, *The Good Food Guide* described the state of English cooking as dire, with the only decent restaurants in London. Kenneth Bell, one of Britain's great pioneering chefs of the 1960s and '70s and best known for his 20-year tenure at Thornbury Castle in Gloucestershire, then one of the top-rated restaurants outside London, rose to the challenge as chef and restaurateur of The Elizabeth from 1961–66. In 1966 he sold The Elizabeth to Antonio Lopez, from Granada, Spain before moving on to Thornbury. In 1974, Kenneth Bell was a judge for the varsity blind-wine tasting competition.

The Elizabeth was in a 15th-century building, in a discreet position opposite Christ Church, and remained popular in Oxford into the 1990s. Both Bell and Lopez ministered to generations of Oxford students and their families, and dons. With its well-heeled clientele, it had a distinct ambience and classic style: plates and glassware with its own crest, and a handsome dining room with an ornate plastered ceiling. Lopez' longstanding chef was Salvador Rodriguez, who stayed 22 years. Aged 75, Lopez sold the restaurant in 2000 and retired.

Anthony Verdin (Merton), owner of The Cherwell Boathouse restaurant in Oxford, remembers The Elizabeth as 'smart and elegant' dining, and the best restaurant in Oxford at the time. 'Lopez was always a great host and would come and have a glass with customers. I have many happy memories of occasions there, including Jasper Morris' stag evening, and my first time tasting Vega Sicilia, a now-famous producer then represented in the UK by Morris & Verdin.'

When the restaurant was about to close in 2000, the cellar needed drinking. Blind wine-tasting competitor Alex Hunt (Worcester), remembers that the wines at his last dinner there with fellow blind-tasters Chris Dark (Trinity) and Tom Bromwich (Trinity) were a half-bottle of Roederer 1989 and a bottle of Château La Chapelle 1978.

ABOVE The Elizabeth restaurant was located in this handsome 15th-century building in St Aldate's.

'If you met a Martian and wanted to introduce him to a real gentleman, it would be Antonio.'

ANTONIO LOPEZ
Kenneth Bell's protégé and restaurateur of The Elizabeth, 1966–2000, remembered by Gabriel Lavelle

Gabriel Lavelle was at Trinity College, Oxford, from 1964–68, and is a friend of the Lopez family.

'I ate at the Elizabeth for the first time in 1966, the year that Elizabeth Taylor and Richard Burton performed *Dr Faustus* at the Oxford Playhouse [see above]. The three-course meal with wine then was £5: a huge amount of money, compared with £1.50 in the Italian restaurant further up St Aldate's.

'Antonio had been born in poverty in Spain, and suffered during the Spanish Civil War. He married his childhood sweetheart, Dolores, and brought her to England, then became the head waiter at The Elizabeth under Kenneth Bell, before Bell sold the restaurant to him when he went on to Thornbury Castle. At first, Antonio continued in the Bell tradition, with a conservative French menu. It didn't matter; you would only go there once or twice a year and be delighted to eat the same thing: *la flamme de volaille* (chicken breast with white wine and cream), *carré d'Agneau* (lamb best end of neck bathed in a mustard sauce served for two), *quenelles de saumon* and *sauce nantua* (salmon fillets) or *truchas Alhambra* (trout). Eventually the menu became a mixture of Spanish and French, including steak with peppers and tomato sauce, which was adventurous for its time.

'Antonio had natural, innate breeding. He would stand at the top of the stairs of The Elizabeth with his hands together, beam at you, and you knew that you were terribly welcome. The restaurant had an amazing wine list: first-, second-, and third-growth clarets, hock and Mosel. He was a loyal customer of Averys and O W Loeb & Co. We once drank a bottle of Clermont 1926, his birth year, together.

'The Elizabeth had a polished wood table with a 1950s Cona Coffee machine that had a glass bowl with steam immersed in the bowl and a burner under the glass. Lewis Carroll drawings adorned the walls because the bay window looked across at Christ Church, where Carroll studied.'

A contribution by JANCIS ROBINSON OBE MW

ST ANNE'S COLLEGE, OXFORD, m.1968

Jancis Robinson writes daily for JancisRobinson.com, weekly for the Financial Times, *and bimonthly for a column that is syndicated around the globe. Her many books include* The Oxford Companion to Wine, The World Atlas of Wine *and, most recently,* Wine Grapes.

'Like so many, I fell in love with wine when I was at Oxford, one of the first three undergraduates reading maths and philosophy. Specifically – and perhaps appropriately – it was a bottle of Chambolle-Musigny Les Amoureuses 1959, shared at the Rose Revived restaurant, that did the trick. I also had a friend at St Anne's, Alison Forbes, who had been brought up, most unusually for the 1960s, in a household familiar with wine-drinking. She would solemnly instruct me "green for Mosel, brown for hock" and give me little sips from two similar but different half-bottles of claret.

'Seeing how interested I was becoming in wine, several friends suggested I join the Oxford University Wine Circle, but I would have none of it. I suspected that this was a gathering of wine snobs whose company I would not enjoy. I now realize that, had I overcome my reservations, I would in fact have enjoyed the company of the circle's members enormously. I would have met my wine-writer contemporaries Oz Clarke and Charles Metcalfe more than a decade earlier than I did, but I'm sure it would have been disastrous for my wine career.

Coming straight from a village of 40 people in Cumbria, I would have had any ounce of confidence knocked out of me. As it was, I went my own way, via three years in travel and a year in Provence, and by the late 1970s I was editing a wine-trade magazine. In that capacity I was regularly invited to the annual Oxbridge wine-tasting competition, then sponsored by Harveys of Bristol.

'I have now written and/or edited more books than I can count, but I can honestly say that my life as an author began at the 1976 varsity blind wine-tasting competition. The wine-loving veteran cricket commentator John Arlott also attended and was particularly taken by the idea of a young woman embarking on a career in such a male-dominated world as wine writing. I was by no means Britain's first female wine writer – Pamela Vandyke Price and several others were already well-established – but perhaps it was my hippie hairstyle that made Arlott think I was a suitable subject for an article on the page then known as *Guardian Women*. He accordingly suggested that one of his newspaper colleagues interview me, and as a direct result, I was subsequently asked to write the wine primer that eventually, in 1979, saw the light of day as *The Wine Book*.

'Back then, the Oxbridge tasting competition, like the Master of Wine exam, was very much easier than it is today. All the competitors had to do was familiarize themselves with the wines on Harveys' list. Sancerre figured strongly in those days, I seem to remember. There certainly weren't any wines I can remember from outside Europe. And I think Bristol Cream-drinking at some point during the festivities was de rigueur.

'I can't remember when Bill Gunn MW of Pol Roger first asked me to be the judge of the competition representing Oxford, and nor do I know who I replaced, but it feels like half a lifetime ago. It was certainly when the competition was still held at the University Women's Club and the person who most frequently represented Cambridge as a judge was my immeasurable late friend, Bill Baker of Reid Wines. My favourite photograph of him was taken at the Oxbridge competition not long before he died, so tragically early, in 2008.

'For the last 20 years I have been, much more often than not, the Oxford judge, with my friend, co-author and founder of *The World Atlas of Wine,* Hugh Johnson, another Cambridge judge. Over those years I have been astounded by the increasing competence of the tasting teams. We pore over the numbered answer papers, which are infuriatingly designed (James Simpson MW, please take note), requiring candidates to squeeze long tasting notes into a tiny box, and often gasp admiringly at how accurately some tasters identify the 12 wines presented to them – often far more accurately than we have done during our own blind-tasting session before undertaking the marking.

'I should point out, incidentally, that we judges make special allowances when we think wine X actually tastes more like a Y. If the answer X is worth, say, 5 points, we tend to give candidates 3 points if they think it's a Y, and possibly 2 if there's a Z we think the wine is rather like. It is also heartening to see that sometimes the reserve tasters outperform the fully fledged team members. And of course, I am always thrilled when, as is so often the case, women team members notch up high scores.

ABOVE Three female Oxford undergraduates standing in front of All Souls College, 1966.

'The most dramatic competition took place in 1993, under mild-mannered Bill Gunn's aegis, when a Cambridge team, dominated by two or three voluble, relatively mature American members, caused an excited ruckus by arguing that Pol Roger was wickedly commandeering the competition. Blithely ignorant of the demands of sponsorship, and the fact that Pol did not exactly have to fend off dozens of other companies anxious to sponsor the event, they claimed to be appealing to the American wine writer Robert M Parker Jr to support their, surely rather hollow, bid for independence.

'I am always overworked. I make work for myself – not least by creating JancisRobinson.com, which needs feeding daily. I therefore rarely accept lunch invitations and find it difficult to shoehorn into my diary anything other than travel and tastings that directly contribute to my knowledge. But I do enjoy my annual reminder of Oxbridge. (Oh, and it goes without saying that I enjoy the wines of Pol Roger; I wouldn't dream of doing this job for many other potential sponsors I could think of.) There is nothing more stimulating than conversation with a nimble and unconstrained mind. My most memorable encounter with an Oxbridge taster at the post-competition lunch was back in the late 1990s, with Oxford psychology, philosophy and physiology student Alex Hunt.

'I'm delighted to say that he is now, like me, a Master of Wine and, more recently, a regular columnist for my website. I still think he's far too bright for the wine trade – but that sentiment almost certainly dates me. He is far from the only ex-competitor to have ended up devoting his professional life to wine. And how could I possibly suggest *that* is unwise?'

ABOVE Judges Bill Baker and Jancis Robinson swopping tasting notes at the varsity match, 2006.

TED HALE MW OF JOHN HARVEY & SONS

AS REMEMBERED by JANE HUNT MW

Jane Hunt worked with John Harvey & Sons in Bristol and in London from 1977, where Ted Hale, who oversaw the blind wine-tasting competition on behalf of Harveys in the 1960s and '70s, became her 'mentor and guiding light'. She now runs Hunt & Coady with business partner Tina Coady, specializing in wine event management.

'The late Ted Hale (d.1991) was an early MW (1960) and an enthusiastic influence on the varsity competition until his retirement from Harveys in 1983. He was very much the protagonist of doing what you shouldn't do. He wouldn't conform to and regularly contravened any regulations imposed on him, regarding driving company cars or opening bottles, but he was so well liked, and so good with wine that Harveys couldn't possibly get rid of him. In those days, Harveys imported Sherry, and Port for Cockburn's Port, in bulk and bottled from cask in Bristol. Originally fine wine merchants, that division had become a very small arm of the big company, which was all about the Sherry and Port. When Sherry and Port, due to EC regulations, had to be bottled in Spain and Portugal, respectively, rather than in the UK this huge operation in Bristol, employing up to 600 people, was forced to contract. The Sherry and Port financed the wine side, and the wine side kept getting smaller and smaller.

'My first job with Harveys was taking people around the museum in the cellars in Bristol. It was a great place,

with a wonderful collection of wine bottles and the little silver neck labels you hang round a bottle, and the most marvellous collection of antique Jacobite Amen 18th-century glass, which even then was worth about £30,000. The restaurant was next door, with the most amazing wine list. Harveys and Averys used to do tastings together at the little West of England Wine and Spirit Association, so we were often together with the Averys lot. I think Harveys considered themselves rather superior, whereas Averys was a much better wine merchant.

'At Harveys, in Bristol, there was the tasting room. And Ted was in his office, James John and John Harvey had their office, and in our office there was myself, the secretaries and Arabella Woodrow, who sat in the middle of the room; she was a funny girl. She'd come from Oxford, and was obviously incredibly bright, but had absolutely no office skills yet whatsoever. She'd leave people hanging on the phone for ten minutes, and then wonder why they had rung off, while she was trying to find something out. She also used to wear diaphanous

ABOVE From left to right: Ted Hale MW tasting wines at Harveys with John Harvey and James John MW.

blouses with no bra underneath, and would go down into the warehouse. In those days, with the unions, you didn't do anything that was somebody else's job, but the boys in the warehouse were happy for Arabella to go down to find the samples that she needed; they used to refer to it as "blackberry picking".

'It was a very amusing time. Ted used to arrive, park the car irregularly (nothing was ever straight with him), come rushing into the office, shut his door, have his phone conversation with his "mistress" in London, open the door, taste lots of wine, and then it was lunch. He had a wonky arm from his first job in Hong Kong as a policeman, when he had had his arm outside of the car window and it got hit by a car coming the other way. His arm was still there; he could move his shoulder and clasp with his hand, but the rest of the arm was withered.

'Michael Broadbent, who had left Harveys in 1966 to join Christie's, used to come to lunch once we'd moved to London. Lunch was quails eggs and cheese and ham, crusty bread and so on. We would have picnic lunches in Harveys, with Ted opening bottles for Michael coming over from Christie's based in King Street across the way. You never got anything done in the afternoon, but then nobody was buying anything in the afternoon, because they'd all had a big lunch, too. We didn't have faxes, email or mobile phones. It really was truly wonderful. You were writing letters and typing with carbon paper.

'I can remember being at 27 Pall Mall in London when my mother came. She was going shopping, and then we were going to the Royal Academy after I had finished work that day. And Ted said, "No, stay for lunch." And bottles were opened: of 1945 Latour from Harveys' cellar. Ted's attitude was that it was there to be enjoyed, not to be stashed away never to be drunk. Of course, this was Harveys' investment and potential profit, so there was a side where the management found him difficult, but I would never have done what I'm doing without his encouragement.

'He was a dear man and charming, and he just had this absolute love of wine. I've got a lovely card Ted wrote me: "To special Jane, good luck in your exams". He was incredibly encouraging to women in the wine business, and very much the instrument in helping me to achieve the Vintners' Scholarship, awarded to a top student at diploma level to further wine studies through travel; he wrote so many letters of introduction for me that on the three-month trip around France, I visited châteaux Latour, Lafite, Mouton-Rothschild, and Margaux with his blessing. My first three nights of the trip were spent in the Château de Saran of Moët et Chandon outside Epernay, and I'd never, ever been in a place like that before. That was down to Ted, and the weight that Harveys carried.

'I also knew Harry Waugh well. He'd had a car accident in France in 1981 where he lost his sense of smell, but he was well into his 80s by then. As Prue Waugh didn't drive, I used sometimes to be their taxi driver.

ABOVE Ted Hale presents a magnum of Harveys' Sherry to Arabella Morris (top) at the varsity match, 1978; and a magnum of Champagne to Claudia Pendred at the varsity match, 1980.

'I didn't particularly want to be in London at first. I had a flat in Bristol, and was happy in Bristol, but was now stuck in Pall Mall, doing a bit of selling and shuffling papers. Then I had a phone call from a man I'd never heard of before called Mark Birley, from Annabel's, a place I'd never heard of before, and would I go and see him. As I didn't know him from a bar of soap, I said, "I'll think about it." He said, "I've been told by Harry Waugh that you must come and see me."

'So I asked a few questions – and, well, Annabel's is the smart society nightclub, and I went to work for Mark Birley in 1982. He had a shop in Fulham Road, Annabel's Wine Cellars, and I used to select the wines for Harry's Bar, which was the Italian side of Annabel's, and do a little bit of wine selection for Annabel's. I was with him until he sold the shop to Ray Gough, who owned a chain of shops called the André Simon Shops, but none of them exist now. They were four retail shops in the most exclusive parts of London, and I worked with them for about five years buying wines, and became an MW in 1985. And that was very much the influence of Harry Waugh.'

The woman...

SUZELLE MOSS of Lady Margaret Hall, Oxford, inspects a glass of wine.

the wine...

KINGSLEY LIU, captain of the Oxford team, receives his cup from John Arlott, left.

and the song!

FIVE MEN and a girl from Oxford University Wine and Food Society won all five prizes in yesterday's annual wine-tasting match against Cambridge University.

They scored 361 points to Cambridge's 354 to record Oxford's 13th victory in 24 matches and regain the silver cup lost last year.

Brasenose third-year Student, Kingsley Liu, from Hong Kong, received a case of wines as the highest-scoring competitor and an autographed copy of John Arlott's book on Burgundy as captain of the winning team.

Suzelle Moss, from Alabama, 23-year-old philosophy Student at Lady Margaret Hall, won a magnum of champagne as top women contestant. Originally a reserve, she beat the Cambridge girl by 52 points to 49.

Wine magazine

Tim Neill of Magdalene was given a year's subscription to a wine magazine as the lowest-scoring competitor.

Judges were wine-writer John Arlott, Dr Bryan Wilson, from Oxford, Dr Denis Marrian, from Cambridge, and Sotheby's wine department head Mr Patrick Grubb.

CHEERS FROM the winners. Oxford's team — Tim Neill, Stephen Parry-Jones, Christopher Johnson-Gilbert, Miss Arabella Morris, Kingsley Liu, Miss Suzelle Moss, Jeremy Wood, Michael Mackenzie and Archie Smith (coach).

The Oxford Mail, February 24, 1977

THE 1970s

The 1970s was a decade of transformation, and the varsity blind wine-tasting competition saw a number of firsts: the first women in the tasting match, in 1970 at Oxford and 1977 at Cambridge, in Oxford in 1971 the first American on the team and, in the late 1970s, the first Chinese competitors. There were also a number of siblings who competed – including Arabella Morris (now Woodrow) and Jasper Morris, to date the only brother and sister both to achieve the Master of Wine. Dr Denis Marrian, notably father of blind taster Christie Marrian and tutor to HRH Prince Charles, was the don of the day at Cambridge, hosting weekly blind-tasting training sessions in his rooms in Trinity College. His tradition was followed on by blind taster and coach Dr Stephen Elliott who shares his knowledge and cellar with students today as Chairman of the Trinity College Wine Committee, along with his wife, Penny (née Johnson) Elliott (the first woman to blind taste competitively at Cambridge), whom he met over a spittoon. Oxford won seven out of the ten varsity matches, possibly due to the tremendous enthusiasm of its blind taster turned peerless varsity match coach, Oz Clarke. But it was Cambridge's Charles Pendred who was the first and only blind wine taster to score 100 per cent in 1974. In the 1970s, total UK wine consumption grew from, at the start of the decade, just over five bottles to almost 11 bottles per capita per annum by the end of the decade. Wines were still predominantly Old World – classic French and German – but wines from Italy, Spain and the New World were on the horizon.

Cambridge

Nigel Allsopp
Robert Clement-Jones
Nicholas de Rothschild
Stephen Elliott
Harry Eyres
Tessa Fawcett (Strickland)
Mark Fitzgerald
Tim Forse
Robert Fraser
Charles Haswell
Jonathan Hippisley
Luke Hughes
Penny Johnson (Elliott)
Sheila Lane
George Leggatt
Raymond Liu
Robert Andrew Luce
John Marks
Christie Marrian
Charles Mercey
Jeremy Passmore

Andy Peacock
Charles Pendred
Dave Richmond
Pippa Robinson
John Shakeshaft
Pippa Robinson (Walker)
Michael Wrobel

Oxford

Brewster Barclay
Roger Bennett
W Jonathan Boyce
Nicholas Butt
Tim Charlton
Oz Clarke
Nicholas Coulson
Selina Elwell
Scott Ewing
Edward Garnier
James Gould
Stephen Hobley
Jasper Morris
Christopher Johnson-Gilbert
Terence Kealey
Rosie Kerslake (MacGregor)
Robin Lane
Martin Lewis
Kingsley Liu
Jane MacHale
Michael MacKenzie
Jonathan Marks
Robert Mather

Martin McNeill
Duncan Menzies
Charles Metcalfe
Jock Miller Stirling
Charles Moore
Arabella Morris (Woodrow) (MW)
Jasper Morris (MW)
Suzelle Moss
Timothy Neill
Antony Northrop
Stephen Parry-Jones
Claudia Pendred
Michael Plumley
Richard Porter
Vicki Pritchard-Davies (Villers)
Christopher Purvis
Mark Savage (MW)
Christopher Sayer
Michael Shires
Sarah Stewart-Brown
Lynne Turner-Warwick
  (Turner-Stokes)
William Wells
Jeremy Wood

OXFORD MAIL, Wednesday, March 3, 1971

SARAH'S TASTE OF A MAN'S WORLD

Sniff . . . twirl . . . spit . . . they say wine-tasting is a man's business, but the first girl ever to take part, Sarah Stewart - Brown of Lady Margaret Hall made history and put all the men to shame (save one) at the Varsity wine-tasting contest in London yesterday.

Of course, the combination of beauty and a palate meant that Oxford were irresistible. They beat Cambridge comfortably by 407 points to 312 in the 23rd match and now lead 12—11 in the series.

Sarah, 20, and a medical student at present reading animal physiology, scored 74 points. The only taster with a better marking was a theologian — Oxford president Robert Owen Clarke (Pembroke) with 85 points. And to emphasise Oxford's cosmopolitan versatility, the first American to take part, Charles Moore (Pembroke) was third with 70 points.

Before the match Mr Owen Clarke said : "I think Sarah has a better palate than I. She has developed a serious interest in wine since spending six weeks in Bordeaux this summer."

The other members of the successful Oxford team were Charles Metcalfe (Christ Church), James Gould (Christ Church), and Mark Savage (University).

ABOVE Dubious maths: Oxford wins the 1971 varsity competition, bringing the tally to 9 wins Oxford and 8 wins Cambridge. The 1971 match was the 18th not the 23rd as stated above – the 1968 match was hazily accounted for as 'no contest'.

An interview with SARAH STEWART-BROWN

LADY MARGARET HALL, OXFORD, m.1968

Sarah Stewart-Brown is a professor of public health at Warwick Medical School, University of Warwick. Her research and teaching focus on mental wellbeing and its potential to contribute to public health.

'I was the first woman in the varsity match – in 1970 and '71. Oz Clarke was the Oxford captain in both years. He was a year ahead of me, reading theology at Pembroke – "Top Four" as it was known. We went out for about a year, and my training was with Oz in the summer holidays; he got all these invitations and we went round the vineyards in the south of France, tripped down to Spain, then Burgundy on the way back.

'My family lived this rather Edwardian life, so I didn't know what went on with my parents. Then my father died when I was 13. It was Oz who got me interested in blind wine tasting, and it was just one of those things that I seemed to be able to do. Oz negotiated with the wine merchants, who would come and put on tastings for the Oxford University Wine Circle (OUWC) and the Oxford University Wine and Food Society (OUWFS). They wanted to cultivate people who were likely to go into or buy from the wine trade in the future. I do remember drinking the odd Italian or Spanish wines, but they were special. Wines were mostly French and German, and certainly no New World.

'The 1971 competition was held in London, at Harveys on Pall Mall. We won in 1970 and in '71, and then I took my finals. I think Oz had taken his finals in 1970. I'm not quite sure what he was doing those extra two terms, because we'd split up by then. He was an actor, quite keen on opera, and he had a lovely voice. Oz and I were both fairly mad, really, so it was all fairly mad when we were going out. There was never a dull moment, but that got to be exhausting, and I suppose because I was a medic I needed to work, and that wasn't part of his plan. Oz was keener on acting and singing than wine then, but

he was carving out a career for himself getting to know these people, and he ended up on a television programme where he identified a wine blind [*Food & Drink* on BBC2] and it made him somewhat famous. It wasn't a viable relationship for the longer term, but fun while it lasted. We had a good time camping all round France and Spain in that long summer of 1970.

'The OUWC and OUWFS would have been present at the freshers' fair, and people would ride around on bicycles and put flyers in pigeonholes so that you would know about events. There was no internet – it was so nice. But I wasn't drawn to the wine societies at that stage, and I wouldn't have been in the tasting competition if I hadn't been going out with Oz. Oz won top taster and I was second in both years, and they gave me a ladies' prize: a bottle of Château Haut-Brion – a bit of a gift, really, because they couldn't give it to anybody else. But I had come second out of both universities; I must have had a reasonably good palate. I have a very good sense of smell, which is 90 per cent the key factor in blind wine tasting. I had no intention of going into the wine trade. Perhaps because there was no pressure I did well.

One in ten

'Partying was a big part of university, but as a medical student I did have a lot of work. There were so few women then at Oxford; it was one in ten. Hundreds of people would know you, but you didn't know all of them; the guys would know who you were because as a woman, you stood out. It was even less than one in ten medical students, and the South Parks Road was not only the anatomy department, but physiology, pathology and pharmacology, too. There was no medical teaching centre, and it was rigidly separated into pre-clinical and clinical. You didn't go near a hospital until you took the medical exam halfway through, and I went on to Westminster Hospital in London. There were few places for clinical training in Oxford then: only 20 or 25. For many of us, certainly for me, it was time for a change.

'My grandfather was a doctor, but he wasn't that kind of a role model for me. I think my father dying when I was young played a part. In my early teens, my mother had a woman lodging with us who was a medical student, and I thought to myself, "You could do this." At the time I went to a small girls' boarding school called West Heath, which is shut now; Princess Diana went there. The school trained us to flower arrange and marry nicely, but medicine wouldn't have been in their forecast for any of us. We wouldn't even have been introduced to the idea we could go to university. My brother got into Cambridge, and I said that I wanted to take the entrance exams for Oxford and Cambridge. The headmistress actually wrote to my mother saying: "This will be a terrible waste of your money to let Sarah sit the exams." I was studying English and history, but was handicapped in the other subjects – they

ABOVE Oz Clarke on his camping tour of France, summer 1970, with Sarah Stewart-Brown.

ABOVE The LMH Summer VIIIs made the cover of *Private Eye*, May 23, 1969. Sarah Stewart-Brown is stroke, far right.

didn't teach science to girls at West Heath. I was studying on my own for the Oxbridge entrance exam. It was beyond their ken.

Summer Eights
'At Oxford I played tennis, and did a bit of acting and rowing, and in the summer of 1969 Lady Margaret Hall (LMH) put a boat on the river in Eights Week. That was the first time women rowed in Eights Week. Until then it had only been men, and we said, "That's ridiculous." So we borrowed a boat, found somebody to coach us and entered the race, but three other women's colleges – St Anne's, St Hugh's and St Hilda's – decided they were going to do it as well. There were too many boats, and so there was a row-off of the bottom Bumps division. LMH didn't get on the river (St Hugh's did), but we got on the front cover of *Private Eye*, which seemed to us to be much more important. Women have been rowing in Eights Week ever since. We were in all the national papers. It was that kind of era, when women were breaking barriers everywhere. We were constantly saying, "Oh my God, we did it."

The English medic-student patient
'On our camping trip Oz and I stayed in a tent in Burgundy. I nearly died in that tent, and didn't realize what had happened until later on in medical school. We were given lovely meals by our hosts, and we ate those white Burgundian sausages, and I was fantastically ill with them.

'In 1970, Sarah Morphew Stephen was the first woman to achieve the Master of Wine, in the same year that I was the first woman on an Oxbridge blind wine-tasting team. It was all happening at the same time.'

ABOVE Sarah Morphew Stephen MW in the 1970s.

The French were known for their cuisine, but were considered primitive as far as food hygiene. Oz's father was a doctor and he'd given us antibiotics to take if we got ill, but he'd been an army doctor, so they were streptomycin pills, which are hopeless for this kind of situation. I took the pills, and Oz left me on my own in the tent because there was a dinner and he needed to go. It was like Kristin Scott Thomas in *The English Patient*. I completely swelled up and was wheezing away, just 19 at the time. I carried on sleeping and hoped it was going to get better, but in retrospect, he could easily have come back and found me gone. I'd had an allergic reaction to the antibiotic.

'I was very much a child of the 1960s. There were sit-ins in 1968, and I was in CND marches. It wasn't Greenham Common, but it was simply the ethos of "This isn't right – let's change it." This attitude has remained with me all my life, but my children really don't have it. All that flower-power stuff I didn't do because I was busy being a medical student, working much too hard, but it was in the fabric of life and the culture. Public health as a career was right for me, because it's about changing how people see health, and what we do sociopolitically about it.

'At university, I would drink wine when I went out for a meal, which was when a boy would ask you out, stand you dinner, and it was a date (I didn't pay; it never seemed wrong, but looking back it was just ridiculous). I never went out like we do today, to have dinner and drinks with girlfriends; it just didn't happen. The Wine Circle would take merchants to The Elizabeth restaurant, which had wonderful wines. The Pimm's parties were in the summer, but there wasn't even a bar at LMH. We had a dining hall where we went for breakfast, lunch and supper. You didn't cater for yourself at all. Wine was something that happened on a dinner date, and at OUWC and OUWFS tastings. Most of the rest of the student body drank beer, cider and gin and tonics. The Bullingdon Club and college dining clubs would certainly have been drinking wine, and Oz was right in there with them, with Charlie Metcalfe, but we weren't, as women.

'There was a lot more serious work that went on in the women's colleges. Plenty of blokes worked seriously as well, but you had to be really good to be a woman at Oxford. You had to be as good as the top ten per cent of the men. I certainly had a good time there.'

THE SUNDAY TIMES, 7 MARCH 1971

Oxbridge faculty for wine tasting

AT the 23rd Oxford-Cambridge wine-tasting contest, held for the first time in London in John Harvey's cellars, the dark blues drew ahead and won from what had been a tie.

There was no affectation about the attitude to wine. Cambridge admit "We do most of our tasting over dinners," and Oxford are reported to have the benefit of inspired coaching sessions from a don.

Those of the Press who tried the ten wines—five each of red and white—found them far harder than the contestants seemed to, though Edward Hale, Master of Wine, one of the judges, said afterwards that he considered only the 1952 Vieux Château Certan (Pomerol) to be "tricky." (I was so wrong about three of the white wines that I retired, snuffling hamster-like behind my inflamed sinuses, hoping no youthful person would see my notes.)

Oxford's captain, Robert Clarke, of Pembroke, had the top score of 85. He hopes to write, which should make some of us start burnishing our taste-vins, and he gets an individual prize of a case of wine selected from those tasted.

My choice would be either the Ruwer, Maximim Grünhauser Herrenberg, 1969, mountain-flower fragrant as only a great Riesling can be, with an elegance plus fruit that would make it a beautiful apéritif or a first-course wine with rather delicate food. (£1.50, estate-bottled.)

Or, of the reds, there's the 1964 Château Palmer, very much a fine claret, with the charm so often associated with this property and a unity and firmness not common among the Médocs of this vintage. Excellent with grills and roasts or—for it will get better—with game next season. (£2.60, château-bottled.)

Second highest score came from the first and only woman to enter the contest, Sarah Stuart-Brown, of Lady Margaret Hall, a pretty girl in violet maxi with the sort of smile and laugh that wine should produce (and good looks often lack).

To demonstrate the delights of a fine wine made in an off year, the hosts, John Harvey, served the 1954 Château Latour at luncheon. (I thought they were being a bit casual by putting horseradish sauce and pickles on the table, but after all one needn't have had them and I didn't.)

This well-proportioned 1954 (£2.81) is a fine example of what I term "a luncheon wine." For occasions when one wants to be pleased, not overwhelmed.

Many directors' chairs in the wine trade are now filled by those who started in their university wine or dining societies to love wine. How civilising and cheering that I came away from the contest sure that future wine lovers and merchants will be at least as good as those who have taught them.

Pamela Vandyke Price

ABOVE Charles Moore playing real tennis at Oxford in 1971.

'I stayed with Edouard Kressmann, the proprietor of Château La-Tour-Martillac, which produces one of the *grands crus* from Graves. We dined well, and drank even better.'

An interview with CHARLES MOORE

PEMBROKE COLLEGE, OXFORD, m.1970

Charles Moore was the first American blind wine-tasting competitor, in the 1971 match. On returning to the USA after Oxford, he became an investment manager and founded the Banc Funds Company in Chicago.

'I was at Oxford from 1970 to 1972. I loved England, but at the time I graduated, tax rates in the country were confiscatory, so no American thought too seriously about staying on. I had a degree from the University of Pennsylvania, and was doing a second undergraduate degree, reading English at Pembroke. There were two wine societies at Oxford: the Oxford University Wine and Food Society (OUWFS) and the Oxford University Wine Circle (OUWC), and London merchants came up and hosted tastings. For me, it was a phenomenal opportunity to taste European wines as well as better wines than most undergraduates would have known, although there were certainly students that came from smart households that would have had large cellars.

Pembroke connection
'I was interested in wine before Oxford, and had read Hugh Johnson's book *Wine* cover to cover. One of my classmates, Andrew Graham, was involved in the Teasel, the dining club at Pembroke, and he knew everybody in both wine societies, including Robert Owen "Oz" Clarke. He was a great host, and on rainy, chilly nights, he'd invite us to his rooms on the first floor, where he'd have a fire going and open an excellent bottle of wine. If Oz was there, we would learn something. I liked Oz enormously – charming individual – and he said, "Why don't you come along to the OUWFS?" Oz introduced me to his friends, and a number of us ended up

on the 1971 team: Charles Metcalfe (Christ Church) was Oz's closest friend, and Sarah Stewart-Brown (Lady Margaret Hall), an attractive woman, was Oz's girlfriend at the time. Our fifth and sixth team members were James Gould (Christ Church), a tall guy with red hair, and Mark Savage (University), who became an MW in 1980.

'There was a match coming up against Cambridge, and another against Imperial College, London. In his house in Boars Hill, Oz would pour a number of wines, serve them blind, and start talking about them. He had what I called (they used to laugh at me when I said this) "a mnemonic tone": this facility, if he'd tasted a wine a week, a year, or ten years ago, to remember the wine. His scores were remarkable. He won top score in 1971, and got to pick a case of wine, and picked Pétrus before anyone had heard of it. Sure enough, years later Pétrus became the wine of the century, and of the world. Oz had this ability to understand wine, to know what he was drinking and why. The rest of us, our brains spinning, were trying to remember everything he said, at the same time trying to form our own understanding: "Is this really what we're tasting?" Oz hosted half-a-dozen wine tutorials, and in the second term he decided it was going to be the six of us on the team.

The 1971 varsity competition
'The match against Cambridge was in March, and Oz gave us strict instructions: "Get up to London the night

before and do not have a thing to drink. Don't eat any flavourful foods. Don't brush your teeth with toothpaste. And for God's sake eat carefully the next morning because if you eat anything too strong you're going to screw up your tasting." We were sitting there, our heads all knotty, when he added: "And don't hang around with any women who wear perfume. That's no good, either." Oz had a lot of ideas about how to get ready for this.

'Bottles were in the middle of a long table in brown paper bags, reds decanted, with unidentified people from Cambridge on the other side. Nobody talked. We were all in the same room and we were not supposed to confer. We tasted the whites first, followed by the reds; nobody swallowed an ounce of wine, but by the time we stumbled out of there you could barely walk: your brain was subsumed by fumes. Oz got the highest score, Sarah second, and I got third. Metcalfe did pretty well. Metcalfe was a proficient wine taster, but I don't think he did well in contests, although he was always right behind Oz in terms of understanding.

'We beat Cambridge, and then we beat Imperial College, London. There was an element of serendipity. As fortune would have it, a week before the match we had a tasting and the merchant brought a 1959 Léoville-Las Cases, and that wine just happened to be in the competition against Cambridge. I got that one exactly right. You had to identify as many characteristics as you could: grape type, country, region, and if you could get the vineyard and the vintage that was a huge bonus. Oz got three or four vineyards right, whereas the rest of us got one, maybe two. If you were even in the right ballpark you were doing well, and it would get harder.

'We had some Italian and Spanish wines at Oxford, but French and German wines were predominant. People didn't mention Australia or New Zealand often, and when people mentioned South America it was not necessarily in a good light. These were emerging wine areas. I don't know that we had

an American wine at all when I was at Oxford, and today California is a huge wine industry, as are Oregon and Washington State. Wine is a far more global phenomenon today than anything we knew in the early 1970s.

Dobermann at Dolamore's

'I worked for Dolamore in its Jericho wine shop in Oxford in the summer of 1971. Stock was heavily French and German, with some Italian. When travelling, people drank Italian wines in Italy, and Spanish wines in Spain, but I don't think much of it came back into the UK due to tariffs. The owner of Dolamore would come up from London to host tastings: pouring wine and offering it, talking about the quality of the vintage, its overtones and influences.

'As the junior summer help at Dolamore, I did anything they asked me to do. Mr Shrimpton and his wife ran the shop. Paddy, an Irishman, was our driver, and when the colleges would order, we would go out in the van and deliver. I did get a privileged view into the college cellars; they were extensive and expensive. The manciple, or wine steward, would come down to meet us, and Paddy and I would unload four to eight cases of wine. We were not afforded the opportunity to spend too much time because we had to get back to the shop in case there was another delivery to be made. There were only

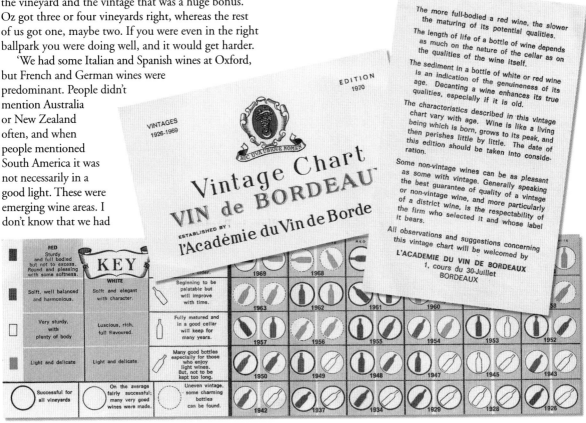

the four of us, and there was walk-in traffic every day. Dolamore wasn't just selling to the colleges; it was selling to the townspeople, the students, and the dons.

'The Shrimptons had a dark Dobermann pinscher by the name of Cocoa. Paddy and I were Cocoa's custodians during the day, and one of my duties was to take the dog to Port Meadow, a big green four blocks from the shop. Cocoa was friendly to people he knew, but was not to be trifled with otherwise. On slow days, if we'd get a little bored we'd tease and torment this poor dog, largely resident upstairs, in the basement or in the tasting room at the front of the shop, blowing on his face or his tail; Cocoa would go crazy.

College life

'Pembroke was not a wealthy college, but it had some nice wines, and a fair amount of resident wine expertise. Across the street in Christ Church, the dining society was called the Lotus, and the joke there was that we were Christ Church's cellar. Financially stronger colleges with the largest endowments, such as Christ Church, had expensive cellars because they had the resources to buy early in the life of the wine. They were buying wines right after they were released, and depending on the opinion of the vintage, buying more or less of it. It was a nice perquisite for those who dined at high table. I have dined at high table at Pembroke once or twice since graduating, but never while I was a student. Students were not served wine at dinner back then.

'There were few Americans and not a lot of women. There were five women's colleges, but other than Sarah, only a handful of women turned out for the tastings. It was a British world in the early 1970s at Oxford. I did have a friend from India, from Pakistan and from Singapore, and at Pembroke there was one guy from Yugoslavia, and a Dutch guy. If the campus was at all international then, it was far more the case at the graduate than the undergraduate level. I rowed for Pembroke, and we had a stroke from New Zealand who also happened to be the heavyweight boxing champion, Michael Hutchins. At the competition, everybody was interested that Sarah, a woman, and I, an American, were on the team. The newspapers played that up, but we were not the two best tasters; they were clearly Oz and Metcalfe. I don't believe anybody was in Oz's class. I am in no way surprised that he has written wine books since then. Oz was witty, fun, engaging and had a tremendous sense of humour; he was a larger-than-life person in the wine world of Oxford. People were drawn to him. Metcalfe wasn't much different. Every five minutes we'd be laughing at some idiocy that somebody had just dreamt up. They were both opera singers, singing and tasting wine: it was a convivial setting. It wasn't competitive, and there wasn't a professional aspect; people weren't going to events to foster a career in wine.

'The French have an expression, *terroir,* and strongly believe that the entire character of the wine is determined by it, and there's a lot of truth in that. At one tasting Oz said, "You know this wine suffered because it rained during

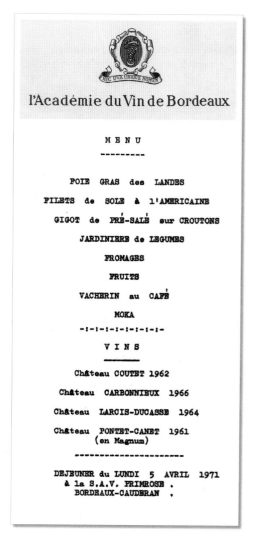

ABOVE Lunch at the Académie du Vin de Bordeaux in Bordeaux after the Blues real tennis team played against the Tennis Club de Bordeaux, April 5, 1971.

the harvest. The wine is thinner and lacks character. A problem in probably one out of every five harvests. They go crazy trying to deal with the rain."

Blues in Bordeaux

'I rowed for the college, and played real tennis for Oxford: I was fifth on the Blues team in my first year and first in my second and we won the varsity match. In 1971, an Oxford-Cambridge Blues team was formed, and we were invited to play in France against teams from Paris and Bordeaux. In Bordeaux, châteaux owners who were also tennis players graciously hosted us. I stayed with Edouard Kressmann, the proprietor of Château Latour-Martillac, which produces one of the Graves *grands crus*. We dined well, and drank even better. At one meal, we had the eponymous *entrecôte Bordelaise* accompanied by a superb, rich claret. Wine engendered great camaraderie at Oxford and was a welcome elixir.'

revue "A Kick In The Stalls" ends tonight after a week at the Robin Hood Theatre, Arnham.

Zany

The Footlights tradition goes back to the last century, when undergraduates provided entertainment for fellow students.

Many famous names in comedy started their careers at Cambridge; 1963, for instance, produced John Cleese, Graham Chapman, Eric Idle, and the Goodies.

Monty rules for satire

THE success enjoyed by the Monty Python team has had one adverse effect: successive highbrow comedy teams have found it difficult to do something completely

different. And if they have used original material, their audiences have still seen a link with Python.

So it is with this year's Cambridge Footlights whose

The cast of the 1976 Cambridge Footlights revue in a pensive mood. Left to right: Michael Murray, Penelope Johnson, Nick Hytner, Jeremy Thomas, Michael Landymore, Oenone Williams, Jimmy Mulville and Charles Shaughnessy.

There is a lot of talent and originality in this year's revue. The humour is zany; the wit intelligent and often biting. It will be interesting to see how many of the eight-strong cast become successful in entertainment.

The revue began with a sketch involving the audience, a shrewd warm-up.

Some other favourites were sketches involving a failed kami-kaze pilot, inept Mafia goldfish-nappers, the Glytta Band, Violentsides (as opposed to Ironsides) and the KGB. — CJ.

An interview with
PENNY (NÉE JOHNSON) ELLIOTT

GIRTON COLLEGE, CAMBRIDGE, m.1974

Penny Elliott is a partner at Forsters LLP in Mayfair, London.

'I applied to John Avery … I went for an interview in Bristol, and I sat among his Louis Kahn furniture and his Baccarat glass. He said, "I'm afraid I tend to sacrifice efficiency for aesthetics." He was just the man for me.'

'I arrived at Girton in 1974. Like lots of colleges it had a "mother system", and my college mother was Jane Moon. Jane sat me down and said, "So, what are you interested in?" I had done drama at school and said, "Theatre." Then she said, "Are you interested in food and drink?" Well, who says no? So she took me along to the freshers' fair for the amateur dramatics club, and then to the first meeting that year of the Cambridge University Wine and Food Society (CUWFS). Jane was going out with Robert Clement-Jones (Trinity) at the time, who was a member, and I signed up. I didn't have any interest in wine prior to that; it was completely from scratch. I was officially the first female CUWFS member in my own right, rather than going as a girlfriend or guest, and I was the first woman at Cambridge on the varsity blind wine-tasting team, in the 1977 match.

'I read archaeology and anthropology (part I), and social and political sciences (part II). I tried to avoid books – I was a thespian and I did 27 plays in nine terms. Many of my contemporaries went on to become incredibly famous in the world of light entertainment; Douglas Adams wrote *The Hitchhiker's Guide to the Galaxy*; there was Griff Rhys Jones; and Rory McGrath and Jimmy Mulville, who were the writers behind *Not the Nine O'Clock News* and co-founders of the production company Hat Trick. I shared a house with Peter Bennett-Jones, who set up the PBJ Agency and represented Rowan

Atkinson. Rowan Atkinson and Richard Curtis were both at Oxford then, and in the Oxford Revue sharing a theatre with the Cambridge Footlights Revue at the Edinburgh Festival Fringe in 1976.

1977 varsity match: got in but didn't win

'I was only in the one match, in 1977; they dropped me resoundingly because I effectively lost the match for Cambridge. There was a seven-mark margin, and I accounted for at least eight marks we didn't get. I remember coming down on the train and feeling quite nervous. There were six whites and six reds. We went to Justerini & Brooks to limber up – for years they had been giving the Cambridge team a pre-match warm-up. They laid out a few whites and reds, to get the palate going, at 10 o'clock in the morning. The match was an hour later in Harveys' basement on Pall Mall.

'Johnny Hugel had given the CUWFS a wonderful and vivid description on the wines of Alsace, telling us the story of how he had changed his nationality three times, and his grandfather six, depending on where the Franco-German border had been. I guessed correctly that one of the whites was a Riesling, and correctly that it was Alsace, but then I put it in Germany, so that was bad news. I had even got the vintage right! It was sad: marks lost for country of origin. I lost it for us putting Alsace in Germany.

THE CAMBRIDGE UNIVERSIT WINE AND FOOD SOCIETY

LENT TERM 1977

OFFICERS

President
Dr D.H. Marrian

Vice-Presidents
Dr Sydney Smith
Michael Roberts, Esq.

Senior Treasurer
Dr D.K. Rose

Cellarer
Raymond Liu (Peterhouse)

Secretary
Anthony Brown (Christ's)

Blind Tasting
Stephen Elliott (Trinity)

Junior Treasurer
Michael Wrobel (Selwyn)

Dinner Secretary
Penelope Johnson (Girton)

Committee Member
Charles Haswell (St. Catharine's)

PROGRAMME

Wednesday 23rd February
The Varsity tasting match, organised by Harveys, to take place at their office in Pall Mall.

Thursday 24th February
M. Jean Hugel from Alsace and Mr de Winton of Dreyfus Ashby will present a tasting of Alsatian wines.

Thursday 3rd March
Mr Wyndham Fletcher, formerly of Cockburn Martinez Mackenzie, will present a tasting of vintage ports, and a film will be shown.

Monday 7th March
Mr Christopher Rowe of Findlater Mackie Todd will present a tasting of white burgundies.

All tastings will take place in the Old Combination Room, Trinity College, at 6.00 p.m. Members are asked to be prompt.

Charge for each guest : £1

Anyone wishing to dine with the speaker after a tasting should contact the dinner secretary.

Blind tastings will be held on Tuesdays in Dr Marrian's rooms at 1.15 p.m.

'The scripts were marked during lunch, downstairs at Harveys because there wasn't any room upstairs. Michael Broadbent was the judge and announced the result. There wasn't any consolation prize – except for 30 years of anecdote about how I lost the 1977 match! Stephen Elliott (Trinity) had been "man of the match" with the top score a year earlier in 1976, with an amazing prize of a case of whichever wine in the tasting line-up he wanted. There was quite a lot of training and spotting, because it was all off of Harveys' list. New World wines were limited; Averys was one of the only importers of Australian wine at the time. There were conventional German wines, but not even obscure French varietals made an appearance.

'The CUWFS had weekly meetings on Tuesday evenings in the Old Combination Room at Trinity College. A merchant would give a tutored tasting, and from time-to-time it degenerated into a cocktail party. So the edict went out: be more deferential, come in a tie and jacket, stop slurping and listen to what was being said. The tastings thereafter were heavily themed, well structured and informative, and everyone took it seriously. It was still sociable, of course, but it wasn't a cocktail party.

'Undergraduates at Cambridge did not go out to dinner much then, with the exception of the end of a theatrical production dinner. There were few restaurants in Cambridge, and we used to be envious of Oxford, which had The Elizabeth. The Hotel de la Poste was in Swavesey, but few undergraduates had cars, so you couldn't get out there. Dinners were usually at King's College, because King's had a number of fellows who had been buying wine for a long time: Kendal Dixon was one of these great bachelor dons who shared wines from the college cellar, and believed in getting the young to drink amazing wines – I remember having Château Batailley 1945, a legendary wine even then. Don Kellaway, a fellow at St Catharine's, and John Rose, a medic at Emmanuel, were also generous. The undergraduate and events cellars were separate from the high table cellars, but if you chose a wine that was particularly old or valuable, catering might clear it to be released through the college wine committee. We paid for the wines, but not at market value; tastings were from your subscription, and dinners you paid at cost. I was dinner secretary in my last year, and the committee formed the core of the team. It

ABOVE Penny Johnson on the steps of Tim Forse's house, Cambridge, before a Riesling tasting and lunch; Stephen Elliott, her future husband, as a young research fellow at Trinity College.

was, in a sense, self-selecting; somebody touched you on the shoulder and said, "Would you like to join the committee?" They identified people who were coming to tastings regularly and taking it seriously. Those people were then invited to go to Tuesday lunchtime trainings with Denis Marrian, a don and member of the Trinity College wine committee, and a great supporter of the CUWFS and the team.

Good heavens! A woman in the wine trade!

'There was not widespread graduate unemployment, so we left university with a degree of self-confidence about the ability to choose jobs that would be remarkable to those leaving now. During my time at Cambridge, I thought about going into the BBC, the Foreign Office and the wine trade. I applied for the Saccone & Speed graduate training programme and when I went for an interview, the chap who interviewed me (the business had just been taken over by Grand Metropolitan) said, "We don't really mind whether we're bottling Château Lafite or toothpaste: it's the margin that's important." So I applied instead to John Avery; I must have asked him at the end of a tasting, "Might I be able to have a job?" I went for an interview in Bristol, and I sat among his Louis Kahn furniture and his Baccarat glass. He said, "I'm afraid I tend to sacrifice efficiency for aesthetics." He was just the man for me.

'I spent two years learning an enormous amount about how not to run a business. It was really interesting. There were quite a lot of like-minded people. Bill Baker, who had been at Cambridge, had gone to Averys the year before me in 1976, and stayed until he set up Reid Wines in 1980. Robin Lane came the year after; he was an Oxford graduate and blind wine-tasting competitor. It became a little Oxbridge melting pot.

'Harveys had sponsored the varsity match, but I took a job at Averys, its Bristol rival. When I went to Averys, Harveys and Averys had both bought a warehouse opposite each other, so there was rivalry. In Bristol there were five independent merchants run by family members. Harveys and Averys were both old, traditional wine merchants, but Harveys had been much more commercial with its exclusivity for Babycham. Harveys had a better commercial brand, with Harveys Bristol Cream on everybody's Christmas lunch table, whereas Averys was a more traditional offering.

Pearls before (s)wine

'Serena Sutcliffe and Sarah Morphew Stephen were the women wine pioneers of the day; Jancis Robinson had not yet been allowed to take the MW course because she was a journalist. The wine trade was male-dominated, with many men from a certain background. It was the preserve of the idle rich and the thick second son: "Hunting on Fridays? Absolutely!" And I saw that even more when I came to London. I circuitously went to work for Green's in the Royal Exchange, and it was Simon Parker Bowles and

Richard Parsons, who was married to a Symington, and Miles Mascall, who set up Green's Champagne bars in the City, who were incredibly well-connected.

'I was mistreated in all sorts of ways, but I didn't get the "Don't worry your pretty little head about it" type of attitude because I didn't have a pretty little head. I had gone through the CUWFS, and adopted the "I'm the honorary chap" role. Probably by modern standards we were treated badly, but I think women who adopted the "I'm an honorary chap" stance in the wine trade held their own quite well. My Footlights training – to be able to laugh at oneself – was an enormous protective ring, because the banter was really quite foul. There were eight of us in our Footlights show in 1976, and six of them have gone on to become incredibly successful in drama one way or another. A chap I last saw selling carpet tiles for Marley and I were the only ones who didn't go into show business. I would not have been a very good actress. I suppose going into the wine trade was a little bit like marching to the beat of your own drum: it was nice to be doing something different from everybody else.

Blind(-tasting) date

'I met my husband over a spittoon. I was sitting down, carefully making notes, and suddenly he came over my shoulder and spat long distance. That was our first encounter and our closest proximity in those days. I had matriculated in 1974 and was a third-year undergraduate, and Stephen had started in '71 and by then was a third-year graduate. We were both in the '77 team.

'Stephen was going out with someone else at university, as was I, but my mother reports that I was quite interested and had "mentionitis". I went down to Averys in Bristol in 1977 and he went off to Malvern. The first autumn I was in Bristol was the first year of the Bristol Wine Fair. Charles Pendred (Trinity) and Nick Stanley, who worked at Simon the Cellarer, then set up the Corney & Barrow wine bars, and Stephen all came to the Bristol Wine Fair. That Christmas he went back to Cambridge and I pursued him; the Bristol Wine Fair was the only contact we had post-May week 1977, and I had a Christmas card saying, "Can't bear research in Malvern. They do it 9 until 5. Going back to Trinity." So I sent him a bottle of Champagne on the Averys delivery van to the Trinity porter's lodge to say congratulations at the beginning of the January term, and he wrote me a postcard saying, "Thank you very much. Come and drink it." And the rest, as they say, is history.

'Stephen was committed to an academic course, although he originally had said to me, "Wouldn't it be wonderful to be the wine expert at Sotheby's?" I vaguely had a not-very-well-formulated career plan on the back of that comment: I would get some trade experience and end up in an auction house. Stephen was always committed to the academic life.

'After two years at Averys, the geography of a Bristol–Cambridge relationship was getting to us. I considered

7 PARK STREET VIADUCT
BRISTOL BS1 5NG
TELEPHONE 24015

27/7/77

Dear Miss Johnson,

I am sorry if I worried you by my last letter on salary and would like to confirm that your starting salary will be £2,500 per annum. As I indicated in my letter I was not certain of the figures discussed and I apologise for any confusion I may have caused. I also confirm that your salary will be increased to £3,020 when you take over full secretarial duties.

I am pleased to see that you are getting in some practice with a typewriter!

Are you able to start work a few days before I go away on holiday so I can show you around?

Once again sorry about the misunderstanding – you can see why I need a good personal secretary!

Yours sincerely

John Avery

P.S. Your salary is of course confidential and would you please ensure that mutual contacts (such as Bill Baker) don't get to know it!

P.P.S I hope you got the letter which was forwarded on to you.

AVERYS OF BRISTOL LIMITED.

1st December 1977

CONTRACT OF EMPLOYMENT
(Weekly Paid)

1.   In this statement under the Contracts of Employment Act 1972 as amended by the Employment Protection Act 1975 Averys of Bristol Ltd gives you:

Name:.........Miss P.Johnson...............................

particulars of the terms and conditions on which it is employing you on

Date:.........8th March 1979...............

2.   Your employment with the Company began on:

Date:...1st September 1977......

and your employment with any previous employer does not count as part of your continuous period of employment.

3.   You are employed as:

Job title:..Audit Clerk................................

4.   Your pay exclusive of overtime is £.43.50.............per week paid weekly in arrears.

5.   Your daily hours of work are from 9.00 a.m. to 5.15 p.m. on Monday to Friday. You are allowed a lunch break of one hour. Your basic working hours, exclusive of overtime are therefore:

Number:....36.............hours per week

Payment will be deducted for lateness after three minutes at a minimum rate of fifteen minutes. You are required to work overtime hours in excess of the basic week as directed by your immediate superior for which you will be paid at over-time rates as follows:

(a)   Other than on Sundays - time plus one-half
(b)   Sundays   - double time

No payment will be made where the period worked is less than fifteen minutes

6.   Your holiday entitlement is laid down in the Companys' Standing Instructions which may be seen on application to the Head of your department.

ABOVE John Avery's letter offering Penny Johnson a job at Averys of Bristol after leaving Cambridge in 1977, and her employment contract.

SYDNEY SMITH by PENNY JOHNSON
St Catharine's College, Cambridge

'Sydney Smith was a big noise in the 1960s and '70s in Cambridge wine circles. He was a fellow of St Catharine's (1939–88) and a great don who was vice-president of the CUWFS for years and introduced us to a lot of wines. He was a bachelor and a charming, generous man. He was a great expert on Ming vases, with his collection of Chinese porcelain in The Fitzwilliam Museum today. He was university lecturer in zoology and a Darwin specialist; it is said he was the only person who could read Darwin's handwriting. Sydney had an amazing cellar, and when he died at age 77, there were seven of us, a group of his protégés, who still get together every six months or so to taste, including me and Stephen, who acquired his cellar. We had 16 cases as our share, and we sold some of the really rich and rare bottles on behalf of Sydney's sister, who was his heir.'

moving to Cambridge, but thought, "This is ridiculous: there's nothing to do in Cambridge." There wasn't any wine activity that wasn't within a college, and all of it was supplied by people from outside of Cambridge, so I moved briefly to Christopher's off Jermyn Street in London.

'Dai Gilbertson gave tastings then; it had just been bought by Scottish Newcastle Breweries, and when I joined it was being decimated as a business. Dai was an old-school wine-trade chap. He would set off to Cambridge to do a tasting, having sent the wine up ahead in a van, with a bottle of gin and a bottle of vodka in his briefcase that I always had to make sure was there. He was completely inebriated. I lasted for three months and then I applied to Green's and spent two years there in the buying department. Then in 1980 there was a big recession. They were cutting back and put me on my bicycle to sell wine in the West End on commission. It was difficult and I had a miserable time. I went into the Athenaeum Club on Pall Mall saying, "Would you like to buy my wine?" and they would say, "No, thank you, but would you like to see where the gentlemen dine?" So I was taken and given a patronizing tour of the Athenaeum's dining rooms.

'I had a Cambridge boyfriend whose father was chairman of The Garrick Club's wine committee, who took pity. He introduced me to their manciple and every time I was really miserable and desperate I would go and sit in the basement of The Garrick and this chap would ply me with glasses of Sherry and occasionally give me an order. So that was nice.'

WINE AND OXFORD
by OZ CLARKE

PEMBROKE COLLEGE, OXFORD, m.1968

Oz blames it all on Oxford. He has made a career out of never having a job, just working very hard at his hobbies, drinking, writing, going on holiday, mucking about on stage and the telly.

'Girls. That's what did it. Or lack of them. And money. I went up to Oxford full of optimism but with very empty pockets. Even so, I thought potential girlfriends would be there. They weren't.

A tasteful victory for Oxford palates

A victory drink of vintage champagne for Oxford captain Robert Clarke, who also made the higher individual score.

The victorious Oxford Wine and Food Society team celebrate with champagne after beating the Cambridge opponents at wine-tasting. From left they are: Charles Moore, James Gould, Mark Savage, Sarah Stewart-Brown, Robert Clarke (captain) and Charles Metcalfe.

ABOVE The Oxford team in 1971.

'I trawled through the University Handbook trying to locate an activity that was a) cheap and b) would render me irresistible to women. And then I saw it. The Oxford University Wine Circle: £2 a term, four tastings. I would be a wine taster: suave, elegant, worldly … Nirvana beckoned.'

I then located a source up the Banbury Road. I worked out that if I signed out from breakfast three days a week at Pembroke, and didn't pay my library dues, I could afford to take a Banbury Road girl out – once, by the last week of term, on the last day, and to lunch, not dinner. A lovely girl called Nu shared steak frites with me that thrilling Friday. And then she scarpered off to Spain. This wasn't looking promising.

'I trawled through the University Handbook trying to locate an activity that was a) cheap and b) would render me irresistible to women. And then I saw it. The Oxford University Wine Circle (OUWC): £2 a term, four tastings. I would be a wine taster: suave, elegant, worldly. And what's this? You can take a guest, free? Nirvana beckoned.

'My first tasting was red Bordeaux. I remember every detail … of Francesca. She was the favoured recipient of my newfound magnetism. I put on my smart jeans (I had two pairs) and a shirt (I had one of those, too). Francesca was a goddess: green hair, green sequins on her face, unfeasibly tight green top, green leather micro-skirt. The rest of her – which was most of her – was covered in green body paint. The courtly Mark Savage (University) opened the doors of the college Red Room to welcome us. Everyone was in a pinstripe suit.

'I took four girls to tastings that term, and none of them gave me a second date. But something in me had changed. As that Bordeaux evening ranged across basic earthy reds to the mellow joys of St-Émilion and Pomerol and finally up to the glittering delights of classed-growth Pauillac and St-Julien, I listened in awe – not to Francesca; she wasn't talking to me by then – about tasting the wines and the flavours described in these splashes of unfamiliar red liquid in front of me. This was all making sense. The final wine was a classic Bordeaux, Léoville-Barton 1962. Just the sight of that name, that vintage, now, fills my brain with a flavour, an aroma, an emotional turmoil. The penetrating blackcurrant was so dry a dragon must have sucked all the sugar from it. And the perfume of cedar and Havana cigar tobacco matched the austere bare ripeness of the fruit.

'Girlfriend-wise things went from nowhere to nowhere. But a flame had been lit in my brain of flavours, scents, perfumes. My mind was packed with keenly remembered aromas from my childhood and adolescence: not only of foods and drinks, but the smell of my cricket bat or my wellington boots, the dust in the lanes at high summer, the grass cuttings after spring rain; my mother's Calèche perfume when she was going out; Daddy's study and his workshop – old books, ink, lathes, lubricating oil and wood shavings; Canterbury Cathedral, cold and pallid on a winter morning, the flagstones smelling of a thousand sunless years, or triumphant and exotic as the incense-swathed clerics swept into the vestry after High Mass. Flavour and scent, emotions, people, place: memories and experiences reverberated in my mind and became part of the wines' flavours. A simple flavour of fruit, a scent of barrel-aging wouldn't do. A great bottle of wine wasn't just a taste; its appreciation depended on my ability to glue its flavours on to everything my life had thus far been.

Driven to the spotlights

'But I wasn't there, yet. The OUWC was full of cultured people from wine-drinking backgrounds, who attended "wine colleges" (Pembroke was a "beer college"), and they were used to drinking decent stuff. I wasn't. Every different glass of wine was a new experience that I soaked up like a sponge. And I quickly came to be seen as the wine swot. Not a member of the group, really – wrong college, school, all that – but I was keen.

'Roger Bennett was the leader, a mighty Melton Mowbray of a man: a cartoonist's dream of a gourmand and an epicure. This jovial bunter of booze had become the face of undergraduate drinking, and ITV television saw an opportunity. Get him on to their top current affairs show. Give him a blind tasting. That'll larn him and his Oxford swells. The first time Roger spoke to me was when he banged on my door at Pembroke. My mother had lent me her car, and I'd obviously told one of the wine bunch. "Have you got a car?" he said. Not "Hello, I'm Roger. Can I come in?" "Yes," I said. "Congratulations. You're a member of the Oxford wine-tasting team. Now, drive to the ITV studios in Birmingham. You're doing a blind tasting." Live, in front of millions – tonight! I could be charitable, and say I was chosen because I was best. But no: they'd wanted Roger. He had more sense. And he didn't have a car. "Get that new squit Clarke to do it. We'll all sit back and watch and have a laugh."

'I'd never done a blind wine tasting. But I thought, if I've tasted it before, I'll remember it. Off I drove. I got there early and went into the canteen. What are they likely to choose? What's on the canteen wine list? Muscadet, Niersteiner, Soave, red Bordeaux, Rioja, and, wow – a five-year-old Beaujolais. I wonder what

that's like. Then make-up, five-minute call, check your mic, try to smile – and you're on.

'Four glasses of wine: two white, two red. An audience, cameras, heat, glaring light. First impressions, I told myself; if you've tasted it, you'll remember. The first one: pale, almost devoid of any smell or taste. The canteen list – Muscadet? Yes. The next: sweetish. Floral mixed with vomit. It's got to be that Niersteiner. Yes, yes. Then the first red. Freddie Price of Dolamore had just given us a Rioja tasting. The creaminess, the strawberry softness … Rioja? Yes, yes, yes. First impressions. This one aging, bricky red, quite light: old Burgundy? Five years old, maybe? The canteen list, you idiot: there's no Burgundy on the canteen list! Beaujolais, five years old, on the canteen list.

'You can barge your way into a tight-knit group, but that doesn't mean you really belong. With the shining exception of Mark Savage, the Wine Circle wasn't a particularly welcoming bunch, and they seemed to exist in a tiny cloistered world. No wonder they shied off that TV tasting. I'm not sure anyone had ever done a blind tasting on TV before, but it gave me a glimpse of two things: the competitive possibilities in blind tasting, and the showbiz. I admit, I *did* like the look of the showbiz. I wasn't going to get much of that in the OUWC. Luckily, I met Charles Metcalfe (Christ Church).

How to stage a coup

'I used to strip off at about half-past eight. He'd join me in the showers at about ten to nine. And we'd set to on each other's torsos: me on him – him on me. It must have taken us five, ten minutes most nights, but finally, we'd remove the last gobbets of stage blood from my death scene at the end of Act 1, and his death scene at the beginning of Act 2, of *Agamemnon*. I was the baritone, he the tenor. We did die well. And we talked as we scrubbed. I told him I was fascinated by wine. I'd heard there was a second wine club at Oxford: the Oxford University Wine and

ABOVE Overacting Prince Paranoid in the Balliol panto.

Food Society (OUWFS), but elitist and elective – full of hoorays. No one was going to elect a Pembroke man from the wrong school. As we enjoyed our final scrubdown on the last night after curtain call, Metcalfe said, "By the way, you're now a member of the OUWFS." "How? I don't know any members." "Yes, you do," he said. "I'm the secretary."

'We planned a coup. Oxford wine was male-only. That needed to change, we said, with a glint in our eyes. The Wine Circle was too mired in the past, but the OUWFS, being an elective society, had become a drinking club for a few students from a few smart schools attending a few smart colleges. That needed to change. And, we'd lost to Cambridge far too often in the tasting competition. So Metcalfe quietly installed himself as president and me as secretary. We opened the society up to everyone, told the hoorays they weren't all that welcome any more – and canvassed the women's colleges. Oh, bliss! I can't remember the numbers, but through a rosy mist of fond memories I tell myself the membership was 50 per cent female in no time flat.

'We beat Cambridge – once, then again, and again. Cambridge trained in the time-honoured fashion: lots of nice bottles from the senior combination room cellars consumed over good dinners. Cheap wines didn't come into it, and no one was put on the spot and made to say what they thought. If you drank enough Mouton and Montrachet, you'd get the hang of it. Colleges like Pembroke didn't have any Mouton and Montrachet, so we decided we'd start at the bottom and build our knowledge block by block. Each week we'd meet for a training session, usually round someone's kitchen table. Sometimes everyone brought a bottle (or half-bottle) and sometimes Metcalfe or I would choose the wines. Affordable, served masked in brown paper bags. Everyone had to write down what they thought. First impressions were the most important things of flavours: however outlandish, note them down, because if you detected

them, they were there, and they could become your personal recognition triggers. We all had to decide what we thought the wines were, and say so, in front of each other. We'd discuss the wines, all giving our opinion, then reveal the bottles – with the labels in front of our eyes, so that the tastes and the names clung together in our memories. And we'd taste them, discuss them, and listen to each other all over again. Then we'd go to the pub.

'This doesn't sound such a big deal now, but it was then. It was the beginning of the 1970s. Oxford's cosy certainties had been buffeted by strong radical winds from the 1960s that were still blowing hard as the decade changed. In the grander scheme of things the world of Oxford wine tasting might not seem that important, but it was our world, and changing it did matter to us. Did we make a difference? We beat Cambridge: once, and again, and again. Same training methods: first impressions; be true to yourself; don't try to second-guess the judges; don't choose the obscure possibility when there's a blatant probability staring you in the face.

'You didn't have to be old and hoary and rich to know about wine. The year after our first win against Cambridge I entered the National Wine-tasting Championships. I came second. The director-general of the BBC came third. I tasted against Reginald Maudling, the Home Secretary, in the semi-final – the innocence of it all. Everyone said, "But you can't know about wine: you're too young." And I said, "I've just proved that I'm not." Well, I didn't say that, but I thought it. We'd proved that you don't have to be wealthy and brought up in wine to love it and understand it – the guy who won the championship ran a garage. As I stood there beaming with my trophy, I felt like a true radical. Beloved Oxford, hotbed of vinous radicalism. I've never lost that desire to be radical, to spread the world of wine as wide as I can, by whatever methods I can bring to bear.

'Wine is tasty, wine is fun, wine makes you happy, witty and wise. And wine might even get you a girlfriend.'

VIEUX-CHÂTEAU-CERTAN 1952
'What an emotional moment. This is the last bottle of my first wine-tasting prize: Oxford vs Cambridge. They all said Cambridge would win – but they didn't. *We* did. Winning that Oxford-Cambridge match gave me the confidence to think that perhaps I could do something, be something, in this wine world. The Vieux-Château-Certan was the last wine in the tasting: tremendous weight, lushness almost, for such a dry wine, brilliant. My prize for top score? My choice: a whole case of it.

ABOVE Oz and Rosie Kerslake in Oxford's revue, *Fool's Paradise* at Edinburgh, 1971. Oz always did think acting was the way to a girl's heart.

A contribution by
CHARLES METCALFE

CHRIST CHURCH, OXFORD, m.1968

After Oxford, Charles Metcalfe co-founded the consumer magazine, Wine International, *and the International Wine Challenge, an annual wine competition, now in its 30th year. He is also a wine writer and television presenter.*

'It was an unconventional start to a career in and around wine. My contemporaries went to open days offered by banks and solicitors, some sat exams for the Civil Service; others were discreetly tapped up for MI5 and MI6. I was approached at a Pimm's tasting.

'I wasn't even a member of the Oxford University Wine and Food Society (OUWFS). David Haddon, from the cathedral choir at Christ Church, had kindly invited me as his guest (I confess I did know it was going to be a Pimm's tasting, held every other year in Oxford, and in Cambridge, respectively). Trinity Gardens were at their most sunnily beguiling. In the spirit of adventure, I set about the different Pimm's Slings, and in those blessed days there were six. No. 1 was the familiar gin sling (I had met this before, and had considerable respect for its powers), No. 2 Scotch, No. 3 brandy, No. 4 rum, No. 5 rye whiskey and No. 6 vodka. I tasted them all, then went back to drink the ones I had enjoyed, socialize and drink more. Towards the end of the evening, I was approached by someone I had never met before: a jolly, rotund man on a mission. "Would you like to be secretary of the OUWFS next year?" was his opening gambit (slightly less precisely articulated). I wasn't capable of saying no to anyone, about anything. Roger Bennett had asked every single member the same question, and knowing this was a job that involved writing letters and organizing tastings, they had all said no. Roger was reduced to asking guests, starting with ones he had met before, moving on to the obviously incapable.

'I was hooked and led into a life of wine willingly. The tasks were light: writing to London wine merchants, organizing tastings, and taking them out to dinner at The Elizabeth afterwards (accounting for the "food" bit of the OUWFS).

The rewards were beyond my limited alcoholic dreams. I learned of great classic regions: Bordeaux, the Rhine and the Douro. Burgundy was somewhat more mysterious: it was a darker, heavier wine than Bordeaux – or was it (we are now in a different era of Burgundy)? Sympathetic characters such as Russell Hone and Sebastian Payne of F & E May and Freddie Price of Dolamore came to impart their wisdom and dispense delights. Life would never be cheap again.

'In our day, there wasn't much coaching (that came at a later period, when the honour of the country was at stake) for the annual varsity blind wine-tasting match. We bought our samples, met, played games on each other, and tried to soak up as much as we could from the visiting merchants – in more ways than one. It helped that my contemporary, Oz Clarke, was one of the most naturally gifted wine tasters it has ever been my privilege to know. Oz was a huge asset to the team. Oz and I, with another friend, Chris Reston, started what we thought was a business, selling wine to our friends, even occasionally to colleges (thank you, William Holmes of St John's!). We made no money, but drank for free. All the while our knowledge growing, we came to love the world of wine and the generous, friendly people who inhabited it.

Banking on team spirit

'Eventually, the time came to move on into the wider world (except for Oz, who stayed on at Oxford for at least two more years to pursue his interest in acting). I realized that selling wine to people who

"Alas Monsieur, ever since the Evening Standard victory, the customers have demanded English wine waiters!"

ABOVE The British team won the first of the three Evening Standard–Le Figaro contests, in 1979, and their victory was celebrated by JAK, the Standard's cartoonist.

had no money to pay the bills was not going to make enough money for me to live on, so I followed my father's advice to get a job in the City. Looking after other people's money, however, was not my greatest talent, and I found myself scraping by as a classical singer, tourist guide, cook and security guard (tourism offered the best pay). Still I was exploring wine.

'One day, Oz, who was working at the National Theatre (playing a long-bearded Irish bard), rang in a state of high excitement. "Have you seen the *Evening Standard*?" he spluttered. "They're going to set up a wine-tasting team to compete against a Paris paper called *Le Figaro*. We have to go in for it. We'll get into the team, and go to Paris and have an amazing time." So we both applied for the team. The first round was a doddle. A few simple wine questions, easily answered. Then came the tasting knockout.

'The wine sponsor was Grant's of St James's, and the contest happened in their cellars in Whitcomb Street (today, I believe, under the Sainsbury Wing of the National Gallery). I felt reasonably confident, but didn't sail into the team (Oz did). In fact, I had to take part in a taste-off for the last place. The two of us were given three glasses. Two were of the same wine, one was different. All three smelled and tasted exactly the same. What to do? Have a wild guess, or find another way. I wandered into a part of the cellar where the light was just a little better, and thought I discerned a faint difference in colour in one of the glasses. It was all I had to go on, so I plumped for that. Right! I squeezed into the last place on the team.

'In fact, the contest was really between Grants of St James's and Nicolas (the *Figaro* team sponsors). We were their puppets. Through weekends of coaching from the redoubtable Angela Muir MW (a friend for life), we started to come to terms with the subtleties and differences of French wines (the French team wasn't going to blind taste "foreign" wines, certainly). My real wine education started there. And we did go to Paris, we had a fabulous time and we won! *Le Figaro* had to have a rematch, of course. The next year (easier to get on the team with the first year's coaching behind me), the French team came to London (not nearly as much fun). There were rumours of their members being given the wines that appeared in the actual competition to train with. Anyway, they won. But they were prepared to compete a third time,

and we slaughtered them. That was the end of the *Evening Standard–Le Figaro* matches.

'Meanwhile, our team had been to California to compete in a contest featuring California and French wines, and to the Rhine to blind taste German wines. And, thanks to expert coaching, we won each time. By now, I was a wine addict. I wanted to learn everything, to travel everywhere. My singing profession took me to lots of places, but eventually, the singing had to give way. I wrote a piece about the last of those Paris contests for the only editor I knew – Kathryn McWhirter, editor of *Wine & Spirit International*, a trade magazine. It had taken me all of a morning of in-depth exposure to Beaujolais Nouveau to pluck up my courage. She was (and still is) a superb editor, and managed to make my little piece funny and readable.

A marriage of true minds

'Kathryn introduced me to her Burgundy correspondent, Robert Joseph. I helped him move his furniture back to England, and we became firm friends. We started a new consumer wine magazine, *What Wine?* (eventually to become *Wine International*). And we created the International Wine Challenge, starting with 43 wines to fill a couple of pages. In 2013, the 30th anniversary of the first IWC, around 12,000 wines were entered.

'Along the way, I worked as a TV wine pundit, married Kathryn (my first and permanent editor), and we wrote books about Spain, Portugal, matching wine with food, and about wine in general. I have travelled to the corners of the world of wine, developing a love for these beautiful places, and their heroic wine farmers. And all because I once went to a Pimm's tasting in Trinity Gardens.'

ABOVE Beaujolais Nouveau Day in London, 1983, the year *What Wine?* was founded. Left to right: Oz Clarke, Charles Metcalfe and Andy Henderson.

Rosemary sinks Cambridge

MYSTIQUE of wine-tasting takes a knock from twenty-year-old **ROSEMARY KERSLAKE**, daughter of a Guinness director.

Rosemary, pictured below, was one of three women in the Oxford University team of six which defeated a Cambridge team in a winesmanship contest last week.

She says: "A month ago I barely knew the difference between red and white. I had just three weeks' intensive coaching from my boyfriend, **ROBERT OWEN CLARKE**, who was runner-up in a recent national wine-tasting competition.

"Cambridge men were flabbergasted to lose with three women against them including me — a rank beginner."

The students were tested on ten wines—sniff it, sip it, identify it—and each marked out of 130 points. Forty was considered good. Rosemary scored fifty.

An interview with ROSIE (NÉE KERSLAKE) MACGREGOR

ST ANNE'S COLLEGE, OXFORD, m.1970

After Oxford, Rosie Kerslake (now MacGregor) appeared in many television productions, including Coronation Street, Lovejoy *and* Star Cops. *She gained a degree in criminology at the LSE and is now a mediator.*

'I did two years in a row on the varsity wine-tasting team: 1972 and '73. Vicki Pritchard-Davies (Lady Margaret Hall) and Sarah Stewart-Brown were the two other women on the team in 1972.

'Coach Oz Clarke said, "The match is in three weeks' time, and I can teach you to blind taste in three weeks." I wasn't that interested in wine tasting, but I thought, "What the hell – why not?" And he did! He was incredibly good at helping you identify tastes and smells you could associate with the wine – and often not what you would think of in connection with anything comestible: wet socks, petrol, cigar boxes. In 1973, I entered the Wine Taster of the Year Competition, sponsored by the *Daily Telegraph*. Martin McNeill (Merton) won it, but I won the ladies' prize: a long weekend trip to Paris for two. I took Oz, and we dined at Pruniers. We drank a lot and had a great time.

'I'd met Oz doing the Oxford Revue, which we took to Edinburgh in the summer of 1971. He had already finished his undergraduate degree. His parents had emigrated to Canada, and I think he rather felt the loss of a family. So he stayed on at Oxford, as he had loved it so much he couldn't bear the idea of leaving. We continued going out for about four years. There were interludes, intermissions on both sides. He was not an easy man to go out with. By that stage I was working

at a theatre in York, and he was working at a theatre in Sheffield with Mel Smith, an actor/comedian who did a series called *Not The Nine O'Clock News* that was very successful. Oz and Mel were good friends; we'd all known each other at Oxford, and had toured the States together in *As You Like It*.

'Oz and Charles set up this company called Metcalfe and Clarke, although they called it "Bum, Tit and Flog" – probably a more appropriate name. Charles had left Oxford and was living in South Kensington, and ran the London end of the business, and Oz, in theory, was meant to be flogging wine in Oxford, but he was disorganized and a lousy salesman – very good at selling, but bad at collecting the money. He would go around with several crates of wine in the boot of his car, and when the wine ran out he would say, "That's okay: I've got a couple of cases of whatever," and everybody would say how wonderful. Then he would forget to bill them and get cross when he didn't get paid. So it wasn't a serious moneymaking organization, it has to be said. They kept it going for a bit, but when Oz did the Oxford Revue he decided that acting was rather fun and he loved it, so he became an actor and it wasn't until later that wine tasting became the main focus of his career.

Separation of the sexes

'I read modern languages at St Anne's. I was there with Tina Brown, who started writing at Oxford for *Isis*, one of the Oxford magazines, and had her sights set on a publishing career from a very early age, which I've always found rather impressive. She was a great party-giver, but she focused only on people who she thought were going places. Once she thought you weren't going anywhere she was less interested. [Oz said she had been out with Metcalfe, who one day saw her driving by in a big black Bentley or similar, where he couldn't see the driver. He waved to Tina and she just looked away; she had dumped him for Dudley Moore, too short to be seen in the driver's seat!] She was tutorial partner with writer Sally Emerson, who married Pete Stothard, who was editor of *The Times* until about five years ago. She was somebody who knew everybody.

'There were five women's colleges and none of the men's colleges were co-ed. We had a ball. There were all kinds of restrictions that don't apply now, in that we had a curfew in the college, and you weren't allowed to have men in your room. The college gates closed at 11pm and after that they would only open every hour on the hour through the night. If you just missed the moment it was a real pain. All the colleges had routes in and out which required various degrees of agility: stepping onto dustbins and over walls, which in an inebriated state was a precarious business. And there were "bulldogs" [the university's private police force] patrolling the grounds, so you hoped you wouldn't get caught coming or going, or letting somebody out who shouldn't have been there in the first place. There was a lot of intrigue. They were trying to keep sex out of the college.

'My parents and my sisters had been to Oxford. My eldest sister was at Cambridge, but then came to do a PhD at Oxford, so we were all Dark Blues, basically. It was easier in those days, so I'm told, to get in. We were geared up to working bloody hard, though, through school, and therefore it was no great surprise when you had to work hard when you got to university. Writing two essays a week is not the kind of thing most students do nowadays. I wouldn't have dreamed of using a credit card. My parents paid my battels – your college bills, as they were called – and gave me £20 a month, which didn't seem absurdly frugal. I wasn't going out and buying lots of clothes, but it was fine.

'The Sorbonne restaurant was considered just below The Elizabeth, and both of them were excellent, and out of my league. I would not have been going to places like that unless I was taken. Fortunately, girls at Oxford had a pretty good time. There was no shortage of people prepared to take you out, which was extremely nice. It's the kind of thing I look back on now with embarrassment, but that was the way it was. I would have felt more comfortable if I was paying my own way.

Wine tasting
'At Oxford, I acted and it took up every waking moment, so my wine tasting was secondary to that. I had done quite a bit of tennis at school, but that stopped when I got to Oxford. Men I knew rowed or did a bit of hockey – a lot of men did a fair amount of sport – but I don't think I knew any women that did, which is a pity. I have no recollection of the Oxford University Wine Circle at all; I went along to the Oxford University Wine and Food Society on occasion, simply because that provided one with essential information in terms of learning how to taste.

'Every other week, a wine merchant would come up and give a tasting either on claret or on Mosel wines. They would bring a range of seriously good wines: the sort of thing most of us couldn't afford to buy. You had a phenomenal opportunity to learn, which I don't think

I have ever experienced since in terms of just being able to taste wines in that very informative way. Russell Hone brought German wines, and he and Oz were good friends. Russell used to come to Oxford regularly and stay at Oz's house. He was a lovely man.

Greater world events
'During the time I was at Oxford, I never read a newspaper or watched TV. All I knew was that "It's third week and I'm doing *As You Like It* in fifth week," that was how I operated. I had absolutely no interest in what was happening elsewhere, which I think is shaming. In 1968 there were protests, when the students tore up Paris, hurling cobblestones at the police. There were sit-ins. Kent State was in 1970, and there were Vietnam War protests. When I went to work with J Walter Thompson we headed into the three-day week. There were miners' strikes. We had no power. That was peculiar: no heating and limited electricity – the whole country went on a three-day week over Christmas, at the end of 1973. The power stations would just stop working.

My acting career at Oxford
'I did a lot of semi-professional acting in Oxford. The first year I was at the Edinburgh Festival, and then I did two productions with the Oxford and Cambridge Shakespeare Company. They used professional directors and a cast from both universities. I did *The Importance of Being Earnest* and *As You Like It*, and we toured the States for about six weeks over Christmas in my last year, which probably wasn't a clever move. The tour was arranged for the Midwest. We started in Madison, Wisconsin, and went on to Ames, Iowa, did a lot of odd dates, and wound up in Washington. In December it was −20°C (−4°F). It was absolutely punishing and completely exhausting. The show lasted over three hours plus a reception. I had a huge part, and we were moving on every day or two, and travelling considerable distances. You never got enough sleep and your voice was always tired. I started with tonsillitis when we left and I never got over it all the time we were there.

'When I got back, spring term had already started, and I was hauled up before the dean who was my tutor, a dreadful woman, and she said to me, "Rosemary, I think we need to sort out what you're going to be doing." She had discovered I played Anita in *West Side Story* the previous term, and we weren't supposed to do any acting without permission in those days. I hadn't got permission, and she wasn't pleased that I'd come back from America, had missed the first week of term, and had finals coming up. I had, however, had rather good reviews, which is how she found out about it. So she pointed out that I was headed for a third-class degree. Well, I was so pleased that I was headed for *any* degree at all that, frankly, I was delighted. I did actually do quite a bit of work, and in the end I got a second.

'I had no sooner finished that interview when I got a call from my father. I hadn't seen my parents over the

Dark blues victorious wine-upmanship test

By Philip Howard

In a haze of rare but free alcohol, Oxford University yesterday beat Cambridge in their twenty-fourth wine-tasting match.

The competitors, six on each side, were required to identify by country, region, district, commune and vintage five white and five red wines from the classic wine-producing regions of France and Germany.

They swirled glasses, dipped

The Cambridge captain Robert Fraser, of Trinity said: " Of course it is a hobby, but it is one th

There were three wi in the Oxford team, and Pritchard-Davies of Lad Hall won a magnum o champagne

Miss Sarah Stewart-B of LMH, who won the wine-upmanship prize said: " It was very unfair did not have an Alsace. tell Alsace a mile off. sulphu

My goodness, my taste—

Graduate wins Wine Taster of Year title

Daily Telegraph Reporter

MR MARTIN McNEILL, 22, a graduate trainee with Hill Samuel, the merchant bankers, became Wine Taster of the Year at the 1973 Grand Final held at the Royal Institute of British Architects in Portland Place.

Mr McNeill, who read Greats at Merton College, Oxford, achieved 540 out of 650 possible points. The competition was the fourth run by The Daily Telegraph in association with Grant's of St James's.

Mr McNeill's winnings included a reservation for a car and two passengers on Normandy Ferries from Southampton to Le Havre, 122 bottles of wines, spirits and liqueurs and a Wolseley Six car, which in six minutes allotted he fitted with 38 out of

innes girl
sie shows
winning
y with wine

By Jill King

E KERSLAKE, 22-
old daughter of
ness's managing
tor, was in high
s yesterday . . .
had won the Special
s Prize in a London
competition.
spitting out
e swallowed

asn't time,"

esults were
l to be called
owder room
a weekend
and some

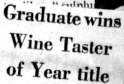

IT'S THAT TASTE OF SUCCESS!

OXFORD University s
ahead to a triple trium
day's 25th annual wine
against a Cambridge tean

They won the contest for the
year (and the 14th time), their c
Northrop of Keble College gaine
prize, and 21-year-old Rosie
Anne's took the women's awar
only woman taking part.

The six-strong teams had to
white and five red French and G
country, region, district, commun
Oxford scored 385 points to Car
They won the whites 211—169,
reds 174—204.

Anthony Northrop, who won a
said: "It wasn't particularly easy
have typical wines like a sauterne
or a beaujolais in the reds."

But Rosie Kerslake, who won a
champagne, considered the con
easier than last year.

Senior judge Mr Harry Yoxall, w
man of the International Wine and
ty, presented the team prize cup to
rop, said the Oxford Captain had sc
equal marks in both sections.

Martin McNeil of Merton, who
standingly well with the whites," was
for the individual prize, while Miss
who is studying French and is the dau
Guinness managing director, was
among the top scorers.

Master of wine Mr Ted Hale — ta
manager for John Harvey and Sons o
who sponsored the contest and supp
wines — suggested that future contests
expanded to involve teams from Oxfo
bridge, and a French university like
bonne.

"heers!" says Rosie Kerslake, who won a magnum of champagne in yesterday's wine tasting contest.

WINE TASTER OF THE YEAR COMPETITION

Telegraph
r of the Year
rbed the tit

ROSIE KERSLAKE, THE ACTRESS WITH EYES LIKE THE
MOON

Christmas holidays because I'd been in America. My
father was a dragon and he said, "Have you decided what
you're going to do next year?" I said, "No." He said,
"Well, you better get on with it. I'm not going to support
you forever." So I thought, "Bloody hell: what do I do?"

'This was January; I popped down to the
appointments board and said, "I need to find a job."
They said, "What do you want to do?" I said, "I don't
know." So they had me fill in this form. It had about 20
boxes, and they said mark a tick – sales, accountancy,
publishing. I had no idea what these things meant –
none of us in those days did work experience, and there
was no careers guidance whatsoever, so I just ticked a
whole load of boxes. I thought the one thing I don't
want to do is act if that's what acting is like, with such a
punishing schedule, thank you very much. And the next
thing I knew I was being interviewed by companies like
Kodak and 3M. I liked the advertising agencies best,
and I was offered a job with J Walter Thompson, in
London on the corner of Berkeley Square.

After Oxford: from shampoo to mediation

'Advertising is what I did, initially. But within a short space
of time I thought, "I really can't spend my life persuading
people to buy one type of shampoo rather than another.
This is completely ridiculous." It wasn't that I didn't enjoy
it; I think it was the first stirring of my social conscience.

I just thought, "You can't be serious to spend your life doing
this." It was then a question of trying to get myself an agent,
to audition, and by that stage Oz was already acting, so I
was going off to see him in shows, and various other friends
from Oxford who had gone into the theatre. I was spending
weekends going to places like Hornchurch and Worthing,
these ghastly repertory theatres that don't exist any longer,
and to see these horrendous productions of Ayckbourn
plays thinking, "If this is professional, I'm sure I could do
this." It took a few months to get going, and then I got
offered a job in Harrogate in Yorkshire and I spent the next
nine months or so working there.

'Beyond 1974, I became a penniless actress and so
wine tasting was not really an option. My so-called
prowess in this field, however, was always bit of a problem
because people were intimidated, and would say, "You
know about wine. Here's the wine list: you choose,"
which is always terrifying if somebody else is paying. I
married an actor, but it didn't last, and shouldn't ever
have happened. But, my husband to whom I have
now been married to for 30 years, was in fact my exact
contemporary at Oxford, at New College. He didn't
do wine tasting, our paths barely crossed, and we never
met all the time we were there. He did see me on stage,
but has little recollection of it. We had about two vague
friends in common; he was much more political than I
was: serious, going to debating societies and the Oxford
Union. I was more a flibbertigibbet social animal.

'I went back to the London School of Economics
when I was 40 and did a degree in criminology and the
contrast with Oxford was extraordinary. I didn't do any
wine tasting or extracurricular activities there, because
by that stage I had two small children. The people who
taught me were not just professors; they were in the field
practising criminal justice: on parole boards, advisers to
the Government, or training judges. I used to do prison
visiting when I was in my twenties and was so appalled
at what I came across. I had always been interested in
sentencing and penology, and it stemmed from that.
I became a mediator: victim–offender mediation and
divorce mediation, several years of that and many grey
hairs later.

'But I had continued acting until my second child was
born. So much of acting involves being away from home.
You've got to be willing to drop everything at a moment's
notice and go – fine when you're single but a nightmare
if you have a young family. I did a year in *Emmerdale*, six
weeks in *Coronation Street*, lots of other telly, and brief
appearances in sitcoms and one or two quite prestigious
BBC films. So I had a reasonably good innings. Of course,
the other problem with women is that once you pass your
mid-30s, you're no longer obviously the mistress, the bit
on the side, the fanciable character, and the parts dry up.
There are more acting parts for women now, as there are
more women in society being police officers, doctors or
whatever, without them having to be designated as "the
woman's role".'

ABOVE Mark Savage MW with daughter Gabriel at her Oxford graduation in 2007.

A contribution by
MARK SAVAGE MW

UNIVERSITY COLLEGE, OXFORD, m.1967

Mark Savage MW is a wine merchant. He owns and runs Savage Selection Ltd, based in the Cotswold town of Northleach.

'I competed in the varsity match in 1970, and in '71 along with Oz Clarke, Charles Metcalfe, Sarah Stewart-Brown, Charles Moore and James Gould – a strong and victorious team, against both Cambridge and Imperial College, London, which I can only attribute to the fact that we trained very hard! And to a congenial *esprit de corps,* with no shortage of mischievous humour, combining the theatrical and operatic talents of Oz and Charles, doses of sanity from Sarah, and an element of transatlantic subversion from Charlie Moore. My study of Tacitus and Thucydides, Aristotle and Plato may have suffered, but I've been rectifying that in recent years – not simply as a cure for insomnia.

'We might not have made it to the Imperial College, London match at all. We piled into Charles' old Saab one dark, winter evening and headed off to Sotheby's in London, when round the Oxford eastern bypass, Charles risked overtaking a large pantechnicon, using an outside lane that was rapidly losing battle against snow and ice. The car, despite (or perhaps because of) its Scandinavian credentials, pirouetted in a perfect 360-degree turn right in front of the juggernaut, but then happily proceeded along the carriageway in the desired direction. How

I wanted to see the expression on the truck driver's face! Without further excitement, we made it to Bond Street, and the team duly retained its unbeaten record.

'The competition today, as with the MW examination, has adapted considerably to changes of emphasis in the marketplace. We were lucky, in an era when the first growths of Bordeaux were not out of reach, and were a regular if not weekly feature of senior common room dining, at any rate in the richer colleges. I only once achieved a perfect score of 15/15, with ticks in all five available boxes: "Burgundy, 1966, Côte de Beaune, Puligny-Montrachet, Les Combettes", and managed a 14/15 with "Bordeaux, 1962, Médoc, St-Julien, Léoville-Barton" (correct answer Léoville-Las Cases). Lest anyone think this boasting, I point out that in the same match I also registered two perfect zeros by mortifyingly mistaking a Mosel with a Rheingau (shock horror!), and an Avelsbacher with an Erbacher. No points at all for Germany. Ten wines; only France and Germany featured. Today's teams may not narrow down to the individual *cru,* but they do agonize over a range of countries.

'The experience at Oxford provided platform and confidence to start backing my own judgement in the selection of young wines with potential. I was also fortunate to become Vintners' Scholar in 1975, giving me the opportunity to travel widely in the vineyards of France, Italy and Germany, and put faces and places to familiar names and labels. Without that experience, I may never have passed the MW exam in 1980, and might well have drifted out of the trade altogether.

'Post-Oxford, with tasting experience under my belt, not to mention a number of useful contacts in the UK wine trade, the temptation to enter the business was strong enough to distract me from doing something more ambitious and important with my life. After a few early experiences with a variety of firms: Moët & Chandon, Harrods, El Vino, O W Loeb and Tanners of Shrewsbury, I was persuaded to launch out on my own. I have remained on that self-imposed treadmill ever since, ploughing my own little furrow both on, and well off, the beaten tracks, pursuing Pinothile passion in such places as Oregon USA. My focus has been on small, idiosyncratic, often rather nonconformist, maverick individualists.

'At Oxford I was president of the Wine Circle, which gave me scope for excellent wine tasting at the expense of generous shippers (the boot is now on the other foot!). A generation further on, my daughter, who had managed, in spite of her father, to get a place to read Greats (*Literae Humaniores*) at his old college, also found herself president of the Wine Circle, but she prudently avoided getting involved in the blind-tasting team, and got a rather better degree as a result.'

An interview with
MICHAEL SHIRES (d.2013)

PEMBROKE COLLEGE, OXFORD, m.1970

Michael Shires looked after hedge-fund and insurance markets for Thomson Reuters.

'I was in the varsity match in 1973. Antony Northrop (Keble) was our captain and president of the Oxford University Wine and Food Society (OUWFS), succeeding James Gould, and I was secretary. Antony and I joined because of our King's School, Canterbury, connections with Oz Clarke. Oz was organizing tastings for the society, and tutoring a smaller group engaged in biweekly blind tastings. He had graduated by then, but was still hanging around Oxford, and at the end of my first year we rented his house out at Boars Hill in order to have a party.

'I was first exposed to wine on holiday in France with my parents. Antony's parents were often abroad and he used to come up and stay with us in Yorkshire. My father helped to nurture his taste, mostly drinking then as opposed to appreciating. I confess my first experience of the OUWFS was a Pimm's tasting at Trinity. Pimm's brought six different cups, and said, "Taste each of them, then stick with the one you like for the rest of the evening," otherwise one would be mixing spirits. It turned into a completely drunken affair, but that party was so hugely successful that everybody decided this was something to take a bit more seriously, and the year after, it became more structured.

'Competition wines were basically French, French and French.'

'Anthony Goldthorp from O W Loeb would come, and Nicholas Clark, before they set up Haynes, Hanson & Clark. John Avery gave tastings. The match itself was at Harveys' cellars in Pall Mall. Competition wines were basically French, French and French: 30 to 40 per cent Bordeaux, 20 per cent Burgundy, a bit of Beaujolais, and some Rhône as far as reds were concerned, and a far higher concentration of German white wine than is typical now. Oz did quite a lot with German wines, the standard Burgundies, some Loire wines, the occasional white Bordeaux and Alsatian whites. Oz also brought in a couple of Australian whites, which confused the hell out of us. In his wine career, he was one of the first people to introduce and talk about New World wines, but they were certainly not in the university match.

'Harveys would come up and do a college tasting, and then one in the evening for the OUWFS. And Ted Hale, the Harveys rep who ran the match, came round for dinner a couple of times. Ted was very independent; he would insist on using a corkscrew, despite the fact that he only had one arm that worked. Cutting French bread was always interesting: he would lean on it with that arm and cut it with the other. We all got on extremely well with him. There was a big generation gap, but I think he enjoyed being around us and the fact that we enjoyed wine, and he enjoyed promoting Harveys.

'During the summer Ted arranged for a few of us to go and see *négociants* and people in France. We started off in Champagne with Laurent-Perrier, were taken out

ABOVE Meister Omers House, King's School, Canterbury, 1966 – a hothouse for future Oxford wine tasters. Michael Shires (back row, 2nd from right), Oz Clarke wearing his hockey colours sweater (2nd row, 4th from the left) and Antony Northrop (front row, far right).

by Ruinart that evening, and spent the next day at Moët & Chandon. We went to Chablis, had a day in the Côte de Nuits and a day in the Côte de Beaune, which was spectacular. We must have tasted 60 wines – going down into tiny cellars through large metal grates – followed by an incredibly long lunch. By the last tasting everyone was exhausted. You really learn about Burgundy when you taste them all side by side.

'We had a day in Beaujolais, a day at Tain-l'Hermitage with Max Chapoutier, and came back through Sancerre. We were supposed to spend a month at Chapoutier, but Antony got ill in Paris and never made it, so instead he worked as a *stagiaire* (trainee) at Moët & Chandon, at Château Saran. In Sancerre, a small grower took us into the caves where they mature the crottins of goat's cheese, and we had lunch. He was clearly not a peasant farmer, but it was not much more than that – *charcuterie* around a long kitchen table with a plastic cloth. Their 11-year old son was listening to the Tour de France on a transistor radio; one of the favourites to win that year was Yves Hézard, who came from the local area.

'Christopher Purvis (Keble) and I visited Loeb in Trier in the Easter vacation of 1973 and stayed with David Rosier, a member of the OUWFS whose father was then second-in-command of NATO forces in western Europe. They had this huge château outside Maastricht. We went

ABOVE The tasting match at Harveys in 1973. Nicholas de Rothschild (Cambridge) (left) sits across the table from Rosie Kerslake (Oxford) and Christie Marrian (Cambridge).

into Germany and had a few days in the Moselle Valley, which was good fun. Christopher worked for Loeb during one of the vacations, and brought Tony Goldthorp up to do a tasting in Yorkshire at our house. My father got a few of his friends around. A lot of German wine was bought, and a load of German wine consumed: at eight per cent ABV you can have more than one bottle. I still drink German whites, and I like some German reds, but I've spent a lot of time since then in Germany. And I had 18 months' living in Vienna, drinking Austrian wine.

'Christopher went to the opera after the match in 1973, and didn't come out to dinner with us, but it was

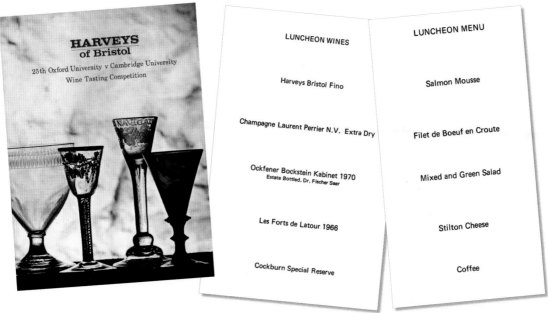

ABOVE Lunch after the 20th (not 25th) match, February 28, 1973.

a memorable lunch. *The Times* sent along Philip Howard, an incredibly intelligent, erudite guy. He started to dominate proceedings by telling people from Harveys that they should open this and that bottle of wine for the lunch. The lunch was spectacular and we drank some very good wine, mostly down to Mr Howard.

'Sarah Stewart-Brown was the first woman on the team, before me, and had gone out with Oz. Everybody used to go out with Oz, but his girlfriend in my time was Rosie Kerslake. Sarah was also family friends with Christopher Purvis. We had a social time. There were quite a few women OUWFS members and guests, as dates. After society events, we'd go out to dinner to The Elizabeth or La Sorbonne with the merchant who was up for that tasting. By the time I'd started my doctorate, Raymond Blanc was working in the kitchen at La Sorbonne. Then he opened a small place in Summertown and later Le Petit Blanc on Walton Street, in Jericho. Alain Desenclos was one of the very good waiters at La Sorbonne, and went with Raymond to Summertown, and to Milton as maître d' at Le Manoir aux Quat' Saisons until he retired recently; the first time I took my wife out we went to La Sorbonne for dinner and he remembered it. And thereafter, every time we turned up for dinner at Le Manoir (not that often), he would give us a bottle of Champagne, which was generous of him.

Oxford in the early 1970s

'I played cricket for the Authentics, and was captain of rugger at Pembroke for two years. I also played hockey and soccer for the college and was a member and on the committee of Vincent's, which was the sports club.

'The early 1970s were grim. Heath was Prime Minister, and in my first term, in December, we had the first power cuts. History prelims were at the end of first term. They still had gas lights on in Merton Street, and the only place you could revise was standing underneath a street lamp to revise Bede and Gibbon and Macaulay. Decimalization came in 1971 and we were coming up to industrial action. It was the time of Nixon and Watergate. But it was a better time than in the late 1970s, with the Winter of Discontent in 1978–79. There were numerous student sit-ins, often about the Vietnam War, but usually over little, odd things: what the bursar was charging you, putting up the price for a pint of Morrells milk from eight to 12 pence, something stupid like that. There was a lot of naive and misdirected left-wing radicalism.

'Sir Hugh Trevor-Roper was still at Oxford as Regius Professor. My first lecture was one of Trevor-Roper's, and he threw out students who were not wearing gowns. The history department was extremely good.

South Africa

'I went to South Africa after I graduated, as an Anglo-American graduate trainee. I was there for two years, when South African wine was at that stage pretty filthy. The decent stuff was hoovered up either by the government, South African Railways or South African Airways. During my first year there, we went down to the Cape, because about four years beforehand they'd replanted the whole of the old Rhodes winery at Boschendal in Franschoek and one of South Africa's oldest wine farms. They'd just opened Boschendal as a restaurant and were in the process of producing the first vintage. That was part of the portfolio of businesses that I was looking after. They also replanted the whole of Rhodes' fruit farm, and were producing a particularly noxious apple drink at the time that became popular. After two years I came back to England and did a doctorate in South African history at Oxford.

'My doctoral thesis was on the development of the Cape Colony from 1854 to 1872, way before Milner, between two different forms of constitutional government. This is the time of the native wars and prior to the discovery of diamonds in 1868. Wine, however, featured in some of the reports I used to read on trade out of South Africa. By that stage, Constantia wine was being exported in considerable volumes. The vines of Constantia were planted in *c*.1680, and the French settlers came into Franschhoek and the Paarl Valley in 1685 and started production. The Brontë books mention the great sweet wines of Constantia in the 1840s and '50s. Constantia wine was already known in the 1700s; it goes back as far as that.

The City and wine

'After my graduate degree, I went into investment management in London. I focused on mining and natural resource stocks, oil and gas stocks, but with no direct involvement with South Africa. We used to do a huge amount of client entertaining, and there was a trip every year to Monaco, to an American technology conference. In the mid-1980s, we would take investment managers to three-star restaurants, and drink as much fine wine as we possibly could on the investment banking account.

'My first City lunch was at The Savoy Hotel. At the age of 28, three months out of university off a postgraduate course, there would be some weeks when I would have two lunches at The Savoy, one dinner at Claridge's and various other meals, taken out by brokers and entertained on expense accounts. This was before the City's relationship with laying down wine as an asset class for investment, which was popular in the mid-1990s, and it became so again fairly recently.

'Oz said that as you get older your palate will change. It seems a lot of younger people, when their palate is developing, prefer Burgundy to Bordeaux, whereas when you get older and your taste buds have developed, it changes. I have a cellar and lay wine down, most of which tends to be claret. I bought mostly the second wines of the well-known growers, before they became ridiculously expensive.'

An interview with
ANTONY NORTHROP

KEBLE COLLEGE, OXFORD, m.1971

Antony Northrop is a senior adviser with
GP Bullhound in London.

'Oz Clarke and I were at school together at The King's School, Canterbury, and when I arrived at Oxford I said I'd like to join the Oxford University Wine and Food Society (OUWFS). He was central at that time in terms of bringing people together, as was Rosie Kerslake, who was also on the team, and his girlfriend. I would go along to tastings with Michael Shires, who lived with me in the same house. Wine merchants were willing to bring decent wines, and we would take them out to dinner afterwards at The Elizabeth.

'Outside of wine, Oz had an acting career. At school he would at times overact, but it was always good fun watching. The last Oxford team captained by Oz was in 1972. Then I was captain, and Christopher Purvis took over from me. Under Oz's stimulus, we would have a blind wine-tasting evening once every two weeks. One person would be responsible for bringing the wine, or everyone would bring a bottle. I read philosophy, politics and economics at Keble, and swam for the university for a year. You only get a Half-Blue for swimming, and we should have got a Half-Blue for wine, so I always pretend that I got a full one.

'Competition wines included Nuits-St-Georges Les St-Georges, Château Rieussec, Meursault Les Perrières and a claret, and the winner got a mixed case of any wines in the competition. Radio 4 interviewed people after

'One of the Chandons was still around then. He used to come to dinner at Saran, and he'd always have ice in his Champagne and use a swizzle stick to take the fizz out.'

the match. I didn't really think about it, until the next morning a friend's mother rang me up and said, "You're on Radio 4! You'd better start listening." Frankly, we all talked absolute rubbish at that stage; we didn't know anything much about wines.

'I'd have dinner with Ted Hale, who was senior buyer at Harveys, with a friend, once a term, down in Bristol where he lived. He was absolutely infuriating because we could not fool him on the wine. He'd say, "I'll cook dinner," but he had a wounded hand, so it was quite difficult for him. Ted would be cooking away in a pompous fashion, and we would bring a few bottles that we had spent hours choosing and serve them blind, but he always got them all right.

Château Saran
'Ted introduced me to Patrick Forbes, who ran Moët & Chandon in the UK, before it was owned by LVMH, and Patrick accepted me to work in Épernay for the summer on a *stagiaire* and *jeune fille* programme, which they had started right after the war. I showed visitors and tourists around the cellars, and we lived in the maison itself, so we were right on top of things. One *stagiaire* and one *jeune fille* were chosen to work at Château Saran, a former hunting lodge up on the hills just outside, where Moët's

ABOVE Antony Northrop (Oxford) tries to concentrate (left) while Rosie Kerslake (Oxford) diverts the opposition, Christie Marrian of Cambridge, in 1973.

DARK BLUES TREBLE
14.3.73 MORNING ADVERTISER

THE 25th Oxford v Cambridge intervarsity annual Wine Tasting Match, sponsored by Harveys of Bristol, was won last week by Oxford for the third year in succession.

The match was held at Harvey's London cellars in Pall Mall. Teams from the wine and food societies of each university had to identify by country, region, district, commune and vintage 5 red and 5 white wines, all selected from Harvey's current list.

Oxford retained the Harry Waugh Cup, named after the former Harvey director who started the competition in 1948.

Oxford captain Anthony Northrop was awarded a case of wine as the most successful individual competitor. Rosie Kerslake, also of Oxford, received the Ladies prize—a magnum of Laurent Perrier Champagne.

In addition, all contestants received a copy of Enjoyment of Wine by Harry Yoxall, chairman of the International Wine and Food Society, and senior competition judge.

big importers and important people are taken for a night and dinner. I gave the tours in English and, depending on language needs, or if they wanted to balance the numbers, they would invite us to dinner. We got fantastic food and Champagne. Once, before lunch, we had an 1895 and a 1911 Champagne. They looked like Sherry, with a slight fizz to them, but faint; you didn't see the bubbles coming out. You met lots of people in the trade as well as side characters. One of the Chandons was still around then. He used to come to dinner at Saran, and he'd always have ice in his Champagne and use a swizzle stick to take the fizz out. The other guests, the importers, would look on with amazement.

'The following year, Ted kindly arranged a tour of French wine regions for us. Michael Shires came, and Tim Charlton (Keble). Through Ted we were invited to lunch at various châteaux, and we went to Château Climens in Barsac. I'd always adored dessert wine, but I'd never been exposed to it in this fashion. They drink it before and throughout the meal, with the fish; it actually goes very well, but it's heavy, so you have to sip rather than drink.

Pimm's and Port to remember

'The culture at Oxford then was coming off the back of a lot of student unrest in 1971. It was more left-wing when we were there, and there was a broader base of people who would be against the OUWFS because they thought it was too exclusive. We invited Pimm's to host the OUWFS summer party in 1973. It was a hot evening – not boiling, but warm – so we decided to hold it in Trinity's gardens. Normally we would get 40 or 50 people, but word spread that it was Pimm's and it invigorated the inert membership. There must have been 100 people. I was worried we wouldn't have enough, but

the guy had brought a case: all flavours, full bottles. It turned into a cocktail party, served with lemonade, and got completely out of control – someone left his signature and threw up all over the guestbook. It went down as one of the better tastings that year.

'At Oxford, I preferred Burgundy to claret, and liked white wines. Now I definitely prefer claret to Burgundy, good Italian reds (which are hard to come by in London) and South African reds. One freshers' ball at Oxford some idiot thought it'd be a good idea to mix industrial alcohol from a chemistry lab with the Port. I was so ill that even today the smell of Port makes me feel sick; I never touch it.

'After university I joined J P Morgan for two years in New York, then came back to the UK. In those days, pre-internet, clients of the bank coming to London didn't know where to go out to eat. A few months after I got back, I found a little book that had 40 restaurants in it published by the bank, but out of date. So I volunteered to update it and rate the venues. The bank paid for the food and wine, and I went to 90 restaurants and distilled them for the book. That was quite a good deal. I did the same thing in South America when I was in Caracas from 1979 to 1982.

'J P Morgan had a spectacular cellar in the Paris office. Whenever you were sent over there, the highlight was a three-hour lunch with fantastic wines. Those wines and those days are gone. And you saw an international cultural gap. I went straight to New York in 1974 on the training programme; there were five of us from overseas, and we wore coloured, pink or blue shirts, and our American contemporaries in New York were in white shirts, had iced tea at lunch, and knew absolutely nothing about wine and had no interest in it. It was probably driven by US drink laws – they aren't allowed to buy or drink alcohol until they're 21 – but even today (my wife is American, so we go there a lot), when I chat to college students it's still beer and spirits.'

ABOVE Château de Saran in the hills outside Épernay.

MICHAEL BROADBENT MW
1911 VINTAGE IN CHAMPAGNE

In his book *Vintage Wine*, Michael Broadbent MW notes that Champagne first appeared in Christie's catalogue in 1768, two years after the start of the auction house, and 'customarily commanded prices twice that of the finest claret'. It was dry and still, with Sillery the most esteemed and expensive label. Broadbent gives the great 1911 vintage five stars, but due to a disastrous harvest the previous year, resulting in one million rather than 30 million bottles produced, *vignerons* were devastated; with serious riots in 1911, 'Champagne was on the verge of civil war'. The oldest vintage and highest-priced Champagne on Harveys of Bristol's retail list in 1929 was 1911, with Krug Private Cuvée costing 290 shillings per dozen: just under £15 in today's currency.

'At the end of my first term, my tutor – an ugly fellow who was teaching me Homer, gravy from his previous ten meals all the way down his tie – spluttered at me: "Purvis, I just want you to know that your family didn't get you in here and, by God, they're not going to keep you here."'

An interview with
CHRISTOPHER PURVIS CBE

KEBLE COLLEGE, OXFORD, m.1970

Christopher Purvis lives in Holland Park, London, where on his shelf David Peppercorn's Bordeaux *sits easily next to an encyclopaedia of opera. Post-Oxford, he joined S G Warburg in the City of London as a banker, and spent much of his career in Japan.*

'We were grotty 20-year olds. People were generous with their time, and it was extraordinary that they thought it worth their while. I have fond memories of Ted Hale of Harveys, who over dinner at The Elizabeth gave us the famous 1945 Latour. It must have cost him a bomb. He thought it was important that we try it once; I've never tasted it again. This led me recently to open a bottle of 1982 Latour and pour it down the throats of my children, now undergraduates at Oxford. Such experiences are important.

'I shared a wonderful flat at 7a Crick Road for two years with Edward Garnier (Jesus), now an MP, in north Oxford, which belonged to the principal of Teddy Hall. We did a lot of match training in this flat. Edward would come along to tastings, but fell ill for the 1974 match, and so Selina Elwell (Lady Margaret Hall) was drafted: "I have a sick team member; what are you doing today? You're tasting wine for Oxford!" It was a certain sense of desperation, and whoever was willing to turn up.

'I read classics at Keble and was in the team in 1973 and captain in '74, when I was also president of the Oxford University Wine and Food Society (OUWFS). We were looked down upon by the Oxford University Wine Circle (OUWC) as being a frivolous cocktail party. There was rivalry between the two. We had an infamous whisky tasting where not one person was left standing at the end of it. We started off with pure grain, just to taste what it was like, and most people were drunk after that, so that was a bad day. It was all rather frivolous. Yet strange, as the university tasters came out of that group, rather than the OUWC. The Wine Circle was a small group, and sat down and went through their wines in a formal way. OUWFS events were held in the Old Taberdars' Room at The Queen's College, and were informal, but the merchants didn't seem to mind because there were lots more people.

'I was brought up in a village called Clifton Hampden, near Oxford, and had been drinking watered-down wine at table since the age of eight. My father was a doctor, and there was nothing silly then about this being bad for children. He always used to serve two wines; everyone was given a bit of both, and then asked which one they would like to drink for the meal. Neither was bad, but one was, say, a Beaujolais, and one a decent claret. Most people chose the Beaujolais. The savvy son quickly realized he should follow whichever one his father was drinking! So there was an element of blind tasting in my life from an early age.

'Oz Clarke, Antony Northrop and Michael Shires had all been to school together at King's, Canterbury. Antony was my contemporary at Quay Hall at Keble, and so several of us from Keble got involved. It was an athletic college, but the idea of me doing any sport is just absurd. I did row for Keble Fifth Eight, which means that you go out on the river once. It was very much a group of friends coming together to taste wine. Oz had stayed on to do a PhD in theology, but he never seemed to do any work, and was always mucking around with us lot as our trainer. Duncan Menzies (Wadham), now a Scottish judge, and Selina, now working for McKinsey, were on the team. Broadbent was the judge; he was frightfully grand and hardly said hello to us!

'The wines were from France, Germany, Italy and, I suppose, Spain – never New World wine, which allowed you to concentrate on distinctions, between, for example, red Burgundy and claret, and get the basics right. It's almost too difficult now. The key thing Oz brought to the party was the ability to use words to describe smells and tastes. He got us thinking: "If it's blackcurrant, it's more likely to be claret; if it's old socks, Côtes du Rhône; if it's raspberries, as opposed to blackcurrant, Burgundy; or if it's apples, Chablis and apricots, southern white Burgundy." Those tips were very helpful.

'A bunch of us competed in the 1973 Grants of St James's Wine Taster of the Year Competition. This was then brought to an end because we wiped the slate with first, second and third. It was a nationwide competition, and these Oxford undergraduates, not Cambridge, were winning it. We didn't talk to the Cambridge lot, and the final was at the Institute of Architects in Portland Place, London. The winner got a Mini Minor stacked up with as many cases of Champagne as he could get inside the car – you won *a car*! There were many rounds up and down the country. I went to the one in London, and on to the final. Martin McNeill won the car. I remember the horror of this group of retired colonels – old middle-class people who drank wine and read the *Daily Telegraph* – who had been beaten by this 22-year old!

'The match had questions about wine, and one of the questions was, "This is the wine of a great producer" – it was a neutral word, it didn't say "château" – "in a very bad year". I got it plum right. It was Château Latour 1963, which we had drunk on one occasion; 1963 was a bum year in Bordeaux, a cold summer with rot in the vineyards, but Latour is a great wine, and '63 Latour was notorious for actually being an interesting wine in a grotty year.

'I was a member of a wonderful old-fashioned all-male dining club at Oxford called The Gridiron or Grid (for short). It was in an attic in Queen Street and like a London gentlemen's club. You paid a subscription, went for lunch and there was a bar, a restaurant and wine. It was snobby – ghastly, actually – and in retrospect awful! There were lots of different dining clubs across the colleges and we had one in Keble; the Bullingdon met once a term and just happened to be the most infamous.

'Keble's background was in the Church of England – the college was actually built by my mother's family. At the end of my first term, my tutor – an ugly fellow who was teaching me Homer, gravy from his previous ten meals all the way down his tie – spluttered at me: "Purvis, I just want you to know that your family didn't get you in here and, by God, they're not going to keep you here." Chunks of Keble were being rebuilt at the time, so many of us, including Antony, had to move out of college after only one year. I didn't have much to do with Keble because I had three years of living out of college. So a different sort of momentum developed in university life that seemed to involve getting up at midday, going down to The Grid for lunch, and then setting off for London for an opera or a jolly and coming back.

'Keble was all-male. The women we tended to know were at Lady Margaret Hall (LMH), as it was closest to Keble. LMH women were brainy, and St Hilda's sporty. Women came to OUWFS events: a much larger proportion than in the university generally. It was an attractive place to come, fun and interesting. Not many took the tasting seriously, though, and went through to the competition. We blew the subscriptions taking visiting wine merchants to The Elizabeth for dinner. This was our reward for all the hard work and wretchedness – shocking!

'When somebody came to your room in college before dinner, the classic thing was to give them a glass of Sherry – an important part of the scene. And the typical thing in the first week of term was to go to pubs. People were drinking beer. Nowadays they go up a week early and have their freshers' fair and get introduced to everything. We didn't do any of that. Mrs Thatcher cut free milk from primary schools in 1973; it was the oil crisis and the tail-end of the Vietnam War. I had friends in the Conservative Association who would go and debate all these serious things, but I didn't; I was too busy listening to music to be marching down the high street.

'I have two children at Oxford now, who are much more serious than we were, putting in hours of study in a way that we didn't. Education at that time taught you about deadlines and bullshitting. The greatest crime was to turn up at a

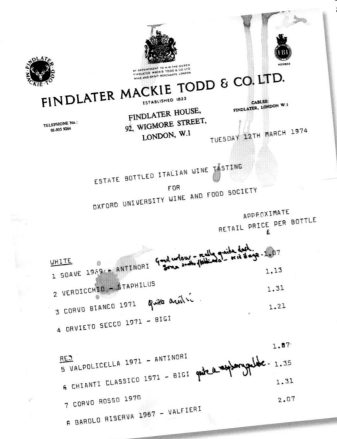

> 'Education at that time taught you about deadlines and bullshitting. The greatest crime was to turn up at a tutorial without anything.'

tutorial without anything. You had to deliver your essay with huge confidence, as though you've been working all week – regardless of the fact that you actually started on the essay only four hours earlier.

'We drank a great deal, but we didn't hit the vodka before going to a party, which my children's generation did. We did drink lots of wine, and because we didn't have much money a lot of it was disgusting. Just sitting down and drinking nice wine doesn't improve your tasting skills. Blind tasting, or tasting wines seriously and taking notes, is the only way. Opening a nice bottle of classed-growth claret at dinner is a lovely experience, but you're not improving your knowledge. My blind-tasting experience at the age of 22 at Oxford influenced my life.

Working in the City and the price of wine

'A bottle of Les Forts de Latour Pauillac then was £4.84, and my starting salary in 1974 at Warburg was £1,750. This was around the time of decimalization. Today an Oxford graduate entering investment banking commands a starting salary of about £40,000. So you need to multiply by about 20+ to see how much a bottle of wine cost. My overdraft when I left Oxford was over £2,000, so relative to today, it was almost £50,000. How did I get an overdraft of £50,000? The answer is simple: wine. When I went to live in Japan and started earning a reasonable amount of money, I bought the 1982s that I've still got. In 1984 I was 33 years old, and was living in Japan earning yen, so it was a different sort of scene. But relative to the price of other things, clarets were still not that expensive compared to what they are now.

'There was a terribly nice man called Raymond Bonham-Carter: Helena's father, but more famous because they're the Asquith family. He was a director of Warburg, and I was in his department when I first arrived in 1974. He had a clot on the brain, couldn't move and so he had to give up work. About 15 years later I found myself going to a cocktail party and there was somebody trying to pull Raymond's wheelchair up the steps. So I jumped in and said, "Hello, Raymond, you don't remember me, but I'm Christopher Purvis." And he said, "Ah yes, Oxford wine-tasting captain, 1974." That's what he remembered about me! Not that I worked for him at Warburg, but the thing that stuck in his head was wine. He thought this was very funny. Sigmund Warburg, who was the founder of the firm and still took an interest when I joined, always considered me slightly bohemian; apparently this comment was written on my file.

'Good wine at lunchtime was an element of City life then. It was a City tradition that you would invite your competitors and clients to lunch to shoot the breeze, and they would arrive at 12.45pm and have Sherry, white wine, red wine and Port, and not be good for much in the afternoon. That was the norm. Warburg was puritanical, German-Jewish; it was almost a dry firm. Warburg was renowned for having two lunches every day: one at 12.30pm and one at 1.30pm so we could see twice as many clients. We shoved them through. They were offered a glass of Sherry or tomato juice before lunch, and a small glass of beer, cider or water at lunchtime – that was considered terribly stingy by the rest of the City. So you had boozy lunches, hardworking lunches, and the third angle was the refined banker in the evening settling in to seriously good wine. Sigmund Warburg himself didn't particularly like drinking, but when he did, he drank serious clarets.

'Then the City wine-story changes. The long, boozy lunch became less and less common. But conversely, young bankers began to make money earlier. I got my first bonus when I was 29. Nowadays, if you don't get a bonus within a year, you've probably been fired! With the money comes wine-drinking. The arrival of the Corney & Barrow wine bar was tied in with younger people who were willing to spend lots of money on bottles of Champagne at six o'clock at night after work. That didn't happen in our day.

'Bankers in the 1970s were expected to be Renaissance men, and we were all men: one minute running investments in Japan; two years later trying to convince Americans to invest outside of the US; two years later writing about tea production in Sri Lanka to help raise funds in the international capital markets. You were thrown in at the deep end and let loose with clients at a very young age.'

ABOVE Christopher Purvis (left) with Cambridge mascot, Paddington Bear, and wine writer Edmund Penning-Rowsell with cigar after the 1973 match.

An interview with
NICHOLAS DE ROTHSCHILD

TRINITY COLLEGE, CAMBRIDGE, m.1970

Nicholas de Rothschild helps to develop Exbury, one of the largest private gardens open to the public in the UK, famous for its rhododendrons and South African nerines.

' I read archeology, anthropology and history of art, and I was in the varsity match in 1973. Certainly Oxford won that year. Christie Marrian (Trinity) was the one who knew everything about wine; he had a fabulous palate and his father, my tutor Dr Denis Marrian, was in charge of the Trinity College cellars. It was Dr Marrian who persuaded me to join the Cambridge University Wine and Food Society (CUWFS). Being a Rothschild, my dad had a fine cellar of Mouton and Château Lafite, but it was very limited in other wines. When they asked me to join the CUWFS, I thought, "Free booze. Sounds good."

Someone once brought along amazing Hungarian Tokaji, which I remember in great detail – delicious. And I bought fantastic wines from a Riesling tasting; I don't drink German wine very often now. Then there was the brandy tasting after

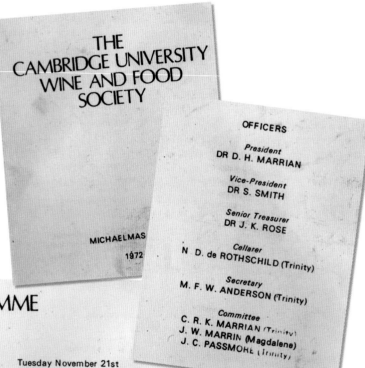

THE CAMBRIDGE UNIVERSITY WINE AND FOOD SOCIETY

MICHAELMAS 1972

OFFICERS

President
DR D. H. MARRIAN

Vice-President
DR S. SMITH

Senior Treasurer
DR J. K. ROSE

Cellarer
N. D. de ROTHSCHILD (Trinity)

Secretary
M. F. W. ANDERSON (Trinity)

Committee
C. R. K. MARRIAN (Trinity)
J. W. MARRIN (Magdalene)
J. C. PASSMORE (Trinity)

PROGRAMME

Wednesday October 18th
Mr Russel Hone of F. E. May and Co. will give a tasting of wines from Hungaria in the O.C.R. Trinity at 6.30 p.m.

Tuesday October 31st
Mr David Gilbertson of Christopher and Co. will give a tasting of red and white Burgundies in Dr Eden's Room, Trinity Hall at 6.30 p.m.

Wednesday November 8th
Mr R. A. M. Goldthorpe of O. W. Loeb and Co. will give a tasting of Rhine wines in Dr Eden's Room, Trinity Hall at 6.30 p.m.

Thursday November 16th
Mr Martin Everett of Mayor, Sworder and Co. will give a tasting of French white wines in the O.C.R. Trinity at 6.30 p.m.

Tuesday November 21st
Mr Victor Hargreaves of J. B. Reynier will give a tasting of wines from the Loire in Dr Eden's Room, Trinity Hall at 6.30 p.m.

Monday November 27th
Mr John Doxat of Buchanan Booth Agencies will give a spirited talk on Drinks and Drinking in Dr Eden's Room, Trinity Hall at 6.30 p.m.

Members are asked to be prompt

Members are respectfully reminded that as a rule no guests are permitted at tastings

ABOVE CUWFS Michaelmas term 1972.

LONDONER'S DIARY

Oxford show better taste than Cambridge

'I got into the tasting competition because they thought they had a ringer in me, but they had a dodo instead.'

OXFORD UNIVERSITY, with a degree of confident superiority, yesterday repeated last year's victory in the annual wine tasting competition against Cambridge, thus putting them two up in the contest which has been sponsored by Harveys of Bristol for the past 24 years.

Deep in Harvey's Pall Mall cellars, they sported three pretty ladies in their team of six and romped home by a large margin against an all-male outfit.

One of their team, Rosemary Kerslake of St Anne's College, whose father is a Guinness director, has only been tasting wine seriously for three weeks, a tribute perhaps to her boyfriend and Oxford coach Oz Clarke, who was last year's dark blue captain and who came second in last year's Wine Taster of the Year competition.

Withdrew

Cambridge were surely without one of their stalwarts, Nicholas de Rothschild, who withdrew from the closely-knit light blue clique at the last minute because of a heavy cold.

Two of the most famous wine properties in the world, Chateaux Lafite and Mouton Rothschild, are owned by his family whose traditional skill and interest in wine would have proved invaluable.

which I drove back to my digs and had a crash, smashed my leg up and ended up in hospital.

'Regarding any knowledge of the vintages, I was good at bullshit – oh, yes! I got into the tasting competition because they thought they had a ringer in me, but they had a dodo instead. The cold noted in the *Evening Standard* in 1972 [see above] could have been an excuse; I don't know. I did it once and thought, "I better not do this again; it will be humiliating next time around."

'The other chap I remember in the wine-tasting team was Robert Fraser (Trinity). He was a big, fat fellow who was very knowledgeable on wines, and organized all the wine for the College May Ball: in 1973, I think. He took all the money to buy the wine, and then disappeared before the end of term with the money. He just vanished and we never knew what happened to him. We got the wine, but it never got paid for and the college did have angry merchants knocking at the door for the funds. Yes, it was a delightful scandal.

'I didn't pay a great deal of attention to life in those days. There was a polarity between the left and right. A march and an ambush took place on Magdalene Bridge; it was entertaining. The little lady who owned the shop at the bottom of Magdalene Bridge was happy to sell eggs and flour to the nice students of Magdalene and Trinity who were going to pelt these "horrible lefties". Some of the students made a cordon across the bridge to bunch the opposition up so that there was a bigger target, and the ones on the roofs of the firehouses doused them – that's one of the memories of the politics of the day! But it was

the era before the trouble started with the petrol crisis and the prices going up. We lived in the golden age, and had a wonderful time. Sex, drugs and rock 'n' roll; it really was great.

'My admissions interview was pretty brief. My father had been there, my grandfather had been there and Dr Marrian thought another Rothschild would be good for the college. We were the last intake where tutors could still pick people they thought would be interesting and amusing, as well as having academic qualifications of a certain standard. We were the cut-off point before they were told to select rigidly on academic qualifications. After that, they could only take A grades and the system became rigid.

'Trinity and the blind wine-tasting team were all-male at that point. There were a number of girls who were of interest to the boys, but generally speaking they tended to be much more serious-minded. There were a few that were really nice; I'm still friends with some of them. I was a member of The University Pitt Club, where gentlemen of a certain breeding would go for their lunches. It was a charming, delightful old club with proper premises and dining room that operated for lunch and dinner, and was run along the lines of a gentlemen's club.

'I became an entrepreneur in Soho. In the early 1970s, a bloke showed me a video machine and I thought, "That's the future: something that can record telly." I went into that business and into the film-processing business. I then started the first digital video-editing company; one of my partners bought me out and I came down to live at the family estate in Hampshire at Exbury, where I've been living happily ever after since 1990. There's a large family wine cellar at Exbury – it floats on the stuff – and at the moment I'm drinking Caro, an Argentinian wine from Catena and Rothschild [Lafite], that is particlarly delicious. Once you become a "country mouse" you like your burrow in the country.'

TECHNICAL FOUL!

Katie Wells was at a technical college of hotel management in Cambridge in the early 1970s. Invited as a guest, she attended a CUWFS event where at the dinner someone stood up and said plainly, 'I abhor the presence of women in this room.' Thankfully, this was followed by a more courteous member's retort, 'I abhor the presence of such bad manners in the room.'

An interview with
ROBERT CLEMENT-JONES

TRINITY COLLEGE, CAMBRIDGE, m.1972

*Robert Clement-Jones has had an international
career in economic and sustainable development.*

'M y parents had a little house in France, and before
I went up to Cambridge I bicycled around the
Dordogne, then via Belgium back to the UK. While
tasting at a winery in Burgundy, wearing ragged shorts
and enjoying myself, a guy asked me if I was *un touriste*
and said, "Would you like to buy a case of wine?" I
wondered how I was going to carry a case of wine on the
back of this bicycle …

'When I went up to Trinity in 1972, I started seeing
mail on my staircase for the secretary of the Cambridge
University Wine and Food Society (CUWFS). I had
done a Cordon Bleu cookery course before Cambridge,
but I didn't know much about wine. I introduced myself

'It was a big win for Cambridge in 1974.
Oxford had won year after year after year.'

LEFT The great Champagne socialist Edmund Penning-
Rowsell (in the foreground, right) wasn't above joining the
post-match lunch in 1973. Duncan Menzies prepares to
drink from the winning Harveys Cup.

to Malcolm Anderson, a third year whose rooms were
just opposite mine, and said, "Are you the secretary of
the CUWFS?" And I joined soon thereafter. Malcolm
was a good friend to all of the society members. He was
on the team in 1973, but was sadly killed in a car crash
at the end of my first year. So I took over for Malcolm.
Once a month I'd buy wine for Footlights. They'd have
a "smoker", where people try out sketches and scenes
and prepare for the pantomime in December, the Revue,
or the Edinburgh Festival at the end of the year. I was in
some of the productions; Griff Rhys Jones went up the
year after me, Clive Anderson was there, and when I was
in *Cinderella* Douglas Adams played the king.

'In my first year in the CUWFS we had eastern
European wines, Yugoslav wines, Hungarian Tokaji
and Bull's Blood. And someone brought a case of Dom
Ruinart: a good excuse to drink. In the 1950s merchants
came primarily to give tastings to dons, but in the '70s our
CUWFS tastings weren't always tacked on to the back of
senior combination room college tastings. The secretary
would write formal letters to merchants, who were
beginning to value the opportunity to develop first-hand
relationships with students, their future clientele.

Training in French vineyards helps Oxford's sensitive palates to victory

By Philip Howard

Oxford beat Cambridge, narrowly
after a recount, in their twenty-
fifth annual wine-tasting contest
over a rough tideway of unlabelled
wines yesterday.

The teams were set to identify
five white and five red wines in
the cellars of Harveys of Bristol in
London. A complicated scale of
points was awarded for distinguishing the country of origin, the
district or region, the commune or
grape variety, and the vintage of
the elusive and exclusive juices.

After hours of earnest sniffing
and swilling, of cleansing the palate
with cheese, Oxford just hiccupped
home.

Their captain, Antony Northrop
of Keble, a college not notable for
its cellar, explained: "The
pleasure of the sport of wine-

tasting is getting the answers right.
We enjoy trying to describe tastes
and smells in words. Some of them
are indescribable. They smell like
old socks, and taste like oatmeal,
which I have never tasted."

He scored the highest individual
marks.

In spite of their characteristic
nonchalance, Oxford had taken the
annual throat race seriously, with
a series of blind, in every connota-
tion of the word, tasting competitions by their wine and food society,
and a tour of the French vineyards
last autumn.

Cambridge included in their team
a Mr Nick de Rothschild, who was
weaned on Château Mouton, and a
mascot of an alcoholic teddy bear
called Paddington. They won the
red wine section of the course, but
not by enough to recover from their

defeat over a testing stretch of
smooth white Bordeaux, burgundy,
Alsace, Loire and hock. Mr Malcolm Anderson, the Cambridge captain, said happily and unoriginally
after the liquid lunch : " Fate cannot harm me, I have dined today."

The guest of honour at the contest was M Jean Perromat, president of the Institut National
d'Appellation et d'Origine, which
makes him a high vinous eminence
of the French wine industry.

He presented a magnum of champagne to the winning and only
female competitor, Miss Rosie
Kerslake of Oxford, and said in
enthusiastic French : " Normally I
never go to these private wine
functions, but I am so impressed
to find English youth sympathetic
to tasting quality French wines that
I intend to start a foundation to
encourage them."

LEFT The 1973
match as reported
in *The Times*.
Malcolm Anderson,
a good friend to
all, spoke fateful
words before he was
killed in a car crash
shortly afterwards.

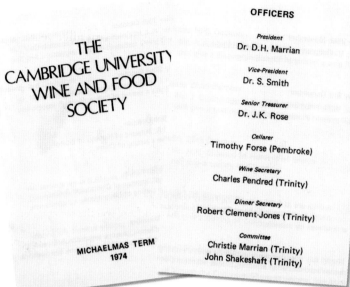

THE CAMBRIDGE UNIVERSITY WINE AND FOOD SOCIETY

OFFICERS

President
Dr. D.H. Marrian

Vice-President
Dr. S. Smith

Senior Treasurer
Dr. J.K. Rose

Cellarer
Timothy Forse (Pembroke)

Wine Secretary
Charles Pendred (Trinity)

Dinner Secretary
Robert Clement-Jones (Trinity)

Committee
Christie Marrian (Trinity)
John Shakeshaft (Trinity)

MICHAELMAS TERM 1974

ABOVE The CUWFS officers 1974–75.

'Leading up to the varsity match we would go to Denis Marrian's rooms once a week on the Great Court at Trinity College. Denis was one of the most beloved dons at Trinity: very popular, a quiet guy and much appreciated by everybody. He would line up wines for us, or call us in last minute: "Come quick! There are 80 wines on display for the college senior common room wine tasting." And we would go. I don't know how we did any work during training. The CUWFS was the only society of its kind then. It was a university society, but our tastings were all at Trinity College.

'Jack Rose was another don who also befriended students. He invited a number of us to dinner and introduced us to wild rice and said, "This is worth more than beef. Whenever you go to the US, make sure you buy this." So the first time I went to the US I bought wild rice – it was unheard of in the UK. Another don, Sydney Smith, had a hell of a cellar and the finest private collection of Chinese porcelain that later went to the Fitzwilliam Museum. He invited the team for a tasting of his wines and that's where I had my first Trockenbeerenauslese. He showed us all of his priceless eighth-century porcelain. There was no burglar alarm on the house.

'There were no women on the Cambridge team and one woman on the Oxford team. Charles Pendred scored 100 per cent. He has the best nose of anybody I've ever come across. It was a big win for Cambridge in 1974. Oxford had won year after year after year. The next year was tragic because we only lost by a few points: confusion on the grape in the Champagne.

'I read archaeology and anthropology, Indian and Chinese. I left Cambridge hoping to get to India to do archaeological research, but couldn't save any money, as it was 1975. So I answered an advertisement to teach English in the Sudan, but a coup broke out just before I went. I did a master's degree at The School for Oriental and African Studies in London, and then I went to Botswana on an Overseas Development Institute fellowship for youngish economists and ministers of finance, and I overlapped for a year with Charles Mercey (Trinity). He went to Swaziland and I went to Papua New Guinea [PNG]. He then came to PNG, and joined Rothschild, which advised the PNG government on gold and copper mines. I worked in the Ministry of Finance as an economist, and met my American wife, Linda, who came on a World Bank mission.

Vranac, the black stallion goes to market

'When we first met, one of Linda's jobs with the World Bank was to go to Montenegro in the 1980s. Montenegro had borrowed money to develop a wine called Vranac, and a huge loan went to the Agrokombinat. They imported equipment from France and brought in the best oenologists. Someone had recognized "incredible" potential in this wine. Vranac, which means "black stallion", is an ancient grape variety indigenous to Montenegro and the Balkans, related to Primitivo and Zinfandel, and produces a unique dry red wine with firm tannins, associated locally with strength, potency and success. The original appraisal team had said, "It's fantastic and compares favourably with Châteauneuf-du-Pape." So they did the economic analysis and thought they could get half the price of a bottle of Châteauneuf-du-Pape. "We'll be selling bottles and it'll help save Montenegro", which was an incredibly poor part of Yugoslavia. But it was a disaster financially; the bottles cost more than they could get on the open market for it. "We can't repay the debt", of course, was heresy as far as the bank was concerned. And they'd also borrowed $20 million from Moët Hennessy or similar, from a manufacturers' trust, another bank that was then merged or went under. They then said, "But we've got a great rehabilitation plan to get us back on track: no one can drink Slivovitz before 11 o'clock in the morning!"

'We put on a blind tasting in Washington DC for Charles Pendred, Charles Mercey and Christie and Nicki Marrian of Vranac and Châteauneuf-du-Pape, and another bottle or two; I said that one of them was a Third World wine. None of them got it because it was such good quality. They've branded Vranac better now and make a bit more money on it, but when Linda was there it was a very dark, dim era in former Yugoslavia.'

Wine-tasters vanquish Oxford

ABOVE After four consecutive losses, a very happy winning Cambridge team in 1974. From left to right: Timothy Forse (Pembroke) with mascot Paddington Bear, and from Trinity College: Christie Marrian (captain), Jeremy Passmore, Robert Clement-Jones, Charles Pendred (top taster with 100 per cent score) and Charles Mercey.

An interview with CHARLES MERCEY

TRINITY COLLEGE, CAMBRIDGE, m.1972

Charles Mercey is managing director for N M Rothschild & Sons in London.

'I've said anecdotally to people in the mining business that I take the view that the price of iron ore and copper will fall when the price of Château Lafite starts going down.'

'I became a member of the Cambridge University Wine and Food Society (CUWFS) in my first year. People with whom I'd been at school at Oundle were members. The food was adjunct to the wine, and boiled down to a dinner held in King's College, because King's had the best chef, reputedly, at that time. King's was also particularly left-wing, so you didn't advertise that you were going there for a CUWFS dinner. We were all English public-school boys, and it was an all-male team. Trinity was an all-male college. There were only two women in the society, as I recall.

Celebrated cellars

'In the prelude to the tasting matches, we underwent arduous training, and had access to very good private cellars owned by fellows. Denis Marrian, who was Prince Charles' tutor at Trinity, had a particularly good selection of Loire wines, and his son, Christian Marrian, was in the tasting team. Sydney Smith, a fellow at St Catharine's,

would let us wander around his fantastic cellar, built up over 50 years, and take bottles. He said, "The trouble is I don't know anything about these New World wines. If you'll replace each bottle you take with a New World wine, then I'll be very happy." We got fantastic wines dating back to the 1940s in return for giving him a few bottles of Australian and US wines. Sydney had a policy that before they left college, his students had to have drunk a first-growth claret and a Trockenbeerenauslese Mosel.

'The run of those two cellars was a remarkable treat. Sydney's tastings were wonderful, but questionable value in terms of training, because if you had a Domaine de la Romanée-Conti Burgundy from, say, 25 years before, you knew you weren't going to get anything like that in the competition, and would probably never drink another one in the rest of your life! As he got older, he became diabetic, and said, "This means I can only drink two glasses of wine a day, but I am sure they have to be the finest."

'Harveys and O W Loeb would come once a year. Harry Waugh gave tastings on Sherry and claret. Tastings were regional, 90 per cent France and Germany. Within France, when it got to the match, Rhône and Alsace were a bit *outré*, and thrown only in for variety and confusion. Harveys played a trick one year and put in a still Champagne. Everyone thought it was unfair to have a Chardonnay that didn't come from Burgundy. The fact that they felt the only other place to take a Chardonnay from was Champagne gives some idea of the extent to which they were not prepared to look beyond Europe.

'There was not a great deal of meritocracy with the team selection. I probably got on to the team because I'm French and that was viewed as being a sufficiently high qualification. My father is French and he used to insist that I had wine. I knew a bit, though not a great deal, but I could bluff. One or two people were clearly very good: Charles Pendred and Denis' son, Christie Marrian. Charles' sister, Claudia (Wadham), played for Oxford about two years later, and was also good. She later worked with me at Rothschild.

'The match was held in Harveys' London cellars. It was done light-heartedly, but we did try to win. Spittoons were not used a great deal. They served Latour at lunch. Then the Cambridge team would repair to Christie's younger brother's flat in Islington, owned by Antony Gormley, the famous sculptor. At the time, we had no idea he was a sculptor, but there were lots of his pictures up on the wall – now worth rather a lot of money, and certainly not to have been entrusted to Antony Marrian during his student days!

'There were two good restaurants in Cambridge then. The Blue Boar Hotel, immediately opposite Trinity, was old-fashioned, traditional British hotel food, and did a nice jugged hare. And there was an Italian restaurant in the marketplace, but that was it. It's amazing the extent to which the town has changed over the last 30 years. It was still in a post-war existence at that point.

'I worked in the City after university, and overseas in the sorts of places where you don't come across terribly good wines most of the time. I then joined Rothschild in London in 1985. I've always bought wine, in quantities I'm sure my doctor doesn't approve of. And I'm now responsible for buying wine for Rothschild to serve at functions. I've been fortunate working at Rothschild because I get to drink some rather nice Lafite. Claudia Pendred used to do a lot of the buying for Rothschild of the non-Rothschild wine and she chose very well. We've got lots of clarets, the 2000s and 2005s, but we've decided to cut back on the amount of non-Rothschild wine because when people have lunch here, they want to have Rothschild wines. We now focus on buying Duhart-Milon, L'Évangile, Carruades or Lafite itself, plus Rothschild's Chilean and the Argentine wines. We obviously have to go elsewhere for whites and to get some variety on the reds for Rhônes and Burgundies, and a few other New World wines.

'The difficulty – or nice problem – we have is the fact that the price of Lafite is at such extraordinary heights that it's difficult, particularly in these austere times, to justify serving it at meals. Should we really be putting out wine at £500 a bottle? And you have to be careful when you serve it. Some clients will take it rather badly that you are spending this much money on what they might view as a frippery.

'Most of the work I do here is natural resources, and mining companies have benefited, probably even more than Château Lafite, from the growth in China. I've said anecdotally to people in the mining business, that I take the view that the price of iron ore and copper will fall when the price of Château Lafite starts going down.

A matter of philosophy

'I went to Trinity because I wanted to do philosophy. Bertrand Russell and Wittgenstein were at Trinity. My supervisor was a fellow called Casimir Lewy, a Polish Jewish émigré, a logician who'd come over to the UK in the 1930s. He studied under Russell and Wittgenstein, who had been at Cambridge in the pre- and immediate post-war years – tremendous. G E Moore was also at Trinity. Keynes was at King's. Ward was at Trinity Hall. So there was a huge collection of very good and well-known philosophers, particularly logicians. Lewy knew them, and had lots of anecdotes. He was a fairly eccentric fellow with a thick Polish accent, which he never lost, and a brilliant lecturer. He left Cambridge at one stage for a lectureship in what was then the new University of Liverpool, and he said to Russell, "Russell, I'm sorry but I'm leaving, and as well as leaving to go to Liverpool, I'm getting married." Russell had just divorced his sixth wife, and he looked up and said, "Well, Lewy, there's nothing else to do in Liverpool."'

A conversation with
CHRISTIE MARRIAN

TRINITY COLLEGE, CAMBRIDGE, m.1970

TIM FORSE

PEMBROKE COLLEGE, CAMBRIDGE, m.1972

'I'm responsible for admitting the first female member and I had to take her to dinner with one of the persons who was not in favour of that.'
Tim Forse

Dr Christie Marrian is a retired electrical engineer who worked with the US Navy, IBM and a memory chip start-up; Dr Tim Forse is founder and chief executive of The Property Database. Since Cambridge, they still meet regularly with tasting team mates to share friendship and wine.

ABOVE Christie Marrian with the Harveys Cup in 1976.

Tim: 'Wine wasn't broadly accessible. My family had a bottle of wine occasionally. But my godfather gave me wine for my christening, and when I became 16 I was faced with this joy of having bottles in the cellar, and I started educating my family in the reverse. We're a farming family and beer and gin was the normal thing in England between the 1950s and 1970s.

'The Cambridge University Wine and Food Society (CUWFS) was a privileged place when Christie and I were there. It was attended mainly by better-off people in the university who had been brought up drinking very fine wine. We were at the transition. It was clear that to grow and thrive the society had to include members who were going to enjoy fine wine for the rest of their lives, and not, in the nicest possible way, be a cocktail party for the upper orders, which had no particular future by about 1975. Anthony Goldthorp of Loeb's said, "Tim, we really like doing this," referring to coming to Cambridge and providing fine wine tastings, "but it's rather disappointing that nobody's gone into the trade in recent years." I think the wine trade also changed dramatically then, significantly.

'It was popular. The question was keeping numbers down, and the size of the society and who we admitted were determined by the committee. I'm responsible for admitting the first female member (Penelope Johnson), and I had to take her to dinner with one of the persons who was not in favour of that. He was utterly persuaded and that was that. These were challenging times. It was all quite sensitive. I think we rode roughshod over quite a few things. Attendance was determined by the size of the Old Combination Room at Trinity. Michael Broadbent from Christie's – then a very spry man in his forties – would insist upon white tablecloths. There were proper standards to be maintained: no duffel coats. We could not have been conscious how generous they were. It was a happy time.'

Christie: 'In the 1970s, CUWFS was the only serious society dedicated to wine and food, and it was responsible for running the blind-tasting team. There weren't that many women around; it was difficult to find one who was prepared to put up with us. Cambridge was only ten per cent female and Trinity was 100 per cent male. There was an incentive for us to have a woman on the team. Wine merchants were doing it to get people to come and work for them, but also in hopes that these people would go out into the City and send large orders to them in the future.

'It was fairly ambitious in retrospect. I was in the society from the word go because my dad was a fellow at Trinity, and president of the CUWFS. We would have a tasting and then take the merchant to dinner. We arranged it so that you could go into formal hall at Trinity after tastings, or we rotated around the colleges, depending on where we'd get the best deal; we got on well with the catering manager at King's. There was at least one formal dinner a term.

'The first match I took part in was 1972. We got absolutely slaughtered. It was all very embarrassing. In 1971 and '72 there was more of this cocktail-party atmosphere about the whole thing; it was ad hoc and chaotic. John Rose, Sydney Smith and my father responded to our requests to help out and organized tastings for us. And as the match got closer, my father would have weekly tastings in his rooms at lunchtime. They were all responding to what they perceived as an interest from the student body, rather than saying "Look, I'm responsible for the society and the team, so we've got to start training." I was a member of the team from 1972 to 1976 and cellarer, captain, dinner secretary. It changed. My father had been doing it for several years before I matriculated, and continued after I went off to Cern in Switzerland in 1977.'

Tim: 'Christie's dad got us up to scratch. The merchants would send samples, and we had to learn about Harveys' list. We had these wonderful evenings when the team would sit down and taste from Sydney Smith's private cellar: "You need to learn about these things." He was a teacher. He would give you a glass and literally tutor you through the wine. Sydney's passion was German wine. He was a great friend of most of the German wine traders, and had the finest, proper German wines.

'The merchants were a distinguished bunch and it was a great big family, really. John Doxat came and gave us a spirited talk on gin. My, oh my, it was a spirited talk on gin! And Jack Fines-Allin, of Simon the Cellarer, on Madeira. David Dugdale, who owned Loeb, was a member of The Saintsbury Club, and Merlin Holland, Oscar Wilde's grandson, now a Saintsbury member, used to share a house with my brother in Cambridge at the same time. Nicholas de Rothschild is our contemporary. Hugh Johnson was and is first class.'

Christie: 'The match was in the cellars of Harveys at Pall Mall. The individual winner was allowed to select a dozen bottles from what was tasted. So of course you chose the dozen of the most expensive claret.'

Tim: 'Harry Waugh dined with the team. Harveys had a bit of an interest in Latour. Every year when we had a competition the national press would cover it. It was quite hard work in the sense that I was learning, and I don't have natural talent. Charles Pendred has a natural talent for it. Christie has a reasonably good talent for it. So you discover among yourselves who actually can and can't. Palate memory is a gift.'

Christie: 'Every time merchants would come we would corner them and say, "Can you help us out with our blind wine-tasting match training programme?" M G L Brendan from Peter Dominic invited us round to his house, near Ashwell & Morden railway station, and put on a blind tasting for us, on a Sunday. Sunday morning is *not* the best day or time for a student. I was captain of the team and somebody had dropped out at the last minute. I thought, "Oh God, this guy has so generously organized this, taken up our request, and for lunch afterwards. I can't show up with half a team." So I coerced my girlfriend, who is now my wife, to come along and I said, "It'll be simple. There'll be four reds, four whites. Just go for the red first. One will really stink – that's probably Beaujolais. One will kind of taste unpleasant, that's probably a claret." We went through this. We get there. There are 13 dry white wines. You're trying to go through them and spot some characteristic. Anyway, she just kept looking at me. It was tough. He said,

ABOVE Tim Forse and Christie Marrian (left and second left) and the 1976 Cambridge winning team celebrate victory with their mascot Paddington Bear.
RIGHT In the 1970s the Cambridge team had a Paddington Bear mascot complete with *tastevin*, seen here at table and admiring his portrait.

"Well, I wanted to make it interesting for you." Nicki did as badly as the rest of us did.

'Paddington Bear was our mascot, dressed up properly, with a *tastevin* around his neck. We had a proper painting of him done. In 1975, when the Cambridge team lost it was attributed to our mascot, who was described as a bucolic, somewhat down-in-the-mouth bear called Paddington. We thought it was a little unfair, and so he wrote a letter to *The Times* in response, saying that he could take it or leave it alone. It's by no means an addiction. He felt the rest of the team had an off day.

'I think Harveys was getting a little pissed off in the 1970s because the Cambridge team just sort of showed up, did incredibly badly, then disappeared and obviously didn't take it all seriously. It was certainly more competitive from '73 onwards. Six reds, six whites, all off the Harveys list, predominantly Old World. I don't recall a single New World wine. After Charles Pendred got 100 per cent, they changed the format and asked you questions. For example, there was one wine with something wrong with it, and the question was, "Which of these wines is faulty and what is the problem?" There was definitely a watershed in '72: a turnover of the personnel. The society became more focused on wine.

Tim: 'The society was declared full and we had a waiting list until the next year to get in.'

Christie: 'Wine was a curiosity. It was pricey and there was a lot of ghastly stuff around. I've been in the States for 30 years now. I come back to the UK and it's extraordinary – even if you spend only £2 on a bottle of wine, at least you can be fairly sure it's represented by the label. If the label says this is grotty cheap wine from Bulgaria, that's what it is. Back then it was hit-and-miss. You could be disappointed after paying a fair amount of money on a bottle of wine, when I don't think that's normally the case these days. Now, it tends to be you don't like what's in it, rather than it's an inferior product.

'In the early to mid-1970s, there was a wine slump. A huge amount of stuff was auctioned off. We bought magnums for about £3. There was inflation; interest rates had gone up and a lot of wine merchants were in trouble. They brought people in to look at the books who said, "Well, you've got all this stock. If you had that in cash, it would be earning ten per cent interest. You need to liquidate." There were extraordinary auctions at Christie's and Sotheby's. It rapidly went round the CUWFS that this was an interesting thing to do. Six people, sitting in this room, and five lots of two dozen came up. We took it in turns to buy one. Then we went to the next auction. It was kind of crazy.'

Tim: 'Buying at auction was much cheaper than buying wine at an off-licence. I've still got an old catalogue from Christie's. And food is the staple stuff of life. Pembroke had good food. One year, we had a house and would cook dinner for the merchants. Michael Broadbent came to our house with a friend of Julian Jeffs. I was learning to cook, and was careful to match the very fine wines with what we were learning to cook. Through the fellows, the college cellars were generous. If you had a good relationship, you'd be in with a chance. 1959 was the greatest year, so in the early 1970s we would go and find 1959 wines, put them with dinner, sit down, eat and drink. Wine is an integral part of showing hospitality.'

ABOVE The post-lunch debris at Canterbury Street, the home of Dr Tim Forse, by now a doyen of the CUWFS in the late 1970s.

THE LIGHTER SIDE OF DR DENIS H MARRIAN, CVO (1915–2008)

by CHRISTIE MARRIAN

Denis Marrian was senior fellow in organic chemistry and chairman of the Wine Committee at Trinity College, Cambridge; he was senior member and president of the Cambridge University Wine and Food Society and indefatigable coach of the varsity blind wine-tasting team in the 1960s and '70s.

'My father was born in Yorkshire but grew up in Scotland, near Glasgow. Of his early schooldays, he said: "Primary schooling in Coatbridge in the 1920s was Dickensian. There would always be a few who came to school in bare feet – not, as happened here in the 1960s, to make some sort of point (I never did fathom what) but because they didn't have any boots. History lessons seemed to focus on a series of heroic Scottish military disasters inflicted by the English, and since I was English it was always my fault. Toward the end of my time there, twin friends were given a chemistry set – I found them distilling water from a retort heated by a little spirit lamp. I was hooked."

'After taking a degree at Manchester, Denis was part of the team of organic chemists (christened 'The Toddlers') that moved to Cambridge with Alex (later Nobel Prize recipient, and Lord) Todd. He completed his PhD and worked in research at Addenbrooke's Hospital, where he met and married Biddy ('Bid') Kingsley-Pillars, a paediatrician. Together they went to the Sloan-Kettering Institute in New York, where Denis worked in the biochemistry department and Bid was attached to the children's leukemia group. "Bid, being a very sociable character, started an acquaintanceship on board the *Île de France* (one travelled by ship in those days) with a family who adopted us on the spot, so that we spent nearly every weekend at their home in New Jersey – with a 30-foot ocean-going yacht moored outside the window. This gave us a taste for sailing which culminated years later in our

ABOVE The Marrians' catamaran, *Cat O'Lafite.*

buying a catamaran, which we moored at Brightlingsea, cruising the East Coast and the nearby continent. By then deeply interested in both felines and wine, we unhesitatingly christened her *Cat O' Lafite.*

"On our return from another year in the States in 1956–57, in Boston (at MIT), now with the family of two potential cricketers (sons Christie and Antony), I began to be invited to play some light-hearted golf on Sunday mornings with Alex Todd, F G Mann and Jackie Roughton. This carried on the tradition started in the early part of the 20th century and described by F G Mann in *Lord Rutherford on the Golf Course* (1976). I mentioned to F G, then directing studies in chemistry at Trinity, that I would like to do supervisions. The following year, F G, being close to retirement, suggested me to the committee, with the result that in 1959 I was offered, as the phrase had it, a lectureship in chemistry 'with the promise of a fellowship'."

'It is worth noting that the golfers developed a particular handicapping system known as "sniffing and snorting", involving a bottle of whisky. A good shot earned a snort, while a poor play got only a sniff; the game was truly self-levelling. As my father was not keen on whisky, he worked his way through his own bottle of wine instead (he admitted to me later that his game would usually improve for at least the first half of the bottle). I recommended he take a Mosel [with a lower abv] next time, which apparently had the desired effect!

'On the sporting side, his talents and interests were broad, ranging across cricket, tennis, bowls, sailing, skiing and bridge; he was president of the University Golf Club, a member of the Real Tennis Club committee, and fixtures secretary for University Rugby.

'As a fellow, my father soon began to establish his sphere of influence on wine and food within Trinity. "At my first traditional cold buffet over the 12 days of Christmas, I was taken aback to notice that although there was a splendid sirloin of beef and a leg of ham, the slices, thoughtfully prepared for us, were not from the same joints. In reply to my comment in the suggestions book, the steward asked why I thought that the slices had come from different joints. I replied that whereas the ham was conventionally leg-shaped, the slices were rectangular and had obviously come from a tin! But my favourite remark was by Michael Vyvyan who wrote, 'There's been altogether too much broken glass in the food lately.' He made his point by attaching the offending piece of glass to the book.

"Just before Christmas each year, fellows would receive a charming letter from the senior bursar telling us that the college estates had some surplus logs and these could be delivered to our rooms or homes. I mention this because it impinged on a Wine Committee innovation, which was to draw lots for bin-ends at the lodge party just before Christmas. This became quite an institution, but was in danger of coming to an end because, as I worriedly mentioned to the senior bursar, we had run out of bin ends. 'Don't worry about that,' was the reply. 'I don't have any logs, either. I just go out and buy them!'"

'In due course my father became senior tutor. There were difficult times, even in Cambridge, as student unrest became a part of everyday life, and Antony Gormley once turned up for a tutorial barefoot. Fortunately, Trinity had had the foresight to have elected Rab Butler as master; his diplomatic skills helped to avoid some of the worst disruption. Along with the tutorship came his most illustrious pupil: "And then, of course, was the unexpected experience of being tutor to Prince Charles. After the announcement was made, I was tied to the telephone all evening as one newspaper after another rang to find out who I was and so on. And I will not forget the day I was asked to go to meet his equerry at the palace. Presenting myself at the Privy Purse Gate and wondering what would happen next, I found myself in a semi-basement room where David Checketts was busy making coffee using Nescafé, powdered milk and saccharine tablets. Informality could scarcely go further, and this

seemed to set the scene for the whole of Prince Charles' time as an undergraduate."

'During their first tutorial, Denis was worried that people might stare in at the window and offered to close the curtains. "Don't worry," responded the prince. "They'll just think you have a huge television." Later, Prince Charles came across my father as he staggered, laden with bottles, from his wine cellar in Trinity. "Ah, so that's where the senior tutor lives," was the prince's observation. I don't know much about Prince Charles' interest in wine, except that on one occasion my father invited him to a tasting organized by Anthony Goldthorp of O W Loeb, where he introduced the prince to Carl von Schubert and the wines of Maximin Grunhaus from the Ruwer.

"Shortly before the installation of the Prince of Wales at Caernarvon I was rung up by an apologetic voice from the BBC who asked me to come to Broadcasting House to record an appreciation of Prince Charles in case he was blown up during the ceremony. So I detoured from the Lord's Test Match and gave an off-the-cuff 'obituary' lasting some 20 minutes. For this I was paid 15 guineas – and when I described the incident to Prince Charles, he fell about, acting out what he imagined to have been my suitably tearful expression."

'By this time, I was beginning to share one of my father's greatest passions: wine. Consequently, there were various holiday detours to visit the noble souls who had devoted their livelihoods to viticulture and winemaking. A sort of substitute grace before a family meal was having me identify (or more often mis-identify) a wine before the meal could start. This introduction to blind tasting taught me much about wine, but also a sense of one's own limitations and not being too afraid of making (in hindsight) obvious mistakes in public.

LEFT Dr Denis Marrian with his pupil and Trinity undergraduate HRH Prince Charles, 1969.

Big enough for two

'I came up to Cambridge in 1970 to read engineering, without much hesitation in deciding on Trinity in spite of my father's obvious presence. Trinity was large and certainly big enough for the both of us. As our subjects were different, our paths did not overlap much, with one exception – and on this, my father was quite firm: "You should really join the Cambridge University Wine and Food Society." I duly did and come spring term 1972, was co-opted onto the blind-tasting team for the annual match with Oxford. We did not do well. As my father was the president of the CUWFS at the time and also looking after the blind-tasting team, I think he was somewhat embarrassed. And for the next year, he instigated a rigorous training schedule with numerous lunchtime tastings in his rooms. What's more, we acquired a mascot, a very fine Paddington Bear presented by my brother for my 21st birthday.

'Denis co-opted other senior members of the university to help: Sydney Smith and Donald Kellaway (both St Catharine's), and Franklin Rose (Emmanuel), and twisted the arms of the various merchants who visited him in his capacity as secretary (later chairman) of the Trinity Wine Committee; samples were procured and special blind tastings arranged. Unfortunately, we still lost the varsity match in 1973, but at least it was close, and Harveys, the sponsor in those days, was rather happier that both sides were taking the event seriously.

'After retirement, my father served as praelector for Trinity College for many years, and continued on the college Wine Committee for 33 years.

'Finally, in my father's words from his 80th birthday celebration in Trinity:

"Master, at lunch the other day I overheard a conversation involving the secretary of the Memorials Committee which, I gathered, is taking a draconian view of future brasses in the Antechapel. It seems that unless we are Nobel Laureates, or Fields Medalists, or have started the Science Park we can forget about being brassed. We ordinary chaps will no longer have our modest achievements or major eccentricities recorded. Well, I suppose that's right. We'll soon run out of wall space, even with the above restrictions. But if we are not to be brassed in the antechapel, Master, might I suggest that we be pewtered and left to weather into indecipherability on the walls of Nevile's Court?

"There, in Latin, future generations might read:

Denysius Marrianum. He drank his way through 132 meetings of the college Wine Committee. His liver withstood countless commercial wine tastings, some of them quite unspeakable, undertaken stoically in the interest of the college. He caused cheese to be served with dessert in the Combination Room and asked council to instigate spouses' nights on the first Saturday of every month.'

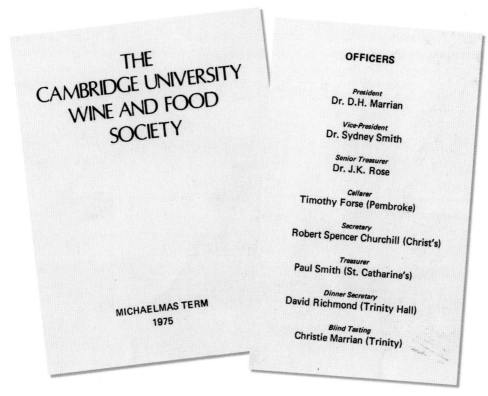

THE
CAMBRIDGE UNIVERSITY
WINE AND FOOD
SOCIETY

MICHAELMAS TERM
1975

OFFICERS

President
Dr. D.H. Marrian

Vice-President
Dr. Sydney Smith

Senior Treasurer
Dr. J.K. Rose

Cellarer
Timothy Forse (Pembroke)

Secretary
Robert Spencer Churchill (Christ's)

Treasurer
Paul Smith (St. Catharine's)

Dinner Secretary
David Richmond (Trinity Hall)

Blind Tasting
Christie Marrian (Trinity)

ABOVE Marrian father and son were both active in the CUWFS.

ABOVE Jonathan Marks of the Oxford Union debating team, shown here in a Sydney setting, considers his major achievement so far is a Blue in wine tasting.

'Oxford politics was unbelievably dirty.'

An interview with JONATHAN MARKS QC

UNIVERSITY COLLEGE, OXFORD, m.1971

Jonathan Marks, Baron Marks of Henley-on-Thames, QC, is a British barrister and Liberal Democrat life peer in the House of Lords.

'New World wines were a revelation. I went to Australia in 1974 and '75 to debate for the Oxford Union, and that was the first time that I'd seriously tasted Australian wine. It was two of us; Simon Walker, now director general of the Institute of Directors, and I were then invited back for the Christchurch and Auckland, New Zealand, festivals with a third person, Simon Carr, now *The Independent*'s political columnist. I hadn't done all the standing for elections, because Oxford politics was unbelievably dirty, and I didn't much like it. But I went in for this; they were show debates, and the Oxford Union, the Foreign Office and the English-Speaking Union chose the team for the tour. Everybody else competing was a former union president, so it caused quite a lot of ruffled feathers at the time.

'For my 21st birthday, my parents bought me a case of Quinta do Noval '55 at £3 a bottle. My uncle was Anthony Blumenthal, of Grierson Blumenthal, the wine shipper; they were Charlie Forte's wine people and, later, sold the business to Trust House Forte. My father and his sister were close, and her husband supplied my household with a lot of nice wine. I had a reasonable knowledge; but I certainly couldn't taste blind before the Oxford University Wine and Food Society (OUWFS). It was a bit of a paradox that it was called a "wine and food society", as we didn't do anything with food at all. We went out for dinner occasionally, but that was adjunct to our purpose, which was to taste wine, seriously – an expensive hobby.

'Bottles would be hidden or decanted, and constructed around the competition. If somebody was coming down and they'd given us good wine,

we'd go to dinner at The Elizabeth, which was gorgeous, and a lovely old Spanish chap ran it. It was the sort of place you got your parents to take you because it cost £3 a head: a lot of money then. La Sorbonne was another good French restaurant. After meetings, we'd go as a group to Le Casse Croûte, off the high street, as students could afford it more easily. That was the "food" bit of the society.

The 1974 match
'I was part of the team in 1974. Captain Christopher Purvis would send a note round saying, "Please bring this wine." We did blind tastings, weekly, building up the memory bank, and would train ourselves about the characteristics of the vintage – 1961 was the great vintage when I was there, and '64s and '66s were lovely. For whites, '71s were thought to be good.

RIGHT Michael Broadbent signed this copy of his book, *Wine tasting*, for Jonathan Marks at the varsity match in 1974.

'The match was in Harveys' tasting room, in the cellar. Michael Broadbent of Christie's came to present the prizes, and he gave me a copy of his book, signed on the date of the tasting. There was multiple choice, with description and elimination. You had to get them all right to get to the last wine. It was stressful, and you were vulnerable if you made one mistake. A Cambridge chap [Charles Pendred] got 100 per cent and as far as I know, he hadn't had breakfast with Michael Broadbent. So that's why we lost. We were given a wonderful reception with Laurent Perrier at lunch. Michael made a speech. It was all quite naive and jolly. We had a good time, and away we went, back to Oxford.

'I went because I was friendly with Duncan Menzies (Wadham), a tremendous, huge character, and I was keen to taste wine. The team was self-selecting. If people weren't any good, they wouldn't continue to come, because they'd feel silly. It is an unusual talent. Duncan is one of the nicest men, funny and a *bon viveur*. He married the girl he was going out with at Oxford, a nurse called Hilary, and they've been together happy ever since. He's had a successful career at the Bar, and became a judge and is now Lord Menzies.

'Oz Clarke was still in Oxford, and our coach. Christopher was quite good. Duncan was very good. The rest of us at times had strokes of genius; sometimes, everything goes right. You've had a wine not that long ago and you get it right and feel absolutely brilliant, but there is no substitute for doing it often. What's really required to taste wine blind is a combination of nose and palate with memory.

'Duncan smoked big cigars. Christopher probably smoked cigars. I smoked the odd cigar. We certainly wouldn't have smoked on the day, because it does spoil it for you. We were mostly men. Selina Elwell was the only girl on the team in my year. It was a time in your life when there were a lot of hormones around, so for most social things, you wanted to be with girls. Duncan, Christopher, Selina and I were all part of a larger social circle and would see each other at parties. I also played rugby in my first year competitively and I played tennis all the way through.

Then and now
'The wine scene at Oxford in the 1970s was small. At the 50th anniversary in 2003, the students were all able to taste Chilean, Argentinean, Australian, New Zealand, and South African wine with real knowledge; my contemporaries and I were completely at sea with that, and awestruck by the ability of the younger tasters to distinguish New World wines in a way that we could only do with France and Germany. We'd hardly even tasted Italian and Spanish wines, although Spanish wine was frequently drunk because Rioja was such good value then. We tasted claret, Burgundy, Alsace, and German wines, Port, Champagne and Sherry, Rhône and the Loire a bit. We didn't taste American wines at all. There was less awareness of grape varieties then, whereas you now have

a tasting of Pinot Noirs from different countries. For us, Pinot Noir was Burgundy and you focused on the grower. We had access to good wine at reasonable prices, more second growth than first; the colleges didn't charge us anything approaching market price. They charged us cost, or replacement cost. Port featured regularly. That made the party. And dry Sherry before dinner. The last day of my Oxford career, my jurisprudence tutor handed me a glass, saying, "This is the last dry Sherry you will ever have to drink compulsorily." In fact, I loved dry Sherry and drink it now. We also had quite a lot of Champagne.

The bar – at the Bar
'I studied law because I wanted to be a barrister; my mother was a barrister and had taken a law degree, and she thought it gave you a better insight into law. I've now been practising law solidly for nearly 40 years, and I think three years studying something different at university would have been broader. Lawyers are serious about wine. The Inns of Court have good cellars. But I've never brought wine into politics, never done a case about wine, which is something that I would do. It's had absolutely nothing to do with my career.

'It isn't necessary to have knowledge of wine to be a successful Liberal Democrat peer. There's a class aspect to wine because of the cost, and because wine tended to be a public-school Oxbridge-type interest. But there are many people in the Labour Party who know lots about wine. The Bar is collegiate and has its own wine committee.'

DUNCAN MENZIES
Wadham College,
Oxford, m.1971

The Rt Hon Lord Menzies is a judge of the Supreme Courts of Scotland.

'I read history and was a member of the wine-tasting team for (I think) three years, having been persuaded to become involved by Oz Clarke, who was and remains a great friend.

'In those days the competition was run by Ted Hale MW of Harveys of Bristol, held in the cellars of the London offices. I was a member of the Oxford University Wine and Food Society and the Wine Circle. Thereafter I read law at Edinburgh. On matters vinous, I founded the Scottish Wine Society in 1976, was chairman and managing director of Ptarmigan Wines Ltd from 1980 to 1991, and chairman of the wine committee of the New Club in Edinburgh for over 20 years; I've been a member of The Saintsbury Club since 1997, and am a *maître* of a new Commanderie de Bordeaux in Edinburgh, inaugurated in 2012.'

An interview with RICK PORTER

UNIVERSITY COLLEGE, OXFORD, m.1969

Dr Richard Porter FRCOG is an obstetrician/ gynaecologist in Bath.

> 'Yesterday's defeat cannot easily be blamed on lack of experience.'
> *Cambridge Evening News*

'I showed initial enthusiasm, so was "conned" into being the treasurer of the Oxford University Wine Circle (OUWC). I thought it was an accolade of sorts, but actually it was because nobody else could be bothered to do it. However, it led to all sorts of enjoyable dinners with visiting wine merchants and an entrée into the big tastings held for the colleges. It was onward and upward from there, or possibly even downwards. A trifle hedonistic perhaps, I ran both the OUWC and the Oxford University Wine and Food Society (OUWFS) for a number of years; it was a perfect way of learning about wine and immense fun. OUWC was the more formal, always seated.

'The generosity of merchants never failed to amaze me; in my opinion the ones listed on the right were the leading lights, and apologies to those I've overlooked. Looking back over the tasting sheets from then, the overriding impression has to be of a sense of naive optimism on the part of the merchants that we would grow up to appreciate fine wines. I hope they were right.

'Ted Hale at Harveys ran the competition against Cambridge, neither an inter-university social occasion nor a boxing weigh-in, held at Harveys' London HQ in Pall Mall. When "training" for the matches, certain home-grown supporters should be remembered with thanks and affection. The splendid Oscar Wood mumbled us through tastings from the Christ Church senior common room cellar, and the wonderful, shy Bryan Wilson held a blind tasting in the cellars at All Souls followed by supper in his rooms – and turned me at least on to Domaine de Chevalier (rouge). These were precious moments with charming, kind people: fairly typical of the wine community in general when you get below the surface.

'The team was created from members of the OUWC and the OUWFS. It was far from democratic, but I doubt if we missed any of the better tasters. The ratio of men to women at the university was about six to one, and in the societies, probably almost representative. There were no wines from New Zealand, South Africa or South America on the market, and precious few from Italy or Spain. Australia was just beginning to be taken seriously. One of my abiding wine memories is of meeting Oz Clarke leaving Lady Margaret Hall one evening in the summer term of 1972, having elected not to stay for an OUWFS tasting being given by John Avery because he was showing "bloody

GENEROUS WINE MERCHANTS

- Definitely *primus inter pares* was the dear and recently departed John Avery. As was true for so many others, my interest in the broad sweep of wine was kindled by John, and his absurdly generous tastings were a regular highlight. I can remember many of his tastings as if it were yesterday, and fortunately I have the tasting sheets, including a vertical tasting of Château Cantemerle given in 1974, ending with the '52!
- Richard Peat of Corney & Barrow gave wonderful tastings in his inimitable style. His enthusiasm was enormous and nobody could forget him. His choice of wines was always instructive: who else would bring Château Cheval Blanc 1968?
- Ted Hale of Harveys was another great supporter, and a huge personality – he treated us to a blind tasting at his house in Gloucestershire, which included Château La Mission Haut-Brion.
- Anthony Goldthorp of O W Loeb gave exemplary tastings, forcing us to take Rhône and Loire wines seriously long before Robin Yapp was on the scene, as well as Alsace (which he insisted on pronouncing as *Al's arse*) and, of course, German wines. Imagine a tasting (in 1976) of the following Jaboulet Aîné wines (all 1972): Crozes-Hermitage Domaine Mule Blanche (blanc), Vacqueyras, Gigondas, St-Joseph le Grand Pompée, Cornas, Crozes-Hermitage Thalabert, Côte-Rôtie les Jumelles, Hermitage la Chapelle, and on top of that Château Rayas blanc and rouge 1967.
- The other German prophet was Russell Hone (for F & E May). This was before he left England and teamed up with Becky Wassermann in Burgundy. His enthusiasm also spilled over into doing tastings of ten Hungarian wines (on numerous occasions). Russell was a gentle giant (literally) and many of us learned about controlling our prejudices from him.
- Freddie Price, then of Dolamore's (and before he became a pre-eminent German promoter), was a great supporter. Again, he was forever trying to persuade us of the merits of Alsace wines. Strange, when we now realize how superb they are, that it was a massively uphill struggle to get anybody to take them seriously.
- Richard Persse of Morgan Furze gave us more modest fare, but always well judged, and with understated charm.
- David Gilbertson of Christopher & Co was another out-and-out eccentric, giving us well-judged tastings with never less than interesting wines.
- Patrick Forbes of Moët – an unrepeatable character.
- Julian Jeffs – imagine: the undisputed English-speaking authority in Sherry giving his time to talk to undergraduates (twice in my time). Another true eccentric.
- Michael Broadbent – how extraordinary that he used to come down to teach us. How lucky we were. It was he who was covered in confusion when telling us how to pronounce Auxey-Duresses, rightly emphasizing the soft 'x' in Auxey, but inexplicably inserting a hard 'x' in Duresses.

boring wines from Australia". Such was the state of our country's catholic taste in wine at that time. Wine was still a bit of an extravagance, but even undergraduates could aspire to tasting all but the first growths from time to time in those days. *O tempora, o mores.*

'We trained in my flat in postgraduate accommodation. The mess that we made still makes my wife cross. We'd bring a bottle each, get them wrong, criticize each other for bringing useless examples, and try unsuccessfully to avoid getting predictably drunk by eating Carr's water biscuits and treading them into the carpet. On occasion, we were allowed to make the same mistakes by generous "patrons". In those days the subtlety of tasting, and of the wines available, was such that Soave was a "banker" – the only wine that was colourless, odourless and tasteless – as was Gewürztraminer (lychees, of course). Sancerre was cat's pee. Rhône was pepper. Coaching was by osmosis, and for this the tastings were crucial, drumming home the basics and developing a sort of syntax.

'My experience with wine was zilch before I went up in 1969. To be fair my grandfather used to serve wine occasionally that said "Beaujolais" on the label that he heated in front of a two-bar electric heater – which may or may not have improved it. My godfather and cousin, Robin Kernick, was in the trade, and latterly keeper of the Royal Cellars, but contact was naturally intermittent until later on, and he wasn't going to waste good wine on wastrels.

'We would dine at The Elizabeth, with its lovely rack of lamb, or alternatively at La Sorbonne

Oxford's winning team in the wine-tasting match. Left to right, Martin Lewis (Keble College), Robin Lane (Brasenose), Richard Porter (University), Jane Machale (St Anne's), Jonathan Boyce (Merton) and Robert Mather (Merton).

No competition for Jane the champagne winner

Jane Machale, who walked away with the Lady's Prize, being the only woman competitor.

LEFT
The *Oxford Mail*,
February 27, 1975.

DIARY

It is difficult to feel any real sympathy for John Marks, of Duxford and Trinity Hall, Cambridge, who had a lovely trip up to London yesterday but complained that there was nowhere to spit.

As a result of there being nowhere to spit, the poor chap had to drink the best part of a dozen glasses of superb wine between 10.45 a.m. and 12.30 p.m. We should all be so unlucky.

Mr. Marks, a second-year English student and son of a Downing Fellow, claimed that all this drinking may have clouded his judgment as a member of the six-man Light Blue team taking part in the 27th annual Oxford and Cambridge wine tasting match organised by Harveys of Bristol at their Pall Mall cellars.

He alone lacked the chair-side box of sawdust into which the rest of them were spitting like village pumps. The only female contestant, Miss Jane MacHale, a frail-

looking girl from St. Anne's, Oxford, had a particularly decorous spitting style.

I have given so much prominence to the trivial matter of the sawdust only because I am loyally casting round for excuses to explain Cambridge's defeat by 317 points to 295. The sandbox is all I can offer, although Cambridge can take comfort in the fact that their captain, Charles Pendred, of Trinity, turned in the best personal achievement by scoring 66 out of 100. Even this was a pale shadow of his 100 per cent success last year, when Cambridge took the title. Cambridge now lag by three matches in the series.

The second best personal score was achieved by Christie Marrian, a research student, also from Trinity, who scored 64. His father, Dr. Denis Marrian, who was Prince

Charles's tutor at Trinity, was one of the judges and was greatly hampered because he had left his spectacles in Cambridge. He had to read the contestants' answers with a magnifying glass. I let him try my spectacles but they were hopelessly unsuitable.

The senior judge was an extremely distinguished Bordeaux wine broker, M. Daniel Lawton, who, in a speech at lunch, made a valiant and sometimes rather touching attempt to dispel the cloud of scandal over Bordeaux. He had a smile like sunlight on a southern slope.

One of the Cambridge team, Timothy Forse, of Pembroke, who was in charge of their Paddington Bear mascot with its yellow, size 20 Dunlop baby wellies, speculated that the reason why four of his colleagues came from Trinity might be

that Trinity reputedly had the most extensive cellars in Cambridge. He said this in a way that indicated that size was not everything.

The truth is that the team does not need college cellars. They are all members of the university Wine and Food Club, which is generouly favoured by the trade. Yesterday's defeat cannot easily be blamed on lack of experience.

I think they should go into stricter training if they wish to win next year. Give up smoking those incendiary French cigarettes, chaps. Stop those beery booze-ups, too.

And another thing. Include your reserve, Dave Richmond, from Trinity Hall, in the team in future. In a dummy run yesterday he did better than any of you on the white wine.

Chris South

ABOVE The *Cambridge Evening News*, February 27, 1975.

(*escalope de chevreuil*), but it became embarrassing to go there and not be able to drink wines anywhere near as good as the merchants had provided, so I persuaded University College to let me buy odd, good bottles from the senior common room cellar specifically for post-tasting dinners, and my wife to cook delicious meals, and so established lifelong friendships with several merchants.

'At that time Pamela Vandyke Price was writing her less-than-bouncy but definitely informative columns for *The Times*, and Eddie Penning-Rowsell was writing his tinder-dry pieces in the *Financial Times* and *Country Life*. Wine journalism was in its infancy. *Decanter* magazine started in the mid-'70s, and my Oxford friends Oz Clarke and Jancis Robinson also moved into wine writing. Michael Broadbent's *Wine Tasting* was very influential then; Hugh Johnson's *World Atlas of Wine* was a fantastic eye-opener.

'I sniff wines first and then hope for divine inspiration. It was all a magical mystery tour. In the period 1970–77 New World wines were just beginning to arrive in the UK and Robin Yapp was taking a huge punt specializing in wines from the Rhône and the Loire. This was also the time of the miners' strike, the oil crisis, devaluation and inflation, and the insanity of the Bordeaux '72s being sold *en primeur* for more than the '70 or '71 vintages, even before the grapes had been picked. This was a strange time for the wine trade.'

YAPP (Agencies)
MERE, WILTSHIRE
Tel. (0747) 860423

VOYAGE DE LA CAVE A L'OFFICE

ABOVE Robin Yapp was the first major British importer of wines from outside the classic regions of France. He introduced many undergraduates to the wines of the Rhône and the Loire.

An interview with
LYNNE (NÉE TURNER-WARWICK) TURNER-STOKES

LADY MARGARET HALL, OXFORD, m.1973

Lynne Turner-Stokes FRCP is a consultant in rehabilitation medicine and professor of rehabilitation at King's College, London.

'My interest in wine started when I was eight, on a family holiday in a villa in Italy in Sestri Levante, on the Ligurian coast. As soon as we arrived my parents got the flu and my sister had German measles. They took to their beds and gave me 100 lire to walk down to the street market and learn Italian. The first shop I came to was a wine merchant, and they had those little miniature Chianti bottles with baskets around them in a bucket for 100 lire. So I bought one a day and wandered down the market drinking my Chianti. And when I got back to the villa, on the top of a hill, I chucked it in the bin and carried on as normal. On the last day of the three-week holiday they'd all recovered, and said, "Come and show us how you spent this 100 lire." So I introduced them to the wine merchant, who said, "Oh good morning, which will it be today: red or white?" My parents were slightly surprised. We'd been brought up having a mini-glass of wine when there was a special occasion.

'My father was a surgeon, and a member of The Wine Society. When I got interested in wine he gave me £100 to buy and lay down bottles of wine that were less than a pound a bottle: the 1970s clarets were coming through, like Château Potensac. We carried on drinking them for 15 years; our cellar at home is double-depth racks. You pull out something, and behind you find an old bottle of 1978. They've kept beautifully – wonderful wines, fantastic. I've always been a claret person.

'I was at Bedales School in Hampshire, which is co-ed, and Richard, my husband, taught me German. He used to bring in German wines at the end of the year for his classes. We'd have a tasting of Rhine and Mosel, and Alsatian wines. He'd been at Oxford, and had a good circle of friends who were keen on wine, one of whom is Sebastian Payne MW, chief buyer for The Wine Society 1985–2012, and his brother, Nicholas Payne, who was director of the English National Opera; they have a fantastic private cellar.

Oxford Blues
'I was at Lady Margaret Hall (LMH) in Oxford from 1973. Oz Clarke was still there when I first started. The Oxford University Wine Circle was a serious, sit-down affair, and the Oxford University Wine and Food Society (OUWFS) was a bigger, mixed social crowd, with various levels of interest. I won a bottle of white Burgundy, guessing closest to its cost – nothing terribly clever –

'I think I have a man's Half-Blue. It was fine; I already had the full Blue for lacrosse.'

and Captain Rick Porter, now a consultant obstetrician in Bath, asked me to join the team, in my third year in 1976.

'I came from a co-ed school, where I'd been since the age of nine, so it was a deep culture shock to arrive in an all-female college. There were about 26 colleges, five of which were female. So I tried to get out and join things like the OUWFS. I was captain of the lacrosse team, and also in the Oxford Bach Choir, which was a mixture of town and gown. I played piano and cello and a lot of my friends went on to be professional musicians. I had a lovely time accompanying violinists who used to practice and perform at the Sheldonian Theatre: a nice place to play and sing. But they worked us hard as medics: a lot of dissection and lectures. You had to sign in to all your lectures, because medical training required that you actually attend them. The sciences block is just across the park from LMH, and it was quite a nice walk.

'Harveys would come and give extraordinary tastings of first and second growths. Michael Broadbent gave a vertical tasting of Lafite. As a student you didn't have much money, but wine wasn't that far out of one's budget; you could go to a restaurant and order a Lynch-Bages perfectly happily.

'In the 1976 match there was a vertical challenge of three clarets; I guessed St-Julien, second growth, and the (slightly strange) years on Harveys' list were 1969, '71 and '72. Only two would fit: Léoville-Las Cases or Ducru Beaucaillou, and I chose the wrong one (it was Beaucaillou!). The match took place in the basement at Harveys, and there was a jolly lunch afterwards. Cambridge won in 1976. I won the Lady's Prize, and when I got back I balanced this magnum of Laurent Perrier Champagne (sadly, before the days of Pol Roger sponsorship, but very nice all the same) in the basket of my bicycle all the way across Oxford. We enjoyed it as a team one evening with Bryan Wilson of All Souls to commiserate.

'I was on the Blues committee because I was captain of the lacrosse team. We voted that year not to have women get Half-Blues for non-sporting events (like tiddlywinks). Hockey and tennis were a full Blue, squash and cricket a Half-Blue. After the varsity blind wine-tasting match everybody was collecting their Half-Blue, and I said, "Women don't get one of those." They said it was unfair, and wrote me down in the men's book. So I think I have a man's Half-Blue. It was fine; I already had the full Blue for lacrosse.

'Julian Jeffs was amazing. I remember him saying, "You're so ignorant: you know nothing about Sherry," and carting us all off to his beautiful house to have a Sherry tasting one Saturday evening, which was the

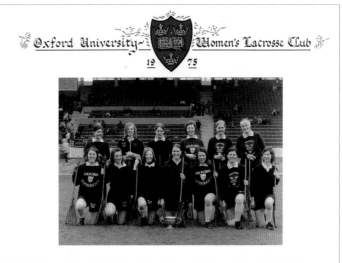

ABOVE Lynne Turner-Warwick (front row, centre) as captain of the Oxford women's lacrosse team.

night of my engagement party; I didn't get to my own engagement party until rather late.

A certain craving
'After Oxford, I came down to London to University College Hospital for the clinical bit, and Richard became a schoolmaster at Westminster (he's now at the Royal Academy of Music coaching young singers on *lieder*). We bought 15 cases of Haut-Brion for £12 a bottle.

'When I was pregnant with my first daughter, I developed this passion for young, tannic claret. We'd just taken delivery of the 1980 clarets and I drank my way stolidly through them; we didn't know in those days that alcohol was bad for you in pregnancy. So the first thing Richard did when I got pregnant with my second daughter was to run out and buy ten cases of some Bourgeois, young claret that I could entertain myself with. Whereupon I announced that this time it was young Burgundy I fancied.

'It used to be common when I was a registrar, and first a consultant, that when a pharmaceutical company came, there would be a bottle of wine for lunch. You'd never have that now; alcohol is not allowed on the premises at all. That's not to say we're not perfectly able to go and have a knees-up if we're not on duty! But the culture has changed. I happened to be down in the Temple recently giving a lecture to a group of lawyers and it was wine, wine and wine – maybe a token carton of orange juice. There's been a change in terms of the medical profession being more conscious of the effects of alcohol.

'I confess I have gone over to "the dark side" and drink more Australian and New Zealand wine now than French, because I have adjunct chairs in Perth and Auckland. I enjoy visiting the wineries in Margaret River. But the cost of good claret has moved disproportionately from other things, and I'm a bit meaner than I was.'

LEFT Robin Lane flew
Chipmunks and Bulldogs
in the University Air
Squadron, which he
described as the best club
ever at Oxford.

An interview with ROBIN LANE

BRASENOSE COLLEGE, OXFORD, m.1972

*Robin Lane worked with Averys of Bristol, then
became one of the first Australian wine buyers
for Sainsbury's before setting up his own agency,
Lane & Tatham.*

'John Avery gave me my first job when I was 17 and still
in school, in 1970. I spent one day working in Averys
bonded warehouse in Bristol, and then they needed
someone in the shop and they said, "He looks alright."
So I got pushed up into the shop to work with a
legendary woman called Miss Mahoney. And I worked
there when I was at Oxford, in the Christmas and Easter
holidays. There was a Bristol Wine Circle, and we used to
meet quite often; it wasn't very serious. There were loads
of wine merchants because Bristol was a port twinned
with Bordeaux, and there's been an association between
the two cities for centuries.

'Having been at Averys, I'd learned quite a bit about
wine, so when I went up to Oxford I joined the Oxford
University Wine Circle (OUWC), and became the
secretary and the president. I was never a member of the
Oxford University Wine and Food Society. The OUWC
used to meet in the New Hall, a lovely room in University
College. I was in the tasting team in 1974, '75 and '76;
we lost, won, and lost, sadly, when I was captain in '76.

'We were trained by Oz Clarke, who came along with
shoulder bag and notebook and told us what to look for.
Lynne Turner-Warwick tasted with me and was very good
indeed – far better than I was; the women in the team were
bloody good tasters. But Charles Pendred at Cambridge
was brilliant and won cases of Latour. He slightly blew it
for us, and we weren't terribly good. And there were colds
around in winter, which is always a problem.

'Guy Gordon Clark, John Avery and Patrick Forbes
from Moët all gave tastings for the OUWC. And
traditional merchants like Loeb and Hallgarten, and
Harveys. Oz arranged for us to visit Edward Sheldon
in Worcestershire, and this chap opened about a dozen
bottles for us and one of them was a Meursault. We tasted
the wines, then he went out of the room to get another
bottle, and Oz immediately turned to us and said, "Right,
that Meursault tasted oxidized to buggery. Just remember
it in case they give you a wine that's got a fault in it
(which they used to). That's what oxidation is."

Magic carpet

'The nicest letter that has ever been written about me was
written by the people who interviewed me at Brasenose.
They offered me a place, and later my housemaster said to
me, "I've received a letter from Brasenose." They wrote to
him specially to say, "We'd like you to tell Mr Lane that
we've just discovered that his father was in this college.
We'd like him to know that we didn't know that when
we offered him a place." I can tell you what questions
they asked me at the admissions interview. They asked
me why the carpet was blue. And they asked me why
the light came through the window and they gave me a
molecule to play with. Now I'm an A-level student, but
we pondered around it for a bit – they just wanted to see
how you thought.

'I read chemistry and played soccer for Brasenose,
a super-sporty college, in a transition period; girls were
accepted when I was there, in 1973 or '74. Chemistry is
a four-year course at Oxford. I was bored by the last year
so I went to my tutor, Jack Barltrop, one of the leading
two photochemists in the world, and he said, "This
making wine out of grapes is way outdated, Robin. We
ought to be able to do something about that." So in the
fourth year I did some oenological research into tannins,
because nobody knew anything about them then. A 30-
page document is the summary of my year's work. They
gave me a third-class degree and I'm very happy with it.

'I was in the University Air Squadron, and I learned
how to fly at Oxford. It was one of the best clubs to be a
member of – fantastic. I used to go flying in the morning,
then go back to the University Air Squadron Club, where
gin was ten pence a shot and Carlsberg Special Brew was
so cheap. I'd have fish and chips and stay in the bar until
about two o'clock, then go home and have a sleep until
the pubs opened at six. That was my perfect day. I was
two years in the air squadron, posting 70 hours flying.

'As far as I was concerned, wine tasting was a Half-
Blue, and so as a bit of a maverick I bought a Half-Blue
tie and I used to wear it quite often. But you don't get
invited to be a member of Vincent's Club; people who
got Blues were invited to be members of Vincent's Club.
Blind wine-tasting wasn't recognized, but we took delight
in just buying the tie and wearing it. As it didn't look like
anything, like any old tie, a dark- and a light-blue stripe,
nobody would ever challenge you.'

LEFT The rather debonair 1978 Cambridge team photographed after the match at Harveys. From left to right (back row): Luke Hughes, Nigel Allsopp, Andy Peacock and Pippa Robinson; (front row): Michael Wrobel (captain), Sheila Lane and Jonathan Hippisley.

An interview with LUKE HUGHES

PETERHOUSE, CAMBRIDGE, m.1975

Luke Hughes FRSA FRGS set up as a furniture designer in 1981 in Covent Garden, London, specializing in furniture for architecturally sensitive buildings. His clients include more than 50 Oxbridge colleges, 17 cathedrals, 90 parish churches, six royal palaces, 20 major institutional libraries (including the library of the UK Supreme Court), three synagogues and the furniture used for the royal wedding in the sanctuary of Westminster Abbey in 2011.

'I was brought up at Wardour, near Salisbury, educated at the choir school there and later at St Paul's School. (I am still living in the same house where I was brought up!)

Tasting at Cambridge

'At Cambridge, there were many college societies with bad claret, on the whole, but college cellars of note included Peterhouse, King's and Trinity. I read history of art and architecture as an undergraduate, and was a member of the Peterhouse Wine Society, as well as the Cambridge University Wine and Food Society (CUWFS). Denis Marrian, Tim Forse and Stephen Elliot were the serious players in my time; others were dilettantes. Much of the team's training was down to Stephen Elliot's guidance, and the abundance of Trinity's cellars. Knockout tasting rounds held over the preceding weeks before the match in Stephen's rooms determined the team.

'The 1978 match was held at Harveys' shop in St James's. There was also a four-way match with Nottingham, Exeter and Oxford. I seem to recall we won that one outright, but then lost to Oxford in the Harveys-sponsored match.

'As CUWFS dinner secretary I organized the dinners at King's College after the tastings (usually held at Trinity), with wine merchants from Berry Bros. & Rudd, Corney & Barrow, Taittinger, Yapp, Averys, Harveys, and David Peppercorn MW – crikey, there were loads! Frank Lawes-Johnson was a legendary host in Paris (and occasional visitor to Cambridge), and another was Aubert de Villaine, who is a family friend and has interests in Burgundy.

'Post-Cambridge, I pursued a career as a furniture designer, specializing in architecturally sensitive buildings, and still enjoy wine as a member of The Garrick Club.'

An interview with
STEPHEN PARRY-JONES

JESUS COLLEGE, OXFORD, m.1973

Stephen Parry-Jones is assistant head of a comprehensive school in south Wales.

'I was born in Wales, and lived my childhood in Cornwall, where the local chemist in my town doubled as wine merchant! My parents believed in us children having a thimbleful. I came up to Oxford knowing "white with fish, red with meat" and the difference between Bordeaux and Burgundy, having been told by my history teacher during A-levels.

The Oxford wine scene
'I read modern history at Jesus, where several family members had previously been. I was in the Oxford University Wine Circle (OUWC), although I did go along to the Oxford University Wine and Food Society (OUWFS) a couple of times. OUWFS seemed like a lot of "hoorays" – doubtless unfair – and OUWC serious without being too earnest. There were two women and six men on the team in 1977, including reserves, whittled down to a core from a preliminary session in Captain Kingsley Liu's room in Brasenose.

'Michael Broadbent of Christie's was an excellent mentor and taught us how to taste, and Hugh Johnson's *Pocket Wine Book* was useful. Ted Hale of Harveys was genial, and also organized a match against Bristol and Exeter. The president of Magdalen had us over one evening, and we focused on Bordeaux. Dinners were at All Souls and Christ Church, in the Cherwell Boathouse, and at The Elizabeth once or twice, where I had a 1914 Armagnac.

'Dr Bryan Wilson of All Souls was our senior member, and gave us a dinner to celebrate our win against Cambridge. I recollect the post-match victory dinner in All Souls with great fondness, as Dr Wilson found bottles from our birth years to accompany the food; I was born in 1955 and this provided a challenge to get something decent. All Souls had complex rituals: fruit brought in with exquisitely fragile glass bowls for us to wash it, and I recall watching Suzelle Moss' fiancé, who had been to dine at All Souls once before, carefully as I negotiated this potential social minefield.

'The don in charge at Jesus used to let us order Château Giscours for college societies. At a dinner at Christ Church, Rémi Krug produced 1966 and '69 bottles of Krug, and there was a '45 Brane-Cantenac from the college cellar. M Krug seemed genuinely impressed – no small compliment from that particular source. Wines were Old World, with the odd bit of North American, as one of our team (Suzelle) was from the US. The Monty Python sketch on Australian wine summed up our own (very ignorant) view of antipodean wines. I got to appreciate Syrah, and to love white Burgundy. I also liked Alsace – underrated then, as now.

'Supermarkets were beginning to stock wine, and Peter Dominic sold Juliénas for 50 pence a bottle. It was the era of Heath as Prime Minister, with frequent general elections and strikes, and with the sense that economically the UK was the "sick man" of Europe. Society seemed more egalitarian, less class-obsessed than now, with less disparity in wealth evident. There was still a belief in the welfare state helping social mobility. Thatcher became party leader while I was an undergraduate, but we had little idea as to her agenda. Fashion was awful; it was the decade taste forgot: platform shoes and extreme flairs, not unknown in Oxford. Also, huge velvet bow ties: cringe-making! I acted, and also went to the Oxford Union fairly often.

'Our team photo was in *Decanter* magazine, and there was a lot of interest in the fact that the Oxford captain was Chinese. Jancis Robinson recently republished it on her blog, making me very nostalgic. All in all, it was one of the most enduringly educative things I did in Oxford.'

Tasty

The Times - Diary
Thursday, 24 Feb., 1977

You have to be at the peak of fitness to take part in a wine tasting contest. Yesterday was the day of the inter-Varsity match at the sport, and one of the Oxford team scratched at the last moment, totally incapacitated, he claimed, by a cold in the head.

The teams train for the event almost as strenuously as their more muscular colleagues do for the Boat Race. "We arrange at least eight blind tastings for practice a term", said a Cambridge tippler enthusiastically, "but this week we have been going at it hammer and tongs, swotting up for the big day".

The tutor in wine at Cambridge University is Dr Denis Marrian, a chemistry don from Trinity who had charge of Prince Charles when he was up. "I imagine our practice tasting supplies have set us back about £50 or £60", he said, "but the undergraduates make a big contribution themselves. They take it very seriously, and can literally talk about wine non-stop for several hours, they are so interested".

His rival from Oxford, Dr Bryan Wilson, reader in sociology and custodian of the cellars at All Souls, had coached his team less: "Really they know as much about it as I do. Cambridge are more ruthless about these things. They really go out to win, you know".

The contest itself was held "in strict examination conditions" in Harvey's cellars. "Knowledge of their wine list helps more than anything", confided one of the Oxford men, "because all the wines come from here". Some of his colleagues had more technical notions though, and carefully dabbed small fingertips of wine on to sheets of clean paper to see how the colours compared when they dried. "That's likely to tell you more about the paper than the wine", scoffed their opponents.

They mostly mistook a Graves for a St Julien or a Pauillac, were all thrown by a 1973 claret which they took to be much older, and turned their noses up at some Sauvignon whites. In the end it was found that Oxford had won, appropriately, by a nose —seven points in 600.

ABOVE *The Times*, February 24, 1977.

KINGSLEY LIU

BRASENOSE COLLEGE, OXFORD, m.1974

RAYMOND LIU

PETERHOUSE COLLEGE, CAMBRIDGE, m.1974

'My brother matriculated the same year as I did; even though he is a year younger, he is brainier! I was reading philosophy, politics and economics at Oxford; my younger brother, Raymond, read law at Cambridge. Several of the national newspapers at that time found it newsworthy that there was a Chinese person in each of the Oxbridge teams, and related to each other, and so they covered the wine-tasting competition in varying details. One reported that our parents were teetotal – a true fact.

'Archie Smith, a lecturer in philosophy originally from the US, was the husband of Suzelle Moss, and not a member of our team. Archie's family owned a vineyard and winery on the east coast of the US, but we did not know it at the time. Unfortunately, Archie passed away a few years ago. Everyone else is alive and well and still enjoying wine, as far as I know. I am afraid, over three decades on, all of us are looking somewhat different from that photograph!'

Kingsley Liu
JancisRobinson.com, May 14, 2010

The Daily Telegraph - Diary
Thursday, 24 Feb., 1977

Brother's revenge

KINGSLEY LIU from Hongkong, on the losing side in last year's annual Oxford v Cambridge wine-tasting match sponsored by Harvey's of Bristol—his brother, Raymond, was in the winning team—redeemed himself with a vengeance yesterday.

Though the margin of victory was only 361 points to 354, he captained a winning Oxford team thus acquiring the cup and John Arlott's book on burgundy. As highest individual scorer he also earned a case of wines of his choice. For a son of teetotal parents who only began to taste wine on arriving at Oxford three years ago, it was an achievement.

It may not be insignificant that his philosophy tutor is also wine buyer for Brasenose and that he has been a particularly assiduous member of the Oxford Wine Circle, a relatively recent offshoot of the more self-indulgent Wine and Food Society. Since the circle was founded in 1964, Oxford have won the contest nine times out of 12.

TOP LEFT Raymond Liu (left) and Kingsley Liu, the first Chinese students in the match. ABOVE Cheers from the winners: the 1977 victorious Oxford team. From left to right: Tim Neill, Stephen Parry-Jones, Christopher Johnson-Gilbert, Arabella Morris, Kingsley Liu (captain), Jeremy Wood, Archie Smith (coach), Suzelle Moss and Michael MacKenzie.

ABOVE The 1978 Oxford winning team. Back row, left to right: Michael MacKenzie, Tim Neill (captain), Christopher Sayer and Stephen Hobley. Front row, left to right: Arabella Morris, Jock Miller Stirling and Claudia Pendred.

'My brother and I joined the trade on exactly the same day!'

'I was up at Oxford for seven years, doing a BA, then a PhD in biochemistry. I joined the Oxford University Wine Circle (OUWC) in my first term, although I knew nothing about wine and no decent wine had ever come my way. My female peers at Lady Margaret Hall assured me that one would meet 'nicer types of men' there, so we all joined in droves. I am not sure any of us met a soulmate at tastings, but we enjoyed the evenings, and learned much about wine.

'In my fifth year I was still a member, but virtually all of my contemporaries had gone down. One or two remained, and asked me if I would like to join the blind wine-tasting group (I'd been a member of OUWC for so long I must've learned a bit by then). I agreed to turn up. Armed with little more than Michael Broadbent's book *Wine Tasting*, an invaluable guide, I tried to link what I read to what I was tasting. My experience grew exponentially in those first few sessions. We practised using wines on the Harveys list. Our tasting group was assisted considerably by the kindness and generosity of several senior members of the university, who hosted blind tastings, and gave us the benefit of their experience of a decade or more of different vintages. We met weekly at the captain's digs or in college rooms, using a set of 50 lovely tasting glasses, property of the OUWC, passed across the group from one year to the next. I participated in 1977 as reserve, and as full team competitor in '78. Oxford won in '78, and I won the Ladies' Prize: a magnum of old bottled Sherry from Harveys' cellars.

'The next year I took on the captain's role, but was hampered by living relatively far from the city centre in small and grubby digs, not really suited to holding weekly tasting sessions. Happily, help was at hand, as my brother, Jasper Morris, was also up at Oxford, and had a magnificent set of rooms in Christ Church. Having

A contribution by
ARABELLA (NÉE MORRIS)
WOODROW MW

LADY MARGARET HALL, OXFORD, m.1972

Arabella Woodrow MW lives in Yorkshire, and is director of wine at Norfolk-based Broadlands Wineries.

not shown any particular interest in wine tasting before this (our family was not brought up drinking wine), I wondered if he might be amenable to bribery. I offered him the loan of the 50 wine glasses, provided I could borrow his rooms every Thursday evening. He was happy to oblige, and duly vacated. By halfway through term, however, he asked if he could join in, as he found the aroma of wine that pervaded his quarters quite irresistible. He joined the OUWC and the tasting group, and, like me, learned fast.

'I selected my team of six and reserve to pit our palates against Cambridge. Off we went to Harveys' Pall Mall offices. Sadly, we didn't win in 1979: possibly my fault as I hadn't spotted that one Chianti had crept onto Harveys' list, which we hadn't tried and weren't expecting. Still, we didn't disgrace ourselves totally. Our heroic, but undesirable, second place was announced in all the broadsheet newspapers the next day. I took a lot of ribbing from friends and family, even though, again, I managed the Ladies' Prize. Although we did not realize it at the time, this competition has had a massive influence on both my brother's and my subsequent careers. All because of a wine competition!'

ABOVE James John MW, John Harvey and Arabella Woodrow, who joined Harveys of Bristol in 1979, tasting in the cellars.

A contribution by JASPER MORRIS MW

CHRIST CHURCH, OXFORD, m.1976

'Arabella and I are the only
brother and sister MWs.'

*Jasper Morris MW co-founded Morris & Verdin specialist wine importers, which was
sold to Berry Bros. & Rudd in 2003; now Berrys' Burgundy director, he writes and
lectures extensively on Burgundy, Beaujolais, California and New Zealand. His book,*
Inside Burgundy, *won the André Simon Drink Award in 2010.*

'We didn't drink wine at home, my father having
become a teetotaller after years of excess and
my mother preferring warm gin and ginger beer to the
exclusion of anything else. Earliest memories of drinking
wine, however, would be summer holidays in Ramatuelle,
in the south of France, the local rosé purchased in ten-litre
demijohns and decanted back into bottles.

During Oxford

'I came up to Oxford in 1976 to read modern history
at Christ Church, having been awarded a Holford
Exhibition: a closed award worth £40 a year for pupils
at Charterhouse, frequently employed, I suspect, while
such awards still existed, by Christ Church to nab
those awarded a place but not a scholarship at more
academically inclined colleges such as Magdalen. My three
years at Oxford coincided with my elder sister Arabella's
second degree. She had already developed an interest in
wine and was keen for me to get involved. It seems natural
enough for a younger brother not to want to do what an
elder sister suggests, and I resisted at first. Other forms of
alcohol seemed easier to access, notably the beer at The
Bear. Alternatively there was house Port, from the buttery:
an essential adjunct to evenings playing bridge.

'Arabella tempted me sufficiently by inviting me as her
guest to the Oxford University Wine Circle's (OUWC)
annual dinner, held at the Cherwell Boathouse, and after
that I never looked back. Much of my exposure to wine at
Oxford came through the OUWC and to a lesser extent
the Oxford University Wine and Food Society (OUWFS).
Later, as a wine merchant, I gave tastings to both these
groups, and it was interesting to see the pendulum swing.
At certain times the OUWC had an avid interest in
learning about wine, while the OUWFS was an excuse for
a party; at other moments OUWFS showed real interest in
wine, while the Wine Circle had become a snobbish clique
aimed at persuading producers to put on vertical tastings of
first growths free of charge.

'During the years I was a member of the OUWC,
those merchants who kindly donated their time and
wines included Harry Waugh, John Avery, Richard Peat
(Corney & Barrow), Robin Yapp, Ted Hale (Harveys)
and Dai Gilbertson (Dolamore's). I also learned a
great deal and had the chance to experience mature
wines, thanks to the generosity of college wine buyers,
among whom the following stand out: Ralph Walker of
Magdalen (special subject: Mosel-Saar-Ruwer), Duncan
Stewart of Wadham (old Beaujolais) and Bryan Wilson
of All Souls (mature claret).

'We had access to good bottles through the Christ
Church cellar. Most memorable, not least because it was
possible to purchase considerable volumes at the amazing
price of £2.50 a bottle, was Cos d'Estournel 1966: a great
vintage, famous château, 12 years old and affordable. It
was not in itself the seminal wine that set me off on a
career in the wine trade – I don't think there was one – but
it was certainly something special that kicked off a long-
term affection for St-Estèphe. I also remember a one-off
bottle of Taylor's 1945 Port, purchased from the buttery
for £6 for a special celebration, and among the whites, a
Meursault Charmes '67.

The 1979 match

'In my last year of a three-year degree, I was encouraged
by Arabella to train for the varsity wine-tasting match
and, indeed, persuaded to host training sessions in my
ground-floor rooms in Peckwater Quad. I suppose these
sessions were helpful, and they were certainly excellent
fun: occasions when drinking wine with friends could be
considered virtuous, as it was doing our homework for
the competition to come. The team selected was Captain
Arabella Morris (Lady Margaret Hall), Jasper Morris
(Christ Church), Nigel Pitel (St Benet's Hall), William
Wells (Christ Church), Claudia Pendred (Wadham),
Brewster Barclay (Brasenose), with John McCallum

ABOVE Jasper and Arabella Morris commiserated with a toast
after Oxford lost the match to Cambridge, 1979.

LEFT The 1979 Oxford
team. From left to right:
Nigel Pitel, William Wells,
Arabella Morris (captain),
Jasper Morris, Claudia
Pendred, Brewster Barclay
and John McCallum.

(Ruskin) in reserve. I don't now recall any of the wines
served at the match itself. We lost by 23 points out
of 1,000 with Arabella easily top-scoring for Oxford,
although still a little behind the overall winner, the light-
blue Harry Eyres (Trinity). Harveys of Bristol sponsored
the competition, and we'd train using their wines. For
several years afterwards I reckoned I could spot blind the
distinctive characteristics of a wine selected by Harveys'
wine buyer, Ted Hale.

After Oxford

'While a member of the OUWC I met Tony Verdin,
proprietor of the Cherwell Boathouse restaurant, regular
attendee at OUWC tastings and father of two daughters.
I never got anywhere much with either Julia or Annie
Verdin, but Tony ended up by marrying my other
sister, Araminta!

'Even while still at Oxford, Tony suggested that it
might be fun to set up a wine business together. As it
happens I had no plans for any job at all, beyond feeling
that something with wine or possibly books might be
enjoyable. I even considered a PhD researching the
drinking habits of 18th-century politicians Pitt and Fox,
a subject that did not particularly impress the Regius
Professor, Hugh Trevor-Roper, when I had an interview
to discuss my plans.

'Instead, I got a phone call from a Cambridge man
(Charles Pendred, brother of Oxford taster Claudia) to
say that a new wine shop was opening in the Fulham
Road and they might have a job. There was and I got
the job – shop assistant and delivery driver – for Birley
& Goedhuis Ltd. The two partners, Mark Birley of
Annabel's fame and Johnny Goedhuis, unfortunately
fell out after a relatively short time, but it was a very

good grounding for me. I had access to some truly
amazing wines out of the Annabel's cellars (staff price
was cost + 10% + VAT, even for rarities like Lafite
1955, though we did not abuse the privilege), while
Johnny showed me that salesmanship was as much
about getting on well with people, and accidentally
selling them a few cases while enjoying a bottle of wine,
or lunch, or both, rather than a skill that one might
be taught.

'In February 1981, Morris & Verdin opened its doors
for business. "Door", actually, since the first office was
an unused bedroom in the Chelsea Arts Club; Marianne
Faithful was living in the room next door. Initially the
company survived on orders from its two big Verdin
accounts, the Cherwell Boathouse and the Chelsea Arts
Club, while connections with the Oxford colleges also
provided valuable early support. The business grew, we
were lucky enough to be in at the start of the new wave
of domaine-bottled Burgundy, and soon developed
a reputation for this lovely region where I now spend
much of my time.

'I became a Master of Wine in 1985, having practised
blind-tasting sessions with Arabella as before; Arabella
and I are the only brother and sister MWs. Oxford set me
on the right path. I couldn't have had a happier working
life. Indeed, when the Christ Church historians of 1976
met for a 30-year reunion dinner, I turned up late and
was greeted with shouts from much wealthier individuals
of "Here's the man with the best job of all!"

'I found the magic of wine during my time at Oxford,
the intellectual appreciation as well as the hedonistic
enjoyment, and made many friends through wine, too–
not least my subsequent business partner and brother-in-
law, Tony Verdin.'

'Wine has been a passion
since university. I'm never
happier than when I've got
a glass in my hand.'

LEFT Charles Pendred (centre) tasting with fellow
blind taster, John Shakeshaft (left) and Richard Peat
of Corney & Barrow (right).

An interview with
CHARLES PENDRED

TRINITY COLLEGE, CAMBRIDGE, m.1972

*Charles Pendred worked in finance and was a
non-executive director for wine merchant Corney
& Barrow in London. He was top taster in the
varsity match for two consecutive years and is the
only competitor ever to score 100 per cent.*

'I'd had a strange and slight exposure to wine before
university. My grandfather would have Blue Nun if it
was white wine, and Burgundy, Nuits-St-Georges, if it
was red. My father liked Right Bank claret; if we went
out to dinner he'd order a St-Émilion, but there was
no genuine wine knowledge in the family. I drank a lot
of Muscadet, the local wine and a natural partner with
seafood, when we used to go to Brittany on holiday, but
I didn't develop any further interest until Cambridge.

Wine tasting at Trinity

'I went up to Cambridge in 1972 and read history.
Robert Clement-Jones was at school with me at
Haileybury, and also at Trinity, living on the same
staircase as Malcolm Anderson, who ran the Cambridge
University Wine and Food Society (CUWFS). They kept
trying to persuade me to join and I thought it was all
a bit funny. To be quite honest, I enjoyed the society at
first because it was a cheap way to get pissed. But then
I was on the committee, and appointed secretary. As
an officer of the society, you got invited to commercial
tastings, held almost every week for the wine buyers for
the colleges. It was an eight-week term and the CUWFS
had at least seven tastings a term – it was intensive. It
was a university-wide society, but there were more people

from Trinity, because tastings took place in Trinity, in
the Old Combination Room and the junior parlour,
and word of mouth got round. The membership fee was
about £7 for the year, and we held the annual formal
dinner at King's; King's had at that stage probably the
best food in Cambridge. Michael Roberts was in charge
of the kitchens. We'd have soup, fish, partridge, sorbet,
main … seven to nine courses with wines. They were big
events and well attended.

Cheese scones and Sydney Smith

'I could fit it all in because I didn't do much work. I ran
the May Ball in my last year as well, and I achieved a good,
solid 2:2 degree. I spent most of my time in the university
library where all the wine books were. I met Sydney Smith
for the first time in the library. I used to potter over at
about 11 in the morning, when the cheese scones came
out; breakfast was often a cheese scone and a hot coffee,
and I introduced myself to him on one occasion. He'd been
ill, and I got him out of retirement and re-involved as vice-
president of the society. Denis Marrian was president, and
John Rose was senior treasurer.

'Sydney and I would buy wine together, and he'd
produce incredible tastings with wines from his cellar
and the St Catharine's College cellar. He was generous,
sharing 1947 Yquem and '47 Château Rayas. Sydney
always looked quite old. He had diabetes and latterly
big problems with his feet, and had to have one of them
removed, I think. He was a bachelor, and his widowed
sister came to live with and help look after him. Sydney
was a polymath. He'd been a visiting professor in Chinese
ceramics at a university in America, and left his own
notable collection to the Fitzwilliam Museum. He was
also a talented harpsichordist, a zoologist and one of the
editors of Darwin's letters. He was eclectic, and would not
have had a cellar just of claret. He had fine German wines
and long connections with Tony Goldthorp at O W Loeb
& Co. In fact, the first tasting I ever went to was given by
Anthony Goldthorp about the Mosel region, and what

Who is Peter Dominic?

There never was a Peter Dominic but the name will always be associated with the late Paul Dauthieu, a Scot whose French parents had become hoteliers in the Highlands. It was he who started it all with one Peter Dominic shop in Horsham in 1939 choosing Peter Dominic as a better name to pronounce than his own.

In 1963, when he sold what had grown to a score of branches to International Distillers and Vintners, Peter Dominic was retained as the best trading name for the attractive modern red and blue wine shops, which are now a familiar sight in some two-hundred and seventy streets of Britain.

In 1972 I.D.V., the parent company, was taken over by Watney's which already owned a considerable part of the equity and within a few months both companies became part of Grand Metropolitan, a group which includes many famous hotels as well as Express Dairies and Mecca.

ABOVE Cambridge undergraduates in the 1970s used to buy wine from the Peter Dominic store, then the UK's largest chain of wine shops.

surprised me was simply that the wines tasted different. I'd never tasted wines side by side before. I tasted ten Mosel wines, all of them genuinely different and clearly recognizable.

'Really, whoever was interested in blind wine tasting was eligible for the team, and it was a relatively small group; it wasn't as if we had 20 people mad-keen on blind tasting. I captained the team in 1975, after I won top taster with 100 per cent score in '74, and I won it again in '75. Oz Clarke and I both won the individual prize twice. The match was a big undertaking. I remember Ted Hale and Colin Fenton from Harveys, and I knew John Harvey, who was a tasting competitor at Cambridge in the '60s. I knew Michael Broadbent rather better than I knew Harry Waugh.

Buying at auction

'I used to come down to London to auctions, when Broadbent was with Christie's and I was starting to set up my cellar. Christie Marrian, a fellow competitor, and I used to come down and taste wines pre-auction, and then bid. I bought at both Christie's and Sotheby's. There had been a big boom in 1972 when the Japanese bought wine prior to the harvest, and then the '72 vintage was an absolute disaster. The year 1970 had been a great vintage, '71 a decent vintage – better on the Right Bank – and there was absolute price speculation. Stock markets were high, and the Japanese decided to buy futures, before the grapes had even been picked. When it went sour they stopped buying.

'Margaux '72 went for something ridiculous like £20 a case in 1975. It was also the oil crisis: the lights went out in the UK and the stock market fell massively in January

1975. There'd been speculation in wine and people just had to get rid of it. I bought magnums of 1970 Château Giscours for £18 a case, and González Byass Port for £12 a case. I knew they were good deals, but I wasn't buying with an eye toward investment and financial appreciation. I couldn't have foretold today's prices ten years ago. China is the big reason why prices have inflated. I don't see how people are ever going to drink these wines. The prices may be nonsense, but that doesn't mean they're going to fall. It means that I'm not interested in buying wines *en primeur* for over £1,000 a case.

'There wasn't the same gap between the prices of first growths and the other lower tiers then that subsequently came about. First growths were expensive, but not unattainable, and you could actually buy these wines in those days rather than only on allocation. The first vintage I bet and won the map on was '82. The wines were expensive in sterling, but they weren't in terms of the dollar. I paid £375 a case for first growths, and similar for late '80s vintage Château Palmer. Pétrus came a bit later. I bought the 1985 Romanée-Conti La Tâche, and today it's worth about £7,000 per case.

'In those days I stored wine in the garage at my parents' home. I then had a smallish cellar in my first house in London near Clapham, before I moved into a bigger house. Now I live in a flat and I've got absolutely no room, so I'm trying to sell wine. If you've got a case of wine that's worth £3,000, you don't want to have it in your flat, because you'll drink it. I buy and store wine with Corney & Barrow. I also buy from Majestic and online. I rather like old Champagne; I've got some 1990 Delamotte, but I'm particularly interested now in wines I didn't know at university – from the Languedoc and southern Italy. I recently bought from a Roman wine merchant because Italian wines are difficult to find in the UK at a sensible price. Chianti and Rioja were on the radar in the early to mid-'70s, but blind tasting was almost always German and French, with little coming in from outside the classic regions.

'In the 1974 match there was a '65 Latour and I got a case for winning the top taster prize. The following year I got a bottle of each of the wines we tasted. Harveys had simplified the scoring format in my first year, and I got everything right: vintage, grape variety, country, region and sub-area. They then realized it was too dumbed down, and went back to a more comprehensive and classic blind wine-tasting format.

'There were no New World wines – nothing from Australia, New Zealand, the US, South Africa or South America. I'm not sure I'd even tasted a Californian wine by the time I left university; if I had, it was once. The first great vintage in California was 1968 or '74 – Georges de Latour and similar. But these were domestic wines that were consumed; they weren't thought of as great wines. It was only 30 years later that people talked about these wines, and no UK merchants would have had them then. Cult wines such as Screaming Eagle and Harlan are relatively recent. Rioja Murrieta was popular from Spain, but in Peter Dominic's shop in Cambridge in the '70s there wasn't anything foreign or from the non-classic regions on the shelves.

'There were only three women's colleges then: Girton, Newnham and New Hall, and Girton was three miles out from the centre of Cambridge. Trinity voted to have women in 1975, and they first came up in '77 or '78. There may have been one or two who had gone up before, but this was the time when things were beginning to happen. It was not deliberately exclusionist, it's just the way it happened. My sister, Claudia, is four years younger than I am; I introduced her to somebody who ran the Oxford University Wine Circle and she was a blind taster at Oxford.

'Wine has been a passion since university. I'm never happier than when I've got a glass in my hand. My career was in finance, and I was a non-executive director of Corney & Barrow for about 15 years (when I joined, I don't think that they even had a single bottle of Rhône on their list). I had a particularly nice cellar, but I had to sell wine to fund my divorce. I sold my 1982s to my sister, Claudia. They were worth £50,000-odd when I sold them to her, and they're probably worth a quarter of a million now.

The Pendred palate

'I have a very good memory for taste. I can only describe it as a library, and when I taste something I put it in a file. So if I taste a Burgundy, a Pommard, I think of other Pommards I've had and it's locked away. But you weren't logging all the wines of the world up there then; it was a relatively small library of French and German classic regions. Now I suspect it's got a bit muddled. The vintage variation was also more marked then as well. I could go through the 1960s and '70s and tell you what every vintage was like, whereas I couldn't do that for the decades since then.

'I love Austrian wines, which are still little known in the UK market since the big scandal when a big producer of not particularly good quality put antifreeze in its wine. And I've blended wine, which was a disastrous investment, to start a single-varietal wine from the Languedoc. It's probably far better to work in finance and buy the wines that you like than try to make money in the wine trade. There is a classic saying "How do you make a small fortune in the wine trade? Start with a large one."'

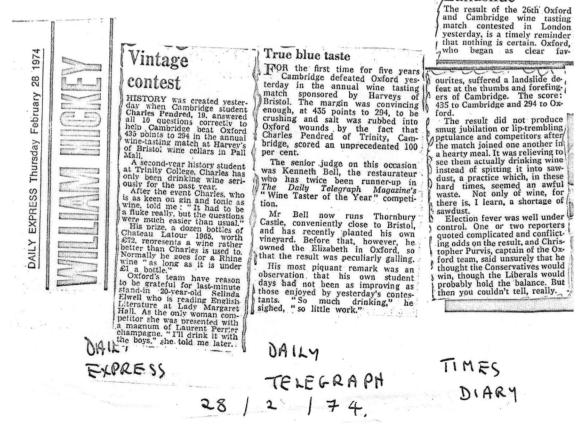

ABOVE Press coverage of the 1974 varsity match.

An interview with CLAUDIA PENDRED

WADHAM COLLEGE, OXFORD, m.1977

Claudia Pendred works with the European Bank of Reconstruction and Development.

'Charles and I constantly discuss and share wines, and often we like the same wines, strangely enough.'

'I competed in 1978, '79 and '80. My brother, Charles, was at Cambridge, in the Cambridge University Wine and Food Society and wine-tasting team, and when I went up to Oxford he said, "You should join the Oxford University Wine Circle (OUWC)." The tasting team came from the OUWC, and he knew the guy in charge from competitions. Tasting is a genetic ability as well as practice; you're either good at it or not. I did quite well and got on to the team in my first year. I was used to drinking wine, but not blind tasting. Arabella Morris was captain in 1979 and Jasper Morris was the year above me. The Oxford team was male-dominated; Arabella and I were pretty much it then as far as women were concerned.

'You got to know wine writers and people in the trade through the OUWC by inviting them to give talks. At my first competition at Harveys in Pall Mall, there were journalists and I sat next to Jancis Robinson at lunch, and we're still good friends. I met Harry Waugh several times, and we had a fascinating dinner with Cyril Ray, who has written books on wine, in his place in London. Ted Hale from Harveys, Richard Peat from Corney & Barrow, O W Loeb, John Avery and Robin Yapp came. I once met Pamela Vandyke Price; she was very dedicated and serious about wine.

'Steven Spurrier was in Paris then, running Les Caves de la Madeleine, and I worked with him in my first summer holidays. I started off in the shop, then at the restaurant Bistro à Vin on the Place de l'Esplanade at La Défence, and at weekends and days off, I would visit vineyards. Steven, and Steven Steed who ran the restaurant, organized for me to spend a day, on my own, with the Krugs. We went around the vineyards, and I saw how they made wine. I remember Rémi Krug saying, "Let's go to lunch," and we went to this little restaurant that didn't seem to have a name. Inside, he knew everybody. "We'll give you this, this and this " – there was no choosing. It was a delicious lunch in this tiny restaurant. I was so lucky. At the time you didn't realize how fortunate you were. It was an incredible experience.

'I worked another summer at Green's, a wine merchant in London in the Royal Exchange. They're not around anymore. When I first asked about joining, they said, "Fine: why don't you do a bit of typing for us?" I said, "I can't type. I can do anything involving the wine." I deliberately did not learn to type. They said okay once they realized I was running the OUWC.

'I got a Half-Blue for swimming, did a few plays with the Oxford University Dramatic Society and I was in the wine-tasting team. I read human sciences, an unusual degree: a combination of physical, physiological, genetics and social sciences. It wasn't one of those subjects where you didn't have to turn up; you actually had to go to lectures. Given I was captain of the tasting team and president of the OUWC that all took up a bit of time.

'Wine Circle tastings were in the Red Room in New College. After Cambridge, Charles came and gave a tasting for the group because I wanted to practise blind, too, and if I organized I knew what the wines were. Charles and I constantly discuss and share wines, and often we like the same wines, strangely enough (he likes Austrian wines). Dinners were hosted at different colleges or by dons, and otherwise at The Cherwell Boathouse. That's how Jasper Morris first became friends with Tony Verdin, later setting up business together as Morris & Verdin. Tony was great because he let us have our events at the restaurant, and we'd have a guest to give a speech at the annual dinner; I remember Cyril Ray reading out a limerick on wine from his book *Lickerish Limericks*.

'For the competition, we went up to London early and had out the Harveys wine list, going through it on the train, testing each other. The tasting was six whites and six reds. It wasn't multiple choice, but literally a blank piece of paper: country, grape, region, sub-region, vintage, and right down to the château. Dons in charge of college cellars would give us blind tasting practice. Bryan

ABOVE Winning team captain Claudia receiving *The Wines of Bordeaux* from author Edmund Penning-Rowsell in 1980.

In the best of taste

LEFT The winning
Oxford team, 1980.
From left to right:
Jonathan Simon, Ian
Todd, Terence Kealey,
Simon Walker, Claudia
Pendred (captain),
Andrew Holroyd,
Marcus Everard and
Nick Butt.

Wilson would give us a celebratory dinner at All Souls
if we won. All Souls was regarded as having a very good
kitchen, and its cellar was mythical. Duncan Stewart
did one from the Wadham cellar, and a don from New
College used to serve 12 German whites blind. We won
in 1978 and in 1980 when I was captain and president of
the OUWC.

Keeping wine as a hobby
'After Oxford, I had a place at University of California
at Davis to study oenology, but I turned it down. I had
the choice of going to Harvard or UC Davis. I discussed
it long and hard. Stephen Hobley, who now works with
Decanter, was in the 1978 team, Brewster Barclay's
parents had a vineyard in Devon, and Michael MacKenzie
now owns a stake in the Champagne house Jacquesson. I
was dying to work in the trade – when you're passionate
you think, "I wouldn't mind having my own vineyard and
making wine," but I remember them all saying "It's great,
but better to do something else and keep it as a hobby."
I'd love to be a winemaker, but I decided to keep wine as
a hobby. I went to medical school, didn't want to do that,
so then I went to Harvard Business School.

'I knew most of my brother's friends at Cambridge
who were in the team. After Harvard, I was in the
German Wine Society with Christie Marrian in
Washington DC, when I was at the World Bank, and I
worked with Charles Mercey when I joined Rothschild
in London before the European Bank of Reconstruction
and Development.

'I chose wine for the Rothschild wine cellar, and for
lunches and dinners, with Leopold de Rothschild. He was
at the bank and responsible for the Lafite. He's wonderful

about wine and food. They have the relationship with
Lafite largely, but also with Mouton, but we bought other
wines outside the family. Charles Mercey joined in. Once
we knew the menus, Leopold and I would choose, with
the chef each week, which wines should be served with
which food. You wouldn't serve Lafite every day; it was
for special occasions. The price did go extremely high
because of the Chinese market.

Going native: Romanian red
'For the past few years, I've lived partly in Romania.
There are beautiful wines and native grapes you almost
never see outside of the country. Fetească Neagră is a
red native grape from Romania; Merlot-Fetească Neagră
gives a delicious well-balanced wine, with a slight kick
of spice to it, and Fetească Albă makes nice white wines.
But the top wines are expensive to produce. The grapes
are all hand-picked, so by the time they get to the UK
and with transport, duty and VAT added on, selling a
red wine from Romania for £20 a bottle is not an easy
thing to do.

'A lot of these wines have sprung up recently since
the Communist period, because during that period, it
was all state controlled. Regional Romanian dishes are
bean soups with ham, sausages and fairly meat-orientated
heavy food, so these wines go well with Italian food, too.
The Romanians now have a wine-tasting fair each year
of their wines. I've become quite friendly with some of
the winemakers and have visited a lot of vineyards, and
I've written for JancisRobinson.com and for magazines in
Romania, translated into Romanian.

'So wine has played a part in everything I've ever done
since I left university.'

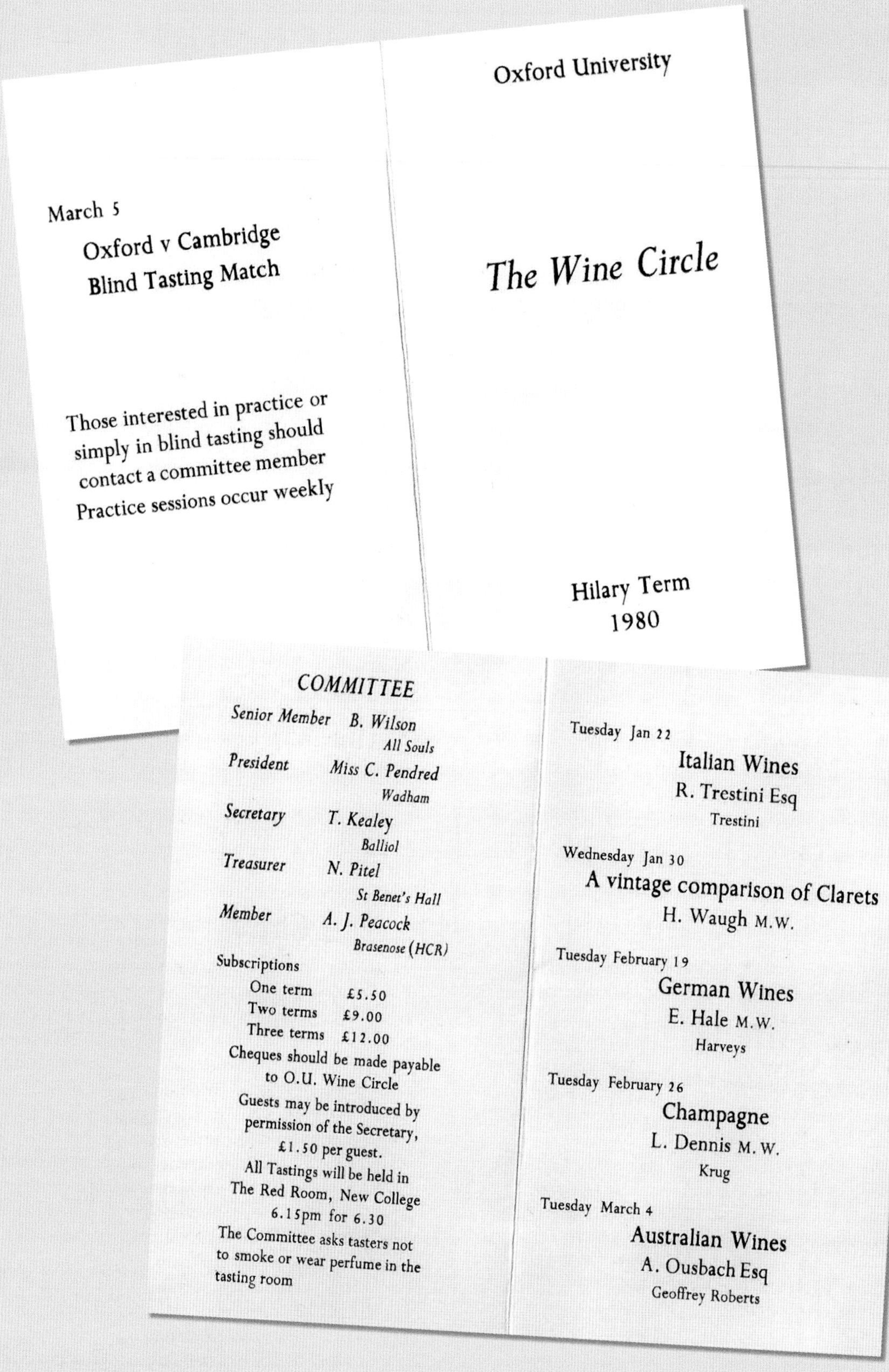

Oxford University

The Wine Circle

Hilary Term
1980

March 5

Oxford v Cambridge
Blind Tasting Match

Those interested in practice or
simply in blind tasting should
contact a committee member
Practice sessions occur weekly

COMMITTEE

Senior Member	B. Wilson	All Souls
President	Miss C. Pendred	Wadham
Secretary	T. Kealey	Balliol
Treasurer	N. Pitel	St Benet's Hall
Member	A. J. Peacock	Brasenose (HCR)

Subscriptions

One term	£5.50
Two terms	£9.00
Three terms	£12.00

Cheques should be made payable
to O.U. Wine Circle

Guests may be introduced by
permission of the Secretary,
£1.50 per guest.

All Tastings will be held in
The Red Room, New College
6.15pm for 6.30

The Committee asks tasters not
to smoke or wear perfume in the
tasting room

Tuesday Jan 22

Italian Wines
R. Trestini Esq
Trestini

Wednesday Jan 30

A vintage comparison of Clarets
H. Waugh M.W.

Tuesday February 19

German Wines
E. Hale M.W.
Harveys

Tuesday February 26

Champagne
L. Dennis M.W.
Krug

Tuesday March 4

Australian Wines
A. Ousbach Esq
Geoffrey Roberts

THE 1980s

The 1980s was a prime era for the tasting match, and fruitful for the wine trade, producing five future Masters of Wine (two of whom are women) – including Pol Roger's own, James Simpson. UK wine consumption increased significantly over the decade, from 11 to 16 bottles per capita per annum; perhaps a result of the initial exposure to wines from Australia and New Zealand, or the growing range of wine on supermarket shelves. Training for the varsity match had become structured, and there was a shift towards meritocracy – with teams sourced from beyond the cloistered membership of the Cambridge University Wine and Food Society. At Oxford, the Wine Circle superseded the Oxford University Wine and Food Society as the training ground which would lead the Dark Blues to win seven out of the ten matches during the decade. Celebrity wine-writing wits Cyril Ray and Auberon Waugh (who was noted to have an 'intellect that could intimidate someone less world weary') balanced the oft stately presence of judge Michael Broadbent MW at competitions, which now alternated between Harveys' cellars and the Oxford and Cambridge Club. Harry Waugh was by now in the US, offering The Harry Waugh Wine Selection with Bruce Templeton, who recalls: 'Harry told me that the "great man" [Winston Churchill] said to him, "Come to supper. If you teach me about wine, I will teach you about cigars." It was the final chapter of Harveys' involvement, for the period that began with Thatcherism and Reaganites, ended not only with the fall of the Berlin Wall, but also with corporate takeovers which would soon signal the end of the grand old era of Harveys.

Cambridge

David Eastwood
Harry Eyres
Tessa Fawcett (Strickland)
Nicholas Fenner
Edward Friend
Simon Gell
Michael Gell
Ben Gladstone
Jamie Guild
Edward Harley
Christina Hippisley
Keith Isaac (MW)
Nicole Jones
Victoria Jones (Baxter)
Richard Keatinge
Helen Kilpatrick
Michael King

Simon Kverndal
Vanessa Kverndal
Sarah Lawman
Madeline Littlewood
Rupert Mathieu
Nigel Medhurst
Kevin Ng
Julian Payne
Richard Phelps
Patrick Porritt
James Simpson (MW)
Stephen Taylor
Charles Taylor (MW)
Campbell Thompson
Nancy Thomson (Gilchrist) (MW)
Stephen Williams
Jeremy Williams

Oxford

Lisa Barnard
Greg Bennett
Roger Brock
Nicholas Butt
Daniel Carey
Christopher Chen
Michelle Chen
Sophia Collins (Lewisohn)
R A Cooper
Marcus Everard
Paul Holloway
Andrew Holroyd
Nicholas Holroyd
Terence Kealey
Charles Mahoney
Peter Martin
Christopher McIntyre

Jonathan Mogford
Angela Mount
Susan Orchard
Claudia Pendred
Fiona Roberts (Barlow) (MW)
Julian Robertson-Kellie
Mark Rolfe
Jonathan Simon
Neil Tallantire
Lucas Taylor
Ian Todd
Simon Walker
Gurdon Wattles
Paul White

FACING PAGE By the 1980s, the Oxford University Wine Circle had established itself as the wine society launching pad and training ground for the Oxford blind-tasting teams.

An interview with ANDREW HOLROYD

ST BENET'S HALL, OXFORD, m.1976

Andrew Holroyd runs a trilingual Spanish property agency,
Cala d'Or Property Services, in Alicante on the Costa Blanca.

'I did a four-year modern and medieval languages degree,
including a third year abroad in Grenoble, France (the
best part, as I learned to ski!).

'The competitors who took part in the blind-tasting
competition of 1980 were given a signed copy of *Lickerish
Limericks* by Cyril Ray. I was fortunate to get my copy
signed by the rest of the winning Oxford team and by
Michael Broadbent, who was one of the judges, plus
a witty limerick dashed off by Arabella Woodrow and
a note by Simon Kverndal, the Cambridge captain,
congratulating us – very sporting of him!

'I was fortunate to be picked for the team, and
unbelievably on the day I got the highest marks for the
white wine section – mainly because I liked white wine,
had a good memory in those days and had drunk virtually
all the white wines in the Harveys catalogue – taking
notes, of course!'

ABOVE Dr Bryan Wilson, a
fellow at All Souls (1963–93),
was a great supporter of the
Oxford tasting team.

ABOVE Dr Bryan Wilson gave a celebratory dinner at
All Souls College for the 1980 winning Oxford team.

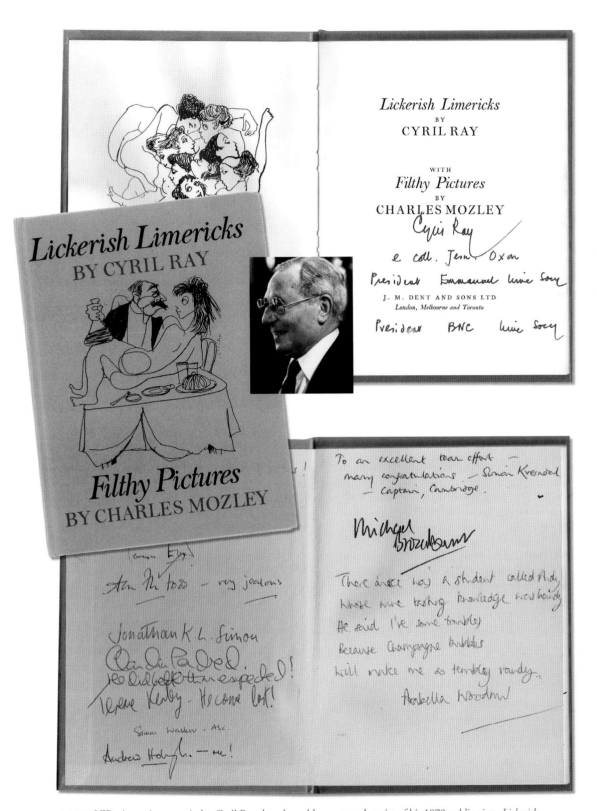

ABOVE VIP wine writer-cum-judge Cyril Ray shared good humour and copies of his 1979 publication, *Lickerish Limericks,* with the 1980 competitors: Cambridge team captain Simon Kverndal epitomized sportsmanship; Arabella (née Morris) Woodrow, by now working with Harveys of Bristol, penned a poem of her own to Andrew Holroyd.

ABOVE Send in the clowns: undergraduate fun post wine tasting at a CUWFS dinner at King's College, February 1980. From left to right: Simon Kverndal, Tessa Fawcett and Harry Eyres (top taster 1979 and '80).

An interview with TESSA (NÉE FAWCETT) STRICKLAND

GIRTON COLLEGE, CAMBRIDGE, m.1977

Tessa Strickland is co-founder and editor-in-chief of Barefoot Books Ltd, an independent children's books publishing company based in Oxford, England, and Cambridge, Massachusetts, USA.

'I was brought up in rural Yorkshire, the second of five children in a semi-dysfunctional Roman Catholic household. My father came from many generations of maltsters, but I greatly preferred wine to beer.

'I spent part of my gap year working for a Swiss banker who had inherited a fabulous cellar, and we drank first-growth clarets for supper on a weekly basis. This kindled my interest in fine wine, although I have yet to drink as well as I did that year. Before I went up to Cambridge, my mother encouraged me to do something, in her words, "non-intellectual". The Cambridge University Wine and Food Society (CUWFS) was listed in the freshers' fair brochure, and joining was the obvious answer. I joined in 1977 at the start of my first year. Apparently, this was atypical, but members of the committee were sufficiently impressed, both by my letter and my handwriting, to invite me to a tasting where I evidently behaved with commensurable impropriety to be invited formally to join the society. I read classics at Cambridge, when Russia invaded Afghanistan, and Margaret Thatcher was elected Prime Minister. I also made batik wall hangings, and was (and still am) a yoga practitioner.

'As CUWFS dining secretary in 1978–79 and 1979–80, I organized dinners at King's College after tastings,

selecting the menus and wines. The most memorable event was, in fact, a lunch held in May Week. Everyone wore white; we ate lobster and drank several varieties and vintages of Champagne (the Taittinger was remarkable!).

'Dr Stephen Elliott at Trinity College trained us for the competition, when New World wines were starting to gain ground. I use all of my senses to blind-taste wines, and we prepared for the varsity match by going on ten-mile runs along the river before dawn. Cambridge won in 1979 and lost in '80. I was the only woman representing the university in both years (men were able to join Girton the year after I graduated).

Post-Cambridge
'After Cambridge, I taught English in Japan on the Japan Exchange and Teaching programme, before returning to England, where I joined Penguin Books as a copywriter, later editor. One of my achievements was publishing a series of books on different grape varieties with fellow Cambridge tasting competitor, writer and editor Harry Eyres (Trinity). I also looked after a book on Château Latour. Thereafter, I was an editorial director at Random House, then founded a children's books publishing company, Barefoot Books.'

PROGRAMME

Tuesday 16th October
Mr Michael Broadbent, M.W.,
director of Christie's Wine Department, will present
a talk 'Wine Tasting' in the Old Kitchens, Trinity
College.

Thursday 25th October
Mr David Gilbertson, of Christopher & Co. Ltd.,
will give a tasting of Claret in the Old Kitchens,
Trinity College.

Wednesday 31st October
Mr Richard Peat, of Corney and Barrow Ltd.,
will present a tasting of Moselle wines in the Old
Kitchens, Trinity College.

Thursday 8th November
Mr Ted Hale, of Harvey's,
will give a tasting of Rhone wines in the Old
Kitchens, Trinity College.

Thursday 15th November
Mr Francis Montague-Jones
will present a Whisky evening on behalf of the
Scotch Whisky Association, with a buffet supper,
in the Garden House Hotel.

Tuesday 20th November
The Michaelmas Term Dinner:
details to be announced. Guest Speaker, Mr Hugh
Johnson.

Thursday 22nd November
Mr Grahame McKenzie, of H. Parrot & Co. Ltd.,
will present a tasting of 1978 Louis Latour White
Burgundies in the Old Kitchens, Trinity College.

Thursday 29th November
Mr Michael Cox, of Matthew Clark & Sons Ltd.,
will give a tasting of Cognac and Armagnac in the
Old Kitchens, Trinity College.

Thursday 6th December
To be arranged.

All tastings be

Members are

Charge for ea

OFFICERS

President
Dr. D. H. Marrian

Vice-Presidents
Michael Roberts Esq.
Dr. Stephen Elliott

Cellarer
Stephen Taylor (Trinity Hall)

Secretary
Andrew Lowe-Watson (Trinity)

Junior Treasurer
Hamish Taylor (Trinity)

Blind Tasting
Simon Kverndal (Sidney Sussex)

Dining Secretary
Tessa Fawcett (Girton)

ABOVE AND BELOW CUWFS term cards, Michaelmas 1979
and Lent 1980. Note that in 1980 the programme started to
explore 'Beyond the Classics', with a tasting of South African
wines and one of 'New World v. Europe'. Tessa Fawcett was the
CUWFS dining secretary for her second and third years
at Cambridge.

PROGRAMME

Thursday 24th January
Mr. Christopher Burr, of Hedges & Butler Limited,
will present a tasting of Krug Champagne in the
Old Combination Room, Trinity College.
MEMBERS ONLY.

Thursday 31st January
Mr. Nicholas Clarke, M.W., of Henry C. Collison &
Sons Ltd., will give a tasting of South African wines
in the Old Combination Room, Trinity College.

Tuesday 5th February
Mr. Anthony Goldthorp, of O. W. Loeb & Co Ltd.,
will present a tasting of Rhine wines in the Old
Kitchens, Trinity College.

Tuesday 12th February
The Lent Term Dinner: details to be announced.

Thursday 21st February
Mr. Andrew Low, of Andrew Low Fine Wines Ltd.,
will present a tasting of select port in the Old
Combination Room, Trinity College.

Thursday 28th February
Mr. George T. D. Sandeman, of The House of
Sandeman, will present a tasting of Sherry in the
Old Combination Room, Trinity College.

Wednesday 5th March
Annual Varsity Blind-Tasting Match in Harveys'
Offices, Pall Mall.

Thursday 6th March
Mr. Bill Baker, of Avery & Co., will present a tasting
entitled "New World v. Europe: a comparison of
Grape Varieties", in the Old Kitchens, Trinity College.

Thursday 13th March
Mr. Russell Hone will present a tasting of Red
Burgundy in the Old Combination Room, Trinity
College.

All tastings begin at 6.00 p.m. sharp.

Members must be prompt

Charge for each guest: £1.50

An interview with
SIMON KVERNDAL QC

SIDNEY SUSSEX COLLEGE, CAMBRIDGE, m.1977

Simon Kverndal QC specializes in maritime litigation and arbitration with Quadrant Chambers in London.

'There was no Half-Blue for wine tasting. I always used to joke that we got a half-blotto instead.'

'I always knew I was going to love wine. My father offered me a present in 1971 for getting a scholarship to school, and I said, "I'll have a case of claret, please." I had a case of Gruaud-Larose 1970 instead of a record player – a much better gift.

'In 1977, Stephen Taylor (Trinity Hall) and I were both about to go up to Cambridge, and I met him through the English community in Paris. He was working at Les Caves de la Madeleine, Steven Spurrier's outfit, and when he arrived at university he went straight into the Cambridge University Wine and Food Society (CUWFS). At the end of my second year Stephen asked, "Will you look after blind tasting?" I'd been appointed captain, although I still had to earn my place to compete.

Sidney Sussex's cellar

'In my fourth year I was on my college wine committee, unusual for an undergraduate. Sidney Sussex couldn't possibly be said to be pinko, but it is quite liberal. It was in its second or third year of being co-ed, and had a junior member on every committee because it felt there should be a student voice. Being on your college wine committee was, and still is, a great perk for the dons. It's terribly hard work going to an excellent wine tasting and having a free lunch, as is the case.

'Sidney Sussex is a small, good, middle-of-the-road college, keen on everything, never wins at anything, but had good endowments relative to its size, and a fellowship that had laid down a good cellar beneath the dining room. From the undergraduates' list, my great favourite

was Château de Pez '71. We had '61 and '66 Beychevelle, and good 1970s from the fellows' list. You could get 1960 Port, but not '63. College consumption of wine was about 6,000 bottles a year, 2,000 bottles each: a third for undergraduates, a third for fellows (formal dinners and commemoration feasts came from the fellows' cellar) and a third for conferences. We had about 18,000 bottles in the cellar: a big turnover.

'We had to buy wines with quick throughput for undergraduates – Côtes du Roussillon would go fast. Students could go to the buttery and sign for a bottle, and wouldn't have to pay until the end-of-term bill. So it was better to go to the buttery than to the local off-licence. For the fellows' cellar, wine was for laying down, and for feasts good wine was important because alumni would be major benefactors. Summer conferences fell in between: good Bourgeois claret laid down for a few years, which the college would sell at a decent profit. Colleges were commercializing, with new buildings and extensions designed with the conference trade in mind. And the conference trade needed good wine.

'We never bought for the college for investment; it was always for consumption, with those three very different groups in mind. A rich college would've been looking to buy first- and second-growth clarets. We were buying second- and third-growth clarets, but not "super seconds", already appearing in those days. Classed growths wouldn't have been for undergraduates. My recommendations as a junior member were taken seriously, I'm happy to say, because I was doing so much wine tasting and I knew a lot about it.

Salad days

'Stephen Elliott was already a fellow at Trinity by 1980. We met weekly for blind-tasting practices in his rooms. We cast the net wide to college societies, and at least two of our number in the 1981 team weren't in the CUWFS. Stephen would introduce a focus, a grape variety and wines from Harveys' list. I confess that made it easy. Blind tasting is always difficult, but competition wines were only from Harveys' list. We had an advantage, but so did Oxford. It was a level playing field. If it tasted like claret, it probably was claret. We knew it wasn't going to be a South African Cabernet Sauvignon – that wasn't on the list.

'During the match in 1981, at half-time I came out into the street from Harveys' cellars on Pall Mall, because we needed air, and a couple of the Oxford chaps were

ABOVE Michael Roberts (left), the beloved catering manager at King's College, with Stephen Taylor, cellarer of the CUWFS, who asked Simon Kverndal to look after blind tasting in 1979.

Sidney Sussex College
Cambridge

September 1980

From the Steward

WINE LIST

Operative from 1st October 1980

(All prices quoted are VAT inclusive)

			£
Bordeaux	(red)	Ch. Bonnet	2.25
		Ch. Liversan 1975	2.50
		Ch. la Vieille Montagne 1975	2.60
		Ch. Lacussade 1975	2.25
		Ch. Raynier 1976	2.80
	(white)	Grand Chevalier	2.25
		Ch. Liot 1973	3.30
		Gaillac Perle	2.50
Burgundy	(red)	Beaujolais Villages 1978	3.00
		Beaujolais Producteurs 1978	2.75
		Cotes de Beaune Villages	3.10
	(white)	Cotes des Luberon 1978	2.10
		Cuvee de Montfort 1973	2.60
		Domaine de Lys 1977	3.25
		Vouvray 1976	2.40
Champagne		Mercier N.V.	5.50
Hock		Liebfraumilch 1978	2.10
		Oppenheimer Krottenbrumen 1978	2.10
		Niersteiner Gutes Domthal 1978	1.95
Loire		Bourguil Rouge 1970	2.65
		Bonnezeaux 1976	2.40
		Saumur 1978	2.75
		Ch. de la Glissoniere 1976	2.15
		Sauvignon 1977	2.60
		Coteaux-de-Layon	2.15
Madiera		Good Company Malmsey	2.75
		Dom Henrique Sercial	2.45
Moselle		Piesporter Michelsburg 1979	2.30
		Berncasteler Kurfurstlay 1975	2.65
		Trittenheimer Altarchen 1975	3.10
		Bereich Bernkastel 1977	2.50
		Zeller Schwarz Katz 1977	2.90
Port		Taylor late bottled 1974	3.30
		Graham	3.00

ABOVE Sidney Sussex College Wine List for 1980–81.

THE 1855 CLASSIFICATION AND 'SUPER SECONDS'

In the 1855 Bordeaux Classification, 62 different Bordeaux châteaux were classified, inspired by the Exposition Universelle de Paris of that same year, when Emperor Napoleon III requested a ranking system for France's best Bordeaux wines on display for visitors from around the world. It took into account a combination of factors, including selling price and quality of the wines, and the châteaux were ranked in five different categories, from first growths (*premiers crus*) to fifth growths. Efforts have been made to update the classification and especially to include Bordeaux's top Right Bank wines, but generally the list is still a fairly reliable indicator of price and quality. Château Mouton-Rothschild was promoted to first growth in 1973, after intensive lobbying by Baron Philippe de Rothschild, and is the most significant change that has been made to the list since 1855, other than changes of name and changes as a result of properties merging and disappearing.

The term 'super second' is a modern invention, and refers to highly praised second growth wines that are almost at, or equal to or even better than, the level of quality of first growths. There is no formal list, but the idea has been adopted by the Bordeaux trade as a way of recognizing the fact that these châteaux are performing way above their official ranking. They typically sell for more money than other second growths, but are not as expensive as first growths.

lighting up. I said, "How on earth can you light up and still go back and taste?" They said, "We wouldn't be able to do anything if we didn't have a cigarette at this moment; we'd be completely hopeless." And they beat us. Cambridge lost in both 1980 and '81.

'Denis Marrian wore glasses strung around his neck on a chain – the glasses were going on, then they'd slip off and down. He was a great man, intellectual, and donnish. I knew him through the CUWFS, and also the Real Tennis Club. Ken Moody was CUWFS and real tennis as well, and our link with King's, where Michael Roberts, the King's catering manager, was terribly important. He opened the superb King's cellar for us, a source of terrific wines from the days of Maynard Keynes in the 1930s. We'd say, "Come on, Michael: can't we have such and such?" – and get lovely wines at good prices. Michael was a vice-president of the CUWFS, and a good chap. He should've been running a wonderful hotel, but he loved being in charge of the food at King's, and all the good wine that went with it. We were fortunate. CUWFS met in the Old Library or the Old Kitchens in Trinity, or in the Saltmarsh or Beves rooms at King's. I well remember the Harveys '78 and '79 *en primeur* tastings

of claret. Then, even for semi-trade like the Oxbridge colleges, it was unusual for the châteaux to send over early bottlings. There was a superb Krug tasting for CUWFS, and Corney's produced Château Trotanoy for a luncheon wine. Michael Broadbent came and talked to us, as did Berry Brothers, among others. In my last year at Cambridge I typically went to five tastings a week! It's not surprising people thought I was going to go into the trade, but I had other things in mind.

Across the (Ox)bridge

'I met Oz Clarke at a wine tasting in Cambridge in about 1980. I bowled up to him because he was on his own wearing a Vincent's Club tie (Vincent's is the sporty club at Oxford). I said, "Good heavens, you're a brave fellow wearing that tie at a tasting here!" and he said, "Kind of you to say. You're the first person who has spoken to me, and to notice the tie. My name's Oz Clarke. I'm an actor performing here at the Arts Theatre, but I'm also a wine writer. I just started a column for the *Sunday Express*." Soon thereafter, Oz took the part of General Perón in *Evita*, a long-running successful production in the West End. Oz was an accomplished actor, particularly in

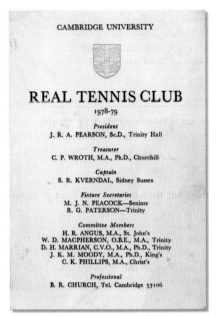

CAMBRIDGE UNIVERSITY

REAL TENNIS CLUB
1978-79

President
J. R. A. PEARSON, Sc.D., Trinity Hall

Treasurer
C. P. WROTH, M.A., Ph.D., Churchill

Captain
S. R. KVERNDAL, Sidney Sussex

Fixture Secretaries
M. J. N. PEACOCK—Seniors
R. G. PATERSON—Trinity

Committee Members
H. R. ANGUS, M.A., St. John's
W. D. MACPHERSON, O.B.E., M.A., Trinity
D. H. MARRIAN, C.V.O., M.A., Ph.D., Trinity
J. K. M. MOODY, M.A., Ph.D., King's
C. K. PHILLIPS, M.A., Christ's

Professional
B. R. CHURCH, Tel. Cambridge 57106

ABOVE Trinity College don Denis Marrian was a committee champion of both real tennis and wine tasting.

musicals, then the wine took over from the acting. I did introduce him to a new girlfriend while he was at the Arts Theatre acting in that run, but best not to say any more about that – ha, ha, ha!

Kind of blue plus greasy spoons

'I was in the Blues team for real tennis four years, and played rackets, college squash and lawn tennis. I sang in my college choral society, and acted in a few college plays. I was doing too many things to get a Half-Blue. I could never have got a Blue – I wasn't that good – but if I'd worked at it, I could've perhaps got a Half-Blue in lawn tennis in the doubles pairings. There was no Half-Blue for wine tasting. I always used to joke that we got a half-blotto instead!

'Everybody went to Greek greasy spoons, with awful Greek wine. Wine in those days in general was dreadful: Côtes du Roussillon was rough, and Yugoslav Laski Riesling still ruled – completely undrinkable, semisweet and foul. If you went to the college bar it was mostly beer, and that goes for the girls as well. Cambridge wasn't 50/50 by a long way: probably two-thirds men and a third women.

Setting the scene

'It was the end of the Cold War, and the American-Russian relationship was near its worst. There was a feeling that fingers were close to the button, and that Brezhnev was going to do the dirty on us. The Iranian Embassy crisis happened. There we were, living this wonderful student life, but we weren't ignorant of the outside world. Religion played a part: Billy Graham came to Cambridge and I went to see a huge debate on the myth of God incarnate. It was extraordinary.

The Conservatives won the 1979 election. Everyone was fed up with a weak Labour government, and I think the undergraduate population was very Tory-voting. I don't suppose they've voted majority for the Conservatives ever since. Even public school undergraduates tend to vote Labour and socialist at university. I suspect it was a highpoint of enthusiasm for Conservative politics.

'Good Lord! We were having a good time. *Chariots of Fire* came out in 1981. There is a scene in the film that is meant to take place in Trinity – the Trinity College Run – but it didn't because the college refused permission. An almost identical court at Eton was used instead, and at the start of the summer term, 1980, the word went round to all of us to be extras. Friends saying, "Come on, Simon, you must. It's a free haircut and a fiver." We didn't know it was going to be an Oscar-winning film. I had glandular fever and thought if I get an *aegrotat*, a sickness chit, for my exams, and am then seen appearing in a film I'll be hauled before the college authorities. But lots of friends were in that opening scene as extras.

'Tom Sharpe (a Pembroke alumnus) wrote a book called *Porterhouse Blue*, published in 1974. The boy gets a crush on his bedder, prepares to have a fling with her, then gets cold feet and can't get rid of the condoms. The chimney explodes. It's a terribly funny scene. Porterhouse, of course, read for a skit on Peterhouse. "Scout" in Oxford, "bedder" in Cambridge. I always thought that Oxford scouts were male; maybe I'm wrong in that, but Cambridge bedders were always female. Your bedder would knock on the door and wake you up in the morning, and clean out your room every day. We all had bedders.

Real tennis, real estate

'In the late 1970s there was a housing crisis, and none of the colleges had enough accommodation. Colleges were accepting more students to offer the Cambridge education to more people. They started buying up hostels on the outskirts of town, and a lot of students were in digs, as paying lodgers in a house. The old double rooms, bedroom and sitting room, if they weren't fellows' rooms, had been made into shared rooms for first-year undergraduates. In your second year, you were out of college – lucky to have a hostel, and if unlucky you would be in digs. After my first year, I didn't like the look of digs, so I bought a three-bedroom house five minutes' cycle ride from the centre of town for the princely sum of £11,500. If only I still had it! I helped relieve the housing crisis by taking two people from college. College was only too delighted.

Wine seller

'I started laying down wine at the age of 13 with the case of Gruaud-Larose '70: my first vintage. At

Cambridge I bought '78s, and when I was just down I bought the '82 clarets. I've been laying down wine consistently since, and have probably got a few thousand bottles. I told my father to sell his shirt to buy '82s, and persuaded him to spend £350 on a case of Château Lafite. We sold the last few bottles, net of commission, for £3,000 each. We bought them for £30 each. I would've got more if I hadn't nicked the labels by mistake. They were wrapped in tissue paper and as I put them in the racks, the paper on the labels caught slightly in the damp– almost imperceptible, but about £500, nicks.

'In town there was a funny restaurant above a bookshop where 1964 and '66 Léoville-Las Cases and '66 Pichon-Longueville Lalande were astonishingly cheap: something silly and ridiculous like £8 a bottle. Mind you, this was when the de Pez '71 was about £2.50 on the college list. Evelyn Waugh's words at the beginning of *Brideshead Revisited*, went something like this: 'At no other time and at no other place do a few hundred pounds one way or the other make so much difference to one's importance and popularity.' But it's not so much importance and popularity as the ability to go out and have an amazing time. And for a few hundred pounds, a thousand pounds, those who had just that bit more

had a fantastic life, and it didn't cost much. I bought white tie and tails from the Oxfam shop for £20, and my dinner jacket for £15; that's all it cost to dress up and look smart.

'I was a member of The University Pitt Club and the Hawks' Club. I wasn't a member of the Union, but had a girlfriend who was vice-president and got invited along all the time. I used to go Scottish dancing once a week to meet people – I won't say "pick up" people. I was sufficiently competent that I didn't tread on the girl's toes before I asked if she'd like to go out to dinner with me.

Tempted by the fruit
'I was tempted to go into the wine trade, but I didn't think I had a sufficiently good palate, and you had to be confident in your abilities as a trader. I would've loved that dilettante existence, but hard work as a wine merchant didn't attract me. After two years of history and two years of law, I went to Bar school and pupillage, an inevitable track from then onwards. I'm not on the Middle Temple wine committee, but I am on the Garrick Club wine committee, and on the wine committee for The Worshipful Company of Shipwrights. The livery company committee is hard work: six dinners a year for 250 people.

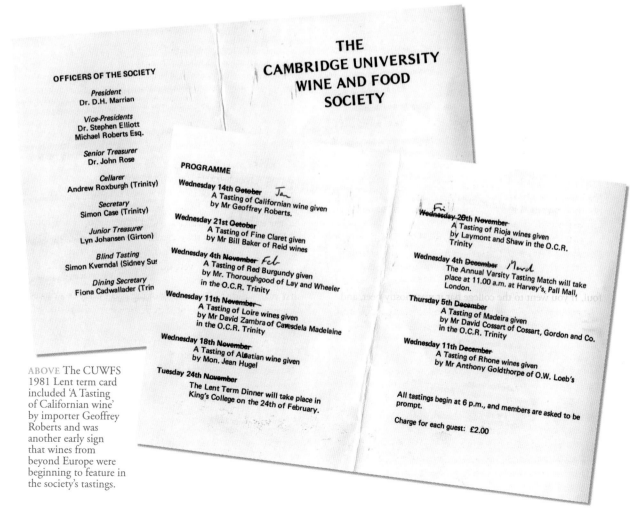

ABOVE The CUWFS 1981 Lent term card included 'A Tasting of Californian wine' by importer Geoffrey Roberts and was another early sign that wines from beyond Europe were beginning to feature in the society's tastings.

OFFICERS OF THE SOCIETY

President
Dr. D.H. Marrian

Vice-Presidents
Dr. Stephen Elliott
Michael Roberts Esq.

Senior Treasurer
Dr. John Rose

Cellarer
Andrew Roxburgh (Trinity)

Secretary
Simon Case (Trinity)

Junior Treasurer
Lyn Johansen (Girton)

Blind Tasting
Simon Kverndal (Sidney Sus

Dining Secretary
Fiona Cadwallader (Trin

THE CAMBRIDGE UNIVERSITY WINE AND FOOD SOCIETY

PROGRAMME

Wednesday 14th October *Jan*
A Tasting of Californian wine given by Mr Geoffrey Roberts.

Wednesday 21st October
A Tasting of Fine Claret given by Mr Bill Baker of Reid wines

Wednesday 4th November *Feb*
A Tasting of Red Burgundy given by Mr. Thoroughgood of Lay and Wheeler in the O.C.R. Trinity

Wednesday 11th November
A Tasting of Loire wines given by Mr David Zambra of Caves de la Madelaine in the O.C.R. Trinity

Wednesday 18th November
A Tasting of Alsatian wine given by Mon. Jean Hugel

Tuesday 24th November
The Lent Term Dinner will take place in King's College on the 24th of February.

Fri
Wednesday 26th November
A Tasting of Rioja wines given by Laymont and Shaw in the O.C.R. Trinity

Wednesday 4th December *March*
The Annual Varsity Tasting Match will take place at 11.00 a.m. at Harvey's, Pall Mall, London.

Thursday 5th December
A Tasting of Madeira given by Mr David Cossart of Cossart, Gordon and Co. in the O.C.R. Trinity

Wednesday 11th December
A Tasting of Rhone wines given by Mr Anthony Goldthorpe of O.W. Loeb's

All tastings begin at 6 p.m., and members are asked to be prompt.

Charge for each guest: £2.00

'The Garrick Club is great fun: 1,200 members, mainly actors and lawyers. Garrick himself was a great actor and the club has always had a slightly offbeat reputation. Why lawyers? We're always told we're failed actors! Actually, a large number of barristers have significant second strings to their bow in terms of artistic talents. There are fine musicians and writers at the Bar and good amateur dramatics put on in the Inns of Court. Several former varsity tasters are on the Garrick Club wine committee, including David Peppercorn MW. Hugh Johnson, Charles Taylor MW and Luke Hughes are members.

Memorable merchants

'I do have a recollection of Harry Waugh at Lords. You have to wear a tie at Lords, and I remember him wearing a cravat instead and getting away with it, saying, "Well, it's a tie!" Ted Hale was a terrific character who lost his right arm hanging out of a window in a taxi in Hong Kong. But it has to be said with great respect to Ted, who was a lovely man, that it was the age of the alcoholic wine merchant, and he was not averse. It put me off going into the trade.

'When I came down from university, Robert Joseph invited me to tastings for Charles Metcalfe's *Wine Magazine*, the precursor to the International Wine Challenge. They used to have ordinary Joes like myself, who knew a bit, come along: always quite fun. Wine has always been a massive enjoyment, hobby and pleasure.'

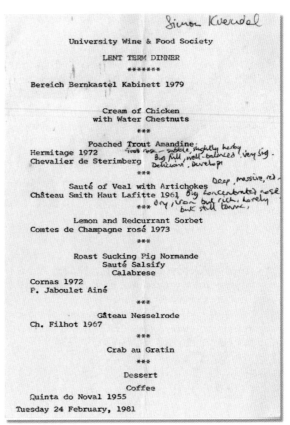

ABOVE The CUWFS Lent Term Dinner, February 1981.

ABOVE The losing 1981 Cambridge varsity blind wine-tasting team. Left to right: Simon Kverndal, A N Other, Charles Taylor, Nancy Thomson, Keith Isaac and David Eastwood.

KEITH ISAAC MW
Selwyn College, Cambridge, m.1978

Keith Isaac MW is general manager with Patriarche Wines in London.

'The year 1981 was not a great one for the Cambridge team; it holds the dubious distinction of having lost badly, and yet still produced two MWs: Nancy Gilchrist and myself. The Cambridge University Wine and Food Society (CUWFS) had widened the search that year for tasters outside its own membership, and a couple of us had been picked from our college societies (I was involved in the Selwyn Wine-Tasting Society). We won a warm-up match against Nottingham, but in sporting parlance lacked strength in depth as a team.

'Having been selected for the match against Oxford, I found I had a clash of dates. I had to apologize to my rowing partner in the University Pairs – the spare man from the Cambridge lightweight crew – that I had to go and drink for the university instead. As the Selwyn stern pair at the time (I was a somewhat fortunate Cambridge University Boat Club trial cap), we had fancied our chances in the absence of Blue boat crews.

'Of the match, I remember losing heavily and drinking heavily, and having an earnest discussion with an attractive young lady who worked at Harveys' Pall Mall offices, where the match was held, about the antique glass collection on display there.

'While we had practised with Rioja and white Rhône from Harveys' list, we were unprepared for the off-vintage Latour that had been outside of our budget. It was a fantastic day with a great lunch, and somehow we got back to Liverpool Street to catch the train.

'As for the MW, I was lucky enough to pass in 1989 and Nancy in '95. Even then the exam was open to candidates from around the world, and in the years since has become recognized universally, cementing its reputation as the pre-eminent international wine qualification. The exam can now be sat in international exam centres, and in different languages.

'When asked if the MW exam is more difficult now than in the early days, I would say only that it is different. The skills needed to answer a question comparing two Bordeaux vintages in considerable detail, as was on the exam in the 1950s, are similar to those needed to contrast techniques and practices in canopy management in different parts of the world today. It is the breadth of topic that differs more than the intellectual rigour.

'I was chair of the MW examination panel for several years. Several of the examiners and panel chairs with whom I've worked were also former members of either the Oxford or Cambridge blind-tasting teams. Long may the match continue to breed future Masters of Wine.'

NANCY (NÉE THOMSON) GILCHRIST MW
Girton College, Cambridge, m.1978

Nancy Gilchrist MW is a wine lecturer and educator with Leiths School of Food and Wine and Le Cordon Bleu, and leads Christie's Wine Education in London.

'Wine came to me early; by the age of 11 I was collecting wine labels, and with the aid of Hugh Johnson's new *World Atlas of Wine*, I was putting them in some sort of geographical order. Getting to Cambridge and discovering the Cambridge University Wine Society (CUWS) was pure joy, with weekly tastings given by luminaries such as Michael Broadbent MW and Claude Taittinger; there was also the quiet inspirational genius of Stephen Elliott, fellow of chemical physics at Trinity College, who arrived as maestro of the university wine-tasting team. Stephen would raid college cellars in the most masterly fashion, and the tastings he put together I still rate as some of the most informative of my career. From him I learned to differentiate, 'blind', the German wine regions, all the different Beaujolais *crus*, the communes of the Médoc, much of the Loire Valley and Madeira. Where else could you get such a grounding?

'In 1981, we did not win the varsity trophy – sorry, Stephen – but I do recall a splendid bit of chauvinism that simply would not happen today: a magnum of Champagne was given to the woman with the highest marks. As I was the only woman in the competition, I was absolutely delighted to receive it! Girton College went mixed only in autumn 1979; I was just in front of 'the wave'.

'The experience shaped my life, and helped to deflect me from my intended goal – to 'save Africa' – and led me in a direction which, instead, allowed me to live my passion. I passed the Master of Wine examination in 1995 (I was about woman No. 32, but no magnums of Champagne were handed out then, more's the pity) and have been working independently as a wine educator ever since. Recently, the wheel of life came a very happy full circle when, after their successful stint of 30 years, Michael Broadbent MW (at a youthful 86) and Steven Spurrier asked me to take over the baton at Christie's Wine Course.

'Wine, and the people I have met through it, have brought nothing but happiness to my life. It is a subject of ceaseless variety and education, delight and passion. It is the perfect excuse to travel and to meet generous, like-minded people. With it has come pleasure and lasting friendships. All I can say is, you may forsake the potential of an overweight bank account when you enter the wine trade, but the riches you gain in experience and opportunity far, far outweigh any monetary compensation.'

OXFORD AND CAMBRIDGE WINE TASTING COMPETITION 1981

A. WHITE WINES:

In front of you are six white wines numbered from 1 to 6. Please identify them as closely as possible using the form below. N.B. There is not necessarily an answer appropriate to each column in respect of every wine. Maximum marks ( ).

Wine No.	Country (1)	Main Viticultural Region (3)	Sub-district (4)	Village or Commune (2)	Predominant Grape Variety (3)	Vintage (3)	Judges use only
1.	Germany	Rhein	Rheingau	Oestricher	Riesling	1971	Oestricher Lenchen Riesling Auslese 1971
2.	France	Burgundy	Chablis or Yonne	or Chablis	Chardonnay (Pinot-Chardonnay)	1977	Chablis Premier Cru Fourchaume 1977
3.	France	Alsace or	Alsace	–	Riesling	1976	Riesling Cuvée Tradition 1976
4.	France	Bordeaux	Sauternes or Barsac	or Barsac	Semillon – Sauvignon	1975	Château Suau 1975
5.	France	Loire	Centre Region or Sancerre	Verdigny or Sancerre	Sauvignon	1979	Sancerre 1979
6.	Germany	Rhein	Rheinpfalz	Kallstadt	Müller-Thurgau	1978	Kallstadter Kobnert Müller-Thurgau 1978

OXFORD AND CAMBRIDGE WINE TASTING COMPETITION 1981

B. RED WINES:

In front of you are six red wines numbered from 7 to 12. Please identify them as closely as possible using the form below. N.B. There is not necessarily an answer appropriate to each column in respect of every wine. Maximum marks ( ).

Wine No.	Country (1)	Main Viticultural Region (3)	Sub-district (4)	Village, Commune or Appellation Controlée (2)	Predominant Grape Variety (3)	Vintage (3)	Judges use only
7.	France	Rhône	Northern Sector or Tain l'Hermitage	Hermitage	Syrah	1976	Hermitage 1976
8.	France	Bordeaux	Médoc	Pauillac	Cabernet-(Sauvignon)	1972	Château Latour 1972
9.	France	Bordeaux	Graves or	(Léognan) Graves	Cabernet-(Sauvignon)	1975	Château Haut Bergey 1975
10.	France	Burgundy	Beaujolais	Brouilly	Gamay	1979	Brouilly 1979
11.	France	Bordeaux	St. Emilion or	St. Emilion	Merlot	1978	Château Canon 1978
12.	France	Burgundy	Côte d'Or or Côte de Beaune	Pommard	Pinot (Noir)	1974	Pommard Clos de la Platière 1974

ABOVE The 1981 competition wine list: on tasting the 1978 Château Canon again recently at a Garrick Club dinner, Simon Kverndal remarked, 'I wish I had aged as well'.

An interview with
FIONA (NÉE ROBERTS) BARLOW MW

KEBLE COLLEGE, OXFORD, m.1981

Fiona Barlow MW is a retired buyer and sales director of the wine trade living in Yorkshire.

ABOVE LEFT Fiona (far right) with members of the Selwyn Wine-Tasting Society at a college garden party. ABOVE RIGHT Fiona on the day she passed the MW, five years after victory in the 1982 Oxford tasting team.

'I had no prior family history of wine apart from my grandmother, who took a nip of brandy for medicinal purposes only. I was an undergraduate at Selwyn College, Cambridge, from 1977 to 1980 where I gained a double-honours MA in French and Russian. In addition to rowing and the chapel choir, I was a staunch member and an officer of the wine-tasting society in Selwyn, having joined in freshers' week because one of the big second-year undergraduates said it was the cheapest way to get a drink on a Friday evening! The Selwyn College Wine Society nurtured my interest and subsequent passion in wine, which led to my eventual career in the wine trade.

'After a year out teaching English in Switzerland, I returned to Keble College, Oxford, to do a PGCE [certificate of education], which I found deadly and absolutely hated, particularly my term's teaching practice in a convent school. The only light at the end of the tunnel was joining the Oxford blind-tasting team in 1982, which gave me a weekly connection with like-minded people. Angela Mount (St Hugh's) and Roger Brock (Worcester) were also in the team. At that time the only wines we tasted were Old World classics, and Hugh Johnson was our main reference. There were other books, too: David Peppercorn's *Bordeaux* stands out as one.

'I never went into teaching and instead joined the wine trade, working for David Scatchard during the summer of the Toxteth riots in Liverpool, before moving on to Grants of St James's, where I spent nine years and during which time became an MW in 1987. I then spent another nine years at Forth Wines in Scotland, followed by a final nine years at Bottle Green in Leeds before retiring from commercial work.

'I have worked in Surrey, Scotland and Yorkshire and have travelled the world both as a buyer and sales director. I still do a lot of work for the Institute of Masters of Wine which I thoroughly enjoy.'

ABOVE LEFT Fiona Barlow MW (left) in Champagne while running the Grants of St James's School of Wine *c*.1988.
ABOVE RIGHT International Judge at the National Australian Wine Competition *c*.1990.

THE INSTITUTE OF MASTERS OF WINE

The Institute of Masters of Wine (IMW) owes its origin to the Wine and Spirit Association and the Vintners' Company, one of the 'Great Twelve' City of London livery companies, which received its first charter in 1363. Soon after World War II these two organizations recognized a need to improve the standard of education in the British wine trade and for a formal certification of its most talented members. They organized the Master of Wine (MW) examination, held for the first time in 1953, in the same year as the first Oxford and Cambridge varsity blind wine-tasting match. In 1955, the IMW was formed by the people who had passed the inaugural exam.

The IMW promotes professional excellence and knowledge of the art, science and business of wine. Membership of 312 MWs spans 24 countries. It is now an independent organization, although the Vintners' Company remains an important supporter, with Vintners' Hall the venue for the IMW Annual General Meeting, awards ceremony and a number of its tastings.

The first examination

In 1953, 21 candidates sat the first MW examination in London. It consisted of five theory and three practical papers. As a reflection of the times, perhaps, one practical paper was entirely devoted to the analysis of faulty wines. Dick Bowes MW (1966) recalled that as most people in the trade at the time started in the cellars, part of the exam was to identify tools of the trade: 'coopers' adzes, bung-tinners and spile hole borers'. Of the 21 original candidates, only six passed, illustrating the rigorous demands of the qualification from the start. It was always open to women but only in 1970 did the first female, Sarah Morphew Stephen, become an MW.

The examination is accepted as the hardest test of knowledge and ability in the world of wine, and currently consists of three parts – theory: four three-hour question papers on viticulture, winemaking, the business of wine and contemporary issues; practical: three 12-wine blind tastings, each lasting 2¼ hours, in which wines must be assessed for variety, origin, winemaking, quality and style; dissertation: a 10,000-word original study, relevant to the wine industry, with the topic selected by the candidate and approved by the institute. Only after successfully passing all three elements is someone eligible for membership of the IMW, with the right to the qualification, and title of Master of Wine.

In 2013, a record number 92 candidates from 24 countries took the MW exam in hopes of achieving the prestigious qualification. Students from China and India competed to become the first MWs in their respective countries. The total student body has grown in recent years to 280 from 36 countries – almost as many in the study programme worldwide as there are Masters of Wine.

KEY DATES

1953
Six candidates out of 21 pass the examination and become Masters of Wine.

1955
The IMW is formed in London.

1970
The first female MW, Sarah Morphew Stephen, is admitted to the membership of the institute.

1984
The IMW opens the examination to people working outside the wine trade (such as winemakers and journalists); Jancis Robinson OBE becomes the first non-trade MW.

1988
Michael Hill Smith AM from Australia becomes the first MW from outside of the UK.

1990
Joel Butler and Tim Hanni become the first MWs from the USA.

1992
The education programme and exam are delivered on three continents: Europe, Australasia, and North America.

2006
The IMW Endowment Fund is established to secure the institute's financial stability and promote its strategic goals. Funds are raised through cash donations from members and by an auction of wine and winery visits provided by MWs and supporters of the institute from around the world.

2008
Jeannie Cho Lee and Debra Meiburg from Hong Kong and Lisa Perrotti-Brown from Singapore, become the first MWs from Asia.

2010
More than 100 MWs are based outside the UK. Ned Goodwin becomes the first MW based in Japan.

2012
The members of the IMW elect its first American chairman, Jean-Michel Valette MW.

2013
The Master of Wine exam celebrates its 60th anniversary.

THE INSTITUTE OF MASTERS of WINE

The Institute of Masters of Wine

Master of Wine Examination 2013
(London, Sydney, Napa)

THEORY PAPER 1 - THE PRODUCTION OF WINE – PART 1
Section A
1. What are the most relevant pests and diseases today? Describe their effects and
2. Many factors can affect flowering and fruit set. Examine what effect these migh
Section B
3. Why, when and how do enzymes work in the winemaking process?
4. You are tasked with establishing new vineyard sites to produce Chardonnay in
in France. What would be your major concerns?
5. Critically assess the role of oxygen during vinification up to the completion of t
6. Define the effects *Botrytis Cinerea* can have on wine quality and explain the m
when both white and red grapes have extensive botrytis infection on entering the

THEORY PAPER 2 - THE PRODUCTION OF WINE – PART 2
Section A
1. What would be the main quality control considerations when considering a change from bottling at source to shipping in bulk and bottling elsewhere?
2. To what extent, following the malolactic conversion, can clarity and stability in wine be controlled? **Section B**
3. Write concise notes on FOUR of the following;
a) Hydrogen Sulphide
b) Volatile Acidity
c) Oak chips
d)Carboxy Methyl Cellulose
e) Isinglass
4. Consider the implications of reducing levels of sulphur dioxide in the post malolactic conversion handling and bulk storage of still wine.
5. "Blending can be an art or a science". What are the main considerations a winemaker must take into account when blending: a) A middle price point red wine AND b) A good quality non-vintage champagne.
6. Consider the advantages and disadvantages of non oak maturation vessels.

THEORY PAPER 3 - THE BUSINESS OF WINE
Section A
1. What matters more to consumers in today's wine market: brand, varietal or appellation?
2. How can the role of the intermediaries between producer and on and off-trade retailers be justified? How is it changing?
Section B
3. Assess the role and importance of generic bodies (such as Wine Australia and Wines of Portugal).
4. As a large corporation taking over a family wine business, should you keep the family values alive and, if so, how?
5. How have the recent fluctuations in grape harvest size changed the global supply and demand of wine? How do you see this affecting the wine market in the next 24 months?
6. As an export manager for a medium sized wine estate, what strategies would you employ in the USA, Europe and China?

THEORY PAPER 4 - CONTEMPORARY ISSUES
1. How important is climate change to the global wine market?
2. Is the global wine market too fragmented?
3. Is the golden age for fine wine investment over?
4. How important is it for countries and wine producing regions to have "signature wines"?
5. To what extent is wine consumption healthy? How much is too much?

VARSITY TASTING TEAM MWs

David Peppercorn MW 1962
Robin Don MW 1965
John Avery MW 1975
Mark Savage MW 1980
Jasper Morris MW 1985
Arabella Woodrow MW 1986
Fiona Barlow MW 1987
Charles Taylor MW 1987
Keith Isaac MW 1989
James Simpson MW 1992
Nancy Gilchrist MW 1995
Mark de Vere MW 1997
Tim Marson MW 2009
Alex Hunt MW 2010

OTHER MWs CONNECTED WITH THE VARSITY COMPETITION

Michael Broadbent MW 1960 *Judge*
Ted Hale MW 1960 *Harveys of Bristol*
Bill Gunn MW 1974 *Pol Roger*
Serena Sutcliffe MW 1976 *Judge*
Jancis Robinson MW 1984 *Judge*

INSTITUTE OF MASTERS OF WINE · 60th ANNIVERSARY · 1953·2013

ABOVE The varsity tasting match has been a hotbed for future MWs. LEFT AND BELOW Part of the 2013 MW examination.

2013 PRACTICAL PAPER THREE

There are three 12-wine blind tasting practical papers, each lasting 2¼ hours.

1 Prosecco Superiore 'Oro Puro', Valdo, NV, Valdobbiadene, Veneto, Italy
2 Lambrusco, Grasparossa di Castelvetro, Villa Cialdini, 2011, Emilia Romagna, Italy
3 Franciacorta Gran Cuvée Brut, Bellavista, 2007, Lombardy, Italy
4 Vat 1 Semillon, Tyrrell's, 2006, Hunter Valley, Australia
5 Château Villa Bel Air Blanc, 2010, Graves, Bordeaux, France
6 Castelnau de Suduiraut, 2007, Sauternes, France
7 Ürziger Würzgarten Riesling Kabinett, Dr Loosen, 2009, Mosel, Germany
8 Jurançon, Château Jolys, Cuvée Jean, 2010, Jurançon, South-West France
9 Tokaji 5 Puttonyos Aszu, Royal Tokaji, 2008, Tokaj, Hungary
10 Cuvée Beerenauslese, Alois Kracher, 2010, Burgenland, Austria
11 Vidal Ice Wine, Peller Estate, 2010, Niagara Peninsula, Canada
12 Chardonnay, Cuvée Sauvage, Franciscan, 2010, Carneros, California

An interview with
JAMES SIMPSON MW

PEMBROKE COLLEGE, CAMBRIDGE, m.1983

'In those days it was still quite glamorous for people to come up to Cambridge and do tastings.'

James Simpson MW is sales and marketing director for Pol Roger in the UK, and oversees the sponsorship of the Oxford and Cambridge varsity blind wine-tasting match.

'I competed in the competition in both 1985 and '86. Nick Fenner, Mike Gell and I all turned up at Pembroke on the same day and got on with each other. Mike thought wouldn't it be fun tasting wine? Mike's elder brother, Simon, had been at Corpus Christi with Charles Taylor, a former blind taster and now MW, and competed in 1984, with our captain Julian Payne (King's). Victoria Jones (Robinson), a fellow classicist, Christina Hippisley (Trinity) and Eddie Friend (Peterhouse), who became a vet up in Oxford, were also on the 1985 team.

'We set up the Pembroke College Wine Society, I suspect, in opposition to the Cambridge University Wine and Food Society (CUWFS) because they were a bit sniffy about us lot. Pembroke wasn't so grand in those days, and CUWFS was posh, but Victoria, who was better connected than I and a member of the CUWFS,

TOP AND ABOVE A mostly Pembroke posse: the 1985 (top) and 1986 Cambridge tasting teams.

dragged me along to occasional dinners. Victoria's father was Tim Jones, a money man for Ackroyd & Smithers, who had a tremendous cellar and knew everyone in the trade. So Victoria invited the great and the good of the wine trade – including David Rutherford – to come up. Once you'd started on some, it spread the net wide. In those days it was still quite glamorous for people to come up to Cambridge and do tastings.

'In 1986, we co-opted more Pembroke people for the team. Campbell Thompson was an Aussie postgraduate who played rugby on the wing, and Richard Keatinge played in the second row. Julian, Nick and Mike were still there and Victoria was reserve in 1986. Pembroke was one of the last of the "public school" type of colleges then. Still all-male, it went mixed only in my second or third year. Stephen Elliott was an absolute star, and coached us with weekly tastings in his fabulous rooms in Trinity. Presumably, I didn't make the grade my first year, but did in my second and third years. Stephen managed to snaffle some bloody good wines from the Trinity cellar, so we drank jolly well. We must have paid something, but it wasn't expensive – replacing the cost of the bottle, if that. I got into terrible trouble once for not turning up, because I was selected to play rugby for the Blues, and blind-tasting training was the same night. I don't think Stephen "got" sport, but one was a good antidote to the other.

A vinous introduction

'I read classics, and played college and university rugby. I might have got a proper Blue, but I did my knee in, in the second match of the last season – a dodgy match under lights at Bedford – and so I got a half-decent degree and competed in the blind-tasting match again.

'Cambridge was my introduction to wine. There were spirits on my grandfather's side of the family (which used to own the Banff Distillery), and the Mackay Brewery in Edinburgh on my grandmother's side. I was brought up in a prep school called Holmewood House, where my father taught, and my godfather, Headmaster Bob Bairamian, was a huge wine fan. I remember him getting frightfully excited about wines, but my parents weren't really that bothered. And so I got up to Cambridge and thought, "Wine: wouldn't that be fun?"

'During my time there, a number of us from the team would disappear off down to Victoria's parents' house in Sussex, the Old Rectory in Berwick – a stunning house on the foot of the Downs, with a stunning cellar. That's where I first drank the 1959 and '61 clarets, both classic years, and some great vintage Port.

A fair trade

'I got a 2:1 – eventually. Everyone was going off to be a merchant banker or management consultant, and it was a big year for advertising; Saatchi & Saatchi was recruiting a hundred people a year. I thought the wine trade looked more fun, despite the fact that everybody would come in to breakfast clutching envelopes, saying, "I've just been offered a huge opening salary."

'The mid-1980s was a prime era – there were lots of jobs and lots of money. Our tuition was paid for, we got a grant, and there were fiddles whereby if your parents gave you money you could claim the tax back. I came out of Cambridge with an overdraft of only £300 – extraordinary. I do remember going to the university careers office, and said, "I want to join the wine trade." They laughed at me and said, "No one's ever asked that before." So I walked out. They had no connections at all.

'My godfather, Bob, had been a cricketing mate of Edward Demery, who was then a very young managing director of Justerini & Brooks. Edward interviewed me one morning, and then happened to be having lunch the same day with Anthony Leschallas from Mentzendorff, the Bollinger agent. Mentzendorff was an old-fashioned agency house, and had a broad range: Bollinger, Fonseca, Faiveley and Delemain. This was the era when Bollinger was the great brand. Anthony and his predecessor had done a huge amount of work promoting 'Bolly' and getting it on the racecourses. Anthony was a slightly scary

old Etonian, but a very good operator. I was asked if I could start the following week.

'I'd left Cambridge without a job at all, and I joined Mentzendorff in September 1986. I haven't stopped since. Shortly thereafter, I was in the office at Mentzendorff and came across Chris Porter (of Porter & Laker, shipper to the wine trade) and Steve Rainbird (whose grandfather, George Rainbird, had been André Simon's publisher). They said, "Do you play rugby?" And I said, "Yes." They were setting up a wine-trade rugby side.

Cellar-bration

'I was playing rugby at Rosslyn Park and having fun matches on Sundays with the wine trade. We set up an annual fixture against the Scottish wine trade with games before the Calcutta Cup, and also had a splendid tour to Spain. We had to raise money, and I remember a huge fundraising event in the cellars at Harveys just before they closed it down. Harveys was still running the match, but the cellars were deserted. Mark Roberts, then at Harveys, was an exact contemporary of mine at Oxford, but not a blind-tasting competitor. He had access to the keys, and managed to blag the cellars. I don't think anybody at Harveys knew we were there. We had a bloody good party – hundreds of people getting paralytically drunk and raising lots for the tour to Spain.

MW

'The MW was the thing to do. I had managed to win a book prize on the Wine & Spirit Education Trust (WSET) higher certificate, and a travel prize in the

ABOVE The Wine Trade Rugby Side on tour to Spain in 1989: James Simpson (back row, third from right); Steve Rainbird, son of publisher George Rainbird, (back row, far right); Alex Waugh, son of tasting match judge and wine writer Auberon Waugh (front row, far right); and Nick Fenner, Cambridge blind taster and a Pembroke friend filling in (top row, fifth from left).

diploma exam, and to sneak my way through the MW, in the days when you could still do it in one year. Again, I had done my knee in playing rugby and was on crutches with nothing else to do. Having passed the MW in 1992, I then joined Pol Roger in 1993 (where I knew Bill Gunn marginally, through the MW, and Peter Winston through wine-trade rugby). Mentzendorff had started to change with the retirement of Anthony Leschallas and there seemed to be a number of "old farts" hanging around who weren't going anywhere. I thought "time to move on".

'Pol Roger UK was run by Bill Gunn and Frank Hart, who had both been with Dent & Reuss. Dent & Reuss had made an awful mess of the brand, and when Bulmers (which bought Dent & Reuss in the 1960s) decided to get out of wine, Bill and Frank had decided to go it alone. The varsity blind wine-tasting competition was the first sponsorship that Bill picked up, and being an ex blind-taster, I took it on fairly swiftly.

Bubbling over

'When I competed in 1985 and 1986, we tasted at the Oxford and Cambridge Club, then went across the road for lunch at Harveys, an old cellar with a proper glossy shop. In 1985 we tasted two sparkling wines (despite, as far as I remember, there being a rule that there should be no sparkling wines in the competition). The first was a Codorníu, a Cava, and the second, a 1976 Pirrot – a lesser Champagne from too hot a year. I'd never even heard of them. I was never top taster. And in 1985, I have a feeling I won the bottle for coming last. I remember trailing around London pissed after lunch, clutching this bottle. We apparently had lost by a point. Auberon Waugh was judge, and John Harvey was there hosting lunch. Harry Waugh had left Harveys by then, and reappeared with his wife, Prue, only when Bill Gunn took it on in 1992 and started inviting him.

Hell hath no fury

'When I joined Pol Roger, the match was still at the Oxford and Cambridge Club, but then there was the row about letting ladies in. So in 1994 the match was held at the Royal Automobile Club and from 1995 at the University Women's Club for a number of years. It was quite funny; there were all-male teams some years at the University Women's Club. The Oxford and Cambridge Club then let women in and so we went back.

Pol-itics

'In 1992, as Pol Roger was taking over the match from Harveys, while I was still with Mentzendorff/Bollinger, I was rung up by two difficult Cambridge competitors – Oliver

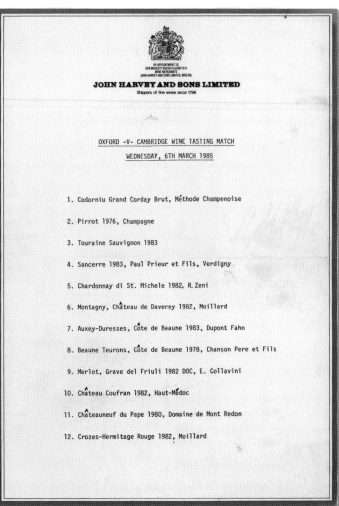

ABOVE The 1985 varsity competition wine list.

Howells and Andrew Barros – who asked, "Would Bollinger be interested in taking on the competition?" They knew I was Cambridge ex-blind tasting. I said, "No, it's a Pol Roger thing, and unless they give it up I wouldn't dream of it." I think Fells was contacted as well, and Tim Stanley-Clarke said the same thing.

'1993 was a nasty year for the match, and only at that time did Bill Gunn have a contract drawn up so they couldn't offer it out. I had said no, but thought, "Wouldn't it be fun to get involved again?" I got my chance when I joined Pol, and for 15 years spent time training the tasting team, and taking them on extended jollies. It was fun, and I was young. Hopefully we continue to give them a jolly time. Part of Bill's original sponsorship was a trip to Champagne for the winners. In the era of Jeremy Seysses [of Domaine Dujac], we extended to Burgundy. We went to the Loire Valley one year, and to the Rhône. I've become too busy to do the extended tours, and they now go to Épernay by train, but I remember driving this amazing Nissan Previa all around France.

'In our day, winners got the Harveys' trophy and a bottle. Harveys paid for first-class return travel, so we all travelled second class and pocketed the difference. It didn't really matter if you won or lost in those days. Early morning train from Cambridge, 10 o'clock start, taste, lunch, get pissed and wander drunken around London trying to find something else to do. I don't really remember chatting much to the Oxford tasters (although I do see Lisa Barnard now, who tasted for Oxford in 1986, as she started with Moët at the same time as I started with Bollinger). We'd been brought up with the university rugby thing, and you didn't really talk to the opposition.

Building a brand

'When I joined, Pol Roger was an under-the-radar brand. We were lucky to sell 9,000 cases a year, of which half was to the Savoy Group – Claridge's, The Connaught, The Berkeley and Simpson's – at a relatively low, if not sub-cost price. It was a struggle and tough in those days. The Savoy Group was a huge account for Pol Roger and great for the profile, but Pol wasn't making much money out of it. Hotels are challenging to sell Champagne to; they want to buy it cheaply, sell it expensively. But we're now selling two-and-a-half times what Bill was selling in those days: 25,000 dozen, at the right price to the right customers. That was Bill's big target when he started to move Pol Roger up level with Bollinger and Roederer as the three key Champagne brands.

'The generation who knew Churchill knew Pol Roger, but that generation was either dying or running out of money. What Bill saw in the varsity competition sponsorship was the chance to get the next generation drinking and talking about Pol Roger. On the back of that we've extended Oxbridge varsity sponsorship through to real tennis, rackets, fives, rugby and cricket – some of them rather esoteric sports. It's sensible and a perfect fit. Pol Roger, having been a bit dull, is now trendy and young – entirely because we're *all* trendy and young at Pol! We seem to be in the right place at the right time. We also work with the old-fashioned independent trade: direct with the livery companies, the clubs, the City of London, and under-the-radar organizations.

'Fongyee Walker and Edward Ragg, ex-Cambridge blind tasters, help in Beijing, and use Pol Roger in educational tastings. China's still a market everyone's talking about, but the volumes are tiny for Champagne. Pol Roger has doubled in Japan, though, since and entirely because of the Royal Wedding in 2011. There was a lot of discreet publicity. It gives authenticity, and you become a nice niche brand without splashing it all over with big headlines. Pol Roger is lucky to have enough supporters, even to the extent that it was served at Kate Moss' wedding. We continue to work with the varsity tastings and varsity sports (extending the tasting matches to Edinburgh and St Andrews, and now Bristol and Bath). If we can fix Pol in their minds at the age of 18, we've got brand loyalty for the next 40 years.

Clubs and committees

'The Wine Trade Sports Club governs all wine-trade sports. I ended up rugby captain and on the committee, and met Julian Bidwell at dinners and events. He said, "We want young chaps like you," and put me up for The Vintners' Company. The Vintners' had, as it were, rediscovered the wine trade when Christopher Berry Green took over as master. The two ways you became a vintner were through patrimony – e.g. your father was – or by redemption: a good chap, come in and be interviewed. They'd had a lot of patrimony, but sons of wine merchants were not necessarily wine merchants, but increasingly accountants and merchant bankers. The wine-trade proportion had decreased to ten or 15 per cent.

'I became a vintner in 2000, and the proportion of wine trade in the livery company is now up to around a third. I'm on the wine committee there, and I'm a trustee of the Wine & Spirit Education Trust. Vintners' helped set up the WSET, and it has three trustees on its governing body. Vintners' also helped set up the Institute of Masters of Wine; I was on the council of the Masters of Wine, and ran the education committee. It's all connected, and yet completely separate.

'The varsity teams today are far more international, from all over the world. We had an Australian in my time and that was fairly exotic, but now there are Asian and Scandinavian kids and far more women coming through. Today, they take it far more seriously, and are better tasters. The wines are so difficult and international now. Hugh Johnson and Jancis Robinson have been the A-team judges since Pol Roger took over.

'Champagne and Burgundy are my niches. The great thing about the wine trade is that you can become extremely expert in not very much. I'm a huge expert in Champagne, which is of no use to anyone else. I can stand up and waffle about Champagne forever if need be. But I also help to run the business, look after staff and try to make money. If I did it all again, I think I'd like to have been a barrister, but being a solicitor would be boring as hell. If lawyers are failed actors, wine merchants are failed everything else. I don't envy the people who went on to merchant banking or consultancy. Those who went into Saatchi and J Walter Thompson – all have now moved on to second-division jobs somewhere else. So the wine trade probably has worked for me.

'At home I've got quite a lot of fizz, a bit of Burgundy and claret, but I have been too busy collecting art to invest in wine. But I'm lucky: I drink jolly good wines on the back of the trade and have just been called up to the Saintsbury Club. I was too busy in Cambridge to worry about what was going on in the world, and I was always taught that you didn't discuss politics or religion with anyone – much easier. I think we were the fortunate generation that got jobs, bought cheapish houses and got away with it. My Cambridge career was wine tasting, rugby, and classics, and my wine-trade career has been wine tasting, rugby, golf and real tennis. The wine trade becomes a way of life rather than just a job.'

TRINITY COLLEGE WINE CELLARS

by PROFESSOR STEPHEN ELLIOTT

TRINITY COLLEGE, CAMBRIDGE, m.1971

Dr Stephen Elliott competed in the varsity match in 1975, '76 and '77. He is Chairman of the Trinity College Wine Committee and was the coach of the Cambridge team until 1991.

'I count myself lucky on at least two counts: I studied Physics at the Cavendish Laboratory in Cambridge in the 1970s when the Physics Nobel Laureate, Professor Sir Nevill Mott, would encourage and inspire students during informal seminars in the tea room; and, I studied wine tasting under the tutelage of Drs Sidney Smith, Kendal Dixon and Denis Marrian, who then looked after the fellows' wine cellars at the colleges of St Catharine's, King's and Trinity, respectively. They were generous and dedicated dons in exposing students to the contents of both their private cellars, and to treasures laid down in these great college cellars by their predecessors. It was from this foundation, I won prize bottles of Château Ducru-Beaucaillou '70 for their correct identification in the varsity match (I drank the last bottle only a couple of years ago), and then also went on to supervise the vinous education of undergraduates.

'Whether my motivation was the fascination with my PhD subject (on arsenic!) or the prospect of having continuing access to the college cellars, I shall never know, but in 1977, I became a fellow of Trinity.

'In popular mythology, the magnificence and sheer size of Oxbridge college wine cellars are unrivalled, perhaps matched only by those of the livery companies. Sadly – like most myths – the reality is rather different. The cellars of Trinity – being the richest and largest of all Oxbridge colleges – are often said to extend under the entire area of the famous Great Court (itself the largest in either Oxford or Cambridge). Not so – they used to be under a small part of the adjoining Whewell's Court (where Ludwig Wittgenstein held rooms in the top of the tower in the 1930s), and are now tucked away beneath a new, unromantic commercial development. The new cellar does, however, have the advantages of proper temperature and humidity control, and contains sufficient wine for the everyday vinous needs of a college with 190 fellows and some 1,000 students. Students are served wine at formal dinners from the buttery; fellows and their guests dining at high table are served with red and white table wines from the fellows' cellar.

'Rather grander wines are served to fellows and guests taking dessert in the Combination Room after formal hall dinner. The rules governing the service of wine in the Combination Room are suitably arcane: Port is always served, but an unfortified wine can be

LEFT Dr Stephen Elliott (left) with the Cambridge team, 1982. From left to right: Kevin Ng, Charles Taylor, Richard Phelps, David Eastwood, Edward Harley and Julian Payne.

served only if three or more persons vote for it at the outset; all wines circulate (clockwise) twice, unless there are any unfinished decanters of unfortified wines left after the second circulation, in which case they continue to circulate until exhausted; each person combining can take a glass of only one wine on any round, except if one happens to finish a decanter while filling a glass, in which case a 'buzz' is awarded, i.e. a fresh glass of wine (fortified or unfortified) can be poured from the new replacement decanter (in order to avoid cross-contamination), after signalling the emptying of the decanter to the presiding fellow who, in turn, notifies the manciple, by means of a hidden electrical buzzer, to bring a new decanter of wine (the *skill* is choosing where to sit around the table so that you get TWO buzzes – one on each round).

'Even grander wines are served to college alumni attending annual gatherings held during each summer, and to fellows and their guests attending several college feasts held during the academic year, the finest wines being reserved for the Fellowship Admission Dinner celebrating the arrival of new fellows at the college. On the evening of the day that I was elected to a research fellowship at Trinity in October 1977, the wines served at the feast were Henriques Sercial, Pouilly-Fumé Les Loges '75, Chateau Lynch-Bages '59, Quarts de Chaume '73 and Graham's Port '45. A decent introduction to life as a junior college fellow. But this list of wines serves to explode a different Oxbridge vinous myth, namely that college fellows drink only first-growth clarets or *grand cru* Burgundies (untrue), and vintage Port (partially true).

'I was first made a member of the Trinity Wine Committee in 1978, and the Minute Book record of my first committee meeting, on May 29 that year, indicates that we tasted, from stock, Château Lynch-Bages '61 ("slightly disappointing, but a first class example of a fifth growth"), Cockburn '67 ("should be drunk fairly soon") and Sandeman '55 ("still rather hard").

'The college had then, and still has to a certain extent, a "traditional" cellar of mainly old-world wines, in which vintage Port and claret predominate. Prior to the 1980s, the college used to order a pipe (60 cases) of each of the better Ports (usually Taylor, Fonseca, Graham and Dow) in every good vintage. Nowadays, the consumption of Port has waned, and it is no longer possible to buy such large quantities from a single merchant, so Port purchases are necessarily smaller. Equally, the college can no longer buy fine (e.g. "super-second") clarets – nor even Château Lynch-Bages – because of the very steep increases in the cost of top clarets in recent vintages. The same is unfortunately true of *premier cru* Burgundies and fine Rhône wines. Thus, college cellars have inevitably changed their focus in recent years. This makes it much harder to continue to educate students in the subtleties of mature fine wine from the Old World, in the way that I could do when, as a young fellow 40 years ago, I trained some of the Cambridge blind tasting teams.'

ABOVE From the Trinity College wine register, 1876.

A contribution by LISA BARNARD

ST ANNE'S COLLEGE, OXFORD, m.1982

Lisa Barnard is the chief executive officer of Illustrated London News Limited in London.

'Auberon Waugh was the chair of the judges, and he inscribed a copy of Michael Broadbent's *Guide to Wine-tasting* for me: "For the Highest Female Score – many condolences".'

'I went up to Oxford to read French and German, and was intrigued to find out what wine societies were on offer, as wine had been a prominent feature at home. My father is an enthusiastic taster and wine collector, mostly of Bordeaux, and family gatherings involved lively debates about accompanying wines, often tasted blind first and unveiled after everyone had had a guess. My parents, both scientists, were members of the wine society at Imperial College, London, where my father ran the Department of Biochemistry. Tasting dinners were occasionally held at our house, led by eminent speakers such as Michael Broadbent MW and Clive Coates MW. As teenagers, my three siblings and I were co-opted to help; I learned to pour 15 tasting measures from one bottle (and leave a small amount for myself!).

'On arrival at Oxford, I kept my palate close to the ground. The Wine and Cheese Society was deemed social, and rather inebriate (where the next day attendees could not even recall if wines they'd drunk were red or white). Far more serious was the Oxford University Wine Circle (OUWC); it attracted great speakers and wine merchants, and had an inner circle of talented tasters who took part in the varsity match.

'You had to be invited to OUWC tastings by a member, so when a college friend, Andrew Nugee, learned of my interest and invited me as his guest, I accepted with alacrity. Wine Circle tastings were formal sit-down events, jacket and tie de rigueur for the chaps, and the ladies nearly all guests rather than members. We were tutored by the great and good of the wine trade, enjoying vertical tastings of wine estates, with concentrated palates, intense discussion and spittoons that were actually used. After attending a few times, I was proposed as a member.

'After a year in France as part of my course, I returned to Oxford for my fourth year and attended an OUWC tasting. One of my tasting companions, now a postgraduate, was on the committee, and informed me that there was a space on the team: would I like to take part in the competition against Cambridge in the spring term? Sure that participants were entitled to a Quarter-Blue (along with tiddlywinks and ballroom dancing), I accepted.

'Training sessions were rigorous. Competition wines would be listed in the John Harvey & Sons

ABOVE Lisa Barnard at Oxford, 1984.

portfolio, but there were hundreds of these from all over the world. Duncan Stewart, a don at Lady Margaret Hall (LMH), sometimes tutored; he could be impatient and had high expectations, and his nickname was Drunken Stewart; this was unfair though memorable (his daughter, Olivia, later became a friend and was amused by this). He generously held an elaborate "dress rehearsal" blind tasting of 40 wines from his cellar in a dining room at LMH – it was reassuring for the team to see how much we had improved at identifying grape varieties, regions, subregions and even individual growers or estates.

'On the day of the competition we travelled to London to Harveys' offices in Pall Mall. On arrival, we learned that the tasting was to be filmed for the BBC – wine celebrities in the making! We applied ourselves in earnest. When I came to the last white, I lingered over the most delicious dessert wine I had ever tasted. I knew exactly what it was: Château d'Yquem '67, and pure nectar. It was the only wine I got 100 per cent on the nail, even though I'd never tasted it before. When I watched the programme later, the main part in which I featured was drinking the Yquem – clearly sipping, not spitting. Sadly, in 1986, Oxford came second (others might say we lost). I was awarded the prize for Highest Female Score – admittedly, there was only one other female, a reserve taster for Cambridge. Auberon Waugh was the chair of the judges, and he inscribed a copy of Michael Broadbent's *Guide to Wine-tasting* for me: "For the Highest Female Score – many condolences." We were treated to an extremely jolly lunch hosted by Harveys with the Cambridge team, and it was there I met an opposite number who was later to become a wine trade colleague and friend: James Simpson, now MW, of Pol Roger.

'The return to Oxford after the match was memorable. Fuelled by our excellent lunch and copious coupes of Champagne and other wines, we boarded the train at Paddington and sat in the first-class compartment. When the inspector arrived and scrutinized our tickets, however, we lowered our boisterous voices and retired to standard – apart from one member of the team who insisted he was a first-class person and refused to budge. He was escorted from the train and duly arrested at Reading by the British Transport Police.

After Oxford

'Participating in the competition undoubtedly had an influence on my future career. During the Easter holidays, before finals, I picked up a book at home: *The Anatomy of the Wine Trade* by Simon Loftus. I was intrigued by a chapter about an Englishman, Steven Spurrier, who had set up a mini-wine empire in Paris: a wine shop, wine bar/restaurant, and a tasting school, the Académie du Vin, where he had the temerity as an Englishman to teach the French about wine. Steven was a brilliant and talented wine

taster, and a champion of French country wines. He had controversially staged the "Judgment of Paris" tasting of 1976, when a Chardonnay and Cabernet Sauvignon from California were ranked above a top Burgundy and Bordeaux. It occurred to me what fun it would be to work in a wine shop in Paris for the summer, before pursuing a "proper career". I looked Steven up in the telephone book and asked him if he had any summer jobs going. I told him about my passion for wine and at the end he said, "I can't take you on in the shop because you're a girl and you'd have to carry heavy wine cases, but I could take you on for a year at the Académie du Vin as a *stagiaire*. You won't be paid much, but you will meet everyone who is anyone in wine in France and taste a lot of interesting wines." He had offered me a job for a year without meeting me and I accepted on the spot.

'I turned up in Paris in August 1986. My job was quite menial – setting up the wine courses, and washing glasses afterwards – but I attended every course, met illustrious châteaux owners and growers and regularly tasted samples with Steven. The Académie du Vin was in a quaint little courtyard just off the Place de la Madeleine – very much *vieux* Paris. I was paid the minimum wage, and after a while I supplemented it by launching a little business called Jeunesse Dorée, organizing the wine side of parties, bringing in "wine waiters" who were all Oxbridge graduates (essentially Brideshead with bottles). My first commission was the St George's Society annual bash, the ex-pat summer party at the British Embassy, when I agreed to do the catering for 500 people for 500 francs. I look back with a frisson at what I took on.

'On my return to London I carried on working in the wine trade, with Moët-Hennessy on the PR side, which is when I ran into James Simpson again, who had also started in the Champagne trade. Much later, I became publisher of *Harpers Wine & Spirit Magazine*, the wine-trade weekly, and applied for the MW course. James agreed to be my sponsor.

'While at *Harpers*, I came full circle when James asked me to be a judge in the competition, which Pol Roger had taken over. I was impressed by how the standards had not just been maintained but were heightened. The students were unbelievably experienced and accurate, and the majority planned to pursue a wine trade career. They were articulate, intelligent and charming individuals.'

ABOVE Judging the tasting match with Hugh Johnson in 1998.

An interview with
VANESSA (née kverndal) ROEBUCK

HOMERTON COLLEGE, CAMBRIDGE, m.1984

Vanessa Roebuck lives in Falmouth and is owner, editor and journalist for the What's On *guide for families in Cornwall.*

'I was reserve in 1987, but on the day I scored higher than everyone else (a Pyrrhic victory, as we lost!), including Oz, and he was furious!'

'I read fine art, history of art and education at Homerton. Through recommendation by family and friends, I was a member of the Cambridge University Wine and Food Society (CUWFS), and also the Cambridge University Wine Society. My older brother, Simon, blind tasted for Cambridge in the early 1980s and my sister blind tasted for Nottingham.

'CUWFS met weekly in the senior combination room at Trinity. It was rather on the Sloaney side, and by the end of the tasting there was always a certain amount of giggling at the back. James Simpson perfected a cold stare that Paddington [the Cambridge mascot] would have been proud of! However, the tastings were brilliant. I still have some tasting notes, and most of them end with the word "Yum". I ran the dining side of the CUWFS for a couple of years, alongside Ben Gladstone (Trinity), who ran the wine side. Midsummer House was a favourite restaurant and I organized dinners in a private dining-room in King's: oak-panelled and bedecked with oil paintings, it made wine merchants feel they hadn't wasted precious jewels on drunken students!

'At Cambridge, in addition to wine tasting, I did drama and choirs, and was real tennis ladies' team captain. I watched Jeffrey Archer get pelted with eggs at Trinity. AIDS had just been discovered, so you had to make sure you were sober enough to run away if necessary! I do remember one wine merchant inviting me to the Loire as his "niece" (I politely declined), and then chasing me round the Tudor dining table in King's – to the amusement of the rest of the diners. People were still reading *The Prophet* and *Jonathan Livingston Seagull*. I also recall being serenaded on a sitar by a friend who now lectures with Bill Clinton on how to save the world.

'Memorable merchants and producers included Louis Latour, Rémi Krug (who stank of Gauloises), Nick Clarke from Hugel, Pol Roger, Yapp Bros, Hennessy, Rothschild, Simon Loftus from Adnams, Tyrrell's, Cloudy Bay and Christiano van Zeller from Quinta do Noval. Without their generosity, I would never have been able to compete. Writers I read then included Émile Peynaud (*The Taste of Wine*), Jancis Robinson and Michael Broadbent.

'Dr Stephen Elliott was a rather serious man with a biblical beard and a delightful rare smile. The Rev James Owen was wonderfully witty, made a perfect Chartreuse and Champagne cocktail and spoke excellent "Burmese" to his cats. At one point, King's cellars flooded, and my brother and James Owen had picked up a load of bottles without labels – only the corks, when opened, gave a clue – real blind tasting!

'I think I made the team because I was spotted as being serious at the university tasting societies. Having asked intelligent and knowledgeable questions, I was invited to attend a few squad tastings and Stephen recommended me. Stephen was incredibly generous, and bought loads of unusual wines for us to try and remember. My preference was, and is, for the superb, subtle and beautifully balanced wines of the Old World, in particular, Alsace – the Hugel family was wonderfully generous. I concentrated hard on how to remember the structure and personality of each wine – rather like a skeleton with veins, muscles and skin. Observe, think. Nose, think. Nose again, check thoughts. Taste, spit, inhale over palate – think. Taste, spit, think again. If in doubt, nose again, depending on how many wines to be tasted.

'Oz Clarke was a judge. I was reserve in 1987, but on the day I scored higher than everyone else (a Pyrrhic victory, as we lost!), including Oz, and he was furious! In 1986 I had been a keen hanger-on. The match was at the Oxford and Cambridge Club. Celebrating afterwards, the team drank from a huge silver bowl. I have a lasting memory of dancing along the middle of Pall Mall after our win, high as a kite on the adrenaline of it all.

'I trained as a teacher with a view to writing and illustrating children's books, but was inspired by wine tasting at university to get a Wine & Spirit Education Trust diploma and go into the wine trade for 14 years. I've been to lots of vineyards, trodden grapes and visited endless bottling lines, and I was pleased to be able to "give back" when I was in the trade and organized Trimbach and Sempé Armagnac tastings for the Cambridge societies.'

An interview with
ROBIN SCOTT-MARTIN

JOHN HARVEY & SONS OF BRISTOL
1969–73; 1983–93

Robin Scott-Martin, formerly of Harveys of Bristol, ran the varsity match in the 1980s. Retired from the wine trade, he has a business selling Chinese furniture in London.

ABOVE Robin Scott-Martin and Michael Broadbent in 1986.

'If I have one small claim to fame, it was moving the tasting match from the Harveys cellars ... back to the Oxford and Cambridge Club in the mid-1980s.'

' I joined Harveys in 1969 and worked there to '73, then joined again in '83. When I first joined I was involved with the match as a pair of hands, with Ted Hale MW who ran the competition before me; it was held in Harveys' cellars at 27 Pall Mall, opposite The Travellers Club, with offices on St James's Square. When I rejoined in '83 they invested in the business and spent money developing a shop and dining rooms downstairs, for use by Allied Lyons before it became Allied Domecq in the early '90s. If I have one small claim to fame, it was moving the tasting match from the Harveys cellars, which became too small to do it effectively with a lot of guests, back to the Oxford and Cambridge Club in the mid-1980s.

'The match was a wonderful promotional opportunity for Harveys, but was made less serious by the fact that wines came only from Harveys' list; if you tasted Gewurztraminer, you knew it was a Hugel Alsace. Teams played for the Harry Waugh Cup, and I went up to the universities once a year to do a mock blind tasting. In each team there were probably two or three good palates; the rest were bright students who memorized the list. Bernard Falk made a BBC film about the match in the mid-1980s. I was nervous about it, as Falk was renowned for being left-wing, but he ended up reasonably sympathetic.

'My father had wanted me to go into the army, but the army and I didn't agree. So I made the most of a tenuous family connection and did a three-year apprenticeship with a wine shipper in Canterbury. But London was Mecca – and an optimistic city in those days – and I moved to Harveys. Harry Waugh had retired, but was still involved, and I sold wine to Harry; he had started his tours to the US. Michael Broadbent had left Harveys and moved to Christie's. John Harvey was on the export side. The wine trade was considered a profession, with hierarchy and apprenticeship. Arabella Woodrow had a doctorate in biochemistry from Oxford, but still joined to do the most menial things; it was all part of the mystique. It was a respectable thing to do. I started off sweeping cellar floors, but tasting as well. I had a fantastic time in the wine trade.

Bogus Burgundy
'The business I worked for in Canterbury, long since gone, had a bonded bottling facility in Ramsgate, and would buy in barrels of Burgundy, and labels. It was all the same wine, but they'd stick the different labels on and charge different prices. Algerian wine was added to give it backbone. The few domaine Burgundy wines we shipped then were expensive, and the rest were light and rather nasty, and didn't express Pinot Noir at all. Harveys did also have its own labels, but they were insignificant wines. Harveys certainly bottled Bristol Cream in 1952 for the Queen's coronation the following year. I used to have one bottle, but I drank it.

Fine wine merchants
'The wine-merchant division organized the blind-tasting contest. In Harry Waugh and Michael Broadbent's days, we were fine-wine merchants, but in my day we were not as good as others like Corney & Barrow, Justerini & Brooks or Berry Bros. & Rudd. Wine became a subsidiary of the brand division once Harveys Bristol Cream became highly successful. Showerings, the Babycham people, had bought Harveys in the 1960s, and injected a lot of money, enabling the company to develop Bristol Cream

as a brand. The company had also acquired Cockburn's Port, based at the back of the offices in St James's Square.

'It was an office for selling to the London clubs, directors' dining rooms, the livery companies and some moneyed private individuals. We weren't geared to do restaurant business, as we didn't have the sales force. It was only one guy, an incredible chap: Major Dick Findlay-Shirras of the Gordon Highlanders. He was one of the directors with George McWatters, his cousin. It was a family business and there was rampant nepotism.

'If people drank wine at all then, it was Blue Nun and Mateus Rosé. The wine trade was largely to blame for that, and had perpetuated the cloistered mystique of the St James's-centred pinstripe suit: that you needed money for the privilege of drinking fine wine. Sainsbury's had the first licences to sell alcohol in about 1968, and it was only when the supermarkets started selling wine, demystifying it and making it accessible, that it became wine for all. This was the subject of my MW thesis, which I failed 40-odd years ago.

'When I left Harveys in 1973 I joined Cockburn & Campbell, wine merchants of London and Edinburgh since 1796, recently bought by Young's Brewery. The fine-wine market had just crashed, and cellars were almost bare. You could buy 1961 first growths at less than £100 a case, but less than ten years later, by 1980, they had risen meteorically to £1,500–£2,000 a case.

'Back at Harveys in 1983, I had limited funds from Robin Frost's budget in PR. We couldn't spend money developing, getting more people involved, with bigger lunches; Harveys was declining. The accountants got hold of the company, and we lost sponsorship of the varsity match in 1992, towards the end of my reign. It was goodbye Harveys. Paul White, an American competitor at Oxford, was upset that it didn't have a high profile, and

wrote to Pol Roger. I don't blame them. It was sad. I left Harveys in 1993.

'In the early 1990s, when Allied Lyons was merging with Pedro Domecq, the accountants were seriously looking at maximizing the profit of Harveys. The wine division existed only to maintain the royal warrant, which we had as wine merchants and not as Sherry shippers. We may have made a small profit, probably cost-neutral, but if we stopped selling wine to the royal household and government hospitality we might lose the royal warrant.

'The writing was on the wall. We were reducing in size. When I rejoined in 1983, I was sales and marketing manager and John Harvey ran the wine-merchant division. Then he went back to the export side and James John MW took over. James John was made redundant and there was an interim guy who looked after the restaurant. It was all very odd. John Harvey came back and we were all summoned to the cellars and made redundant [this was in 1993]. Fortunately they were extremely generous, and I got a load of money to go and join Averys, which was fine by me.

Jumping ship

'For Averys, I also put on tastings for the senior common and combination rooms (SCRs). John Avery was cheeky, though. He'd say, "Yes, I'll come and help you, Robin." I'd organize a tasting for 20 SCRs, with 40 tasters, in a buttery in Oxford or Cambridge, and John never turned up. John Avery was a pioneer as far as New World wines are concerned, and his father, Ronald, was a legend of the trade. The majority shareholding was owned by an American. Eventually, Averys was bought by Laithwaite's because it had some key agencies – for Klein Constantia, Sonoma-Cutrer, Tyrrell's, Nobilo and others. The trouble

'*If that is Bristol Milk, then this must be the cream.*'

when you've got an agency is that you've got to market the good vintages with the bad, whereas if you are a merchant like Corney & Barrow or Berry Bros. & Rudd, you can just buy the good vintage wines. It may have changed now, though, with arrangements for annual purchase volumes with certain producers.

'At Cambridge, I used to stay with Denis and Biddy Marrian, lovely couple, and I know Stephen Elliott. Recruitment to the company was never my objective; it was PR. The competition underpinned the SCR business, and kept Harveys' name in with fellows and dons. They were the great claret and vintage Port buyers; significant, as we had Cockburn's on our list.

'When I first joined Harveys, the 1967 vintage Port was hailed by Wyndham Fletcher, MD of Cockburn's, as one of the finest. Maybe wishful thinking that 1967 was going to be so wonderful, but we sold a huge amount of it, in pipes. It was not yet the golden age for Bordeaux, from 1982 on, and *en primeur* wasn't happening yet, but we were doing sort of *en primeur*, selling the wine before it was bottled.

Master regret

'We all aimed for the MW. I used to go to Grants of St James's, where all the young students of wine would be tutored by existing MWs. Before Grants of St James's, Harveys was seen as the training ground for the trade because it had Harry Waugh, a great mentor for young people. Later there was Wyndham Fletcher at Cockburn's, and lots of notable early MWs: Michael Broadbent, Robin Don and Ronnie Hicks. They felt they had to raise the next generation – very much the wine trade's attitude then, but not in the 1980s.

'Ted Hale MW was good, but unfortunately lost his driving licence, and when I rejoined Harveys in 1983 I took over his job. So he left under a bit of a cloud. He wasn't an alcoholic, but he wasn't particularly sensible with drinking and driving. But then most of us weren't in those days. I eventually took the diploma in 1973, but the standard of the diploma now is the same as the standard of the MW in those days. There was no dissertation for the MW at that time, and it was dead easy to pass if you applied yourself, which I never did. I kick myself.

Master of the match

'The varsity teams came up to London in the morning, suited, with ties – it was mainly male. I'd give a briefing with Mark Roberts from Oxford, who worked for me then, and we'd try to get a figure to present the prize to make it more memorable: David Peppercorn MW was the man on Bordeaux, and Hugh Johnson had a shop in Pall Mall selling glassware then. Michael Broadbent MW was with Christie's, and Serena Sutcliffe MW with Sotheby's. Auberon Waugh was a distant cousin of Harry Waugh, and a well-known wine journalist. Cyril Ray, a well-known wine writer, was around, too, but in decline; Jancis Robinson MW, I suppose, was starting.

'Auberon would sit and have a glass of white wine while we did the marking, then we'd put the cup in his hand to present it, and have lunch. Serena Sutcliffe came in 1990, and was extremely, quite rightly, most rude about the wines, a bit acerbic. Wines were predominantly French – a wine from Alsace would be rather dramatic. I don't think I ever included Champagne. We'd have lunch at the Oxford and Cambridge Club, and then the students would disappear absolutely out of their skulls, clutching this valuable silver trophy, which we got

engraved the moment the winner was known. The Harry Waugh Cup was rushed up to Mappin & Webb and the winner inscribed. There wasn't a prize – maybe wines from the day; it was just for the glory of the cup.

'I was only at Averys for a year. One of my customers was part of a group that had three big 200-seater American diner-style restaurants. The two main shareholders were David Linley and Patrick Lichfield. They asked me to set up their wine merchant arm, and I spent three incredible years with them in London. The MD was a guy called Eddie Lim. He'd come into my office in the morning, when he got up, about 10 or 11am, because he lived in the flat above the office, and say, "Right, Robin, where are we going for lunch? There's a new restaurant. We've got to see what they're doing. I've heard their sushi is particularly good." I spent five days a week lunching with Eddie Lim, when I had to produce a new wine list. The company sadly folded. I retired from the wine trade then. I thought, "I'm not going to do this any more; what was the point of all that?"

'As an old wine-drinker, there has never been a better time to drink wine. I'm still a Francophile, not so much Bordeaux now, but the South of France produces stunning wines. In my declining years, I'd like to do something with Sherry. I think it is the most underrated wine, an acquired taste.'

OXFORD VERSUS CAMBRIDGE – 2nd March 1988.

WHITE WINES.

1. Chablis Mont de Milieu 1985, Regnard.
2. Savennieres 1985 – Clos de Coulaine.
3. Chardonnay 1986, Orlando.
4. Vouvray 1986, Chateau de Valmer.
5. Geisenheimer Klauserweg Riesling Auslese 1976, Rosankenberg.
6. Gewurztraminer 1985, Hugel.

RED WINES.

7. Chateau Lanessan 1979, Haut-Medoc.
8. Sancerre 1985, Paul Prieur.
9. Chateau de Fleurie 1986, Loron.
10. Beaune-Boucherottes 1980, Jadot.
11. Morgon 1985, Brisson.
12. Cabernet Sauvignon 1980, Inglenook.

ABOVE Near the end of an era, the 1988 Harveys competition wines.

181

A conversation with
PAUL WHITE

HERTFORD COLLEGE, OXFORD, m.1986

Dr Paul White is a wine writer.

PAUL DAY

WADHAM COLLEGE, OXFORD, m.1988

Dr Paul Day works in finance in the City of London.

White: 'I was at Hertford College doing a PhD in music, and captain of the team (1990, '91 and '92) through the two final years of Harveys, before the transition. There had been a corporate takeover. Harveys had been taken over for the Sherry, and they were in the process of throwing away the old wine merchants. In 1987 we were a handful of people – barely enough for a team. Greg Bennett was on the team from 1988, when Peter Martin (Magdalen), studying medicine, was captain. Michelle Chen (St Hilda's), from Singapore, was the first Asian woman to compete, in 1987, '88 and '89. She had trained before Oxford with a friend who changed the wine and food culture at Singapore Air which put the airline on the map.

'The Harveys list had remains of tired older vintages they weren't selling through. The company was making the transition to a new kind of client base. It was limiting the essence of the competition, because you could guess, and the quality of the wines wasn't representing *terroirs* as it should've been. Harveys couldn't carry on the stewardship of the competition; the company was shrinking and you could see what was coming.

'It was the start of the early 1990s recession, and I sought advice from Jasper Morris MW and Mark Savage MW, old hands who had been in the team, and merchants about the change of sponsorship. I said, "We've got a problem." We were worried they could go belly-up, and there wouldn't be sponsorship at all. Robin Scott-Martin at Harveys was running the match. He was a nice man and we had a lot of sympathy with Harveys. It was a grand old name, but the company was falling on difficult times.

'I was looking at a tradition that had gone on since the 1950s, an institution I thought had to survive. I went to Jonathan Black, the captain at Cambridge, with the idea that we should have a neutral kind of agency on the periphery, like a Port or a Champagne house – a prestige brand. I talked to Graham's or Taylor's. I wanted companies that had been around not just 50 but hundreds of years, that would think about carrying it on for another hundred years.

'It was expensive to practise blind wine tasting. I had to find a way to make it financially viable for everybody,

'We had a lot of sympathy with Harveys. It was a grand old name, but the company was falling on difficult times.'
Paul White

and to expand to get as many good participants as I could. I wanted 30 people trying to be blind tasters so that we had the very best people for the team. I'd read papers that said that women are better wine tasters than men and I also wanted to shift the gender dynamic to 50/50. And I found it was a different dynamic: men were more fact and details – fantastic for base knowledge; women were more in touch with their senses, for smelling, tasting and description. If I could bring the two together, the team would be much better. We were undefeated from 1987 to 1993 but for one year: 1988. The first time I competed, the celebrity judge was Alexis Lichine, who died shortly afterwards in 1989. I won top score, and got a case of his wine: 1981 Château Prieuré-Lichine. The following year I also won top score and received a half-case of Les Forts de Latour 1983 from Harveys. Hugh Johnson was judge in 1989 and Serena Sutcliffe in 1990. Our team would judge at the International Wine Challenge (IWC) every summer to enhance our training regime. At that time Charles Metcalfe and Oz Clarke, previous competitors, were trying to make wine accessible to the public.

Day: 'I was at Jesus College, Cambridge, as an undergraduate, before going to Wadham at Oxford for my doctorate. I was a member of the Cambridge University Wine Society (CUWS), but wasn't aware of the opportunity for blind tasting. When I went to Oxford and joined the Oxford University Wine Circle (OUWC), Paul White asked anybody who was interested to stay behind at the end of a tasting. It was open. Finding good examples at a reasonable price was always tough. We were struggling to get £2.50 together each week to blind taste supermarket wines or wines from Oddbins.

'Serena Sutcliffe MW came as guest judge in 1990. She laid into the wines and said they were appalling examples – these were the last days of Harveys. It was quite staggering. She's a very good taster, and was totally right, but it was surprising to hear her say they were terrible, with Robin Scott-Martin, the buyer, sitting right next to her. It was a bit like *University Challenge*. Mark de Vere (Christ Church) went through the team and became Mondavi's MW in the US, then the youngest MW to pass the exam, and Paul White is a wine writer.

'Serena Sutcliffe MW came as guest judge in 1990. She laid into the wines and said they were appalling examples – these were the last days of Harveys.'
Paul Day

LEFT The1989 Oxford tasting team receives the Harveys Cup from VIP judge Hugh Johnson. Left to right: A N Other, Paul White, Charles Mahoney, Michelle Chen, Peter Martin (captain), James John MW of Harveys, Hugh Johnson, Greg Bennett and Daniel Carey.

GREG BENNETT
Christ Church, Oxford, m.1987

Greg Bennett lives in London, funding his wine habits through working in finance. He is married, with three daughters, all of whom are fortunately too young to be a threat to his cellar – yet.

'Before going up to Oxford as an undergraduate, I was a complete ignoramus about wine. Tastings and blind-tasting practice sessions were the route by which I learned about and started to appreciate wine. I joined the Oxford University Wine Circle (OUWC) through the freshers' fair in 1987, became its treasurer for the following two academic years, and was on the team in 1988, '89 and '90. Apart from studying modern history and wine tasting, my other activities included music, pool, snooker, the Oxford Union and the junior common room. The Hillsborough tragedy happened in the spring of 1989, and the period was marked by the fall of the Berlin Wall in autumn 1989.

'Practice wines were funded by individuals in the squad, and Harveys arranged a mock tasting for us just before the match. The team was chosen from the ranks of the OUWC. In 1988 there were two women in the team, and in 1989, there was one, Michelle Chen. Ahead of the match, we practised with increasing frequency: two to three times a week, increasing to

'My wine-tasting peak was reached in March 1990, on Pall Mall.'

five or six times a week in the two weeks immediately before the competition. The captain was coach for my first two years; in the last year, the captain (Paul White) and I shared the coaching role.

'The match was at Harveys on Pall Mall. We met the other side (the Cambridge team) for only a few hours one day in March each year, so there was little chance to connect – a shame.

'There was still a far higher percentage of French (Bordeaux, Burgundy), particularly on college wine lists, compared to now, although the main sources of wines then were the high-street chains of Oddbins and Bottoms Up, both of which had a wide range of Old and New World wines. I've passed the Wine & Spirit Education Trust intermediate and advanced certificates, but I've never been tempted to enter the trade or try winemaking itself. I'll leave that to the experts.

'After leaving Oxford in 1990, I moved down to London and have now spent over 22 years working in the City of London. I've continued to enjoy wine since Oxford, and am certainly more able to afford to drink the good stuff now, but I have always thought that my wine-tasting peak was reached in March 1990, on Pall Mall. I'd never been better trained and prepared to taste, and never will be again!'

College wine buyer

'I went on to be an academic at Lady Margaret Hall (LMH), and despite my relative junior position, through politics and opportunity I was buying wine for an Oxford college.

'I was 15 when my father gave me an unwanted Hugh Johnson *Pocket Wine Guide*, because my parents weren't regular wine drinkers, and I remember ordering books on wine when I was still at school. At Cambridge, a group of friends dined in college every night, and we took it in turns to bring a bottle. I got involved with the CUWS in my last year. I didn't think too deeply about wine, though, until I started blind tasting at Oxford. It was the discipline of associating words with tasting that gave me a mental framework, and it was a steep learning curve. Paul had

honed it quite well in terms of a simple sheet of grape types, and we were forced to come up with words to attach with wine – most totally irrelevant to wine. Wine doesn't really smell of blackcurrants – blackcurrants smell of blackcurrants. But once you get that vocabulary, it builds a framework to appreciate, to stick in the memory.

'A wine steward could be a college employee or a fellow who buys wine for the college, and there's a big difference between the two. When a fellow is in charge, it's normally a sinecure. These ideas of legendary Oxford cellars are romantic and a myth. Some have good bottles, but even at famous college cellars, where they might have a few bottles of old first growths, everyday wines could be appallingly bought. The interesting stories are about everyday wines. At Cambridge, a senior fellow

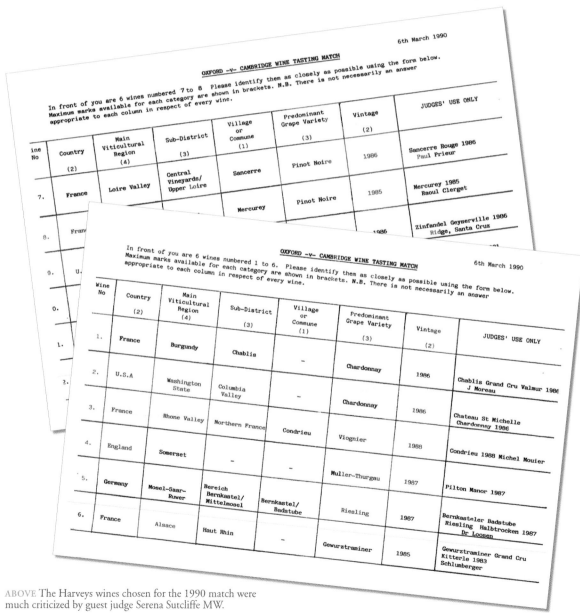

ABOVE The Harveys wines chosen for the 1990 match were much criticized by guest judge Serena Sutcliffe MW.

went on holiday in Germany, obviously enjoyed a tasting and ended up buying a whole juggernaut of wine to be brought back to a college. It wasn't even Riesling; it was mostly Albalonga. The college paid up because it didn't want any embarrassment. The way things were purchased was amateurish in many cases, but not in all. There were colleges where people took care of the whole wine list, from top to bottom.

'While doing my PhD at Wadham, I had a senior scholarship that entitled me to high-table dining rights once a week. The butler would leave the red wine on the radiator; it was basically mulled wine, whatever it was – incredible. They heated the wine because they thought wine should be brought up to room temperature, but nobody complained. When I went to LMH, nobody had ever sent a bottle back from high table for being corked. At one of my first dinners the principal accepted a Meursault, and it came to me about three places down, and I said, "Sorry, this is corked." I was not banned from high table; people respected the truth.

'At LMH, traditionally three decanters were served up after dinner. You went to a separate room for formal dessert, and there was a sweet wine, a claret (popular to be drunk after the meal) and Port. There were people who would never touch Port and only claret, and vice versa. On one occasion the decanters went around twice, and on the second circuit somebody on the wine committee said to me, "Paul, I find the claret a little sweet this evening." He'd been drinking the dessert wine, and they'd got the little silver tags for claret and Port switched round.

White: 'And the steward would be back in the kitchen laughing.

Day: 'Oxford colleges curiously varied. At Wadham, one of the people who knew most about wine was very junior in the college hierarchy, Hanneke Wirtjes [now Dr Hanneke Wilson]. She wrote large sections of the *Oxford Companion to Wine*, but wasn't allowed anywhere near the cellar or the wine committee, as again, it was a sinecure, and often went to the person who was most senior in college. King's was the one Cambridge cellar that had good wine to sell, and that you could buy from; certainly not Jesus (although I managed to get a few good wines through the steward). Once, I got a couple of bottles out of Wadham.

'One of the other reasons colleges drank old wine was that most academics don't have that much money, and they like to have reasonable bills for dinner. If colleges keep wine, they can charge cost price plus ten per cent: that was the formula. There was a tax reason why you had to charge a minimum of ten per cent, and you couldn't charge cost or sell it at a loss. Old Port might be costed at £1.10 a bottle, because the 1963s were probably bought at just under a pound a bottle. The way to balance the books was to charge conferences for wines that had expanded in value. There are a few tricks, but it's not

such a black-and-white picture as 'this very clever group of people who know how to pick great investments consistently'. I don't think there was any particular great skill. There were a few people on top of things as buyers, but not many, and wines bought to be offered in colleges regularly, were often not particularly good.

White: 'As captain of the team, merchants invited me to senior common room tastings for dons. College wine stewards also had a tasting group, and for £1 Nick Davies did the entire line of Domaine de la Romanée-Conti (DRC) for one vintage (1982: my first DRC tasting) for them. He may have misunderstood the membership, or was hoping that the dons, who were buying, would be influenced by what the stewards told them they'd tasted. Nick also brought DRC wines for the OUWC: I think 1956. Putting those tastings on for the Wine Circle was in hope that Oxbridge people would be influential in the future; the idea is to hook them in and have them buying wine later in life when they're successful.

'For a new sponsor I wanted a pinstriped MW who understood the varsity match and that many wine writers and people in the trade had come out of the teams. We put the sponsorship out to tender, and Bill Gunn and Pol Roger came up with the best offer. I had a sense that they were going to keep it neutral, make it educational, and nurture the competition tastefully – not make a circus out of it, or exploit it in a gross way, but run it the way it had always been run: with subtlety. I didn't demand prizes; we just wanted to make sure it lasted into the future. Bill Gunn was such a gentleman. Great old wine-trade guy in many ways and confident he would make enough money to make sure it kept going.

'There was a Cambridge undergraduate studying law, Oliver Howells, who threw all kinds of nasty spanners into the works prior to the 1993 match. Jonathan Black was trying to bat him away, but Howells and his cohorts were the only glitch. We just said go away. They were just a bunch of spoiled brats.

Day: 'In retrospect, you couldn't have chosen a better sponsor. Pol Roger is privately run. It makes great wine, but it's also a passionate, family-run company and has been around for a long time. The one condition applied was that there wouldn't be Champagne or sparkling wine in the blind tasting, because it would be embarrassing if they poured a competitor's wine, and too easy if they poured their own. Before my time, a decanted bottle of Champagne had been served which had lost all of its fizz. People were largely guessing it was Muscadet, and that had created an incident.

'Harveys' marking was digital: six whites, six reds; grape type, country, region, subregion, vintage and there was an allotted score out of 15 for each wine. It was either right or wrong. It was a bit like Oxford exams: you spend two terms learning the subject, one term learning the exam – the Harveys wine list – although compressed. The

ABOVE VIPs at the 1992 match, the first year sponsored by Pol Roger. From left to right: Hubert de Billy (Pol Roger), Jancis Robinson (judge), Paul White (Oxford captain), Hugh Johnson (judge), Anthony Rose (journalist) and Bill Gunn (Pol Roger).

goal was to change that with Pol Roger. So that like the MW exam, if you're close, but off on the actual wine, as long as your reasoning is correct you would get points. Initially, under Pol Roger, Oxford was, for whatever reason, a far more experienced team. In 1992 there was such a discrepancy of marks before the competition in practices that they started to introduce this new format.

White: 'I had to teach people quickly. I looked at what Ann Noble was doing with the tasting wheel and thought about music: building intervals, chords, chord progressions, and natural style and historic periods. The previous 20 vintages would be coming up on the test, and things had suddenly opened up in the New World. It wasn't just Europe, such as Alsace Gewurztraminer versus Sancerre from the Loire. It was a watershed moment: New World wines with lots of fruit you'd never tasted before. Australian and New Zealand wines came into the UK market for the first time. You were starting to get South American wines, and to see more Italian wines. American wines never played in, although Harveys had a few on their list, including a Ridge Zinfandel. You weren't tasting only classic *terroirs*. I looked at the basic flavours of Chardonnay, Riesling, Chenin Blanc or Gewürztraminer and how those fruit flavours and structure change, depending on how much sun and rain, whether it was a cool or a hot climate. In Burgundy, a Chardonnay in Chablis is lemony and flinty; in the middle of Beaune, going into Meursault, it's big and more yellow, with graceful and refined characteristics in Montrachet and Mâcon and into peach flavours through southern Burgundy. But in Australia, suddenly you're talking tropical fruits, and acidity levels change considerably from what they would be in Chablis.

'Bill Gunn understood this. In the first competition there was a St-Joseph that was as Australian as you could get, and we had a Rothbury Estate Hunter Valley Shiraz

that was about as Côte-Rôtie as you could get. He played games with us – a great challenge. After I left, I covered one of the events for *Wine Magazine*, about the inner workings of your mind when blind tasting.

Down under, with new zeal
'I'm from Oregon. My family didn't drink wine, but I learned a bit about Pinot Noir in Oregon in the 1970s by visiting new wineries. Before Oxford, I'd been in Holland studying music at the Royal Conservatory, and I drank cheap European wines. The opportunity to learn about wine is why I joined the tasting team at Oxford. When I finished the PhD, my now ex-wife was from Wellington, New Zealand, and wanted to go back. I had already tasted New Zealand wines: I remember judging a 1992 Rippon Pinot Noir at the 1993 IWC, thinking, "Wow: pure ruby in the rough; they're going to make a fantastic Pinot Noir someday." I'd done Europe and America, and thought, "I'll check out Australia and move to New Zealand." Little did I know there are only four million people in the place: small and insular.

The thin red wine
'Marlborough is a factory. The first time I went to New Zealand in 1993, Mark Savage suggested I visit Danny Shuster in Wairarapa, the only guy talking about *terroir*. It was primitive when I moved there – instant coffee, bad food and dodgy wine – but there were a handful of good producers who had vision. I also went to Rippon, which made the Pinot Noir I awarded a gold medal to in 1993 at the IWC. When I made the pilgrimage from London and told them they're making fantastic wine, they said, "Our resident guru MW said we should pull our Pinot Noir because nobody wants to drink thin red wine."

Screwing with screwcaps
'I showed up with a PhD from Oxford, but in New Zealand I put out 80 applications in the wine industry, and got one reply. Bill Gunn came down to judge the Air New Zealand Wine Awards. I used to judge next to Bill at IWC, and I said, "They didn't reply to me." It was a closed shop, but then the grand wine writer of New Zealand, John Graham, died, and the newspaper put the job out to tender. I sent in articles and they gave me the job. My first newspaper job was the top column in *The New Zealand Herald*. I also wrote for Australia's biggest wine magazine, *Gourmet Traveller Wine*, and Wellington's newspaper, *The Dominion Post*. But I was the first person to expose the problems with screwcaps and sulphide reduction, and they circled the wagons and I got fired. They shut me out.

'It wasn't about screwcaps, an anaerobic system, or corks; it was about oxidization versus reduction. I blind tasted 240 Sauvignon Blancs for a column, and found that 50 per cent of the screwcap wines were faulty, and I wrote about it to my readers and that caused the first stir. Then I wrote an article for the Australian magazine, and was literally told by one of the top guys in the industry – he came up and grabbed me by the shirt collars and said, "If you don't shut up about this, we're going to ruin your career; we've done it to other people." Interestingly, two kings of screwcaps, who had been adamant about how wonderful they are, have now publicly gone back to cork. Neil Beckett from *World of Fine Wine* threw me a lifeline, and I've written for the magazine since the second or third issue. I write for other magazines, too.

Day: 'I stayed on in academia briefly at LMH as a mathematician, then went into the City as an analyst. When I had more money, I started to lay wine down. My speciality is Madeira, and classic wines: Bordeaux, Burgundy and Germany. I was in Germany for the Trier auction. With the blind-tasting team, you were forced to try everything; one of my first interests was Loire reds – Cabernet Franc – and I got to taste Australian wines from Oddbins and specialist importers like John Avery MW.

White: 'I'm an explorer and go to under-known places. Earlier this year, I did a tour of 12 natural wine producers in Italy: no sulphur and low sulphur, biodynamic and organic; and the amphorae producers. In Campagna, they're all reading texts about how wine was made in Greece and Rome 2,000 years ago, a production process that goes straight back to the Romans in southern Portugal. Nobody knows how to reproduce the amphorae any more. The big ones are thick and have three types of clay: one for structure in the middle, and the other two have different porosities. It's a sophisticated system and what everybody did before French oak; clay ceramic is porous like an old barrel. José de Sousa bought an old winery years ago and found old amphorae, the earliest from *c.*1819. They're trying to make it commercial again, and the processing is brilliant. It's fantastic wine.'

JONATHAN BLACK
St John's College, Cambridge, m.1989

Dr Jonathan Black FRSA, AICA is senior research fellow in history of art with the Dorich House Museum at Kingston University in London.

'I read history at St John's College. I was a member of the team in 1991 under captain Jeremy Williams. I was captain for the '92 competition and supported the idea that Pol Roger should take over as sponsor. I recall meeting with Bill Gunn MW on the subject (an absolute gent of the old school) plus my opposite number at Oxford, Paul White.

'Since, I've worked for the National Portrait Gallery, curated half a dozen exhibitions, and picked up a PhD in history of art (at University College, London). I specialize in 20th-century British art. Oddly enough, I have recently begun work on a book about the sculptor Ivor Roberts-Jones (1913–96), who is responsible for the statue of Churchill in Parliament Square. I recall that Winston was rather a fan of Pol Roger Champagne.'

ABOVE LEFT Paul White (centre) and Jonathan Black (right) in battle at the 1992 match, now sponsored by Pol Roger.
ABOVE RIGHT United in front of the United Oxford and Cambridge University Club to save the competition.

Scholarly Rivalry: Cambridge Noses Vs. Oxford Palates

By FRANK J. PRIAL

Special to The New York Times

LONDON, March 16 — Before Harvard and Yale, long before Army and Notre Dame, before even the Red Sox and the Yankees, there were Oxford and Cambridge. Friendly rivals since the Middle Ages, they continue to compete in every field of scholarly endeavor.

And some not so scholarly. Like wine tasting. For almost 40 years, the best palates and noses of the two great universities have battled with tasting glass and spittoon to capture what must be the academic world's most prestigious wine title. Of course, it's probably the academic world's only wine title.

This year's Oxford versus Cambridge Annual Blind Tasting Match took place last Thursday at the Oxford-Cambridge Club on Pall Mall here. Oxford won. Hands down.

"Well, why not?" said Coralie Evans, 19 years old, of Newnham College, Cambridge. "They are all graduate students, except one. We're all undergraduates, except one."

The Oxford tasters characterized this as sour grapes, which they noted was a particularly apt simile.

Each team consisted of six tasters, with two reservists. Clearly, the Oxford team was older and more experienced. Three of its members were doctoral candidates.

Paul Day, for example, was on the varsity tasting team in 1990 and 1991 and when he isn't lecturing in mathematics at Lady Margaret Hall, helps out as a wine buyer for his college. Piers Hillier, who is working for a master's degree in management at Templeton College, comes from a family in the wine trade in the Bahamas. He was on last year's varsity team and was vice president of the Bristol University Wine Society before coming to Oxford.

The competition, which is sponsored by Pol Roger Champagne, was in two sections, white wine and red wine. The rules were simple: taste the six wines in each section and identify them.

Forty minutes was allotted to each section. The 12 contestants, studies in deep concentration, sat around a long mahogany table covered with a white tablecloth. An overhead skylight pro-

Continued on Page C10

Michael Klein

Wine Talk

Continued From Page C1

vided good light for studying wine color, in spite of the low March sky and intermittent showers that drummed on the glass.

The reserve tasters relaxed in an adjoining room, ready to step in if fatigue, panic or indigestion felled a colleague. They were given their own sets of the wines so as to be up to speed if called upon suddenly. Tasting with them were the judges, three of Britain's best-known wine writers: Jancis Robinson, Hugh Johnson and Anthony Rose. Ms. Robinson is a product of Oxford; Mr. Johnson of Cambridge.

Each wine group consisted of two pairs from the same grape but from different countries, plus two for which the only information given was that they were from different countries.

The first pair of white wines were 1989 gewürztraminers; the first was a Herrenweg Turckheim from Alsace and the second a Durkheimer Deuerberg Spätlese from Germany. The second pair were both 1989 chardonnays; the first was from the Edna Valley Vineyards in California, the second was a Rully from the Côtes Chalonnaise in Burgundy. The fifth wine was a 1988 semillon from the Clare Valley in South Australia. The sixth was a 1990 viognier from Condrieu in the Rhône Valley of France.

The first two reds were pinot noirs, one a 1990 from Martinborough in New Zealand, the other, a 1988 San-

In the varsity taste test, Oxford won handily.

tenay, Clos de la Confrèrie, from Burgundy. The second pair consisted of syrahs; one a 1987 from Australia's Hunter Valley, the second a St.-Joseph from the Rhône Valley. The fifth wine was a 1985 Beringer Private Reserve cabernet sauvignon from California, followed by a 1985 Château Lynch-Bages, made primarily of cabernet sauvignon, from Bordeaux.

Tasters were marked on their ability to identify the grape varieties; to place the wines as close as possible to their origins, and to explain how they reached their conclusions.

"In this kind of thing, you can get points for being wrong for the right reasons," said Bill Gunn, Pol Roger's managing director in Britain and the organizer of this year's tasting.

Oxford won easily with a score of 761 to Cambridge's 523. It was Oxford's fourth victory in a row. The winners will spend two days at Pol Roger, in Epernay, France, during their Easter break. Alan Sheppard, 23, of Christ Church College, Oxford, won a case of Pol Roger for amassing the highest individual score. He was the only one to completely identify one of the wines, the 1985 Lynch-Bages.

Michael Klein

Contrary to the myths about wine, even experts rarely guess individual wines in blind tastings. Bottle variation and the fact that tasting is meant to determine the quality of a wine and not its name militate against showy identifications of individual wines.

"It was a tough, tough competition," said Mr. Johnson, who participated himself in the 1960's. "The kids had to work quite hard. I was rather proud that I picked out the viognier."

Only two women participated this year: Ms. Evans for Cambridge and Katrina Mullen, 20, of Keble College, Oxford. One Cambridge reservist was a woman. "Two is low," Mr. Gunn said. "We usually have three or four women competing."

One American competed: Paul White, 32, of Portland, Ore., who has

lived in England since 1978. Mr. White builds reproductions of 17th- and 18th-century bassoons and is doing a doctoral thesis at Hertford College, Oxford, on the evolution of the bassoon reed. He captained the Oxford team in 1991, 1990 and 1989 and was the individual high scorer in 1989 and 1990. He has also worked as a wine buyer in London.

Dennis Harrington, 23, an Oxford reservist, also is an American, a graduate of Georgetown University.

Next year, the 40th anniversary of the competion will be marked by a reunion of former stars. They include David Peppercorn and Oz Clarke, both prominent British wine writers, and Sir Ewen Fergusson, the British Ambassador in Paris.

THE 1990s

The 1990s were a time of transition. After 38 years of a grand tradition, Harveys ceased organizing the varsity match, and by its 40th annniversary, would close their London cellar doors. With the 1992 Oxford and Cambridge team captains working in tandem, Pol Roger took over the sponsorship under the mantle of Bill Gunn MW. The match was rescued but was not yet in the clear – a few sorely misguided mavericks, with a penchant for creative legalese and crude commentary, would sour the scene in 1993, while the Oxford and Cambridge Club refused to budge on its policies relating to women's membership, excluding female blind tasters from post-match festivities, and forcing a change of venue. But by the mid-1990s in came a new wave of formidable tasters, many of whom were postgraduates – and a new Oxford coach in Dr Hanneke Wilson. Oxford won eight out of the ten matches of the decade. In spite of the recession in the early 1990s, UK wine consumption grew from 16 to just over 21 bottles per capita per annum.

Cambridge

Barry Appleton, 1991
Kate Archer, 1996
Andrew Barros, 1993
Pascal Bates, 1991, 1992, 1993
Jonathan Bevan, 1998 T, 1999 C and T
Rufus Bird, 1995
Jonathan Black, 1991, 1992 C
M S Brauss, 1991
Rupert Britton, 1994, 1995, 1996 C
Jacques Callaghan, 1993
Kean Chung, 1999
Colette Clement, 1998, 1999
Keith Conway, 1992
Rachel Couzens (Santamaria), 1992
Tom Crispin, 1996, 1997
Julian Danvers, 1992
Coralie Evans (Evison), 1992
Jonathan Foweraker, 1993
Charlotte Frith, 1999
Laurent Gervat, 1990
Nicolene Gibbons, 1994
Andrew Gibbons, 1994
Tim Hancock, 1994, 1995 C and T, 1996
Chris Hart, 1994
Karen Hart, 1994

Thomas Heide, 1999
Juha Heikkilä, 1997, 1998
Oliver Howells, 1992, 1993 C
Nicole Jones, 1990, 1991
Michael King, 1990
Justin King/Jin, 1993, 1994 C and T, 1995
Sarah Lawman, 1990
Albert Lee, 1998, 1999
Richard Lewin, 1997
Spyro Markesinis, 1996, 1997, 1998
Klaus Martin, 1995, 1996, 1997 C
David Metcalfe, 1997, 1998 C
Laura Miller, 1991
Stephen Park, 1995
Brendan Pearson, 1991
Marek Pitera, 1997
Joel Smith, 1992
Dean Stanton, 1993
J Alistair Swiffen, 1998
Hakan Tarras-Whalberg, 1996
Greg Thomas, 1994, 1995
Fabian Wagner, 1999
Mike Warner, 1993
Jeremy Williams, 1990 C, 1991 C and T

Oxford

Frederika Adam, 1999
Lucy Astill, 1996
Tima Bansal, 1993, 1994
Matthew Barr, 1997
Greg Bennett, 1990
Julia Black, 1993
Simon Bucknall, 1998
Daniel Carey, 1990, 1991
Andrew Comrie-Picard, 1997, 1998
Tim Cross, 1993
Paul Day, 1990, 1991, 1992
Mark de Vere, 1990, 1991
Thomas Drastik, 1996, 1998
Nicola Fearnhead, 1993
Danielle Follett, 1994
James Hardy, 1995, 1996, 1998 C
Dennis Harrington, 1992
Piers Hillier, 1991, 1992
Alex Hunt (MW), 1999
Sophie Jourdier, 1997
Daniel Kim, 1999
Simon Lloyd, 1995
Sara Lodge, 1998, 1999
Tim Marson (MW), 1997
Guy Morris, 1990
Katrina Mullen, 1992
Mark Oldman, 1990, 1991

Ed O'Malley, 1999
Peter Palmer, 1993, 1994 C, 1995
James Pennefather, 1994
Lynnette Peterson, 1998, 1999
Rosy Rathbone, 1994
James Semple, 1991, 1992, 1993 Co-C
Jeremy Seysses, 1995, 1996, 1997
Alan Sheppard, 1992 T, 1993 Co-C and T, 1994 T
Andrew Sheriff, 1990
Andrew Sleightholme, 1998, 1999 C
Barney Smith, 1992, 1993
David Strange, 1994, 1995 C, 1996, 1997
Freda Sze, 1993
Greg Thomas, 1996
Jack Tsao, 1994
Edward Tully, 1995, 1996 C and T, 1997 C and T
Paul White, 1990 C and T, 1991 C, 1992 C
Anthony Whittaker, 1995

C = captain T = top taster

'Like the Boat Race, they used to ply it with PhDs who were ten years older than we were.'

An interview with
JEREMY WILLIAMS

ST JOHN'S COLLEGE, CAMBRIDGE, m.1987

Jeremy Williams is an independent documentary film producer.

'My dad was an academic. Growing up, I had the odd glass of wine, but there was a fascinating and wistful documentary in the mid-1980s about John Arlott, the cricket correspondent. Arlott was down rummaging in his fantastic cellar, which he bequeathed to Ian Botham, I think, for all these dusty old bottles. In our house, we had a cellar with nothing in it. So I was about 13 when I became interested in the concept of a wine that could age, or was revered in some way. I read Jancis Robinson's *The Great Wine Book*, and was glued to *The Wine Programme*, the television series she did in the 1980s. I was interested in winemaking when I was young and bought a starter wine kit from Boots, the chemist. It was a cheap way of providing your friends with alcohol.

Taking a leap
'In 1987, before Cambridge, I got an under-the-counter job for eight weeks at Stag's Leap Wine Cellars in the Napa Valley. Warren Winiarski was there, and I got him to come to Cambridge in 1988. He's a great character. If you compare him to Robert Mondavi, they were chalk and cheese, but wonderful in that period of renaissance of the Napa Valley and great wines. He sold Stag's Leap in 2007 and made a fortune: $185 million. This guy was a lecturer in international relations at the University of Chicago, and decided to go west with his family. He worked in a cellar at Mondavi in the late '60s, got his little plot of land and established his own winery in what became known as the Stags Leap District. With his second (first commercial) vintage, the 1973 Cabernet Sauvignon SLV, he beat all the Bordeaux first growths in the US bicentennial blind tasting of 1976 in Paris, organized by Steven Spurrier. He was an inspirational chap. They would put on blind tastings at the winery

for staff – Sauvignon Blanc or Chardonnay – and there'd be French stuff in there. It was great listening to the mistakes.

'When I went to university the following autumn, I joined the Cambridge University Wine Society (CUWS). It was a huge society – the third largest. I was never a member of the Cambridge University Wine and Food Society. The blind-tasting team wasn't a club, but it was separate. I was president of CUWS in 1989–90 and 1990–91, and captain of the tasting team in 1990 and '91. I also ran the May Ball committee for St John's. We'd do tasting techniques with a local merchant, Stuart Purdie, who subsequently headed the wine-buying team at Morrisons. He was a great salesman and ran the Bottoms Up shop opposite St John's College.

A funny old bunch
'I did geography at St John's and an MPhil in international relations, and I played college cricket. St John's fellows were a funny old bunch. At the time Conway Morris was in charge of the college cellar. The St John's College Wine Society was a meagre affair. CUWS was getting in good people like Simon Loftus [of Adnams] to do Italian tastings, and Winiarski did a vertical of Stag's Leap wines back to the 1970s, and a tasting for the fellows back to '74: a great Californian vintage. CUWS was more interesting than any of the college societies. At one point, we were asked independently to value the Latour held at Jesus College. I hope they held on to it. Even then it seemed pricey, but it's probably worth a hell of a lot more now.

For he's a jolly good fellow
'Dr Stephen Elliott is probably still wearing corduroy! After 1991, he went on sabbatical to Belgium – for the beer, presumably. In his rooms there would be unidentified decanters of white and red, and we would literally just write down what we thought of each wine and select the best team we could to try and win. It was not subsidized; we paid for samples, but Stephen would generously share wines out of his cellar, so we'd get to look at wines that had a certain maturity with specific benchmarks; a '79 Gruaud-Larose was the benchmark St-Julien. A classic style would be cleverly picked so that we could get a handle on what that really was.

False lead
'The year before my first match, the 1988 Cambridge team had been very successful. "Charismatic" is the wrong word, but they had a high opinion of themselves and were confident. They weren't necessarily the most attractive bunch of people, but they thrashed Oxford and came back swaggering. It seemed an amazing event to participate in.

'On match day we went on the train to London, mugging up on the Harveys list on the way; if it was a St-Julien and they'd only got '86 Langoa-Barton, it must be that. In the last year (1991), Robin Scott-Martin introduced the idea of there being one wine that wasn't from the list; consequently, there was a fig leaf of "It may or may not be the wines you think".

'Hugh Johnson was judge in 1989. We hadn't had anything to eat, so I had to pop out for a bit of fresh air on Pall Mall. You were so focused during the event that by the time you came up for a few glasses of Champagne afterwards – like finishing your exams – it knocked you out completely. You were always right with your first thought and tended to make a horrendous mistake at the last minute. It's like the Boat Race – competitive. And like the Boat Race, they used to ply it with PhDs who were ten years older than we were.

'In 1991, I got a prize for highest individual score: a case of wine from Harveys. That was some kind of consolation we could take home, but it was so depressing losing to Oxford again that frankly I have no recollection of what happened after. We lost every year – the last time by a very small margin – to the same guy: Paul White. He was the real McCoy; I couldn't believe it. It was such a great competition to test senses and your ability to focus memory, recognition and judgement. Malcolm Gladwell would be fascinating on this, in terms of the "blink idea": that thin slicing comes with immediate judgement about something. That's relevant to both blind tasting and the judgements you make about people instantly.

Teammates

'The team was Trinity-dominated. Stephen Williams was in the 1988 team the year before I first took part. They beat Oxford with a high score and he ended up with a magnum. He was an ostentatious, extravagant chap and I think quite wealthy. Nigel Medhurst, in the 1989 team, was also at Trinity. They were drinking a lot of fine stuff. It did open a different window on that kind of world.

'Laurent Gervat (Fitzwilliam) was a Frenchman on the team in 1990. He effectively did his national service doing education rather than in the French army; at the time there was a choice. He'd got an amazing cellar in France with wines that went back to the 19th century, and his radar was skewed years before ours. He couldn't believe we were drinking wines from the 1980s, rather than the 1880s.

'Brendan Pearson (St Edmund's) is an Australian I met in my fourth and last year, who now works for a global mining company. He was also doing the MPhil in international relations and had done part of the Roseworthy wine correspondence course. I met him on the cross-Channel ferry on a trip to see the institutions of Europe. I chatted with him over a few beers, and thought I could get him on the team to see what his palate was like. He was, I think, second-highest scorer in 1991.

'I played cricket for the university second team, but missed the varsity match because I went to graduation. I used to play county cricket for my age group, and had a dream of being a professional cricketer, but realized that I couldn't make any less money doing film. Today it's quite a lucrative sport, but then it wasn't: a couple of thousand quid for a summer contract with the county.

ABOVE Jeremy with James Halliday and the Coldstream Hills team, 1996; digging out a vat of Pinot Noir prior to pressing.

ABOVE Warren Winiarski (second from left) with CUWS, 1988.

From tastings to television

'Post-Cambridge I made current affairs programmes for Juniper, for Channel 4. And I was writing for *Decanter*; I wrote for the magazine at Cambridge, and did work experience with them when David Rowe was editor. I helped out with a *cru classé* tasting of '86 Bordeaux. The night before, I could hardly get to sleep. I was a little office junior, and everyone was coming: Anthony Rose, who had just become the *Independent* wine correspondent; Steven Spurrier; Tony Lord, *Decanter*'s publisher; Serena Sutcliffe; David Peppercorn and the doyen of Bordeaux writers, Edmund Penning-Rowsell – a Champagne socialist. The notes for his toast were written in green ink.

'I tried to keep up with wine peripatetically around the TV career. I did a summer at Petaluma in Australia with Brian Croser – a military operation, but it was an interesting approach to wine. You wouldn't describe Croser as fun, although he's knowledgeable. Don Hewitson was on the staff there then and has now got a label of his own. Croser is the Australian old guard; with people like James Halliday of Coldstream Hills in the Yarra Valley, outside Melbourne, and (the late) Len Evans, who was on the board at Petaluma at the time.

'After about five years in television I took a year off, and did three vintages, in France, and a vintage with James Halliday in February. I'd never had so much fun in my life. James would cook three-course meals every night. He'd rack bottles of wine out of his cellar in the winery, and we played blind-tasting options every night for eight weeks. It was fantastic. We'd be half-cut most evenings, but determined to win to beat James. It was a bit, I imagine, like being with Len Evans; he had a great cellar and wanted to share it with people who were young.

'I did *Kitchen Nightmares* with Gordon Ramsay in 2008 at Optimum, which is where Jamie Oliver started. Gordon was professional and a nice person to work with, but that sort of telly is so uninteresting. I was fortunate in that the film I made was shot more like a conventional documentary. Things went wrong spectacularly, so we just kept filming and in the end the story was really about the things that went wrong. But you're encouraged to set up so much of the film that it feels incredibly contrived. I'm much more interested in character-driven organic films – more complicated to fund now, but much more rewarding to make – like *Mondovino*.

'I have a slightly complicated life because my wife works for the EU. We've got an apartment in London but live in Kosovo, in Pristina, a lot of the year. I've got a wine blog, winewordsandvideotape.com, and I go to *en primeur* tastings of Bordeaux, but my day job is filmmaking. As much as I can afford to, I still buy wine, mainly Bordeaux. The first time I went to Bordeaux I did a grape harvest at Château Palmer in 1988 – such great fun. And I like California wines, but they often get bad press.'

ABOVE A 1989 tasting-team dinner at St John's College. Left to right: Rupert Mathieu (Pembroke), Nigel Medhurst (Trinity) and Jeremy Williams.

LAURENT GERVAT
Fitzwilliam College, Cambridge, m.1988

Dr Laurent Gervat is a chemical engineer with Renault and lives in Versailles, France.

'I grew up in Versailles and went to school in Paris. I've been blind tasting with my father, who was a member of the Wine and Food Academy in France, since I was eight. I would ask what the dinner would be and then go to the cellar to select an appropriate wine. My father had divided the cellar into four categories: "good" was a simple appellation (Bourgogne, Beaujolais, Bordeaux, etc); "very good" was a village wine in Burgundy (e.g. Gevrey-Chambertin) or a Cru Bourgeois; "great" was a Burgundy *premier cru* or a Bordeaux *cru classé*; and "very great" was a Burgundy *grand cru* or a Bordeaux first growth. He would tell me which category to choose from, but I had the right to play dice, and if I threw a '6' I could take the next higher category. I would then ask my father to identify the wine; the next day, he would choose and challenge me to recognize the wine. We did this every night for more than ten years, and any time I returned to France to visit my parents.

'When I arrived to read for a PhD in chemistry at Fitzwilliam, I had a comprehensive knowledge of French wines but no idea of the wine world outside. I was shocked when I first entered the Bottoms Up shop in Cambridge. Instead of a shelf for Burgundy, another for Bordeaux, another for Côtes du Rhône, etc, I discovered a shelf for the US, Australia, Bulgaria, Chile, and just one shelf for French wines! At that time in France, it was impossible to find wine from outside of France, so I took the opportunity to discover, in particular, Spanish, Californian and Australian wines. I was a member of the Cambridge University Wine Society and the Fitzwilliam Wine Society, and because I knew French wines it wasn't too difficult to convince the management (Jeremy Williams) that I should be part of the team.

'Every Tuesday at 11am (hangover or not) we tasted a diverse selection of wines at Trinity College. I pay a particular attention to the difference of what we call in France "first nose" and "second nose": i.e., the smell of the wine without swirling the glass versus after the swirl. This gives a precious indication on its maturity. Not many tasters pay attention to these two distinct phases of a wine. I was amazed to discover tropical-fruit Chardonnays from Australia, and during training I learned to distinguish them from Californian – and, of course, French, ones. At the 1990 competition in London, one of the whites had this tropical/pineapple fruit taste that I recognized as typical of Australian Chardonnay. To my greatest shame and nightmares for several years after, it was a Condrieu!

'Drinking wine is a pleasure. Yet waking up with a hangover after a good evening and being obliged to go straight to a wine tasting is not a pleasant experience, so I thought I'd better keep wine as a hobby.'

Cambridge University 19 91 Varsity Wine Tasting Team

Mr. B.M.Pearson   Mr.B.W.Appleton   Miss L.Miller Thompson   Mr. M.S.Brauss

Miss H.Y.Jones   Mr. J.P.Bates   Mr. J.L.Williams   Mr. J.A.Black

C.U.Wine Society Dinner
Saturday 2nd February,1991

1983 Norheimer Klosterzerg Kerner Spatlese
(Weingut Hans Crusius)
Courtesy of Deinhard & Co.Ltd.

French Onion Soup
with toasted flutes

———

———

1987 Brown Brothers Sémillon
Courtesy of Michael Druitt Wines

Poached Salmon in Dill Sauce

———

———

1988 Moulin a Vent Clos De La Roche
(Prosper Maufoux)
Courtesy of Deinhard & Co.Ltd.

Roast Pheasant
Chateau Potatoes
Cauliflower Mornay
Carrots

———

———

1990 Brown Brothers Late Harvest Orange
Muscat and Flora
Courtesy of Michael Druitt Wines

Orange Syllabub

———

———

Blandy's 10 year Old Malmsy
Courtesy of Blandy's Madeira Estab.1811

Assorted Cheese and Biscuits

———

Coffee and Petit Fours

An interview with PASCAL BATES

GONVILLE & CAIUS COLLEGE,
CAMBRIDGE, m.1990

Pascal Bates practises law in London.

'In 1993 we had a team, half
of whom loathed the other half.
We were trying to keep a lid on it.'

'The Cambridge team in the early 1990s had a substantial undergraduate presence. It was probably the reason why we lost consistently, and didn't come close to achieving the level of competence of the current teams, made up of mostly older graduate students.

Blind beginnings

'My mother died when I was 12 years old, and so there was less rigour at the dining table than there might have been, and I was allowed to have the occasional glass of wine with an evening meal. My exposure was shaped by the wines my father was drinking: New World, claret and Sauternes, but almost never dry white Bordeaux because for decades most of them had been foul and over-sulphured. And rarely Italian: he'd had bad experiences in the 1960s and '70s, when the wines imported to the UK were dreadful. He would serve wines blind at dinner parties and I got to the point where I could, with reasonable accuracy, tell you whether a claret was Left or Right Bank and whether it was a '61 or a '67. But I was tasting a small spectrum of wines of considerable quality – not tasting the great gamut of wines I was suddenly exposed to when I came up to Cambridge.

'My father went to St Catharine's, but didn't become interested in wine until well into his undergraduate years. It was a classic situation: he was one of those people who thought a lot of fuss was being made about nothing, then one of the old fellows said, "I think you ought to come and taste this." My father then kept a cellar; he was a customer of O W Loeb and a member of the Wednesday Club, which met in a restaurant in London called The Cabin. The only requirement was that you brought an interesting bottle to taste. It was driven by an association with Hedges & Butler on Regent Street close by.

'I joined Stephen Elliott's blind-tasting sessions within ten days of arriving at Cambridge. One of the first things I learned through Stephen Elliott's coaching was quite how many different wines there were.

'You had advantages as a beginner, in that your ignorance meant you were less likely to fret about terribly obscure things. Also in the early 1990s, New World offerings were not aping European styles to the same extent as they do now, and it was obvious whether a Chardonnay was from the Hunter Valley or the Côte d'Or. Jancis Robinson refers to this in her book *Confessions of a Wine Lover*: why MWs frequently get given something blind to taste, often in unpropitious circumstances, then they are made fun of when they don't immediately identify the wine. The more you know, the more difficult it gets.

'During my Cambridge vacations, I used to travel quite a lot to Alsace, which had an open tradition of *dégustation du vin*, and to Burgundy. Because of the economic situation of the time, people in Burgundy who for years had been saying "No, we don't have any wine other than for our existing clients" began to offer tastings. With my father I had the chance to taste and buy at Sauzet, Coche-Dury, D'Angerville and Dujac. Coche-Dury was the most difficult (nothing has changed) and he agreed to sell to us only once, but he continued to sell to a friend of my father's, based in Geneva, whom he counted as part of his Swiss clientele. But at D'Angerville and Dujac we bought wine from the 1990 vintage through every vintage up to '05. I met Jeremy Seysses of Dujac, a blind taster at Oxford a few years after me, when he went to work for O W Loeb & Co, one of our main wine merchants; my father had known his father, Jacques.

CUWS versus CUWFS

'The Cambridge University Wine Society (CUWS) was well established in 1990. I didn't know there was a Cambridge University Wine and Food Society (CUWFS) because they didn't advertise at the freshers' fair. Trinity, one of the largest, richest colleges, dominated the CUWFS membership, which was by invitation only, and it tended to be rather grander than the CUWS. At that time, there was economic recession; grunge and goth were in, and it was considered unfashionable to be associated with Old Etonians (which was how much of the rest of the university regarded the CUWFS). The CUWS was open to all, and by then had a membership of about 200, including a number from Trinity. With the economic and social pressures to keep things grounded, though, the committee had a constant battle to avoid degenerating into a source of cheap drink, while not putting on functions that were too expensive.

'Three-quarters of the wines we were tasting were New World, and Oddbins, the dominant retailer at the time, had a fantastically good-value selection. You had a choice between "Ronseal" wines – wines from specific European appellations that were exactly what they said on the label, but no more – the sort of wines restaurants would snap up or that Oddbins or a big supermarket could buy in bulk (they had no character and were absolutely standard); or New World (Penfolds, in particular, was strong in the early 1990s).

'The CUWFS had relations with a number of figures in the trade for free or subsidized tastings. The CUWS had established similar links, but when we contacted a merchant who hadn't previously given a tasting for the

CUWS, the answer was often, "Sorry, we already do an annual tasting at Cambridge for the other people." CUWS did have generous support from Simon Loftus MW, who ran Adnams. He gave Italian tastings, superbly presented, and while hugely knowledgeable, wore it lightly and was good with an undergraduate crowd. Members paid an annual fee, about £5, that would cover the cost of a term booklet with forthcoming tastings; the cost of the wine and the room were covered by tickets. We tried to have eight functions in an eight-week term, a few parties and one annual dinner, and to make sure we didn't run any single tasting at a loss. Some we were able to make a profit on because of the generosity of people who provided the wines.

'Life was still paper-based. If you wanted to advertise you needed to put up a poster or place flyers in people's pigeonholes in the porter's lodges of each college. Thus clubs were fairly chaotic, and the university didn't heavily regulate them. CUWS elections came up at the end of the spring term. At the end of my first year I was elected secretary, and in my second year, president. As secretary I organized the advertising with considerable help from Laura Miller (Newnham), who did the artwork, which was important because emails weren't all singing and dancing then (there was a Xerox copy shop in the centre of town). I was also secretary of a couple of other societies, and doing about 75 miles a week on my bicycle delivering flyers to about 30 colleges (I would try to get somebody else to do Girton, three miles out of town). It was a good workout. I was much thinner then, and it worked off the hangovers.

From red to black

'The president when I was secretary was Andy Pile at Christ's College. When he took over, the CUWS was in a parlous financial state. Budgetary constraints had not been imposed and tastings had lost money. He started off in the red, and the only reason it had kept going was by not paying bills as they fell due. There was nothing to pay them with. Andy did the most fantastic job turning around the finances. He said, "This has got to be run as a business. We can't make people wait a month to be paid for the wine," which is what he'd been forced to do at the beginning of the season. By the time I took over as president we were flat financially, and the person after me took over with a healthy surplus.

'We were turning over about £10,000 a year: peanuts in commercial terms, but for a university society it was a substantial sum – big enough that if we let the finances run away, we would've been in a sticky position because the bank looked to us for two signatures on cheques to make it good personally.

'I am immensely pleased with what we managed to achieve at CUWS. For undergraduates just beginning to be interested in wine, we did an introductory tasting at the beginning of the autumn term along the lines of "This is a red wine from Bordeaux, often known as claret, and this next wine is Burgundy, from somewhere else in France" and built up from there. The committee served as waiting staff, and with careful pouring, we'd make a bottle produce 16–20 tasting samples. If we got the number of samples wrong, or if we failed to sell the optimum number of tickets, we quickly slid from profit to loss.

'One of the most fantastic events was by Pol Roger; Bill Gunn and Hubert de Billy brought four bottles of each wine so we were able to host 80 people, but we had to get a special venue. A lot of colleges wouldn't let you

TOP AND ABOVE The 1992 Oxford and Cambridge teams at the first match sponsored by Pol Roger. Hubert de Billy of Pol Roger is far left and Pascal Bates is front row, far right.

195

book a venue unless you were a college member, and had venues suitable for 50 or 60 people, but not for more, which meant the whole thing became more expensive. It was critical to bring in the cost for a tasting at between £6–£9 a head, because if you charged £10 a ticket for anything except Champagne, the undergrads wouldn't buy it. It would go from an extravagant but affordable night out to an unaffordable extravagance (and in the recession, you couldn't afford not to look at the numbers). The largest annual dinner we had was 120. Members were keen to go because it was heavily subsidized and a fantastic dinner: on par with some of the smaller balls. In keeping with the times, we introduced a vegetarian option by 1993.

'We held tastings in the Upper Hall at Jesus. They had an amenable restaurant manager and a venue often used for trade tastings for the dons. And they were prepared to put out tables and provide catering staff, and for a tasting with 60 people, at least 120 clean glasses, and cooperation to clear them up afterwards.

Harveys
'Harveys had been arguably the most influential British wine merchant since 1945. But by the early 1990s, it was no longer a small company, or even a major part of a larger company; it was a tiny part of a huge company. Senior management took the view that the way to go forward was with the Sherry brands – the way most of the trade had run between the wars. Since joining the EU, exclusive agencies were rapidly becoming a thing of the past, demolished by parallel importers, and while I was at Cambridge one of the most high-profile casualties was Madame Bize-Leroy of Domaine de la Romanée-Conti (DRC), who was forced out of DRC in 1992.

'Merchants had to look carefully at the bottom line. It became apparent, even in those three years, that the idea of giving undergraduates a free tasting – so that in ten years when they had a bit of money they might buy wine from you – was going out the window. They had to be more hard-nosed if they wanted to stay in business. The days of the "good old boys" of Harveys and Averys were on the way out. There was still a willingness to proselytize. Yet proselytizing and being paid for the wine you serve versus giving up an evening and coming to Cambridge for thanks and a dinner in one of the colleges, but no more – and also throwing in a couple hundred pounds' worth of wine – is a different thing.

The last Harveys team: 1991
'In my first year, Harveys was still the sponsor of the varsity match. I had no idea it was on its last legs. Jeremy Williams was captain in his final year, and was seriously thinking about a career in the trade, and his right-hand man was Jonathan Black, an art historian who was doing a long-running PhD at St John's. Barry Appleton, a Canadian, was at Queens' for a year doing a master of philosophy and now runs Appleton & Associates law firm

in Toronto. Nicole Jones was a veterinary student, I think, at Caius. Laura Miller came to the first blind-tasting session only because her friend fancied Jeremy. The friend was plainly not going to make the team, whereas Laura, who had worked in a wine bar in Norwood, got the wine bug, and she and I were the reserves in 1991. But many were in their final year, and we lost most of the team after 1991, with the exception of Jonathan and me.

'After 1991, Harveys said, "We're not taking this competition any further." Luckily, Jonathan was a genius at anything related to applying for grants and free money (by his own admission what he was doing through his PhD years). He and Paul White, the captain at Oxford, got together, and there were two potential sponsors, one of them Pol Roger. Pol Roger was the most attractive. They were prepared to run the competition in the spirit in which it had been run, and indeed, to restore it, because in the final years of Harveys there was a perception of diminishing interest – that this was something they did every year, so they'd better do it, but they were doing it without huge enthusiasm. Understandably, but counter-productively, almost every wine you tasted blind was on the Harveys list – a biggish list by the standards of the times, but lists before computerized stock control were much smaller. Everyone read the Harveys list because it was ridiculous not to. Those who conducted the negotiations were keen to get a sponsor who was not only enthusiastic and well capitalized, but who would be prepared to source wines through the trade at large so that there wasn't this artificiality.

'One of many superb things Bill Gunn, of Pol Roger, did for the competition was to source wines from different places, despite the fact that Pol Roger UK was taking on a number of agencies, including Pipers Brook and Faiveley. You might've thought there was temptation for him to put these wines in as part of the line-up, but he never did, and it made for more interesting and challenging competitions. The scores after 1991 go down for both teams, not just because the Cambridge team was junior, but because all of a sudden there was a reinvigorated competition with more difficult things to taste.

DIY
'In the autumn of 1991, Bill Gunn was in the process of accepting the sponsorship – and, I think, wondering whether we were going to hold up our end of actually fielding a team. Stephen Elliott had gone on sabbatical. So we went from a position where Dr Elliott was laying on quality weekly trainings to having to train and select ourselves. I acquired six-dozen glasses from Eaden Lilley's sale at 50p a glass, and Jonathan and I devised training sessions, hoping that we would identify bottles representative of what we were trying to illustrate. We'd be lucky to get three peak examples of Chardonnay: a Hunter Valley, a Chablis and a Meursault. And since Jonathan and I knew what the wines were, we were getting less training than the rest of the team. We tried to do it weekly, but had obligations to other societies, including the CUWS, and I needed to show my face at

tastings, either because I wished to or because it was one of our major sponsors. I was going to about three tastings a week: the limit if you wanted to do undergraduate work at all seriously.

'It looked at one point like the competition might end altogether. Helen Thomson at O W Loeb & Co said to me, "Things are not looking good for this trade, full stop." There was a huge amount of stuff coming in on white vans that was undercutting business in the south and southeast. We were lucky to find anyone who could sponsor the competition, let alone on such generous terms as Pol Roger offered. The Oxford people were at least as proactive as Jonathan, because more of their 1991 team survived. It was a challenging period; we lost more than half the team – all the able and experienced members – and it was not a great time economically. We had some support from a kind don, the wine steward at Queens', when he heard we'd lost the assistance of Stephen Elliott. But one tasting, with generous gems from the Queens' cellar that were unlikely to turn up in the match, doesn't make a training regime.

Matching memories

'In 1992, I remember not doing particularly well, but avoided the embarrassment of being the single worst taster, and the further embarrassment of doing less well than the reserves. Hubert de Billy came over from Pol Roger in France to the Oxford and Cambridge Club. Hubert was in his twenties then, a bit older than we were, but of our generation; Bill Gunn was of our parents' generation. One of our reserves, a charming girl called Rachel Couzens (Newnham), was enthusiastic after an incredible performance, but I'm not sure she spat everything, possibly out of nervousness. The combination of whatever she'd sipped and the relief of getting through the competition meant that she decided a good way of greeting Hubert at lunch, whom she'd met previously at a Pol Roger tasting, was to yell, "Hubert!" from the other side of the room, and to run and launch herself at him, wrapping her arms around his neck and her legs around his middle. While she was only about 100 pounds, it's a good thing Hubert was as substantial a member of the trade as he was – but he did seem to enjoy it.

'The year 1993 was a less happy one. Having lost in the previous two years, we were keen to come forward, but also keen to keep it predominantly undergraduate; many competitions were becoming

dominated by graduates and postgraduates, and weren't truly representative of the university. With the benefit of hindsight, that was unrealistic. As with rowing, you won't have the physique at 20 that you'll have at 25, and you will not, even if you start young, have the wine knowledge at 20 that you'll have at 25.

'When I was president of the CUWS, two members – an American postgraduate called Andrew Barros (Sidney Sussex) and a British law undergraduate at Queens' called Oliver Howells (who'd been in the 1992 team), weren't on the CUWS committee and hadn't put themselves forward for election at end of spring term 1992. Training for the 1993 competition began in the autumn of '92, and they indicated a willingness to be involved, but on their terms. I wasn't interested, frankly, in plans, which had already been laid by a committee that had already been elected, being derailed by people who weren't on the committee, so I was not receptive to their suggestions (they wanted to have tastings of expensive wines I knew I couldn't sell to the membership-at-large). They went off and looked at the university statutes, which no one ever

Wine No.	Predominant Grape Variety (5)	Country of Origin (3)	Main Viticultural Region (2)	Sub-District (3)	Vintage (2)	Comments & Closer Identification (5)
1	Gewurztraminer	France	Alsace	-	1989	Herrenweg Turckheim Zind-Humbrecht
2	Gewurztraminer	Germany	Rhein	Pfalz	1989	Durkheimer Feuerberg Spatlese WzG. Vier Jahreszeiten
3	Chardonnay	U.S.A.	California	Santa Barbara	1989	Edna Valley Vineyard
4	Chardonnay	France	Burgundy	Cote Chalonnaise	1989	Rully Meix Cadot, Sounit
5	Semillon	Australia	South Australia	Clare Valley	1988	Mt. Horrocks, wood-aged Semillon
6	Viognier	France	Rhone	Condrieu	1990	Coteau de Chery, Andre Perret
7	Pinot Noir	New Zealand	North Island	Martinborough	1990	Martinborough Vineyard
8	Pinot Noir	France	Burgundy	Cote de Beaune	1988	Santenay, Clos de la Confrerie, V. Girardin
9	Syrah	Australia	Hunter Valley	-	1987	Rothbury Estate Syrah
10	Syrah	France	Rhone	(Sept.) (2) St. Joseph (1)	1989	St. Joseph, Clos de Cuminaille, P. Gaillard
11	Cabernet Sauvignon	U.S.A.	California	Napa Valley	1985	Beringer Private Reserve
12	Cabernet Sauvignon	France	Bordeaux	Pauillac	1985	Ch. Lynch-Bages C.B.

OXFORD vs CAMBRIDGE 1992 BLIND TASTING MATCH   TASTER:.........................
United Oxford and Cambridge Universities Club, 12th March 1992.   UNIVERSITY:...................

ABOVE The wines from the first Pol Roger-sponsored competition in 1992.

looks at, and discovered that neither the CUWS nor the CUWFS had ever been officially registered on behalf of the university. The CUWFS had grown out of Trinity, and the CUWS had grown up organically. So they put forward the argument that neither was entitled to represent the university, and registered a new society of which they were its three officers (along with Dean Stanton at Clare), called the Cambridge University Wine Circle (CUWC), and said they had the exclusive rights to field a tasting team on behalf of the university. They wanted to run it, before it became apparent that that they couldn't put together the rest of a team. This caused a great deal of emotion, and people did not take kindly to these sorts of tactics. We had to tell Bill Gunn, who was extremely supportive.

'Barros and Howells started writing letters to merchants and sponsors, saying effectively, "We are now the Cambridge team," and purporting to represent Cambridge in wine-related matters. People we already had contacts with sent them off with a flea in their ear, and said, "What's this about Cambridge students writing up asking for free wine?" Olivier Humbrecht MW had been approached on behalf of this duo with a letter asking him to send a couple of cases of free samples. The two of them tasted their way through cases of free wine.

'The situation got progressively more difficult. Jonathan was eventually able to make peace with them (he was better at compromise; I'm more of a litigator), sufficiently so that we did field a team. But the cost of it was that Howells was allowed to be captain and his sidekick, Andrew the American, was on the team. In 1993 we had a team, half

ABOVE Keeping a lid on loathing at the 1993 match. Left to right: Pascal Bates (Cambridge), Barney Smith (Oxford) and Andrew Barros (Cambridge).

of whom loathed the other half. We were trying to keep a lid on it. It was Howells' last year as an undergraduate, and he wasn't going to remain at Cambridge, and it was the American's only year as a postgraduate. We got through the tasting and lost, for pretty much the same reasons: we were too junior a team against an established and strong, largely graduate, Oxford team.

Louts at lunch

'After the match, at the Oxford and Cambridge Club, Bill Gunn was generous enough to cover a superb luncheon at Pol Roger's expense, during which he showcased the Pipers Brook wines. Jancis Robinson was a judge that year and joined us for lunch. Jancis was, at the time, putting together the first edition of *The Oxford Companion to Wine*. In her autobiography she says that there were only six events she went to that year, one of which was this competition that descended into a brawl.

'By the time the Pipers Brook red was served towards the end of lunch, Barros and Howells were well-oiled (I'm not saying the rest of us were wholly sober). They started passing remarks about how inferior the wines were, which simply wasn't accurate, never mind how impolite to the sponsors. They were terribly keen on Robert Parker's view that "Tasmanian wines were under-powered, like all the New Zealand wines" and said they'd been given rubbish to drink because the sponsor had the agency for it. They were loud, swinging back on their dining chairs like 12-year-olds in a classroom. We did our best to smooth it over, but they just got worse. There was appalling behaviour at the lunch.

'Had I been Bill, I'd've said, "Gentleman, I'm sorry I think you need to go and have a sit down or leave." But Bill, as always, was almost too polite for his own good, and it became apparent that Jancis had not been sufficiently distracted by my attempts to divert her. There was a particularly bad remark, and she started to storm out. The remarks weren't directed at her, but at the wines and Pol Roger. I went out with Bill to say, "Look I am very sorry about this," but she wasn't having any of it. Her back was up. Bill was unable to smooth it over and the lunch ended. Jancis then published an article in the *Financial Times* (*FT*) in which she absolutely castigated, at considerable length, someone she described without naming as the captain of the Cambridge team.

'Over the next year, I did interviews for law pupillage – the apprenticeship for the Bar – and my CV stated that I'd been president of the CUWS and on the blind-tasting team. On at least two occasions I was asked if I read the *FT* by people who read the *FT*, who assumed I was the person described in the article. It almost certainly cost me a well-remunerated pupillage. So I did one that was unfunded – but it was a silver lining because the set I would've gone to, but for that issue, subsequently broke up, and the one I went to turned out to be much better. It all came out fine in the end, but it has, however, given me a healthy arm's-length attitude towards journalists ever since.'

Why a varsity match gave *Jancis Robinson* that sinking feeling ...

Before the fracas — hands on glasses, no conferring

Reds, whites and blues

OXBRIDGE rivalry is supposed to run deepest on the river Thames between Putney and Mortlake, isn't it? But this year's Boat Race can hardly be more acrimonious than the Oxford v Cambridge Wine Tasting Match held in London on Tuesday.

This, the 40th annual such blind tasting, had all the usual hallmarks of varsity confrontation: Cambridge accusing Oxford of weighting the boat with too many graduates; women in a minority; and a certain amount of exhibitionism. The cocktail was headily spiked, however, with a few distinctly 1990s ingredients: gratuitous legal wrangling, the strong whiff of hard-edged commercialism, and calculated yobbism.

The Cambridge captain, a law student currently choosing between offers of employment from four investment banks, was proud of the contract he had spent "hundreds of pounds worth of faxes and paper" drawing up between his team and the competition's sponsors, Pol Roger champagne.

"We're the first team to realise the commercial value of all this," he said proudly, nodding at his fellow competitors slurping Pol Roger wines around the celebratory lunch table at London's Oxford & Cambridge Club.

"Yeah," said his vice captain, an American who declared, not entirely coherently, that he could be as rude as he liked since next week he would be at Yale, "teaching scumbags European History".

This charming fellow, seated just two places away from the the event's organiser, Bill Gunn, the mild-mannered Master of Wine who represents Pol Roger in England, noisily (and erroneously) laid into the quality of the champagne being hosed into our glasses. The vice captain boasted that Cambridge had talked about offering the sponsorship deal to Bollinger, its preferred champagne house, and that it was only by agreeing to the lawyer captain's strict terms and conditions that Pol Roger had secured the privilege of laying on this competition and lunch.

With an eye to relatively extensive press coverage last year (helped enormously by *New York Times* wine writer Frank Prial's entirely coincidental presence in London SW1 that day), the Cambridge captain had decided to polish up the participants' image.

In order to present a less privileged and more "caring" image, he had insisted that Pol Roger changed the prize from champagne to a cheque for £1,000 for a charity of the winner's choice.

No, he had not actually thought about *which* charity, which was perhaps just as well since Cambridge lost, by 744 points to 855 (out of a possible 1,440), in spite of fielding one young Australian who dropped only 12 points out of a maximum of 120 in the white wine paper. The captain/business manager had clearly put more energy into the subclauses than into coaching his team. Younger Cambridge tasters talked wistfully of how much they could have learnt by tasting together and sharing impressions before the big day, a process assiduously encouraged at Oxford.

While Cambridge fielded the regulation stubble-wearer with *FT* folded ostentatiously into a Samuel Beckett paperback, Oxford's team was long on neatly dressed mathematicians and democracy (joint captains and a positive bias in favour of women).

The opposing captains nearly came to blows across the table when the question of graduate participation was broached. "But our graduates are relatively inexperienced tasters", was Oxford's defence of the maturity of its team.

Oh and the wines themselves? Forgive me, they seemed rather peripheral to the event. A New Zealand Sauvignon Blanc (1991 from Selaks) was spotted by almost everyone, even the judges — myself and Hugh Johnson — along with a full throttle Australian Chardonnay (1990 from Tim Knappstein) and a mature rioja, Viña Ardanza Reserva 1985.

Best wines there were probably Ch Léoville Las-Cases 1985 (Cambridge had contracted Pol Roger to lay on some smart wines) and Mascarello's Barbaresco Marcarini 1985 (£17.99 from Winecellars of London SW18).

The worst wine, by far, was an unexpectedly oxidised Meursault, Narvaux 1989 from Boyer-Martinot, which some participants loved. This did not surprise me one little bit.

JR

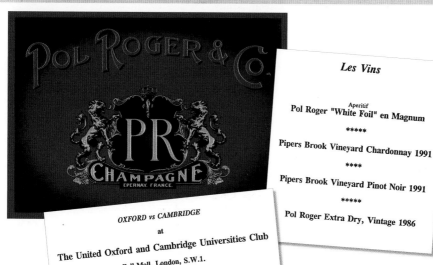

POL ROGER & CO.

PR CHAMPAGNE
ÉPERNAY. FRANCE.

Les Vins

Aperitif
Pol Roger "White Foil" en Magnum

*****

Pipers Brook Vineyard Chardonnay 1991

****

Pipers Brook Vineyard Pinot Noir 1991

*****

Pol Roger Extra Dry, Vintage 1986

OXFORD vs CAMBRIDGE

at

The United Oxford and Cambridge Universities Club

Pall Mall, London, S.W.1.

Tuesday, 2nd March, 1993

ABOVE The *Financial Times*, March 6, 1993.

Oxford Win the 40th Varsity Wine Tasting Match

Pol Roger again sponsored the Varsity Wine Tasting Match, which this year celebrates its 40th Anniversary. The match was contested in the traditional surroundings of the United Oxford and Cambridge University Club, Pall Mall, and resulted in a win for Oxford by 855 points to 744. Hubert de Billy presented the Trophy to the joint captains of the Oxford team. Oxford have now won 25 victories in comparison to Cambridge's 15. The standard of the competition this year was extremely high, and both teams were warmly congratulated by the judges, Jancis Robinson and Hugh Johnson. We were also delighted to welcome as our guest Harry Waugh, who founded the Match in the 1950s.

Later this year, we will be hosting a Champagne Reception for former competitors and many of those who have been associated with the Match over the years.

The scene in The King Edward Room as the Match gets under way.

Hugh Johnson in conversation with Harry Waugh (left) and Hubert de Billy (centre).

The Oxford team relax between sessions. (Left to right) Pratima Bansal (Reserve), Jim Semple (Joint Captain), and Barney Smith.

Hubert de Billy presents the Pol Roger Trophy to the Oxford Joint Captains, Jim Semple (centre) and Alan Sheppard (right).

The judges hard at work, Jancis Robinson and Hugh Johnson.

Jancis Robinson presents a cheque for £1000 to Charities nominated by the winning team.

Extracting every ounce of information: Jonathan Foweraker of Cambridge.

ABOVE A salute from members of the 1953 Cambridge team at the 40th anniversary party, at The United Oxford & Cambridge University Club, 1993. Left to right: Robin Don MW, David Peppercorn MW, Harry Waugh, Hubert de Billy, Jonathan Janson and Roger Richardson. BELOW Oz Clarke and Rosie Kerslake at the 40th anniversary party. LEFT Oxford win the 40th match.

Below: Oliver Howells (Captain, Cambridge), Jim Semple (Joint Captain, Oxford), and Dean Stanton (Cambridge).

Nicola Fearnhead (Oxford) who won a prize as the top scoring Reserve.

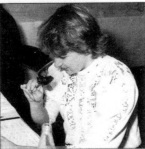

Cambridge team members enjoy a break after the Match.

OXFORD vs CAMBRIDGE

WINE TASTING MATCH

1953 - 1993

40th ANNIVERSARY REUNION

at

The United Oxford & Cambridge University Club
71, Pall Mall, London, SW1

Tuesday, 9th November, 1993

CAMBRIDGE UNIVERSITY WINE SOCIETY

ABOVE CUWS programme designed by Laura Miller.

An interview with LAURA MILLER

NEWNHAM COLLEGE, CAMBRIDGE, m.1989

Laura Miller is a librarian at St George's University of London, and a writer and artist.

'I'm a Lambeth girl, and one of the first members of my family to go to university. I entered Cambridge a couple of years older than most, so I was not a typical entrant. I read history of art at Newnham College, and was on the College Bar and Ball committees; I was also the Cambridge University Wine Society (CUWS) publicity officer and produced a lot of artwork for various societies and events. I'd drunk a hell of a lot of wine before going to Cambridge and simply carried on. I was a trained cocktail bartender so knew my way around liqueurs and spirits, and had been a civil servant. In those days the Civil Service seemed to run on claret.

'I was unwillingly dragged to the CUWS squash in 1989 by a fellow Newnhamite who wanted to "meet men". As we entered the room, the president left insensible, supported by a couple of members; he'd been checking the strength of the pre-mixed cocktails for some time before. I did, however, end up dating a local wine merchant I met via a CUWS member – convenient at the time – and so became a member through 1992.

'The CUWS was an eccentric, wide-ranging society, and was taken seriously by fellows, who were likely to produce a bottle of something special, as it would be appreciated. Several fellows raided their cellars for rarities, and I recall Berry Bros. & Rudd being particularly nice. Other notable wine and food societies were orientated towards public-school types who wanted to pretend they were in a Waugh novel; the wine and food was often good, but the company dull. I did like some of the

'I tended to use word associations – rude ones when possible – and memorized them so that I could place a wine.'

drinking societies, however, because of their largesse with Champagne on Suicide Sunday.

'There were two women on the team in 1991. The CUWS had a good ratio of female members who actually turned out for tastings: often at least a third of attendees. But in general, there were more men than women at Cambridge at the time; it was quite a macho place. Jeremy Williams, our captain in 1991, was a talented wine taster and directed us, and we prepared for the competition with small-scale tastings of wines by region, grape or year. I tended to use word associations – rude ones when possible – and memorized them so that I could place a wine. South African wines were beginning to appear, but my favourite tipples were and remain white Burgundies and Champagnes. Two fellow competitors were respectively obsessed with regional Italian and Alsace wines (they wore me down). We'd sometimes repair to Browns, but I most associate the Gardenia Burger Bar in Rose Crescent with wine tastings, due to the fact that a few CUWS members conveniently had a flat close by.

'When I competed at the Oxford and Cambridge Club, we could not dine there as a team due to having two female team members (one of whom was me). This was the first time in my life I had ever been excluded from something due to my gender, and I was inwardly fuming. So some of us went back to Cambridge and drank at Browns. The club has since seen sense and I am now a member. We lost by a narrow margin, with the observation made that our tendency not to spit out the tastier wines might've been to our detriment. Oxford competitors seemed to take it far more seriously, and were mainly postgraduates.

'Geopolitically, it was a curiously transitional period, with the implosion of the Eastern bloc. And computers were rare: only just beginning to appear in bedrooms of wealthy students. A friend and I broke into the King's computer room – I was shown how a Mac worked, and decided it wasn't for me!

'Wine in supermarkets took off, and wine celebrities such as Oz Clarke started to get a lot of air time. Wine also started to become cheaper and far more alcoholic. Sadly, a lot of old-style wine merchants gave up in the face of the supermarket challenge. It was a good time for penniless students, though.

'I have led a fairly nomadic existence, including a long period in the Far East, and now divide my time between working as a university librarian, writing and painting. My great enthusiasm is for the 1930s and '40s, and I spend too much time hunting for pre-war hats and costume jewellery. I still drink a lot of wine, and fellow CUWS members form the core of friends I have to this day: Pascal Bates, Jonathan Black, Joel Smith (Caius) and Coralie Evans (Newnham) were all in the blind-tasting team.'

ABOVE The 'Gang of Four' started up Pol Roger Ltd UK in Ledbury in 1990. From left to right: Elizabeth Vaughan, Bill Gunn MW, Isobel Mills and Frank Hart.

An interview with BILL GUNN MW

CORPUS CHRISTI COLLEGE, OXFORD, m.1965

Bill Gunn MW is retired managing director of Pol Roger UK.

'I went up to Oxford in 1965. I wasn't a member of the tasting team, nor of the Oxford University Wine and Food Society, but I belonged to the Corpus Christi Dining Club. The people who ran the college dining club knew what they were about. They'd had private cellars at home and would buy from merchants direct. Looking back at the menus, it was pearls before swine.

'Corpus Christi is an old college, founded in 1517, and it was a small college with only 120 undergraduates then. I read history and I rowed for the college, and played squash – my particular forte. I didn't get a Blue, but I played seriously. I had a good time, but I left at the end of three years not really knowing what I wanted to do. I had a cousin in the wine trade, and by that stage, through the dining club, I had become quite interested in wine.

Grants of St James's

'I got a job with Grants of St James's as a trainee marketer, not realizing there were such things as wine exams. Grants encouraged me to get a diploma, and passing the MW in 1974 gave me access to join the buying department. It was an exciting place to be.

'Grants had a full-time training school and cleverly put all its trainees through the school as lecturers. If you've got to stand up and talk to a class of 30 publicans about Bordeaux, you jolly well do your homework. It was a fairly painless way of getting trainees to learn the subject. Grants was part of the Allied estate, so pub,

'The first year went very well ... Then in 1993 there was a lot of very vicious in-fighting at Cambridge. It was good undergraduate politics.'

brewery managers and tenants came on the course. And the Wine Trade Educational Foundation ran courses at Smithfield Market. We'd follow the bacon boning class and as you'd go into the room they would be sweeping away blood and sawdust for the next lecture on German wines (tasting wines when the room smelled like bacon was not ideal).

'The abolition of resale price maintenance was the big breakthrough in about 1973. Somebody from Asda came to talk to Grants about it; it was revolutionary, with explosive growth, and the wine world was going through a dynamic phase. When I joined the trade it was Bordeaux, Germany and Port. Maybe Burgundy, but it was the old Europe and the concept of wines coming from anywhere else was still foreign. Then all of a sudden the market started opening out. Before this, if you wanted to buy an Australian wine in London there was literally only one place you could do it: the Australian Wine Centre in Soho.

Asda and the supermarket scene

'At Asda I was responsible for wines, spirits and beers. It was a steep learning curve and there was a simple measure: profit margin. If it was going down, you had serious questions to answer. Wine was a small percentage, but growing fast – on supermarket shelves for the first time – and we used it as a traffic builder. Everyone wanted to be part of the supermarket scene. We'd have all the Champagne at keen prices, purely and simply for getting people in the door; it was a PR effort. Customers had been going to the supermarket and to a separate merchant to get beer and wine. Once they came together it was a new concept called "a bottle in a trolley".

'Four years at Asda was worth 40 years at Grants in terms of pace of business. I'd loved Grants, but my boss had made it clear that he didn't want to move on, and Asda offered me twice the salary. But the benchmark was only profitability. I did introduce an educational taste index: a merchandising concept to distinguish dry wines from medium, medium from sweet, and so on. Basic stuff, but it worked well and was a landmark in that department.

'Big-selling brands were things like Black Tower, Liebfraumilch, Lambrusco, Mateus Rosé and Mouton Cadet. Liebfraumilch was arguably the brand responsible for making people stop drinking German wine. German wine is a specialist importers' market with wonderful wines catering to a specialist clientele, but the Germans screwed up the perception of their market with ever-cheaper and nastier products – Blue Nun, Niersteiner Gutes Domtal, Oppenheimer Krötenbrunnen – and it has never recovered. It was Müller-Thurgau, sugar and lemonade – a huge shame.

Bulmers, Dent & Reuss, Pol Roger

'Post-Asda, I was headhunted to work for the wine and spirit division at Bulmers. Bulmers was expanding, and building its range, about the time it got into water with the Perrier franchise and took on Red Stripe Lager. In the 1960s it had bought lock, stock and barrel a traditional London wine merchant, Dent & Reuss, the sole agent in the UK for Pol Roger for a very long time.

'When Bulmers bought the business, Dent & Reuss had a good portfolio, including Pol Roger, Louis Latour, Taylor's Port and Hine Cognac. But what Bulmers didn't realize was that it wasn't buying the rights to the agencies. So Hine, Louis Latour and Taylor's took one look at Bulmers and said, "We don't want to be part of a cider company." But Pol Roger was taken by surprise, and it's made up of loyal people. As far as they were concerned, they'd shaken hands on this and stayed aboard. Christian de Billy was the boss, having taken over in 1959, and Christian Pol-Roger was his lieutenant.

'Pol Roger was not a big brand in the UK then, but proportionately the UK has always been an important market, with 20 per cent of sales. My brief by Bulmers was to improve the breed of the portfolio and to build the Dent & Reuss agency list. The company had had it for 20 years, but wasn't making a success of it. Having seen both sides of the desk as a buyer for Grants and Asda, and with an MW, I knew the language and the way to sell to supermarkets. I suppose they thought having been gamekeeper I could turn poacher. But things came full cycle. Bulmers, having been on a diversification programme, brought in consultants in the late 1980s who said, "Forget about all this diversification nonsense. What you want to do is concentrate on cider and the apple." So Bulmers put Dent & Reuss up for sale in 1989.

A new start: Pol Roger UK

'By that stage I'd got to know Christian de Billy quite well. He had been tempted for a while to see whether Pol Roger could go it alone. Frank Hart, the Dent sales director, and I put our heads together and came up with a business plan we put to Christian to say, "Why don't we give it a go?" Christian said "okay" and get on with it. That was the start of Pol Roger in the UK. It was always accepted that we'd bring in other things, but that Pol Roger would be the flagpole around which the other brands would congregate, and we would not have competing Champagne brands (anything with a bubble – sparkling wine – was off the radar) or give priority to a lower-level spirit making money.

'Frank and I were also up for sale with Dent & Reuss, but the first we knew about it was when we read it in the Saturday business section of *The Telegraph*. It was unbelievable. We had a lot of guys coming in to Bulmers on Monday saying, "I'm not for sale. Are you for sale?" There was a diaspora of people; Frank and I stuck together. We recruited Isobel Mills and Elizabeth Vaughan, who had both been at Dent & Reuss, and in 1990 we started as a gang of four in a small office in

Ledbury. We wanted blue water between us and Bulmers, and Hereford was all about Bulmers. In the first six months we sold more than the Dent & Reuss sales team of 30 had sold in the previous year. We got off to a jolly good start, with tremendous reception and support from our customers, but as it turned out, it was a bit of a honeymoon because a year later we hit recession.

Champagne setback

'By the second half of 1991 we were in trouble because a lot of our customers had been small and independent wine merchants who started going to the wall. We had to rebuild our customer list radically over the next few years, and didn't really come out of recession until 1994. We resisted going straight to private clientele because we felt that the trade was a necessary evil, and that once you started bypassing the trade you were stacking up problems. Our critical mass of volume then was actually The Savoy contract. We had the exclusive contract and were its house Champagne – a dangerous situation because it was about 40 per cent of our sales. And, eventually that came to an end, but we had a number of other house-Champagne businesses.

A hint from Harveys

'In 1991 I was talking to Robin Scott-Martin of Harveys. To paraphrase, he said, "Harveys is falling apart. We've got this sponsorship; are you interested in taking it on?" I think that was the gist of it. For years Ted Hale, who was a super character, was a driving force and great enthusiast within Harveys for the competition. Then he was off the scene, and the sponsorship was up for grabs, and it suited us. It was absolutely what we were looking for at the time.

It was Black and White

'The two key players were Paul White at Oxford and Jonathan Black at Cambridge. Paul was the first person I spoke to and he was instrumental in going with us. We had a gentlemen's agreement from the start, with representatives from both universities, and after that a contract. We took it on as a trial in fairness, to see whether it worked for all three parties, and it did. The first year went very well.

ABOVE Christian de Billy and Lady Soames toast the success of the newly released 1985 Sir Winston Churchill Cuvée, 1992.

'Then in 1993 there was a lot of very vicious in-fighting at Cambridge. It was good undergraduate politics. There was one bad apple, the ringleader of all the trouble: Oliver Howells. He certainly clouded the atmosphere for one year. Pascal Bates came in and smoothed the waters, and after that we were back on an even keel. Our feeling was that it was a blip and would blow over. It was the only hassle we ever had, and in my time, sweetness and light since.

'The sponsorship has been absolutely wonderful in terms of the network that's been built. A galaxy of people turned up for the 40th party in 1993 and the 50th in 2003, with an extraordinary range of professions and talent, and all Pol Roger enthusiasts. That was the whole point: to establish the relationship at a formative age and remain friends for life. It is a very long-term view, and it has blossomed for us. It was an issue that the age profile of the Pol customer back in the early 1990s was heavily weighted to the top end. Pol Roger was known by everyone's fathers and grandfathers, by colonels and majors. We had to do something, and paying for a presence in hotel nightclubs was neither profitable nor palatable. Sponsorship of the tasting competition was consistent with the aim to try and build a younger audience.

'Harry Waugh was a charming man and an old-fashioned gent. The match was his idea and to his credit, he still came along to competitions under the new Pol Roger sponsorship. I went to the last match at Harveys' cellars on Pall Mall in 1991, and all the wines came up from the Harveys list. So we said that we'd go wider than that, but our range was very limited in the early 1990s (only one New Zealand wine), and so we sourced competition wines from the trade at large. I would do a training session in both Oxford and Cambridge, before James Simpson MW came on board and took that over, and I also took the first prizewinners to Épernay.

Women, wine and white water

'The only other white water was venue-related. We held the match at the Oxford and Cambridge Club, at that time a gentlemen's club. In the early 1990s there was a higher proportion of women on both teams; a feisty girl on the Cambridge team said, "I'm not coming up the back stairs of the Oxford and Cambridge Club. Unless I come on equal terms, I'm not coming." So we said, "We'll move." We bent with the wind and went to the RAC, and then to the University Women's Club for a few years. At the Oxford and Cambridge Club it was uncomfortable, frankly; there was a side door and back stairs. It was all very much second-class citizens. Then the rules changed. When women were admitted on equal terms, we came back to the Oxford and Cambridge Club. It's a natural venue, and banqueting managers Joe Inglott and Neil Greer have been magic over the years: especially supportive with competition-morning bacon butties. Hugh Johnson and Jancis Robinson have always been our A-team judges, and if they couldn't make it we'd find a special guest star, like Bill Baker. We never scraped the barrel. We've had some very good people.'

THE OXFORD & CAMBRIDGE CLUB

The United University Club was founded in 1821, with premises on 1 Suffolk Street at the corner of Pall Mall near the northwest corner of Trafalgar Square. A long waiting list beyond the allowed 1,000 members (500 Oxford and 500 Cambridge) prompted Lord Palmerston and other committee members to form a second club in 1830 called the Oxford and Cambridge University Club (housed at 18 St James's Square until 1836, when it moved to 71 Pall Mall). After 1945, when gentlemen's clubs fell into decline, the United University Club closed its doors, and in 1972 its membership was merged with the Oxford and Cambridge University Club, together now called the United Oxford and Cambridge University Club. The joint club admitted Oxford and Cambridge men, and lady associates (with restrictions): Oxford and Cambridge women and close female relatives of members. Lady associate members were not allowed to use the main staircase or the library.

Across from Harveys' offices in London, the club had been a venue for the blind-tasting contest on occasions prior to and regularly since the 1980s, but its policy on women's membership came under attack in the 1990s. In 1991, female blind tasters were not allowed to dine with their teams at the club restaurant, and in 1992 were in an uproar after being required to use the side entrance to enter the club for the competition. In 1993, despite strong objections, the match was held again at the club, and two female Oxford competitors linked arms and walked defiantly up the staircase that was forbidden to women. Sponsor Pol Roger then moved the match to the RAC in 1994 and to the University Women's Club in 1995 (with, ironically, two all-male teams). In 1995, the club's policy was attacked as 'discriminatory' and 'offensive to women' in a statement signed by the heads of more than 70 Oxford and Cambridge colleges and two vice-chancellors, and the two universities threatened to disassociate from the club. Dr Peter North, then vice-chancellor of Oxford, considered the legal position on the club's continued use of the universities' names and coats of arms. In 1996 it finally admitted women as full members, and reverted to the Oxford and Cambridge Club name in 2001. The match returned in 2002.

Today the Oxford and Cambridge Club has over 4,500 undergraduate and graduate members internationally, and hosts The Oxford & Cambridge Alumni Wine Society (ocaws.co.uk), founded in 2009 by Oxford blind-taster Charlie Pistorius (Oriel).

An interview with
CORALIE (née evans) EVISON

NEWNHAM COLLEGE, CAMBRIDGE, m.1990

Coralie Evison studied accountancy and works as a project manager with EDF Trading in London.

> 'I remember being outraged: Oxbridge women weren't allowed to be members, but we could be lady associate members and use the side entrance.'

ABOVE Still in good spirits, the losing Cambridge team in 1992. Left to right: Oliver Howells, Jonathan Black (captain), Joel Smith, Rachel Couzens, Keith Conway, Coralie Evans, Julian Danvers and Pascal Bates.

'I read economics as an undergraduate. At the time, there was a big focus on the liberalization of Eastern Europe, moving from communism to capitalism. Margaret Thatcher resigned on TV, and sterling fell out of the European Exchange Rate Mechanism. Newnham, New Hall and Lucy Cavendish (for mature women) were women's colleges. Co-ed colleges varied a lot, but the university in general was maybe one-third women. One of my friends is an engineer – there were 16 women out of 300 in that programme – but the arts subjects were more even. Rachel Couzens and I were both at Newnham, and the only women on the Cambridge team in 1992. There was one woman on the Oxford team that year (Katrina Mullen, Keble).

'I drank wine but with limited knowledge until I joined the Cambridge University Wine Society (CUWS). My father and stepmother had lived abroad a lot and drank local wines but not in any serious way. My mother didn't drink at all. The CUWS sounded like fun. It was at the freshers' fair, and Rachel and I joined with another friend. There were a lot of people from Newnham in the CUWS. Newnham didn't have a college wine society then.

Crackers about crackers
'Pascal Bates took blind tasting very seriously and was strict about crackers. He got terribly upset if people brought any other type but water biscuits because the flavour would contaminate the tasting experience. We drank a lot of New World: Australian and New Zealand Sauvignon Blancs from the Oddbins shop on King's Parade. I definitely formed some strong dislikes – Chenin Blanc and Semillon, particularly – and I'm good at avoiding them.

'For CUWS, you had to get your booking in early. Pre-email and mobile phones, you took your piece of paper and dropped it off at somebody's pigeonhole, or we used to queue up for the phone boxes. And everybody had a notebook, and a pencil on a little piece of string, hung on a hook outside their door, and people would come round and leave you notes. Some had cute girly ones, but most just went for the cheap ones with the spirals across the top. I still have all these notebooks from university with random drunk messages from people.

'I got drawn into blind tasting with Rachel by Pascal and other friends. I vaguely remember some conversation that Oxford never had any girls and I think they wanted some token girls on the team. I knew Pol Roger was the sponsor of the match, but I don't think I knew it was the company's first year. Pascal and Jonathan Black ran tutored sessions. I showed up and did what I was told. If you have lunch at Pascal's house now, it's still very similar: you get tastings, you have to give opinions and it's full-on. He's very opinionated.

Oxford and Cambridge rub
'The match was at the Oxford and Cambridge Club, which was extremely stuffy. Afterwards, they said, "If you'd like, you could become lady associate members." I remember being outraged: Oxbridge women weren't allowed to be members, but we could be lady associate members and use the side entrance. You weren't allowed in the main bar and restaurant, and there were other restrictions. I remember the toilets, bizarrely: *very* pink, little hand basins with frilly pink skirts around them and sewing kits. I was like, "Why would you want a sewing kit?" But I guess it was in case you tore your dress: you could go and sew it in the toilet. It was very archaic, and still like that when I graduated in 1993. We weren't remotely interested in becoming members then.

'We had an alcoholic lunch afterwards, and headed back to Cambridge on the train with bottles of Pol Roger Champagne. The actual match I'm hazy on, but I don't think I did very well. Pascal had been trying to train us on grape varieties and countries. He would argue about specific fields that grapes came from, whereas the rest of us were going, "Oh, we got the country! That's good!" Or the type of wine, or maybe vaguely the vintage. But Oxford won in 1992.

'We had a lot of fun, though, and on the day everybody was given a bottle of Champagne in a white box with gold writing.'

An interview with
PETER PALMER

BRASENOSE COLLEGE, OXFORD, m.1992

Dr Peter Palmer is a freelance political analyst and election expert, with international organizations in the Balkans, the former Soviet Union and Africa.

'On one occasion with the blind-tasting group, I commented that I liked a wine. I was rebuked and told not to be so judgemental.'

'My time at Oxford was dominated by the wars in the former Yugoslavia, and as a PhD student in Yugoslav history, I spent Michaelmas term 1993 abroad carrying out research. I returned to Oxford in early '94 to find that the blind-tasting group of the Oxford University Wine Circle (OUWC) had been inactive, and that there had been no preparation for the varsity match. Expressing disquiet at this state of affairs, I was asked to take on the job of tasting-team captain. I did not manage to knock a winning team into shape in time (although we did pretty well, considering: 739–721), but I did succeed in persuading David Strange (New), who was surprisingly reticent and modest at that time, that he was up to being on the team. Unfortunately, I picked him as reserve. Had I picked him as a full team member, Oxford would have won.

'While the OUWC was taken seriously, it was also fun, and lifelong friendships were made. It was exclusive to the extent that there was a ceiling of 45 members (the main criterion was the level of interest displayed at the freshers' fair), for practical reasons. Lance Foyster MW traditionally presented the first meeting of the year, an introduction to wine tasting. Hanneke Wilson, then a lecturer at Wadham, and Geoff Nicholls, then a post-doctoral researcher and now a fellow of St Peter's, were both stalwart supporters of the OUWC and the blind-tasting group. Oddbins was particularly valuable in educating people to broaden their tastes, and staff from branches on the high street and on Little Clarendon Street sometimes joined us at tastings.

'It was near the start of Pol Roger's engagement with Bill Gunn MW, James Simpson MW and Hubert de Billy. The ratio of men to women in the team varied considerably. In 1993, there was one woman and five men, with two women as reserves, at the Oxford and Cambridge Club. In 1994, three women and three men, with two men as reserves, competed at the RAC. In 1995, an all-male team of six with one reserve competed at the University Women's Club.

'A graduate OUWC member at Christ Church was able to obtain fine wines from the college cellar at ludicrously low prices. Brasenose had a good cellar (but I never benefitted), and I was told the college wine buyer was one of only a few in the university who really knew what he was doing. Lady Margaret Hall had a good, imaginatively put-together cellar, thanks to Paul Day, acting wine buyer for a time, and an active member of the OUWC and former member of the blind-tasting team.

'Oxford was not well served by good restaurants then. We'd go to the Chiang Mai Kitchen, a good Thai restaurant, and drink beer, or to a burger bar in a caravan, not far from the railway station, but the best food we had was prepared by superlative cooks among our own number, most notably Ed Tully (Christ Church), whose genius in the kitchen had already blossomed, and also Jeremy Seysses (University).

'I'd first become enthusiastic about wine as a teenager, courtesy of distant cousins in the Port trade in Portugal. In my 20s, I joined a wine club in my home village, run by a local merchant, and made trips to the Loire Valley, Bordeaux and Burgundy. My tastes did change while in Oxford. I'd had little exposure to the wines of Alsace or Germany before then, both of which I came to love. I made a conscious decision not to go into the wine trade, preferring to keep wine as a hobby. I've found reading Hugh Johnson and Jancis Robinson MW particularly useful, and since Oxford, I have often referred to Robert Parker, although I do not share his taste. Nowadays, more than anything else, I read the wine blog of David Strange – with some satisfaction that I first introduced him to the Oxford blind-tasting group. Blind wine tasters I met at Oxford are still close friends, including David Strange, Jeremy Seysses, Edward Tully and James Hardy (Brasenose).'

ABOVE The losing 1994 Oxford team. Left to right: Alan Sheppard, Jack Tsao, Danielle Follett, David Strange, Peter Palmer (captain), Rosie Rathbone, James Pennefather and Tima Bansal.

FROM THE ARCHIVES BY PETER PALMER

- In my first year, one young man made a gaffe from which he never recovered. There were jars on the table for spittoons, but he, unfortunately, spat into one of the tasting bottles. We were nice about it. It was his first [and last] time with the group, and we did not want to humiliate him.
- On one occasion with the group, I commented that I liked a wine. I was rebuked, and told not to be so judgemental.
- On the trip to Champagne following our 1993 win, one of our number was a citizen of Zimbabwe who did not have the required French visa. Waiting in the queue at French passport control, Bill Gunn noticed that there was no one in the next booth and the barrier was up. The Zimbabwean revved his engine and raced through. Thankfully none of the French police took any notice.
- Early in the academic year 1994–95, Captain David Strange provided an Australian Shiraz, which Edward Tully, then a beginner, but later one of the strongest team members, guessed was a Beaujolais. Overcome with

laughter, David lay on a bench, shaking his arms and legs in the air. Edward was not put off.
- At one competition, Edward Tully turned to spit in the spittoon next to his chair, missed, and spat into the turned-up leg of the trousers of the Cambridge team member sitting next to him.
- On a sour note, I've never forgotten the appalling behaviour of three members of the Cambridge team at the 1993 match. In her anger, Jancis Robinson wrote an article for the *FT* slating the event. It was unfortunate that the match and all of its participants were thus tarnished, as it was only certain members of the Cambridge team who spoiled it. Other team members were charming, including one young Australian who got an astonishingly high score for his whites (unfortunately his reds let him down).
- In one year, we were chuffed when Jancis Robinson and Hugh Johnson told us that they'd also tasted the wines blind, had scored themselves, and that several members of the teams had done better than they had.

CAMBRIDGE UNIVERSITY WINE SOCIETIES

CUWFS: 'Almost' a Blind Tasting
The first meeting of the Cambridge University Wine and Food Society (CUWFS) was held in December 1951 in Christ's College with a competition: 'Members were invited to taste three groups of four wines each, from bottles fully labelled. They were then asked to identify the same wines in decanters. Finally, they were asked to name a single white wine as a "Joker".' CUWFS, led in its early years by Tony Hepworth and B C Robertson, was a strong feeder for the tasting team until the 1990s, becoming dormant after the turn of the century; the Cambridge University Wine Society (CUWS) then gained ground, developing a diverse and large membership by the 1990s that continues to date.

Naughty Nineties: A Cambridge Coup
Unbeknown to the unregistered CUWFS and CUWS committees, a disgruntled Oliver Howells (Queens') registered a new society, the Cambridge University Wine Circle (CUWC), in May 1992, after competing in the first Pol Roger-sponsored match. He appointed himself president, with cohorts Andrew Barros (Sidney Sussex) as secretary and Dean Stanton (Clare) as treasurer; the CUWC's constitution declared organizational rights to field the concurrently registered Cambridge University Wine Tasting Team (CUWTT) to 'represent Cambridge University at all intra- and inter-University wine tasting competitions, events such as the annual Oxford vs Cambridge Blind Tasting Match, and any wine trade or public occasions', usurping the tasting match in a vulnerable moment when long-time tasting coach Dr Stephen Elliott had gone on sabbatical, and

the team was only just recovering from the transition of sponsorship from Harveys to Pol Roger. Records show only one CUWC tasting was held in the 1992–93 academic year, put on by 1953 blind-tasting competitor David Peppercorn MW.

CUDOS
Blind taster David Metcalfe (Trinity Hall) registered the Cambridge University Débouché Oenological Society in December 1997: 'The Society aims to improve the ability of its members to discern one wine from another in preparation for the annual Oxford-Cambridge Blind Wine-Tasting Varsity match.' The society was deregistered in 2003 in favour of the Cambridge University Blind Wine Tasting Society (CUBWTS).

CUBWTS
Blind taster Fongyee Walker (Queens'), co-author of the *CUBWTS Official Guide to Blind Wine Tasting*, registered the Cambridge University Blind Wine Tasting Society in December 2003 'to field, from its members, the team for the annual Oxford-Cambridge Blind Wine Tasting Varsity Match'. It continues today as the organization behind the team (cubwts.co.uk).

CUWS
With purported roots back to 1792, the CUWS was finally officially registered (or possibly re-registered) by Jennie Matthews (Newnham) in 1998 'to hold termly events and tasting to discover wines from different regions all over the world, and to become aware of their relevant social and cultural impacts'. The society highlights are its annual dinner in Lent term, and a post 'Suicide Sunday' summer-term garden party of Champagne and strawberries (cuws.co.uk).

THE 41ˢᵗ VARSITY WINE TASTING MATCH

V

R·A·C· CLUB 1ˢᵗ MARCH 1994

The Winning Cambridge Team

ABOVE Left to right: Rupert Britton, Nicolene Gibbons, Greg Thomas, Andrew Gibbons, Justin King (captain and top taster), Chris Hart, Karen Hart and Tim Hancock. Note the two married couples in this team, probably the only time in the history of the match.

'It was the first time Cambridge had won in six years. It was all incredibly exciting on our prize trip to Épernay, shown round by minibus, eating, and drinking lovely Champagne – like being in a rock band on tour.'

An interview with
RUPERT BRITTON

PETERHOUSE, CAMBRIDGE, m.1993

Rupert Britton works with LiquidThread, a creative media and communications agency in London.

'Rufus Bird (Peterhouse) told me about the blind-tasting competition, which I'd never heard about before. At that point my background in wine was drinking rather cheap plonk from Tesco with Mum and Dad. So I bought Michael Broadbent's *Pocket Guide to Winetasting*, a Christmas stocking-filler, learned my claret from my Beaujolais and I treated it like an exam. I never expected to achieve the top score in the qualification trial and they offered me the captaincy; I declined in favour of a veteran taster, but on the proviso that I would be asked again. After tasting decent wine for a good year or two, I then got a very low score, but they still allowed me to be captain in 1996.

'In 1994, the match was held at the RAC in London, and we won. It was the first time Cambridge had won in six years. It was all incredibly exciting on our prize trip to Épernay, shown round by minibus, eating, and drinking lovely Champagne – like being in a rock band on tour. I competed for three years, but after that first match we had a bit of complacency, and another bad run of defeats. We were democratic with how we recruited. The blind-tasting team took it seriously and was separate from the Cambridge University Wine and Food Society (CUWFS). A bunch of mates met up every other week, often in a lovely, oak-panelled room in Jesus College, and we all brought a bottle to decant so that you wouldn't know what it was. The match was competitive, and, like an exam, deadly quiet. Six whites, six reds: grape variety, country, region, subdistrict, vintage; and notes and comments leading to identification. In the 1994 match we had an English wine; they were trying to trip us up. I brought my Michael Broadbent book for good luck, but I didn't cheat.

'I was not a member of the CUWFS, but I went to Peterhouse Wine Society events. I studied archaeology as an undergraduate, and went on a dig in Belize with Professor Norman Hammond (archaeology correspondent for *The Times*), who'd been at Peterhouse and also in the blind-tasting team in the 1960s. Hammond loved the fact that I, too, did Central American archaeology at Peterhouse and was on the team. People from Oddbins would come, but we were really teaching ourselves. Blokes who'd done it in previous years would pass down knowledge. We had a lot of graduate students, and there was always a divide: the graduates were anoraks who read natural sciences and mathematics, many at Darwin College, whereas the undergrads, who read archaeology, history and history of art, just enjoyed it – it was quite fun socializing. Roderick Munday, a fellow who looked after the Peterhouse Wine Society, gave us tastings. And if people had tastings within their colleges, we would go to those as well. Occasionally we would have merchants, but more often than not we'd hire out a room in Jesus, Peterhouse or Darwin, and use their decanters.

'I had friends who played rugby and thought, "Look at them with their Blue and Half-Blue ties. The match has gone on for so long, and we beat Oxford; surely we should have some sort of recognition." I sounded it out with the university authorities about getting a Half-Blue, and they just laughed at me. So I designed a team tie: Cambridge blue with champagne and burgundy stripes. The tie was symbolic: "Yes, we represented the university." It was a secret society; people wouldn't have known about it but for word of mouth.

'People in years above would recruit from years below. There was a strong Peterhouse contingent then, considering it's one of the smallest colleges in Cambridge. Justin King was captain and tied for top taster [with Alan Sheppard, Christ Church, Oxford] in 1994, and Rufus Bird, an Old Etonian who was at Christie's and who now looks after paintings for Prince Charles, was in the team in 1995 (Tim Hancock at Wolfson was captain and top taster in 1995). Kate Archer was the reserve in the Cambridge team in 1996.

'Peterhouse was predominately historians, who were very driven to get firsts. They all loved their subject passionately, but as soon as they left it was like, "Right, we're doing law-conversion courses," and they're barristers now. The Michaelmas term was fun – a lot of partying – and a group of us kept setting up drinking and dining societies beyond wine tasting. There was a terrible (all-male) society called the '85s based on when they admitted women into Peterhouse. We were members, but thought the whole point was to meet up with girls from other colleges. So Rufus and I set up the Cocoa Tree Club, which was far more civilized; we would have nice wines, nice food and invite girls from other colleges.

Rebelling against old traditions

'Although many of us were from public school we liked rebelling against old traditions, putting a twist on things. A bunch of us had rowed for college, but thought, "Why are we getting up so early in the mornings? What's the point in it all?" So we set up the Gentlemen's VIII; you'd only row in the afternoon if the weather conditions were right. We'd row up the river a bit, then crack open a bottle of Champagne, smoking at the side of the river, watching the other boats go by. We were recognized by the college, and actually went into Bumps, but it was so stupid; we went into Bumps with bugger all exercise

behind us. You can imagine the state of us – I've never felt so ill and horrid, coughing out our lungs. It was a Peterhouse thing, but symptomatic of that era: on the one hand, going quite hard with your partying, sticking your tongue out at authority, but on the other hand full-on competitive.

'The Authenticators was another comedic society set up in honour of Lord Dacre of Glanton, Hugh Trevor-Roper, a former master of Peterhouse, who (mis-)authenticated *The Hitler Diaries* for *The Times*. Basically it was taking the piss out of the former master. The dress code was red hosiery. Girls had to wear red tights, guys red socks, because that's what Lord Dacre would always be seen wearing. For one dinner Germaine Greer, who had been at Newnham, attended and I sat next to her. All the undergraduates were flirting with this older woman feminist. She was great fun, as was May Week, with garden parties and Suicide Sunday.

'The recession was quite political, and there were definite factions: Conservative and Labour. One chap called Nick Boyes-Smith started off very Labour and then suddenly switched. There was a lot of that, and a lot going on with the Cambridge Union Society. Comedian David Mitchell was in my year and in Footlights; Zadie Smith and Thandie Newton were also there. It was fantastic: some of the best days of my life. I started a PhD but then gave up, mainly because my friends had all gone off to London to do law, and my girlfriend at the time left and went into the greater world. I went into TV as a graduate trainee for a production company that morphed into Endemol, which churns out a lot of stuff like *Big Brother*. They originally did *Food and Drink* with Oz Clarke and Jilly Goolden. Peter Bazalgette at Endemol, who was also at Cambridge, was instrumental in introducing reality TV, like *Ready Steady Cook*. I work in advertising now, in a creative agency with LiquidThread.

'I still enjoy wine, but in London I don't have a cellar so I should set up an account with Berry Bros. & Rudd and store wine there. Quite a good idea.'

ABOVE Studies in concentration at the 1994 match: Nicolene Gibbons (Cambridge), David Strange (Oxford) and Rupert Britton (Cambridge).

THE FIRST CAMBRIDGE TEAM TIE

designed by RUPERT BRITTON (1994)

"*Even bloody tiddlywinks gets a quarter-blue!*" I cannot remember who slurred those infamous words in the Peterhouse bar. It was 1994, and Cambridge had just won the varsity blind wine-tasting match. It was all a Blur versus Oasis; we barely had time to digest the victory tour of Épernay, a weekend feast of Pol Roger Champagne and ten-course meals, when an undergraduate's sense of injustice was finally flicked, like a plastic counter flying off a table. Tiddlywinks and cheap lager prompted direct action and I couldn't care less about the stuffy Blues Committee or anyone else who might stand in our way. Our noses, taste buds, livers and boozy bedsits (our underfunded and unsponsored training grounds) deserved proper recognition. We needed a damn fine tie.

'The early 1990s in Cambridge were imbued, and in the team's case imbibed, with competitiveness. Against the odds John Major had returned the Tories to power and student politics was a bit of a joke. One day your student union hack neighbour would be a terrifying Trotskyist, the next a putative Portillo. No more so was this the case than in Peterhouse. This oldest and smallest of the Cambridge colleges, the birthplace of Thatcherism and the Conservatism of Maurice Cowling, was now building its reputation as the cradle of ironic and extremely good-fun dining societies. The Authenticators paid homage to former master Lord Dacre, (mis-) authenticator of the fake Hitler diaries and a fan of red socks (dress code: red hosiery), and the Cocoa Tree was a riposte to the all-male bulimia favoured by sportsmen. Humour was paramount and the perfect antidote to the more perennial Cambridge trait of outdoing each other in academic results. It's no surprise that the most famous Petrean to have emerged from that era is the popular comedian David Mitchell.

'A friend of mine who had a Half-Blue in rugby told me to forget about approaching the Blues Committee; he was worried about my safety among former prop forwards. Further investigation also revealed that the tiddlywinks Quarter-Blue was a joke (our honour was at least intact on that front). However, our achievement in beating the old enemy against all the odds after a prolonged period of defeats deserved to be commemorated. We were a ramshackle bunch, and I (happily) became the Stella McCartney to this elite group of wine drinkers.

'I approached Ryder & Amies, Cambridge's university outfitters, with a simple design. A light-blue

'It was all a Blur versus Oasis ... We were at long last properly armed, and attired, for competition.'

background was to be crossed by fine lines of burgundy and champagne, evocative of those six mysterious red and white wines we had to identify. Bow ties were made for the evenings. The look was unmistakeably Cambridge, and even official Blues were envious of our style. We were at long last properly armed, and attired, for competition. What a shame we lost the next year.'

THE SECOND CAMBRIDGE TEAM TIE

designed by DAVID METCALFE (1998)
TRINITY HALL, CAMBRIDGE, m.1996

'When I became captain in 1998, I wrote a letter to the Blues Committee asking to have the match recognized as an official Oxford–Cambridge 'sport', but was turned down. I was not surprised, but I wasn't going to leave it there. In autumn 1998 I went to Harvard to finish my PhD, and from the 'other Cambridge' I began faxing designs to Thom Heide (Clare) who liaised with Ede & Ravenscroft (university tailor and robemaker). We debated and varied the width of the stripes in search of a touch of distinction, but quickly agreed on the colours: burgundy, champagne and Cambridge blue. Since 2000, blind-tasting team members now wear this unofficial Cambridge 'Quarter-Blue' tie. Importantly, the tie should only ever be worn by people who compete – including the reserve tasters, of course, since they can swing the match!'

ABOVE (Left) Natasha Redcliffe (St John's) and (right) Matthew Richardson (Queens') sporting team ties in 2012.

ABOVE Members of the 1995 and '96 winning Oxford teams: (left to right) Peter Palmer, Jeremy Seysses, David Strange, Greg Thomas and Ed Tully with designer Annabel Symington and winemakers, Jean-Pierre de Smet and Alain Graillot.

ALL TIED UP

Oxford blind tasters from the 1995 and 1996 teams showed off their renowned individuality with a range of striking ties, following a tasting given by Jean-Pierre de Smet, of Domaine d'Arlot in Burgundy, and Alain Graillot, of Crozes-Hermitage fame (also both in ties). As Oxford did not award a Half-Blue for blind tasting, local artist Annabel Symington designed the ties (with full artistic licence) in 1996; each tie features a unique, scantily clad woman – with strategically placed bunches of grapes!

ABOVE David Strange (in bacchanalian Oxford tie) had a cheeky chat with Harry Waugh in 1997.

'Suddenly I had to charm the daughter
of the owner of Château Margaux.'

An interview with
DAVID STRANGE

NEW COLLEGE and LINCOLN COLLEGE,
OXFORD, m.1993

Dr David Strange writes about wine (and food) for his blog, www.elitistreview.com.

'I was at New College, then Lincoln for my postgraduate degree, and was in the 1994 (reserve), '95 (captain), '96 and '97 competitions. I took my studies, wine-tasting and rowing extremely seriously. And I drilled a sense of seriousness into the people I trained. Before me, they had one session a week; I had three sessions a week. And if anybody was particularly keen, they would come to my room afterwards and taste wines blind from my personal collection (and get shouted at if they didn't get it right!). In 1995, when I was captain, a Cambridge chap from the '94 winning team who had got a very high score walked in with a big smile. We thought we didn't stand a chance – and then we creamed them!

'My mother got *The World Atlas of Wine* as a Book Club gift when I was five, and I would spend hours poring over the maps and wine labels. Then, when I was nine, she and my stepfather brought back a bottle of Trimbach Riesling Cuvée Frédéric Emile '79 from Alsace, which I'd read about in my book. I asked if I could try some, and commented, "Wow: wine can taste of lots of different things (for an underage drinker I knew quite a lot)!" I was the first wine nut in my family and in sixth form I'd take trips into London to wine merchants to pick up interesting things – and drink them with my teachers.

'At Oxford, I went looking for wine societies at the freshers' fair. I paid my tenner for the Oxford University Wine Circle (OUWC) introductory session, and got sent all the tickets by mistake, because they had taped them together. I got myself a place by resending all these tickets, sending a note to the person who ran it at the time saying, "You've sent them all to me; I've sent them on." The OUWC had about 50 places; 120 people would apply to join each year, and there would be people from the previous year wanting to stay in. The male-to-female ratio was nearly 50:50, but the blind-tasting sessions and the team were male-dominated. I'd been too shy to turn up to blind tastings in my first term, as they seemed filled with expert graduates. But one merchant gave a blind-tasting challenge in the OUWC, and I got them all right. Captain Peter Palmer came up to me and said if I could do that I should be on the team. I started turning up and almost never left!

'The Oxford University Wine and Food Society (OUWFS) was social, sitting around with a few bottles chatting to people, whereas the OUWC was a presentation: you sat and listened and asked questions. I was an OUWFS member for two years, but only turned up to the cheap meals they had at White's, a fairly flash restaurant on Turl Street where rich parents took their offspring. It has long since gone, and Michael White now owns the pub on the other side of the station.

'The OUWC would treat luminaries of the wine world to Singha beer and fiery-hot Thai food at the Chiang Mai Kitchen, or to dinner at The Cherwell Boathouse, owned by Tony Verdin. The Boathouse wine list was amazing and affordable, and our well-heeled guests would delight in buying bottles for us to try. We did stupendous verticals of off vintages of Lafon's Le Montrachet.

'At the end of every tasting, I would say, "Please turn up to blind-tasting sessions. We've got plenty of space, interesting wines and I won't laugh too loudly if you get them wrong!" The captain and senior members chose the team – six and a reserve, drawn from the OUWC – based on the scores of the last few tastings before the competition.

'Jeremy Seysses arrived in 1994. Dealing with OUWC membership, I thought, "I know that name; bloody hell, it's Jeremy, Jacques Seysses' son. He's in!" His application said begrudgingly, "I should become a member of the OUWC and blind-tasting team because my father is quite famous in wine." But in the space of a year he turned from being not terribly interested to rabidly fascinated and taking it all incredibly seriously. Now he's a brilliant winemaker, of course – one of the best I know. So we did well there! In his second year, he was president of the OUWC.

'The OUWC had amazing guests, and when Jeremy took over it was mostly producers who came. Egon Müller opened thousands of pounds' worth of wine for a sparsely attended tasting, because even though we had told people he made the most expensive white wines in the world, a lot of people still thought German wines were a bit naff. Jacques Seysses of Domaine Dujac, who rarely gave tastings, came himself and gave a stunning tasting of wines going back to '69 (his second vintage). It was my first taste of seriously good, mature Burgundy and it shaped my tastes to this day.

'Javier Hidalgo brought enough Sherry across the range for 100 people; 30 turned up, but he insisted we drink everything. Those of us who were at the tasting still buy his wines, and pop a bottle with great chortles of mirth. It was incredibly positive and formative.

'Margaux, Latour and Palmer gave enlightening claret tastings. We took the owner of Château Margaux to the Thai restaurant, and at one point she said, "I wonder how things are at home?" I asked, "Why? Have you left an eligible daughter behind?" She replied, "Yes, I'll ring her so you can have a chat!" She whipped out her mobile phone, dialled a number and handed it to me. Suddenly I had to charm the daughter of the owner of Château Margaux.

'Josh Jensen of Calera Wine in southern California came, a great bloke who did his masters degree in anthropology at Oxford. He was in the OUWFS, or whatever it was before the OUWC, but didn't make it into the tasting team [he did, however, earn a Guinness World Record in the late 1960s as the heaviest man at 212 pounds – height more than girth – ever to row in a varsity boat race, which Oxford won].

'Hanneke Wilson of Wadham was invaluable, and brought wine from the college cellar, and from her private collection. She once put a bottle of Margaux '83 in a blind tasting and asked, "What do you think?" We all said, "Fantastic! Brilliant! Amazing! It's obviously claret." Hanneke said, "That's as good as claret gets. You don't need to bother anymore with that rubbish," because we weren't going to get that in the competition. We had English wine in my first competition, which was dreadful – not quite the same. We also got wines from the cellars of Christ Church, New, University and Lincoln colleges, and the '78 to '95 vertical of Hermitage La Chapelle I organized by raiding the New College cellar was a real joy!

'Lance Foyster MW, who now runs Clark Foyster Wines in Ealing, London, gave frighteningly difficult blind tastings of anonymous northern Italian white wines. We had no idea what these wines were. "It's Gavi," he'd explain, "the kind of basic thing that everyone should be able to identify instantly." Water tasted less of water than Gavi did. He often went away with a smug smile, having taken us down a peg or two, and we'd all feel crushed and woefully awful. He's got a great list with flash Burgundy: Sylvain Cathiard, Henri Jouan, Fourrier, and loads of good

Austrian wines. We held competitions against local Oddbins staff, who were helpful, and thrashed them. And it wasn't unusual to take a trip into London before a blind-tasting session to buy wines from beyond the usual Oddbins outlets so that we could taste a broader range. Bill Gunn MW was running Pol Roger UK, and James Simpson MW would give the OUWC a Pol Roger tasting once a year, and the team one practice tasting a month before the competition.

'We had to be in London for 9.30am (for a 10am start). There would be an introductory talk, and anyone who took up the offer of coffee was severely reprimanded for ruining their palate! Hubert de Billy would go around pouring wines: six whites, a short break, six reds; then James would drive us all off in a minibus to do something in London (in 1994, a guided tour of the Government Hospitality Cellar in Lancaster House). Of course, none of us cared about this; we wanted to know the result! As winning captain in 1995, I was prodded to give a speech. I was a touch tired and emotional, and it was difficult

ABOVE The 1997 Cambridge team with consolation prizes of Pol Roger White Foil. Left to right: Marek Pitera, Juka Heikkilä, Klaus Martin (captain), Hubert de Billy (Pol Roger), David Metcalfe, Tom Crispin, Richard Lewin and Spyro Markesinis.

ABOVE 1996 and 1997 Oxford captain and top taster Edward Tully (Christ Church, right) with Hugh Johnson, in 1997.

ABOVE The 1995 Oxford team's victory visit to Champagne.

finding the right phrases to say, "Thank you very much to Cambridge for losing," without saying that exactly!

'After the trip to Champagne in 1995, we spent another four days in Burgundy. We stayed at Domaine Dujac and visited the great and good producers in the area. We tried all the '95s in barrel, and back to '69 of La Tâche! We visited such luminaries as Aubert de Villaine of Domaine de la Romanée-Conti, Gérard Jaboulet, Etienne Guigal and Charles Joguet. James was driving us around in a Previa. There were a couple of times when he'd say, "David, can you hold my Champagne glass? I need to change gear!" It was a long time ago …

'The only Cambridge competitor I know is Greg Thomas, who was at Oundle School with me in Northamptonshire, and in the Cambridge team (Jesus) in 1994 and 1995. A doctor, he switched to do his clinical side and joined the Oxford team (St John's) in 1996. James Hardy is a lawyer who works for Clifford Chance. Peter Palmer could be a spy, but we don't know; he travels around eastern European, ex-Balkan countries doing things that no one understands, and somehow has this massive income from it all. Edward Tully, who was captain after me and top taster in two years, is a teacher on Jersey; he once finished his six wines in five minutes, and then got out a newspaper and started reading during the match. He has a picture of the 1997 team clustered around Harry Waugh, who was one of the most charming people it was possible to meet [see page 4]. I was a real shit, actually. When I found out he was going to turn up, I thought, "I bet I can get him on a blind-tasting challenge," and I took along a bottle of La Chapelle '83. Harry said, "Well, you know, I've lost my sense of smell. I can't blind taste anymore, but it's got the texture of La Chapelle '88." Pretty good!

'My first degree was in biological science, and I did a PhD in epidemiology, but as I was finishing off my doctorate I developed paranoid schizophrenia, which torpedoed my academic career. So I went and joined the wine trade. I worked for Lea & Sandeman, as an advisor to the Australian Wine Club, and as a panel-tasting contributor to *Decanter*. I worked for Fosters, selling

Australian fine wine on the phone, which was awful! I hated ringing people up to sell (usually) well-made, if not terribly interesting, £10 Australian Shiraz. They'd all say: "Ten pounds! I could buy a case of wine for that!" And I thought, "You just want something cheap to get drunk on. I'm going to be polite and get off the phone as quickly as possible." Pleasure is important; good wine provides a large amount of pleasure, and a £3.99 wine provides none.

Blogging away

'I now run a hilariously successful wine and food site. There are loads that I read. Keith Levenberg is a bit off-track, but well thought out. I used to do more writing for magazines – *Decanter*, *Wine Spectator* – that paid slightly better, but they didn't want you to be rude. On my blog I have a fantastic degree of freedom. If I don't like something I can say precisely why, and winkle out all the flaws and faults: "This is rubbish. If you buy this you're being robbed!" I don't have advertisers who are going to stop advertising with me, and Google will keep paying per click. I've had between 8–9,000 visitors a month, going up by about five per cent a month. As far as I'm concerned, success is if I can write an article and feel happy I've achieved a little piece of argument that might entertain people. It's a little clique: you communicate with other wine bloggers, email each other what's worth trying, discuss things and then slag each other off violently online – great fun!

'But Robert Parker is right about most wine trade journalists really writing marketing and promotional copy. There's money to be lost if you're not polite about the right things. That doesn't mean they're not nice people; I'm quite popular with a lot of wine merchants, and I often get emails saying, "I agree entirely: that wine is horrible and tastes of rubber and burnt glue, but I sell it, so I'm not going to leave a comment on your site!" I get samples from generous merchants. I go to Burgundy *en primeur* tastings, Howard Ripley's German tastings and portfolio tastings. I have a Wine & Spirit Education Trust diploma, and made wine in Burgundy in 1997 and '98.

'Training for the varsity match is the best wine education one can get. The competition has enabled me to judge wine competitively, buy wines for a variety of organizations, make wine with at least a moderate degree of competence and now write about it with a rich and broad store of information to draw upon. Blind tasting moved me on from being a Champagne, Alsace and Australian wine drinker to Burgundy and German Riesling, and I drink far more Sherry than I used to.

'I now live in Winchester, which makes me immeasurably more relaxed. My best friends are former members of the team: Jeremy Seysses, Edward Tully, Peter Palmer and James Hardy. We still meet up regularly and go on wine trips together, and they all leave rude comments on my site. We visit Jeremy every summer in Burgundy and hang around with the family for a week while tasting wine, and Jeremy stays with Edward Tully every New Year in Jersey. I could not wish for better friends.'

ABOVE Jeremy Seysses receiving a cheque for Oxford Kidney Relief from judge and former Oxford blind taster Charles Metcalfe at the match in 1997.

'It was more important to distinguish between California Chardonnay and French counterparts, than to distinguish the various *crus* of the Côte d'Or, or to learn to recognize Bourboulenc and Clairette.'

An interview with
JEREMY SEYSSES

UNIVERSITY COLLEGE, OXFORD, m.1994

Jeremy Seysses is a managing partner and co-proprietor of Domaine Dujac.

'My parents make wine in Burgundy, although I paid no attention and had little knowledge until I came to university. I am half French and American, grew up in Morey-St-Denis and left for St Clare's, an international boarding school in Oxford, at the age of 17. I hadn't tasted much up until then. Wine tasting was something my parents did, not something young people did.

'I found my way into the Oxford University Wine Circle (OUWC) through the freshers' fair, and was a member for three years and its president for two. At the time, the OUWC ran the blind-tasting team as one and the same society; they've since separated. Annual membership was £45, raised to £50 thereafter. The OUWC was dedicated to tastings of good-calibre wines put on by merchants and producers representing the world's important wine regions (e.g. Jasper Morris MW gave a tasting each year on Burgundy). The Oxford University Wine and Food Society (OUWFS) was also active, with events ranging from a pizza tasting with Pizza Express to tea tastings. Actual wine tastings, however, were infrequent, and typically a taste through the range of a given supermarket – not so interesting to me.

'When I became OUWC president in 1995–96, most of my contacts were producers, so we began to host more winemakers: Josh Jensen (Calera), Alain Graillot, Jean-Pierre de Smet (Domaine de l'Arlot), Egon Müller, Jean-Marc Roulot and a Bordeaux first growth with Frédéric Engerer from Château Latour. Egon Müller was unbelievably generous, providing both younger wines and more mature examples: a 1971 Kabinett, '76 and '59 Auslesen, and finishing with a '85 Eiswein, all from the Scharzhofberg.

'Dr Julian Jack and Nick Rawlins, wine stewards at University College, kindly gave me access to the senior common room college cellar and a few special wines (e.g. Jamet Côte-Rotie '78). The Christ Church cellar was more open, and thanks to Edward Tully, we drank a fair few bottles of Figeac '85 and La Mission Haut-Brion '83. Hanneke Wilson was more than helpful in her counsel. David Strange was captain and coach in my first year, assisted by Peter Palmer. Mark de Vere, a former blind taster studying for his MW, helped on occasion.

'I lacked consistency in 1995, and was selected as reserve (I won the reserve match). With more experience, I became a full team member in 1996 and 1997, and in those years, James Hardy, Edward Tully and I pitched in to train new people. Any member could take part in blind-tasting practice sessions by paying £5 towards the purchase of the wines. We met once to a few times a week, more often as core friendships developed (in my last year some of us met almost every day), and tasted six to eight wines blind – one session white, one session red – and took notes: practice, practice, practice.

'There was only so much time to train, and prioritizing was important. It was more important, for example, to distinguish between California Chardonnay and French counterparts, than to distinguish the various *crus* of the Côte d'Or, or to learn to recognize Bourboulenc and Clairette.

Women in the circle

'The OUWC accepted the first 25 male and the first 25 female applicants. If we'd just taken the first 50, it would've been a male-dominated society, probably reinforcing itself over time. Women were typically slower in sending in their applications, requiring convincing that this was not a drinking club. But there were only so many women willing to join into the competitive aspect of blind tasting, and fewer willing to commit the time necessary to becoming good enough. We did have two women come through the team ranks in my time – Lucy Astill (Christ Church) and Sophie Jourdier (Worcester) – and in subsequent years Lynnette Peterson (Wolfson) and Frederika Adam (Lincoln).

'Socially, we drank with an open mind, though our parents' cellars had a big influence on a number of us, most being Old World-heavy. An Austrian friend gave us exposure to the wines of the Wachau and of Burgenland. New Zealand Sauvignon Blanc was a big deal at the time; not recognizing it in a blind tasting would have been inexcusable. At Oxford, I was introduced to Riesling, of which my parents drank little; I now drink a lot of it and love it. Tasting also made me love Zinfandel for a while. Chilean wine was taking off, for all varieties including Pinot Noir (now seldom seen); Chilean Merlot had not yet been identified as Carmenère.

'Chiang Mai Kitchen's Thai food was good, and not out of budget, but they were never very gracious about bringing in our own wine, even if we offered to pay corkage. Ma Belle was very accepting (corkage £5), but the food was ordinary.

'I played college rugby for three years, but while a member of the first XV, I was never close to being good enough to play for the university team. I dabbled in rowing, but there were only so many hours in the day, and wine was more important. I read biology when DNA and genomic sequencing was undergoing a revolution with polymerase chain-reaction analysis, and genetic modifications were a big focus of study. The internet was in its early stages. As a science student, I was one of the first to be given an email address by faculty, but I rarely received more than an email per week. No one trusted it enough to rely on it, so any email was usually followed by a note or a phone call. Cell phones began to gain popularity, but felt expensive and unessential.

'Until university, I'd been wavering between a career in marine biology or winemaking, but post-Oxford, I studied vine sciences at the Université de Bourgogne (Dijon), committing to wine, and worked two years as a sales representative for O W Loeb & Co in London, dealing mostly with restaurants. In July 2000, I returned to France to work, initially for my father, in the family wineries: Domaine Dujac (Burgundy) and Domaine de Triennes (Provence). I am now president of Domaine Dujac, and share winemaking duties with my brother, Alec, and my wife, Diana Snowden, who works with me at Domaine Dujac as our oenologist. We have two sons: Aubert, born 2007, and Blaise, born 2010.

'The OUWC always ran the risk of becoming a social gathering instead of a club of people serious and passionate about wine. It has been a regret, when I've returned to give tastings, to find the room filled mostly with postgraduate students on two-year masters courses. The continuity and mentoring longer membership can afford has disappeared as a consequence. I hope to see more undergraduates interested in blind tasting and the OUWC in future.

LEFT La famille Seysses: Jacques Seysses (front left) with his daughter-in-law, oenologist Diana Snowden Seysses, and sons Alec (back left) and Jeremy (back right). Jeremy joined the family firm in 2000 and Alec in 2003. Jacques Seysses has owned Domaine Dujac, in Burgundy's Morey-St-Denis, since 1968. Today Domaine Dujac boasts 15.56 hectares of vines in the most prestigious appellations in the Côte de Nuits. Its wines are hugely in demand – with particular interest from Asia.

'Oxford won in all three years I competed at the University Women's Club. My best results came when I tasted fast and went by first impressions. A look at colour, a sniff, a taste to confirm, a few quick notes, and on to the next, returning to fill in the details. I don't think I ever changed my initial impression during the competition without moving from a correct to a wrong answer – which unfortunately I did several times.

'In 1995, only two of our group had competed before. The Cambridge side, with many returning members, felt intimidating, experienced, confident and rightly so. Their captain Tim Hancock (Wolfson) won the highest score that year, but Oxford did well enough (817–760) and we won.

Trips to France's wine regions

'After the winning prize visits to Pol Roger in Épernay, I organized trips to several wine regions. James Simpson was kind enough to join us (and to drive!). In 1995, we went to Burgundy; in '96, to the northern Rhône; and in '97 to Anjou and Touraine. Some of us also went on a separate trip to Alsace that year.

'The trips were fantastic, with Pol Roger Champagne consumed, of course – mostly White Foil, but we also had the extraordinary privilege to taste 1914 Pol Roger during a lunch at the *maison* in Épernay with Hubert de Billy. What a treat, and by a long way the oldest wine any of us had ever tasted. It was still very much alive and delicious, and I remember honey and mushrooms. More recreational moments involved riding around vineyards on bicycles under torrential rain: more fun than I thought possible. On the same trip, Edward Tully and David Strange bought pistols that shot little rubber bullets, and spent the entire drive from Épernay to Savennières in Anjou (five-plus hours), shooting at each other, confirming everyone's suspicions about their mental age.

'Going to bed early in Épernay was never an option, and we explored the local nightlife: pinball was available until 11pm. What then? A nightclub: Club Diamond provided a spacious and empty dance floor. We were close to being the only ones there, but for a single woman who provided James Hardy with the opportunity to use his well-honed pickup line: *La piste de dance est comme un désert sans vous.* Sadly, she was unimpressed. On another night, we were pointed in the direction of Bar Kris. The price of the beers, let alone the Champagne, proved prohibitive, while the shortness of the hostesses' skirts and depth of *décolletés* suggested that perhaps this place was dedicated to more than providing customers with drink. We were proud, however, to see that all the Champagne buckets had been provided by Pol Roger (a testament to the dedication of the Pol sales team).

'Meals were plentiful and terrific. On one trip, having been away from France for much too long, I craved cheese. The restaurant we lunched in did honour to French cheese, but choice proved too difficult. I took the easy and brave way out, and told the waiter, "One of each." I finished my plate of 25 varieties without

flinching under the watchful eye of the table, determined not to admit this might've been a bit much after the previous four courses. The visit to press house that afternoon proved challenging during the digestive coma that ensued.

'I met a number of my best friends through blind tasting, and am indebted to David Strange in mentoring me in wine tasting that first year. Edward Tully (godfather to my younger son) and his wife, Kathryn (née Nunn, also a former member of the OUWC), James Hardy (godfather to my older son) and I talk regularly and meet at every chance, and Peter Palmer's endless patience has made him a favourite among the now numerous children running around whenever our group reunites. I also remain in touch with Anthony Whittaker (Oriel), Thomas Drastik (St Edmund Hall) and Tim Marson (Oriel).

'I am deeply grateful to Pol Roger for hosting us so generously, giving us good memories, and friendships that will last a lifetime. I remember thinking at the time that it was unlikely Pol Roger would ever see any sort of return on investment from a hapless bunch like ours. How little I knew! All of us have been loyal clients since, and there has not been a reunion that has not involved a bottle of Pol Roger – or several. All of them taste that little bit more special because of the associated memories.'

DOMAINE DUJAC APPELLATIONS

Bourgogne Blanc
Morey-St-Denis blanc
Morey-St-Denis 1er Cru Les Monts Luisants blanc

Morey St-Denis
Chambolle-Musigny

Morey-St-Denis 1er Cru
Chambolle-Musigny 1er Cru Les Gruenchers
Gevrey-Chambertin 1er Cru Aux Combottes
Vosne-Romanée 1er Cru Les Beaux-Monts
Vosne-Romanée 1er Cru Aux Malconsorts

Charmes-Chambertin
Clos de la Roche
Clos St-Denis
Échézeaux
Bonnes-Mares
Chambertin
Romanée St-Vivant

2001 CLOS ST-DENIS: ANATOMY OF A WINE

by JEREMY SEYSSES

'When villages affixed the name of their most prestigious vineyard – the *clos* – to the name of their town, such as Le Musigny to Chambolle or Le Chambertin to Gevrey, Morey chose the *grand cru* Clos St-Denis. This choice, made in 1927, has been subject to some controversy. Some people argue that Clos de la Roche is the *tête de cuvée* of Morey, while others think the Clos de Tart should have pride of place. I would argue that, based on those qualities that make a red wine quintessentially Burgundian – elegance, finesse of tannin, weightlessness, perfume, length and complexity – Clos St-Denis was the correct choice. From Clos St-Denis come some of the most elegant wines of the Côte de Nuits.

'Few people know Clos St-Denis very well. The vineyard is 6.62 hectares (ha), with an annual production of under 25,000 bottles, so it is a rare wine. Like many other Burgundian *grands crus*, it is composed of several *climats* (individually named vineyards), namely the original Clos St-Denis, Maison Brûlée, les Chaffots and Calouère. Domaine Dujac is the second-largest owner, with 1.47ha lying mostly in Calouère (1.11ha), the remainder in Clos St-Denis and Chaffots.

'When discussing Clos St-Denis, it is only natural to compare it to its immediate neighbour, Clos de la Roche. These two vineyards co-exist in many *domaines*, including ours. Geologically, they are similar. Clos de la Roche is perhaps a bit rockier, and the clay of Clos St-Denis is a bit redder, indicating a higher iron content. My feeling is that most of the differences are to be attributed to the fact that Clos St-Denis is located at the bottom of the Combe de Morey, a small canyon leading in to the plateau above. These *combes* channel air masses and contribute greatly to the microclimates that make the Côte so diverse. Cold air pockets behave like liquids, pouring out of the *combes*, so I suspect Clos St-Denis sees more air movement and bigger temperature fluctuations than Clos de la Roche – subtle things, but defining over the course of a growing season.

Viticulture

'The year 2001 marked the beginning of organic and biodynamic farming at Domaine Dujac. We had stopped herbicides in the early 1990s and felt ready to take the next step. About a third of the *domaine* was farmed organically that first year, and, following a *stage* in biodynamics, we decided to apply biodynamic preparations to the vineyards. Organic is by no means the ideal way of farming, but we feel that it is one of the better ways and have had excellent results with it. Using no synthetic compounds means that whatever you're spraying – e.g. copper sulphate or sulphur – can be washed off easily and protects only existing growth. Any new leaves that grow after a spray are open to contamination from fungal disease. By contrast, in conventional production, systemic pesticides protect a plant, including new growth, against disease for a period of time.

'This has several implications. The first is that organics contain a higher element of risk: the margin of error is much smaller. Viticulture is essentially intensive monoculture and *Vitis vinifera* is sensitive to a bevy of fungal disease. In our area, downy and powdery mildew (oïdium) are the two main fungal pathogens affecting vines. The best defence is prophylactic. Training your vine so as to maximize air flow and reduce humidity in the canopy and on the grapes is crucial. As with anything that involves greater risk, you have to become very good at what you do: better at observing conditions (the life cycle of downy mildew is well known, whereas oïdium contaminations are harder to predict); better at timing and positioning your spraying – i.e. better at making the right choices. Experience counts for a lot, and writing this just before our 12th organic and biodynamic harvest comes in, at the end of the toughest growing seasons in many decades, I can say with confidence that our vineyard team has become very good at what they do.

The vintage

'The 2001 vintage was, in many ways, a typical Burgundian vintage. A late budbreak was followed by a normal flowering time in mid-June, under good weather conditions. The summer went from hot to cold and dry to humid several times and was followed by a cool, overcast September – cool enough to delay picking by a week. Typically, we count 100 days from full flowering to picking. In 2001, we began the harvest 107 days post-flowering, on September 26, taking advantage of an eight-day window of good weather between rains.

'We get this type of varied weather more often than not in Burgundy. With recent improvements in viticulture, mainly our ability to keep the canopy healthy and controlling the size of the crop, this does not impact our ability to get the crop ripe. However, despite best efforts, there is often, as in 2001, some botrytis or grey rot infection on the grapes. Around harvest time, the choice of picking date is crucial. Does one allow

ABOVE A view of the village of Morey from the northwest corner of Clos St-Denis, encompassing most of Clos St-Denis itself, taken by Jeremy Seysses just after harvest in September 2012.

the botrytis to progress, hoping for a few days of extra ripening to make a difference? What will the weather be like? Experience, observation and luck are required.

Winemaking

'The Clos St-Denis was picked on September 27–28. Our pickers sort as they go along rather than on a hypnotic, mind-numbing sorting table. Thanks to their rigorous work, only healthy, ripe grapes made it into the tank. Potential alcohols were 12 per cent, at the lower end, but the grapes showed all the hallmarks of ripeness: partially lignified stems, pulp easily separated from the seeds, brown pips, etc. Domaine Dujac has a long history of whole-cluster fermentations. However, in 2001, we took the unusual step of destemming a significant proportion of the grapes. The Clos St-Denis was about 60 per cent destemmed, 40 per cent whole cluster. The yield was 34 hectolitres per ha.

'Winemaking was straightforward. The grapes came in cool and took about four days before they began fermenting spontaneously with native yeasts. The

ripeness was evident when the must became deeply coloured after just a few punch-downs; extractability is a good indicator of ripeness. We chaptalized the fermenting must using cane sugar so that it would end up at 13 per cent, punching down regularly. Fermentation and maceration lasted ten days, at which point we pressed, settled the wine and put it in barrel. Malolactic fermentation was slow, beginning in spring and finishing in late June 2002. Until 2001, the malolactic had always taken place before the winter following harvest. We use a high proportion of new oak on our *grands crus*: in this case, about 90 per cent. We bottled the unfined, unfiltered wine in March 2003.

The wine, as tasted in August 2013

'Dark garnet, bricking at the rim; darker than many older vintages of Dujac, partly due to the later malolactic. At almost 12 years old, some evolution in the colour is normal. The deeply aromatic nose shows spices that I strongly associate with Morey St-Denis, such as cinnamon and nutmeg. Floral components, violets and rose petals, point more specifically to the Clos St-Denis. Some Pinot [Noir] fruit – sour cherries and plums – is in the background. A sappy quality is indicative of the partial whole-cluster fermentation, and sandalwood and oak notes reflect the time in new-oak barrels. Age is beginning to show in hints of forest floor, mushroom and earth. On the palate, the transparent, cool nature of the vintage is palpable. The wine is still firm with some dusty tannins. But the tannins are elegant and show some of the Clos St-Denis silkiness. Bright acidity and length indicate its pedigree.'

CHAMPAGNE AND RACE CARS
by ANDREW COMRIE-PICARD

TRINITY COLLEGE, OXFORD, m.1996

Andrew Comrie-Picard started rally racing while at Oxford, where he ran the Oxford University Wine Circle in 1997–98 and was on the blind-tasting team in 1997 and 1998. After a brief stint as an entertainment lawyer in New York City, he left to race full time. He is a stunt driver for film and television, a producer, writer and precision driver on the US version of BBC's Top Gear, *and hosts other shows about automobiles.*

'Champagne is much harder to clean off a car than you would expect. The first documented use of Champagne spray as a motor-racing victory celebration was in fact by an American at the 24 Hours of Le Mans (the world's oldest active sports-car race in endurance racing), and it was spontaneous. Dan Gurney, the unexpected 1967 victor, took the bottle he was holding after the race and sprayed everyone in his vicinity: Henry Ford II, A J Foyt, and Carroll Shelby, among others.

'My crew hates me for this – or rather, they love it when we're on the podium after the race (having satisfied goals, sponsors and egos), spraying Champagne everywhere, but they hate the last thing I always do, which is to pour it over the still-hot hood of the car, from whence it trickles down onto the molten, ticking engine, where it boils off and turns to sticky glue. But I can't have all the Champagne and not share it with the car! I reckon the car earned it; I just operated the controls. My team has had the fortunate opportunity to waste a lot of Champagne on race cars.

'It's turning into a tough race and we've had our share of troubles, but I'm confident we'll be tasting Champagne at the end.'

'For the last decade, we've been competing on the pointy end of the North American Rally Championship (which we won in 2009), and at five consecutive ESPN X Games, where we medalled in 2010. Along the way we've seen some good, and some not-so-good, fizzy stuff sprayed on us and our cars. And I have come to rate events in part on how good the bubbly is at the end. Most races pimp for the Proper Stuff, but the sad truth is that some races cheap out – *méthode Champenoise* be damned – and in Missouri the ban against open liquor in public places actually meant that we had to spray some kind of non-alcoholic fizzy fruit wine on the podium. That bottle I neither drank nor subjected the car to.

'For the first five years we kept all the bottles and labelled them with the race name and result and put them on a shelf back at the shop, but eventually the shelf became full and we became blasé and this tradition has fizzled out. We keep spare brake fluid on that shelf now, but Champagne still remains prominent in our minds. I often rate probable success on the basis of the chance for Champagne. One of my common quotes to the media mid-event is, "It's turning into a tough race and we've had our share of troubles, but I'm confident we'll be tasting Champagne at the end."

'On a recent competition, a 2000km road race, our margin of victory was so considerable, and the significance of the win sufficiently large, that one of our supporters brought out a bottle of 1990 Pol Roger rosé after the race. We allowed the cork to blow right off and drank it straight from the bottle, and truly, there's nothing better – damage to the wine and insult to the nose be damned! Fortunately, as the driver, I got the first crack at it. But old habits die hard. As the bottle came around to me a second time, I poured the dregs over the car hood. Hey, it may have been vintage Pol Roger, but the car earned it. I'm sure the crew will be only too pleased to clean it off.'

ABOVE Andrew Comrie-Picard (fourth from the left) celebrates a first place finish, Lewiston, Michigan, 2013.

An interview with ALEX HUNT MW

WORCESTER COLLEGE, OXFORD, m.1997

Alex Hunt MW is purchasing director at Berkmann Wine Cellars in London.

'I competed in 1999 and 2000 (as captain), and Oxford won in both years. I was part of the Oxford University Wine Circle (OUWC), but it was about the time of the founding of a new university wine society called Bacchus. Dr Hanneke Wilson was the OUWC senior common room presence, and integral to getting the tasting team up to scratch. In 1998–99, Captain Andrew Sleightholme had us meet in rooms at Christ Church. After that, we tended to meet in New College. At that point, the OUWC was stable and ran stupendous tastings (for a capacity of around 60), and also ran the blind-tasting team. The fragmentation between the two groups happened shortly after my time.

'Prior to Oxford, I'd been in a loosely structured wine society at Winchester College, where a singular maths teacher presented treasures from his cellar a couple of times a term. We had Château Pédesclaux '90, vintages of Beaucastel and Musar, and a '59 Riesling Auslese, which he encouraged us to guess the age of: we were all 20 years too young.

Joining the Wine Circle

'You had to write a detailed letter of application on why you should be allowed to join the OUWC. In my first term, I failed to write convincingly enough and I didn't get in, but I made it into the OUWC in my second year, by which time I was already working for Oddbins in north Oxford over the holidays. During my two years in the OUWC, we had three of the first growths and numerous second growths, nice Burgundy, and Javier Hidalgo did his annual Sherry tastings. I decided I wanted to work in the trade at the point at which Paul Draper was midway through his presentation (which coincided with my failure to think of a career alternative). There was something about the combination of spectacular wines and the way Draper spoke about them that clicked. But Oddbins was a holiday job, and I vowed that it would only ever be that (I'd seen people who'd fallen into its enjoyable lifestyle still there six years later). Mayfair Cellars had just been bought by Champagne Jacquesson, and Michael MacKenzie, a blind taster from the 1970s who owned a stake in Jacquesson, had done a presentation to the OUWC when Frederika Adam (Linacre) tipped me off that they had a position going. I joined Mayfair Cellars in 2000, and I've been at Berkmann Wine Cellars since 2006.

'The match was held at the University Women's Club on Audley Square, and Jancis Robinson and Hugh Johnson were judges, de rigueur. We went on a jolly prize visit to Épernay, but didn't yet compete against the French (it was all very humble and simple at that time). That started not long afterwards, with the Chris

ABOVE The 1999 match with (left to right) Oxford captain Andrew Sleightholme, Colette Clement (Cambridge) and Alex Hunt (Oxford). Hubert de Billy and James Simpson look on.

> 'All these fundamental parts of analytical tasting were a means to an end, which was getting the wines right and beating Cambridge. Ultimately, it's not a party trick.'

Dark/Tom Bromwich (both Trinity) era winning double magnums of Lafite in Champagne. [Since 2003, as part of the prize-winning trip to Épernay, the winning Oxbridge team competes against the best French university team.]

'It's unfair to suggest that if you're not interested in learning to blind taste, you're only there for the label. A middle category would be the majority: people who have a non-academic, non-competitive interest in wine for its own sake. Blind tasting is difficult. You need to be committed, and have an endless store of humility and patience.

Varsity match vs MW, identification vs analysis

'My palate is good from exposure and practice. Blind tasting in the varsity match actually puts you at a disadvantage when you then go and learn it in the trade. The way it's scored in trade exams, be it diploma or MW, is that the majority of marks are given for the description and analysis of the wine, and the minority for the identification. In a sense, that's how it should be, because ultimately, in the trade, you're working with an open knowledge of the label. I think it's correct that analysis is favoured in the trade exams, but it makes it difficult and most people don't pass. However, in the varsity matches, inversely, 75 per cent of the marks are for spotting the wine, and 25 per cent for the justificatory description.

'For two years at Oxford I was focused on getting the wine right. You had an advantage in not having to work so hard from first principles every time, with the knack of recognition, but as MW students we were almost told you don't have to get all the wines right, and you can still pass. I aimed to get them right and also to write intelligently about them. I think it's probably easier to learn recognition first and analysis second. Certainly, though, we would be castigated by Hanneke if we wrote stupid things in the description box.

'We weren't idiot savants, tasting in a completely subconscious, intuitive way. We would be writing notes on the wine to deduce what it was, if it wasn't immediately recognized. It's simply that the emphasis, the ultimate goal in the varsity match was not to do a nice analysis; the ultimate goal was to get the identification right, and to use the analysis as a tool. So we were training ourselves to identify alcohol levels to within half a degree, to learn to taste sugar, to taste the difference between alcohol and acidity, to recognize and describe tannins. And all these fundamental parts of analytical tasting were a means to an end, which was getting the wines right and beating Cambridge. Ultimately, it's not a party trick.

Mastering the art of tasting – and description

'I did the Wine & Spirit Education Trust higher certificate as soon as I joined Mayfair Cellars, and then went into the diploma within months. I was keen to do the MW, was supported by successive bosses through the whole process, and won the Madame Bollinger prize for the tasting papers. I don't know quite what class to think of myself in because I passed the exams in 2004, but only finally got the letters in 2010. I definitely took it seriously, and I enjoyed socializing with other wine geeks. The best part of blind tasting is participation with like-minded people in a difficult enterprise. With blind tasting, there is nowhere to hide. You get it right or you get it wrong, and you try and get better. I wrote a series on the language of wine description for *World of Fine Wine* commissioned by Neil Beckett. We must have

ABOVE The 1999 captains shake hands. Andrew Sleightholme (Oxford) (left) and top taster Jonathan Bevan (Cambridge).

been discussing my first MW dissertation – a philosophy of criticism piece that failed. My first dissertation was about objectivity in wine criticism, and whether such a thing can exist. The thrust of most of it was to look at parallel lines of enquiry in the arts, where philosophers have questioned whether there can be an objective basis for judgements of quality of painting and literature. But it turned out that the methods by which one writes a philosophical paper were not considered by the Institute of Masters of Wine (IMW) to constitute research. The IMW takes a narrower definition of research than any university. The MW dissertation in its present form is a very young thing, and the criteria required for passing are continually redefined over time. They want original research, by which they mean original data.

'My second dissertation was titled *Increasing Must Weight in California: Trends, Causes and Implications for Winemaking*. There were two sources of original data: a questionnaire I sent to everyone making Chardonnay, Cabernet or Zinfandel in the state; and follow-up interviews with the winemakers. Then I gathered data from the two main de-alcoholization consultancy companies, detailed ripeness data from state authorities, and US weather station data over 100 years. The conclusion was that, however much people would like to claim it, climate change has had no effect on increasing ripeness of grapes in California. It's a combination of viticultural factors, and a paradigm shift in the criteria used by winemakers to determine when they pick their grapes. In chasing a certain flavour style, the sugar content of grapes, when they're deemed ripe, has rocketed to unprecedented levels.

'There aren't legal alcohol limits in the US; there are tax boundaries, but the wine can be as strong as you like. There's a hard tax boundary at 14 per cent (ABV) that cuts across most wines (in the UK it's 15 per cent). So you'll find that, with quite a lot of people, if they end up with wines at 14.1 per cent and it's a big production, what they spend in reducing the alcohol to 13.9 per cent, they will more than recoup in the tax benefit.

'This explicitly sanctions the replacement, in the winery, of water lost through field dehydration: in other words, waiting to pick grapes until they've turned into raisins. Cynics among us might argue that because a lot of wineries in California buy fruit rather than pick it from their own vineyards, and a lot of them pay by weight, it's better to have 20 per cent of the water evaporate in the grapes, pay 20 per cent less for expensive grapes, and then replace that water in the winery, dollars per megalitre. Other people say the best vineyards are paid on a per-acre rather than a per-ton basis, so that wouldn't have any effect. So there are sides.

'Recently, Jancis Robinson commissioned me to do a monthly column for her website. In the announcement she made before the first piece was published, she cited our first meeting at the blind-tasting match, when she was a judge. So it all goes back to that.'

An interview with ED FITZGERALD
Bacchus: Oxford University Wine Society

MAGDALEN COLLEGE, OXFORD, m.1997

Ed Fitzgerald MRCS is a surgical registrar in London.

'Drink no longer water, but use a little wine for thy stomach's sake and thine often infirmities.' 1 Timothy 5:23.

'My parents packaged me off up to Oxford to read medicine with a six-bottle wine rack, a half case of wine, and a copy of *Oz Clarke's Pocket Wine Guide*. My friends thought, 'This chap must know something about wine,' and I've tried to live up to that as much possible.

'Magdalen has a strong wine tradition, and was unique in that it had its own JCR wine shop - a mini version of Oddbins – underneath the main college hall which was staffed, stocked and run entirely by students for students. When it came to the end of my first year, I got involved in running the wine shop. Terry Newport, a phenomenal fellow with 30 years of service as SCR wine steward, and I spent evenings in the college cellar, and if something special had been opened at high table he would let me taste a glass. Magdalen had a spectacular college wine society, with one particularly generous individual, Marcus Malkmus, who was a major wine collector. He put on fabulous tastings, which used to start at eight in the evening and finish at about five in the morning: a vertical of 15 vintages of Penfolds Grange with accompanying foods, partnered with good vintages of La Chapelle for comparison. It was remarkable.

'Peter Pound, an American, was running the Oxford University Wine Circle (OUWC) then, and I went to a Frog's Leap tasting at New College at the end of my first year. Alex Hunt, now MW, was a member. I never formally joined OUWC, but I went to tastings when there was space. By my second year, the idea came together to set up Bacchus: Oxford University Wine Society (I did hear it raised a few eyebrows at the time). There was a market for another society that could cater for people who were not so knowledgeable about wine already. OUWC was formal and capped its number of memberships, a big influence on surplus demand for wine tasting at the university level. College wine societies were good, but congregated around the college cellar, and didn't have the gravitas or following to pull in a big international winery or producer.

'Within a year or two, quite a few people were members of both groups, including OUWC committee members. And at the freshers' fair in the second year 1,000 people expressed an interest. There's always been student interest in wine, but by the late '90s and through the supermarkets wine reached a much wider audience. Bacchus was involved in capturing that upswing of exposure and interest. In 2002, Nina Wilson (University), who competed in the varsity match that year, Beth Shapiro (Balliol) and I won the Australian University Wine Challenge (in its second year) and awareness took off. Professor John Stein, brother of chef Rick Stein and a neuro-physiologist, was our first senior member. He joined Magdalen in the '60s when Latour and Lafite were only a couple of pounds from the college cellar. We had a number of fellows in a broad membership – it was good fun. But setting up a new society was hard work. We paid out of pocket, and didn't have any contacts or connections in the trade, but gained momentum and organized weekly tastings with world famous wineries. With over 300 members, it was starting to get a bit tricky, but we never capped membership. We launched an online sign-up system in the spring of 2000, to regulate the number of people at events; it made it more business-like.

'In 2002–03, we started beginner wine courses, which tapped into an immense need in Oxford. They would book out within a couple of days every time. We took people who knew nothing about wine and introduced them to how to taste professionally, to different grape varieties, dispelled a lot of myth and intrigue and addressed the basic science behind wine and winemaking. We did blind tasting, but the society wasn't built around that. Membership was £20, and £2 for tastings on the door. It was a terribly ambitious project. If I was at Oxford today, I'd taste the best of all worlds.'

OXFORD UNIVERSITY WINE SOCIETIES

- Oxford University Wine and Food Society (OUWFS) was founded in association with André Simon's Wine and Food Society in 1951. Headed by early presidents David d'Ambrumenil (New) and H B G Montgomery (Lincoln), it was the sole society behind the blind-tasting match until the 1960s. By the 1990s, OUWFS had changed focus, away from serious wine tastings toward food and novelty tastings.
- Oxford University Wine Circle (OUWC) was established in the early 1960s; in 1965 its members first joined forces with the OUWFS to field a stronger Oxford blind-tasting team. OUWC became the society to train the blind-tasting teams from the 1980s until 2008.
- Bacchus was the third university-wide wine society founded in 1998–99 by its first president Edward Fitzgerald (Magdalen), to address a growing widespread university interest in wine not fulfilled by the limited (and more expert) membership of OUWC. It has a strong and diverse membership today.
- Oxford University Blind Tasting Society (oxfordblindtasting. com) became a distinct organization from OUWC in 2008–09; its founding captain and first president was John Mead (St Hugh's).

CHAMPAGNE
POL ROGER

A lunch to celebrate the
60th Anniversary of the Oxford and Cambridge Blind
Wine-Tasting Competition

at Berry Brothers & Rudd
on Thursday February 21st 2013

Reds, whites and Blues

Oxbridge rivalry goes beyond the Boat Race
– the wine-tasting contest is hard-fought, too

Team profiles have evolved considerably since 1953. ABOVE The 2013 Cambridge team included five women, five PhD students, with six tasters competing for the first time; from seven different colleges, they hailed from South Korea, the Netherlands, Poland, the UK, Canada, Lithuania and the US. Front row, left to right: Ellie Kim (captain), Vaiva Imbrasaite, Lucy Yang, Madeline Huberth and Jennifer Yen; (back row) Antoni Wrobel, Stefan Kuppen (tied for top taster) and David Beall (coach). They tasted valiantly – losing by only 12 points to an experienced Oxford team (TOP): (front row) Ren Lim (captain), Swii Yii Lim, Henry Little, Hanneke Wilson (coach), George Scratcherd (coach) and Tao (L J) Ruan; (back row) David Soud, Tom Arnold (tied for top taster – his father Charles Arnold tasted for Oxford in the early 1960s) and James Anderson.

THE 2000s

Facebook; Twitter; Obama; the Queen's Diamond Jubilee; the London Olympics. By the 2010s, UK wine consumption, which was only 1.7 per cent of alcohol consumption in the 1950s, climbed to 20 per cent and 28 bottles per capita per annum (while beer dropped, 94 to 66 per cent). Wine education is no longer only for those in the trade. The tasting teams are transfigured. Eight wins to Oxford; six wins to Cambridge. The 60th competition wines included a 1953 Vega Sicilia. Noted by Jancis Robinson as 'expressive, with strong overtones of vanilla oak and slight cheesiness', it was as old, and as alive, as the varsity blind wine-tasting match.

Cambridge

Nicholas Aldridge, 2001
Jeff Bailey, 2007
Mark Barber, 2010
David Beall, 2011
Bettina Beinhoff, 2008
Dominic Brittain, 2001, 2002
John Burman, 2007
Andrew Butt, 2007, 2008, 2009
Freya Cameron, 2002, 2003 C
Dexter Canoy, 2003
Simon Chin, 2006
Victor Chun, 2000
Aaron Coble, 2008, 2009
Ian Colman, 2006
Aidan Craig, 2004, 2005, 2006 C and T
Molly Crockett, 2007, 2008
Rodolphe d'Arjuzon, 2000, 2002 C
Rafael de Haan, 2001
Carlos del Cueto, 2010, 2011
Eric Denton, 2011
Benjamin Drew, 2004, 2005 C
Robert Fenster, 2004, 2005
Jeremy Fialko, 2001
Dominic Forsythe, 2002
Pierre Gaudillat, 2002, 2003
Alastair Green, 2006
Rohan Gulrajani, 2004
(Anthony) John Harrison, 2003, 2004 Co-C
Madeline Huberth, 2013
James Hutchinson, 2007, 2008 C, 2009 C
Vaiva Imbrasaite, 2013
Nicholas Jackson, 2011
Rhys James, 2012
Ellie Kim, 2012, 2013 C

James Kirkbride, 2005, 2006, 2007 C
Rachel Kulick, 2010
Stefan Kuppen, 2013 T
Albert Lee, 2000
Ryan Marien, 2010
David Metcalfe, 2000
Monica Morrill, 2006
Lionel Nierop, 2005
Felix Nissen, 2012
Claire Novorol, 2010 C, 2011 C
Anna Oates, 2003
Lynnette Peterson, 2007
Gareth Powell, 2010, 2011
Hannah Price, 2011, 2012 C
Edward Ragg, 2000, 2001 C, 2002
Natasha Redcliffe, 2012
Matthew Richardson, 2012
Alexandria Richart, 2009
John (Jack) Rose, 2010
Ainsley Mayhew Seers, 2004, 2005
Daniel Simon, 2000 C
Katherine Smith, 2008, 2009 T
Daniel Thornton, 2002
Cain Todd, 2001, 2003
Gillian Todd, 2006
Thijs Venema, 2008
Michelle Vickers, 2012
Fabian Wagner, 2000
Fongyee Walker, 2003, 2004 Co-C and T, 2005
Rosalynne Watt, 2009
James Whyte, 2001
Robert Williams, 2009
Antoni Wrobel, 2013
Lucy Yang, 2013
Jennifer Yen, 2013

Oxford

Frederika Adam, 2000, 2001 T
James Anderson, 2013
Tom Arnold, 2013 T
Piers Barclay, 2006, 2007 C, 2008 T
Lukas Brandt, 2011
Sean Breen, 2005
Tom Bromwich, 2001, 2002, 2003 C
Torquil Carlisle, 2004
Caroline Conner, 2009 T
Chris Dark, 2000, 2001 C, 2002 C and T
Omar Farid, 2011
James Flewellen, 2010 T, 2011 C and T, 2012 C
Alexander Foulkes 2002, 2003, 2004 C
Yohan Graham, 2003 T, 2004, 2005 C and T
Adam Harmon, 2009, 2010
Alun Harris, 2004, 2005, 2006
Daniel Hasler, 2003
Rob Hayward, 2004, 2006 Co-C
Lucian Holland, 2005
Alex Hunt (MW), 2000 C
Stephen Knights, 2005
Sarah Knowles, 2006
Paulius Kuncinas, 2002, 2003
Ren Lim, 2011, 2012 T, 2013 C
Swii Yii Lim, 2013
Henry Little, 2012, 2013
Mark Martin, 2000, 2001, 2002
Rumbidzai Maweni, 2010
John Mead, 2007, 2008 C, 2009
Cecilia Muldoon 2008, 2009, 2010
Ed O'Malley, 2000 T
YiXin Ong, 2001

Tom Parker, 2011
Ciaran Patrick, 2001, 2002, 2003
Charles Pattison, 2005
William Pearce, 2007 T
Paul Phelps, 2010, 2011
Daniel Phillips, 2005
Jan-Karel Pinxten, 2012
Charlie Pistorius, 2007, 2008
William Pooley, 2007, 2008, 2011
Adam Porter, 2004
Peter Power, 2012
Tao (L J) Ruan, 2012, 2013
Andras Salamon, 2007, 2008
Michael Saller, 2000
Jorg Scheibe, 2003
Janet Scott, 2004, 2006 Co-C
George Scratcherd, 2008, 2009 C, 2010 C
David Soud, 2012, 2013
Daniel Thornton, 2001
Gareth Tilley, 2006
Hsien Min Toh, 2000
Justin Walker, 2006, 2007
Lisa Welze, 2010
Robert West, 2009
Nina Wilson, 2002
Alex Woodham, 2009

C = captain T = top taster

ABOVE Frederika Adam with Hugh Johnson in 1999.

An interview with
FREDERIKA ADAM

LINACRE COLLEGE, OXFORD, m.1996

Frederika Adam read for a doctorate in post-war British art history at Oxford and has since settled in the UK with a portfolio career as a photographer, sommelier, co-founder of the Real Tennis Society and co-creator of Realtennis.tv. She is a top female real tennis player and has won the British, French and US Open doubles titles.

'With the US drinking laws, learning about wine is something many North American students feel they miss out on until graduate school. I had been an undergraduate at the University of Michigan, and did my masters degree at St Andrews in Scotland, where I had been a member of the St Andrews Quaich Society – but unfortunately in the days before the St Andrews versus Edinburgh blind-tasting match (also now sponsored by Pol Roger). So I joined the Oxford University Wine Circle (OUWC) in my first term as a PhD student, and started blind tasting in my second year.

'My first year in the OUWC caught the end of the David Strange, Ed Tully and Jeremy Seysses era. They were huge personalities, with David often making excited announcements about blind-tasting sessions, and their success in the 1997 tasting match (731 to 605!). In the autumn of 1997, Jeremy, who had graduated, came back to do a tasting for the OUWC and convinced me by saying that, "If you really want to learn about wine, you have to do blind tasting." From that moment I started attending blind-tasting workouts and Jeremy became my mentor. We were expected to memorize a crib sheet listing grape varieties and key characteristics across various regions within a few weeks. Early grape memories are of varieties and wines that you had to know for the match, but which did not always merit much respect: commercial Chilean Merlot, young California Cabernet Sauvignon and "white Rioja", aka Viura (no Albariño in those days).

Blind tasters on tour: the northern Rhône

'I went on my first comprehensive tasting trip to the northern Rhône over the Easter holiday in 1998. The Seysses-Strange-Tully-Hardy blind-tasting team was joined by James Simpson MW, Gernot Schleiss (an Oxford-based Austrian friend) and blind tasters Peter Palmer and Simon Bucknall (University). Jeremy, who had organized the trip, used Remington Norman's book

Rhône Renaissance (1995) as his guide, and over four days we visited Robert Jasmin, René Rostaing, Jaboulet, Alain Graillot, Auguste and Pierre-Marie Clape, Jean-Louis Grippat, Alain Voge, Jean Lionnet, Jean-Paul Jamet, Joel Champet and Bernard Burgaud. In the evenings, we would taste wines blind before heading out to dinner, and blind tasting continued when we returned to Domaine Dujac for our final dinner on the Saturday evening, where I had – for the first, and only, time – Domaine de la Romanée-Conti Richebourg 1978.

'Having a sense of place – of where grapes are grown and wine is made – and to be in the landscape, with a feeling of season, meeting the people and recognizing the smells of winemaking all provide a completely new dimension to the picture. It's similar to learning about art, where a pilgrimage to see an altarpiece in a remote Tuscan hill town, or trekking to the East End of London to visit the latest gallery, reveals and rewards.

'In 1998, Cambridge had interrupted Oxford's three-year winning streak, and so Captain Andrew Sleightholme (Christ Church) asked Hanneke Wilson to coach us for the 1999 match (she had been less active for a spell, perhaps because Strange & Co were incredibly self-sufficient). Hanneke is a fantastic teacher; you want to please her and do well. When you take a wrong turn or jump to a conclusion, she guides you to figure out where you went wrong, and gives you the memorable clues to prevent you from making the same mistake twice.

'Blind tasting is a fickle sport. Just as you start to recognize the "bankers", human doubt creeps in. The revelation of blind tasting is that, little by little – almost miraculously – one starts to remember types of wines, then more specifically individual wines, as sensory impressions are stored in the memory bank. Blind tasting is tasting wines by comparison, side by side, six wines in the case of the match. First impressions first: colour and smell provide big clues. Then taste: palate, weight, acidity, alcohol and tannins "should confirm your first impression" (to quote Hanneke). Blind tasting changes your whole perspective on how to understand and appreciate wine; most profoundly, it takes the pretension out of wine.

'And as soon as you start blind tasting you become hypersensitive: "Why is the light so bad in the Red Room?" and "Can we please get the person wearing perfume *out* of the room?"!

Party like it's 1999

'After my first match in 1999, we were very worried to hear shouts of excitement from the Cambridge team when John Bevan (Trinity) realized he had gotten all the reds right. On our tense return trip from the pub back to the University Women's Club (UWC), Bill Gunn MW announced John as top taster and we were ready to accept defeat. However, an exceptional magnum prize was awarded to me for being one point off John's score – and the Oxford team had in fact won by 12 points and so *we* were going to Épernay!

L'Equipe 2000

'In the following year, Alex Hunt took over as captain and I ran the OUWC. We raised the annual fee to £80, which is a lot of money for a student, and we were still oversubscribed. OUWC secretary Ed O'Malley (New) looked after logistics, from designing term cards to sourcing candles from the New College chapel for Jean-Bernard Delmas – who insisted on double-decanting the Haut-Brion wines by candlelight. The highlight of Michaelmas term was an uninterrupted hour-and-a-half tasting with Paul Draper. Normally 40 minutes is the magic moment when the attention starts to go, the noise level rises and the wine takes effect, but Paul had completely mesmerized his audience. I visited Ridge twice while I was at Oxford (my parents live in the San Francisco Bay Area of California) and Paul Draper's wines will always be a favourite.

'That year we were feeling pretty confident. Self-appointed "head of research" Hsien Min Toh (Keble) had compiled a master list of UK wine merchants in the hope of identifying which one James Simpson might choose the wines from for the match! In preparation, we had a match against Oddbins staff – former blind taster Tim Marson, now MW, was then based at Oddbins on the high street. This was the final phase of the wonderful world of Oddbins and its quirky and knowledgeable staff (which included Alex Hunt, who was working at Oddbins in Summertown during the holidays).

'By this time, we also had a good sense of James Simpson's *modus operandi* for selecting match wines. Pale Sangiovese or Pinot Noir often appeared near the top of the red line-up, followed by an American-oaked Tempranillo or fuller Cabernet Franc (Joguet being a favourite producer), and if not an eucalyptus-infused Shiraz, then inevitably a "sweaty farmyard full of blackberries" Syrah from the northern Rhône. Syrah of

ABOVE The 1998 Oxford ladies varsity lawn tennis team, the first year James Simpson (left) and Pol Roger sponsored the match. Frederika Adam is second from right.

the northern Rhône is one of my favourites and I can recognize it immediately – even out of the glass! On arriving at the 2000 match, on the stairs of the UWC I met James, who had just emerged from tasting the wines, and was greeted with a big, black smile and two kisses on either cheek. I detected the smell of Syrah from the northern Rhône (Cornas) and once he was out of earshot gathered the team together to give them the news. Sure enough, it was wine number five, and to this day Alex Hunt still can't believe he didn't put it down for the reds. In any event, we won the match comfortably in 2000, with Ed O'Malley winning top taster, and were thrilled to have lunch with Harry Waugh and his wife, Prue, after the match. That year, Pol hosted us in Épernay in their brand-new white-marbled tasting room [see page 4].

On the Hunt

'I had a strong feeling that Alex was destined for the wine world. As fate would have it, the evening after his final exam in aesthetics at Oxford, he arrived late to the OUWC tasting I was hosting with Bérénice Lurton. I silently mouthed to him: "How did it go?" His big smile and thumbs up were good signs. Afterwards, he came up to me, and said, "You're not going to believe it. One of the questions I had was: could one wine be better than another?" That was his final exam at Oxford.

'When Michael MacKenzie (New) of Mayfair Cellars, a former blind taster and OUWC president, visited Oxford to do a tasting of Champagne Jacquesson, he mentioned he was looking for a new recruit. I immediately told him about Alex, who then started at Mayfair Cellars the following autumn.

My final match

'For the 2001 match we gained a group of new and formidable tasters: Ciaran Patrick (Christ Church), Tom

Bromwich (Trinity), Dan Thornton (Trinity) and YiXin Ong (Exeter) arrived – and joined me, Mark Martin (Trinity) and Captain Chris Dark (Trinity) in the team. Our workouts included a number of keen tasters who would eventually compete, including Ciaran's future husband, Dr Alex Foulkes (Christ Church). In 2001, the team had a relaxed but focused confidence, and I remember a long and happy final tasting session for everyone at my house the week before the match. I broke the cardinal rule on the morning of the match by having strong coffee, while YiXin started his own tradition by bringing along wines to taste on the train into London – the morning commuters looked on with amazement!

'Competition wines that year were less predictable than those of the previous two years, with a few unusual locations and grape varieties thrown into the expected Simpson line-up. Memorably, a juicy Gamay prompted me to note enthusiastically: "Ideal for a summer picnic." Apparently this set off a minor discussion among the judges as to whether a qualitative comment belonged in the notes. I heard later that Hugh Johnson accepted the odd enthusiasm "if appropriate". Again, holding on to one's first impressions was critical; when going back over the wines before completing the reds, I realized I had second-guessed myself on two wines and decided to correct accordingly. We won by a good margin, and because of sticking to first impressions, I was awarded top taster in 2001.

Post-match at Berry Bros. & Rudd

'The year 2001 also saw the firm establishment of a new tradition: the Berry Bros. & Rudd post-match tasting and tour. In May 1999, Lance Jefferson had hosted an annual lunch for the Linacre Wine Committee that included a tour of "his new baby": a beautiful new tasting room in the Berry Bros. & Rudd cellars at St James's just round the corner from the match venue at the Oxford and Cambridge Club. He was keen to promote this new space, and I thought, "You can test it out on us!" It was a great opportunity for the teams to get to know each other better after the match, but it also extended our drinking intake for the day considerably. The extra tasting proved to be one too many for YiXin; in the taxi on the way to dinner he threw up all over my prize magnum of Churchill 1990!

The wine-tasting "Blue"

'I spent more time on blind tasting than on any other sport I played while at Oxford, and I always thought it deserved a Half-Blue, alongside other "non-sporting" or "mind-sport" categories such as chess, bridge and backgammon. The blind-tasting match has something akin to *University Challenge*, and it was certainly as fiercely competitive as any other sporting varsity I competed in (i.e., lawn tennis, real tennis, golf and basketball). It is also one of the best organized – and sponsored – varsity matches.'

THE CHERWELL BOATHOUSE RESTAURANT

by Frederika Adam, Sommelier (2006–08), The Cherwell Boathouse

'The Cherwell Boathouse, beside the River Cherwell in north Oxford, has provided a place of pilgrimage for blind tasters since the early 1970s. Anthony "Tony" Verdin went up to Merton College to read chemistry in 1953. In 1968 he bought The Boathouse, a simple café established in 1964. He initially offered three white and three red wines by the glass, then started buying wine from Freddy Price at Dolomore, and through college tastings he became good friends with both Ronald Avery and John Harvey. To build up the restaurant list, he bought his first *en primeur* vintage of Bordeaux in 1970, and notably four cases of Échézeaux '61 from Michael Broadbent MW at Christie's. As a student dealing in unusual wines and odd lots, Oz Clarke sold him a memorable purchase of vintage Krug, and Jancis Robinson celebrated her 21st birthday party at The Boathouse.

'In the late 1970s, Arabella Morris recommended that Tony meet her brother, Jasper, who had just arrived at Oxford, since "he doesn't know much about wine"(!). In 1981, their friendship culminated in the wine partnership Morris & Verdin. Tony notes: "With Jasper, it was all about 'personality' – from producer to inside the glass". It was a rocky start, however, when on the first day of their first tasting trip to Burgundy, with none other than Harry Waugh, they had a car crash, and Harry had to return to the UK suffering from shock! But it was a successful run thereafter until they sold the agency to Berry Bros. & Rudd in 2003. Tony and his wife, Araminta (*née* Morris, sister to Arabella and Jasper), and family have now run the business for over 45 years. Oxford students have often entertained merchants and producers there after Wine Circle events, and fondly recall its wine list.

'OUWC presidents Andrew Comrie-Picard (1997–98) and Peter Pound (1998–99) had each organized a summer party, and in 2000, it seemed a good idea to turn it into an annual event. With its historical connections to the OUWC and reputation for fine wine, The Boathouse was the ideal venue: we could go punting first (in black tie!), while sipping Pol Roger Champagne, then retire to a wine bar on the marquee terrace, followed by a buffet dinner and raffle. The response was generous and overwhelming. Wine – and more wine – started coming in for the party. A magnum of 1986 Haut-Brion was the star prize donated by Prince Robert of Luxembourg.'

OXFORD UNIVERSITY WINE CIRCLE   MONDAY 19 JUNE 2000   THE FIRST ANNUAL BALNC ET ROUGE SUMMER PARTY

CHERWELL BOATHOUSE RESTAURANT

PUNTING

WINE BAR

DINNER UNDER THE MARQUEE

'I remember heeding the advice of our steely coach, Hanneke Wilson, to trust one's instincts or first impressions.'

An interview with
ED O'MALLEY

NEW COLLEGE, OXFORD, m.1997

Ed O'Malley works with Cambridge Associates, an investment consulting firm, in London.

'I competed in 1999 and 2000 and got the highest score in 2000. With elder brothers who had got a boxing Blue and a rifle-shooting Half-Blue, it was always a disappointment to me that blind tasting was not recognized by the Blues Committee. My father's solution to this was simply to tell friends that his son drank for Oxford. Certainly the intensity of training for the competition was a match for most sports.

'One notable feature of the varsity competition is that it is held in the morning, at 10am, and so in the final weeks the team would meet for morning tastings – at that hour one's palate is particularly sensitive. We were tasting a hundred or so wines a week, and certainly tasting, rather than drinking, at that hour.

'In effect I was recruited to join the Oxford University Wine Circle (OUWC), first for being an undergraduate, and second for being British. There were a very limited number of spaces each year, and it was so popular among postgraduates (especially Americans and continental Europeans) that the committee was keen to attract some younger undergraduates. I was very lucky, therefore, to get to know someone who was a member. One particularly striking memory is of the Château Margaux tasting on the evening of my 21st birthday, with Corinne Mentzelopolous presenting a vertical tasting dating back to 1959.

Tasting instinctively
'As for the competition itself, I remember heeding the advice of our steely coach, Hanneke Wilson, to trust one's instincts or first impressions. There were a couple of instances of opting for my initial identification rather than going with what was perhaps a more considered or nuanced conclusion, and those first impressions turned out to be correct. If the preparation was the equal of

early-morning rowing, then the prestige of the event itself and the prizes on offer far surpassed most varsity matches. It was a great honour to have Harry Waugh, such a luminary of the wine world, in attendance, and the magnum of Winston Churchill 1988 that I'm clutching in this photo still remains unopened in my cellar. It's probably finally ready to open now.'

ABOVE Ed O'Malley with Harry Waugh after the 2000 match. He is holding his prize magnum for top taster that year.
RIGHT Celebrating after his exams at Oxford.

THE POL ROGER VARSITY TASTING MATCH
Tuesday, February 22, 2000

1 Scharzhofberger Riesling Kabinett 1996
Egon Müller (Saar)

2 Savennières 1997
Château de Chamboureau (Anjou-Saumur)

3 Thelema Mountain Sauvignon Blanc 1998
(Stellenbosch)

4 Pierro Chardonnay 1998
Margaret River (Western Australia)

5 Gewurztraminer Grand Cru Pfersigberg 1997
Domaine Bruno Sorg

6 Deidesheimer Paradiesgarten Riesling Auslese 1995
Reichsrat von Buhl (Rheinpfalz)

7 Fleurie Vieilles Vignes 1998
Domaine Métrat

8 Rioja Imperial Reserva 1994
CVNE

9 Santenay Premier Cru Les Gravières 1997
Nicolas Potel

10 Hanna Merlot 1996
Alexander Valley (Sonoma County)

11 Domaine de Rochepertuis Cornas 1996
Jean Lionnet

12 Barolo Bricco Luciani 1995
Silvio Grasso

COACHING THE OXFORD UNIVERSITY BLIND-TASTING TEAM

by DR HANNEKE WILSON

Dr Hanneke Wilson has coached the Oxford team since 1994 and is the senior member of the Oxford University Blind-Tasting Society. She has held a British Academy Post-Doctoral Fellowship which enabled her to write Wine and Words in the Middle Ages and Classical Antiquity. *She works for Haynes Hanson & Clark wine merchants, is the wine steward of Exeter College and continues to teach for various Oxford colleges.*

LEFT 'Coach' Hanneke against a backdrop of Pinot Meunier vines at Redfold Vineyard, Pulborough, West Sussex, England.

'If there is any undermining of the incompetent to be done, Oxford students will do it briskly.'

'In 1994 I got a peremptory postcard from Jancis Robinson. She had just acted as the Oxford judge, and some of the competitors had not taken the match as seriously as they should have done. "Oxford lost. They need a firm hand. I told them you would coach them. Squeal if you object."

'You always know where you are with Jancis. The first time I met her was when she called on me in my room in Wadham, bringing a bottle of Domaine de Chevalier as a present. "We're going to have to do a lot of work together," she said, "so we'd better see if we get on". The "work" was the first edition of *The Oxford Companion to Wine*. I decided that there was a lot to be said for being straightforward, and Jancis must have concluded that I was all right, really, because our next meeting was dinner at her house in Hampstead: "But you'd better come early, so that we can do a bit of work first."

'"Work", an activity of which Jancis proved to be exceedingly fond, turned out to be not just the *Companion* itself, but also a test that I foolishly had not anticipated. "These are three Chardonnays. Do please tell me what you think of them." *Honesty is the best policy*, I thought nervously, as I found myself blurting out that the Californian wine had a nose of apricots and cigarette smoke. What did I think I was doing? I don't even smoke! "Hmmm," Jancis said, taking a good sniff. "Filter-tips." After an interruption for "work" (the proposed entries on the history of wine in classical antiquity and the Middle Ages), I found myself once more at the kitchen table: "Here is a sample that Oddbins has sent me. They're thinking of making this their generic German Riesling."

'"Bad idea: sugar water," I opined, hoping I was right. A quick nod from my hostess ushered in the serious drinking: a glass of a deliciously refreshing Kabinett by J J Prüm was put into my hand. What a relief: *nunc est bibendum*! We ate the best roast duck I have ever tasted, cooked by Jancis' husband, and, among other things, drank a fascinating Latricières-Chambertin '59, an Averys' bottling in a somewhat old-fashioned style, in all probability neither 100 per cent Pinot Noir nor 100 per cent Burgundy.

'I didn't squeal, and soon after that postcard I got a letter from the president of the Oxford University Wine Circle (OUWC), James Pennefather (Christ Church), inviting me to become its senior member. I met various blind tasters at a dinner party in the study of Paul Day, then a college lecturer in maths at Lady Margaret Hall. The principal's cat, Oscar, a large handsome Burmese, was an uninvited but remarkably well-behaved guest, and naturally the wines were served blind. The entire company was stumped by a red table wine from the Douro, which was a novelty then, but we did well collectively.

'So this is how, in 1994, I found myself "the firm hand". I had plenty of experience teaching undergraduates, but coaching a sports team, even if it wasn't a Blues sport, was a different matter. Was I good enough at this stuff? "Those who can't, teach", as G B Shaw has it, but one should not allow oneself to be intimidated by a teetotal vegetarian with dodgy political views and a beard; if there is any undermining of the incompetent to be done, Oxford students will do it briskly. Quite properly and always politely, they make me taste something blind from time to time, but I have survived.

'I inherited "the crib sheet" and a small band of enthusiastic and talented tasters; to my relief all

I needed to do was impose structure and a sense of order. I had always found tasting with others congenial, and the training sessions were really a formalized version of trying out wines with fellow anoraks: a class of person that abounds in Oxford. For quite a few years this light-touch approach worked rather well. The blind-tasting group was part of the OUWC, the blind-tasting captain being one of the officers. Victory in the varsity match gave added lustre to the OUWC, a core of proficient tasters raised the tone of its meetings, and the OUWC was happy to subsidize blind tasting.

'It couldn't last. Looking back, our run of victories was surprising, however good my first vintage of Oxford tasters were – and it has to be said that some were truly excellent. But I realized that for the first few years I had been blessed with a rare, close-knit group of "natural" tasters, and as coach I just had to be a friendly presence. Once they had left Oxford, I found that their successors tended to be beginners who really did need something that should probably be called "teaching". I rewrote and expanded the crib sheet and ran themed tastings, often twice a week, and even produced handouts; meanwhile someone had clearly had a word with Cambridge, because victory no longer seemed assured.

'When the OUWC could not afford to subsidize the blind tasters any more, the captain's presence on the committee ceased to be useful, so one late afternoon in Hilary 2008, as the captain, John Mead, and I trudged to St Hugh's (his college) with our bottles, John remarked, "At Cambridge, blind tasting is a separate society," and we agreed that there should be a velvet divorce. A constitution was written and officers elected; John was our founding captain, and his dynamic presidency established the

Oxford University Blind-Tasting Society (OUBTS) on a sound financial basis. We decided on a small annual membership fee, and after that, given enough participants, attending a tasting need cost no more than going for a couple of drinks with a friend. The formula worked, and has done ever since.

'Now that we were on our own, we could be as nerdish as we liked. Handouts proliferated. I said "methoxypyrazines", and nobody fainted. We were the subject of an hilariously ignorant profile in *The Oxford Student*, which expressed puzzlement at how so many people could sit in a room talking about wine, drinking almost nothing and in some cases even spitting out the little they tasted. Weren't students meant to get drunk? Er, no. What *The Oxford Student* had witnessed was one of the sessions in our introductory course, which is devised and run by the committee and has proved a great success. It attracts new people and gives committee members a chance to present tastings and develop their didactic skills. When we were part of the OUWC we could not invite guests to give blind tastings, but now the OUBTS has acquired a number of loyal friends from outside Oxford, and this, too, ensures that a variety of voices is heard. That some of our visitors are former blind tasters is a source of great pride.

'So what goes on in these tastings? I think I'll keep the opposition (known as "the Tabs" when we are in competitive mood) guessing. If they sent a spy (who would be promptly debagged), they might be surprised at all the giggling. We are Cavaliers, not Roundheads. Deference to the captain or the coach is firmly discouraged, pomposity is stamped on and Parker-style tasting notes are banned. I will admit to occasional ferocity. Recently there has been an influx of Wine &

LEFT The winning Oxford team, 2008. From left to right: Andras Salamon, William Pooley, Piers Barclay (top taster), John Mead (captain), Charlie Pistorius, Cecilia Muldoon, George Scratcherd and Hanneke Wilson (coach).

Spirit Education Trust terminology, which purports to be exact but sounds like Orwell's Newspeak. Anyone claiming that the acidity of a sample is 'medium minus' can expect a verbal rugby tackle in response. As long as we all know that we have to be able to take it if we are to dish it out, the system works: I remember the Homeric laughter when I was given a Chianti blind and described the colour as "red", by which I meant "not purple" – but I have been well aware ever since that my perception of colour is below average.

'As a tutor one is used to making quick assessments of undergraduates' intellectual capabilities, but blind tasting is not like that. "X is a very nice chap to have around and I'm glad he keeps turning up, but he has a cloth palate" is likely to be wrong; often the tortoise beats the hare, because the tortoise's willingness to learn from his mistakes is a huge asset. Arrogance is counterproductive, but confidence is vital, because a line-up of six samples is a daunting sight – all the more reason to ensure that the hares do not intimidate the tortoises.

'As the world of wine has changed, so has the match. Fine wine has rocketed in price, and gone are the days when a training session could be a line-up of high-grade white Burgundies. Standards of viticulture and winemaking have improved, and this has not made blind tasting any easier: the pale, old-style Chiantis, made from high-yielding vines and compulsorily adulterated with Trebbiano, no longer exist, and modern Chianti is nowhere near as easy to spot. Spain now produces a range of delicious white wines: those white Riojas that spent far too long in horrid American oak barrels are hard to find these days. The first time an Albariño figured in the competition, we all thought that was a bit outré – except for the Cambridge woman who got it bang on and won the Tabs the match. It now has a firm place in the crib sheet. The teams themselves have changed, too: graduates had been part of the team when I first took over, but these days they predominate; and because today's graduate students are drawn from all over the world, the teams are far more international in composition.

'What has not changed is the enjoyment that we all derive from blind tasting. The effort, commitment, sportsmanship and talent that the Oxford tasters display make me raise my game continually and strive for excellence. I have had the good fortune to get to know lots of splendid people, many of whom keep in touch, and I am grateful to Pol Roger for sponsoring and organizing the varsity match. In 2012 James Simpson, presiding at lunch, invited the Reverend Gareth Powell, a former Cambridge taster, to say grace: simply and eloquently, he gave thanks for the gifts of friendship and good wine. Amen to that.'

ABOVE Serena Sutcliffe MW tasting historic wines from the Massandra Collection in the Crimea in 1991, the year in which she joined Sotheby's.

WINE AT AUCTION

by SERENA SUTCLIFFE MW

Serena Sutcliffe MW is the head of Sotheby's International Wine Department, and a former varsity blind wine-tasting competition judge.

'There are days when I wonder how I came to be running Sotheby's International Wine Department – the route was so circuitous it could have been a maze. At other times, it seems entirely logical, since my personal system of osmosis had been taking wine on board for years before I joined the wine trade. There was a certain inevitability about my vinous route, given that smell and taste had always meant so much to me, but harnessing this was another matter. History, literature and languages absorbed me completely and I was headed in a Light Blue direction when the full impact of having to wait until I was "old enough" and, even more, to be part of an all-woman college, hit home and promptly sent me abroad. I earned my living by translating and interpreting, trying out northern and southern Europe, but it was my time in France that turned wine into an obsession, a state of mind that is allowed only if it is a hobby!

'It took a bit of courage, in the early 1970s, to join the wine trade and return to a very drab England, but it led to a rapid realization that the only way to be taken seriously (patronizing remarks by the pinstripes at that epoch could fill a book – a boring one at that) was to become a Master of Wine. Someone once said to me that "the MW is the best club in the world", a difficult claim for me to verify as I am not very clubbable. However, it was a relief to join the club in 1976, at my first attempt, celebrated if I remember correctly by three Campari sodas on the trot. Not long after, the celebration was more important, as I met and married David Peppercorn, a very illustrious wine man and the world's best drinking partner. We ran our own business until 1991, when I joined Sotheby's to head the Wine Department, pushed by David, who obviously wanted me out of the house!

'It has been a terrific roller coaster of a ride. When I faced a completely empty, barrack-like office in a Battersea warehouse, I did think of scampering back over the Channel. The challenge was huge and the market for "fine wine" at auction was tiny and London-centric. We built up the business with painstaking care, deciding right from the start that we would only sell The Best. Experience, energy and sheer grind all come into it and I remember working on catalogues until well into the night, pasting and sticking, proofreading and writing deathless prose. We went to see cellars, we went right back to origins, we opened cases, we checked facts – and we learnt a lot along the way.

'We also had headline-making sales, such as das Fürstenhaus Thurn und Taxis (still the largest wine auction, with 75,000 bottles), the Imperial Cellar of Massandra and the Andrew Lloyd Webber Wine Collection. The breakthrough in New York came in 1994, when authorities allowed wine auctions to be held in their exciting city. It was bonanza time leading up to the end of the century, culminating in pre-millennium record-making euphoria. In 2009, we launched regular sales in Hong Kong, following the enlightened decision there to abolish taxes on wine. We spend more time in airports, but no less time on checking condition and provenance: an absolute necessity at a time when prices for top wines can be stratospheric.

'Sotheby's has led in holding exceptional sales of historic wines direct from the cellars of Bordeaux first growths, from the top Champagne houses and wonders such as Vega Sicilia, the ultimate in perfect provenance. We have set world records, such as for a single lot (50 cases of Château Mouton Rothschild 1982, $1,051,600, New York, 2006), for any-sized bottle (a jeroboam of Château Mouton-Rothschild 1945, $310,700, New York 2007), and for a standard bottle (Château Lafite 1869, $232,692, Hong Kong, 2010). And, since 2010, we have also been retailers in New York, a great new adjunct to our business.

'The market is now truly global. Buyers and sellers come from every continent, and international participation in wine sales crosses all time zones, particularly since the advent of online bidding. Our job is to bring to the party great cellars and fascinating collections of wine, and the only part of the work I find difficult is watching them pass through our hands! Oh yes, we do sometimes taste them and even, daringly, drink them and this makes it all worthwhile, plus the pleasure of working with my colleagues in London, New York and Hong Kong, the most recent recruit being Nicholas Jackson, a member of the 2011 (winning) Cambridge wine-tasting team.'

ABOVE The 2011 match in progress. Nicholas Jackson (Cambridge) is on the far left.

An interview with
CHRIS DARK

TRINITY COLLEGE, OXFORD, m.1998

Dr Chris Dark invests in tech companies (most famously Angry Birds) with Atomico, a venture capital firm started by the founder of Skype, in London.

'Dr Hanneke Wilson was for years the master trainer – she was our secret weapon!'

'I was reading a master of engineering in materials science, followed by a PhD in superconductors, and was in the Trinity College Wine Society from 1998 to 2005. I'd had little exposure to wine until I went to university, and I worked in a wine shop in the holidays. Through friends Mark Martin and Frederika Adam I joined the Oxford University Wine Circle (OUWC) in 1999, and competed in the blind wine-tasting team in 2000, 2001 (captain), and 2002 (captain/top taster). I was president of the OUWC in 2002–03.

'We met weekly, first in the Red Room at New College, then the Oxford Union, and then the Danson Room at Trinity College. Dr Hanneke Wilson was for years the master trainer – she was our secret weapon! Lincoln College wine cellars were generous with wines to help us train. The team was chosen by the captain from the people who came to the training sessions; you didn't need to belong to the OUWC or Bacchus, the Oxford University Wine Society. Preparation in advance of the match was a lot of training, at least twice a week; the wines we tasted were about 60 per cent French, 20 per cent other Europe, 20 per cent New World. The up-and-coming styles in the late '90s into the 2000s were "Parker" Shiraz from Australia and Argentinean Malbec.

'In 2001 I was captain, and Frederika Adam was the top taster. It was a fairly tough year. Looking back at the wines, there were not really any that were that weird, but for some reason no one got a killer score. As per usual the first red was a Cabernet Franc (in 2001 a Baudry Chinon La Croix Boissée 1997) or a Beaujolais, and James Simpson MW often ended the competition with a heavy Shiraz.

'Tasting is instinct, but we did tell our team members what to default guess if they didn't know: i.e. we knew that James wouldn't put a 17 per cent Zinfandel as Wine No. 1 of the red flight. Whether these default guesses got us any points I don't know, but I know they focused people's minds on things like the first red. If there was a dry German Riesling, it would most likely be No. 1 or 2 of the white wines, as it's so light; if the wine was a bit sweeter it would be later in the line-up. To look at the wine is sometimes enough (e.g. Beaujolais). Then sniff – this is often enough to write most of the answer down.

Then taste – if you don't know it immediately, then it's likely you will not get it right.

'In 2002 we had an experienced team, very much the next generation from Freddy Adam, Alex Hunt and Ed O'Malley. It was my and Mark Martin's third match in a row, and Tom Bromwich's and Ciaran Patrick's second. I remember smelling the whites; I got five pretty much correct (I mucked up the Pinot Grigio), and Wines 1, 3, 5 and 6 didn't need tasting: the grape and region were obvious. In the break before the reds we knew we had very consistent answers, which generally means you're getting a super-high (or -low) score. We were confident, though. For the white wines I got 100/120: the highest score for six I ever got.

'The reds started with (surprise!) a Beaujolais. I just looked at it, saw the purple, slightly nuclear glow, and wrote the tasting note – only checking it by smelling/tasting after it was written. The South African Pinotage split people (I got it wrong, I'm sure), and the Valpolicella Classico was guessable as Italian, but I can't remember if anyone got the grape. Then it got easier again with the Pinot Noir, and Bordeaux, followed by a monster Shiraz at the end.

'Comparing notes, we'd been less consistent with the whites but got the actual list of wines and knew we had a great score. Cambridge also knew they'd done well; funnily enough, in '02 Dan Thornton, who had tasted for Oxford in '01, was on their team. The years of 2000 (931/853) and '02 (898/794) ended with Oxford having the highest and second highest scores ever since Pol Roger had taken on the competition.

'Perhaps the coolest thing that came from all this tasting is the Winston Synod of Oxonian Cellarers, a dining society founded by myself, Tom Bromwich, Alex Hunt and Dan Thornton. Since '02, we've met 18 times, taking turns to cook for the other members, and often their other halves. We drink great wine and the food takes second stage!

'The funniest part of the winning team trips to Champagne was James Simpson's face when Nina Wilson (2002) walked downstairs at our hotel, ready for a bike ride, with shorts so short they were a belt. It's fair to say the rest of the team took notice as well!'

ABOVE Cycling among the Champagne vineyards in 2002. Chris Dark is second from left and Nina Wilson is far right.

An interview with
HSIEN MIN TOH

KEBLE COLLEGE, OXFORD, m.1996

Hsien Min Toh works as a credit risk quantitative analyst with a bank in Singapore. He studied English literature at Oxford, was president of the Oxford University Poetry Society, and is founding editor of the Quarterly Literary Review Singapore.

> 'When I started writing about wine in the 1970s I was told firmly that the Asians would never become wine drinkers. When, for example, the Liu brothers from Hong Kong starred in the Oxbridge wine-tasting teams in the late 1970s, they were considered the exceptions who proved the rule. Today, more fine wine is auctioned on Hong Kong island than anywhere else in the world ... But the Asian wine scene is very much more than Hong Kong and China. Japan and Singapore have long histories of connoisseurship.'
> – Jancis Robinson MW

'When I first got to Oxford in 1996, I hardly knew anything about wine; I was teetotal, even. It wasn't an Asian cultural thing then; it has completely changed now. But we did the usual student thing, and bought odd bottles of Bulgarian Chardonnay from Oddbins. One day I decided I would splash out and buy a £9 half-bottle of Château Rieussec Reserve '93. It was one of those strange things I've never seen or heard of since. Château Rieussec had apparently thought that the '93 vintage was not worthy of its name on the label, so they declassified it and bottled it under another label. Interested, I thought, "Oh, I'll go and get some bottles of this," and I shared it with friends in my room, in my first year. We tasted through it, and I went, "Whoa! You mean wine can taste like *this*?" I had that magic "aha" moment, and I started tasting wines regularly with a group of similarly interested friends. We had this spectacular tasting at a friend's place in Denmark Street,

ABOVE Judges Jancis Robinson and Bill Baker considered 2000 one of the best matches in recent years (Oxford won 931/853), with some exceptional scores on both sides. From left to right: Hsien Min Toh, Chris Dark, Frederika Adam, Ed O'Malley, Mark Martin, Alex Hunt (captain) and Michael Saller (reserve).

south of Oxford, and each person brought a bottle that they thought was really something. One was a Château de Chamboureau Cuvée d'Avant, a dry Savennières from the 1995 vintage so it had rather low botrytis – you could smell it as a sweet wine, but once you poured it from the bottle it was completely dry.

'The slight tragedy was that I didn't know about the existence of the Oxford University Wine Circle (OUWC) until 1999–2000. But after my finals, in the summer of 1999, I went through the freshers' fair all over again. And the moment I saw the OUWC, £25 membership, with all of these events generally free or nominal (for the big events you might pay £25 to join a Haut-Brion tasting), I said, "Yes, sign me up!" We had some memorable tastings: in 2000, Haut-Brion did a vertical tasting of 1982, '85, '88, '90, '93 and '94, and Latour came as well in the same year and showed '93, '94 and '96.

'The only year that I was in the OUWC and on the team was 1999–2000. There was an open call for the varsity blind-tasting match, with weekly practice sessions, and at the end of that a qualification session. I went to all of those training sessions with Dr Hanneke Wilson. Coach Hanneke was our secret weapon, because we got the sense from some of the Cambridge people that they didn't train quite as seriously – maybe "seriously" is the wrong word, but that they didn't train quite as systematically as we did. Thirty people showed up for the first training session, and when it came to the last qualification session, it was 15 to 18. There were six competitors and one reserve. I can't remember the top four qualifications in order, but I know that Michael Saller (Brasesnose), a graduate student, was the reserve, Mark Martin (Trinity) qualified sixth, and I qualified fifth. We were five undergraduates and two graduate students. Alex Hunt was the captain of the team and the most gifted taster, apparent to everyone. Ed O'Malley might have been top taster that year, but only by a narrow lead to Alex. On a consistent basis we all accepted that Alex was the best taster, because he was able to explain wine to us in simple and lucid terms that people could deal with.

'After the match we went into the pub next door to wait for the results, and to drink beer – since we'd only had 12 glasses of wine! The Cambridge team was in the same pub, but we were relaxed and it was friendly; I got to know one of the Cambridge tasters subsequently.

'It was while we were at the pub that we figured we'd won, because, as you do, you finish an exam paper and you compare notes: "Oh, what did you think that was? My answer was this." And we realized that everybody in the Oxford team had nailed and identified the Rioja, and everybody in the Cambridge team had not. And it was indeed the Rioja that made the difference in this competition, because of the systematic training that we'd all gone through. That summer was the first time I went to Champagne, with the winning Oxford team.

'At Oxford, I was also the president of the Poetry Society. We had about 110 members and would invite famous writers to speak to us, like Wendy Hope and Benjamin Zephaniah. Singapore is a fairly tight literary scene, and I've now run the *Quarterly Literary Review Singapore* for over ten years. The most prestigious award for the arts in Singapore is the Cultural Medallion, and the baby version is the Young Artist Award, which I received in 2010. Apparently, I'm famous back in Singapore!

Wine in Singapore

'After Oxford, I was the captain of our Singapore wine-tasting team, and we had the Singapore Blind-Tasting Competition, which was created in 2001 by one of the Antipodean wine importers using a formula that Len Evans had come up with years before. Another Singaporean from our tasting group at Oxford, Elaine Teo (now Mosimann) (St Hilda's) was in our team. I imported the Oxford system of training to bring discipline to our blind-tasting sessions, and we organized themed tastings every fortnight. The group would taste regularly, but we were not always high-flown. We liked to throw in the odd curiosity: a Japanese Merlot, which was absolutely awful, but the Thai Chenin Blanc was not half bad!

'I don't know if I'd say I was surprised by the turn in the Asian market with regard to wine – but in hindsight there has certainly been a paradigm shift in Singapore, Hong Kong and China. It became not just acceptable, and maybe not even just fashionable to drink wine, but it became something that you did, something that is a part of your life in a sense. Tax on wine was the single biggest influence for Hong Kong. It went down from 80 per cent to 40 per cent, then to zero in 2008. I do not like to draw a distinction between the markets of Hong Kong, Singapore and China, but China has been driving the trade in first growths and super seconds in recent years, and now they're starting to turn their attention to Burgundy. In terms of Hong Kong and Singapore, it's a more expert market; people take trips to Burgundy to visit producers, and to find out which plots are better and why. China is still in the learning curve, but they have the hunger to learn and the wealth to help buy everything they want!

'In the late 1980s, Michelle Chen was the first blind taster from Singapore in the team. Then I came along in 2000, and in the next year another friend from Singapore, YiXin Ong, who studied philosophy, politics and economics at Exeter, got on the team as well. Another Singaporean at Oxford, Tan Ying Sien, was not in the team, but was the recipient of the Institute of Masters of Wine Champagne Trinity Scholarship [sponsored by Pol Roger, Bollinger and Roederer] in 2010.

'I joined Standard Chartered in 2005, and I now work in a bank building mathematical models, which is strange considering I read English. As a hobby – and it is strictly a hobby – I built a master database for wine tasting, and a model to help me to predict what the wine is going to be based on all of my tasting notes. I can set the machine to compete against me. As in, if I picked up, say, apple and peach in a wine, I could key them in and it would tell me "This has a 70 per cent chance of being a Chardonnay".'

RIESLING
by Hsien Min Toh

There's nothing finer for the summer
than a glass of Mosel Riesling, its light green
colour dancing with so much breaking sunlight
it scatters a shadow play all over the straw mat.
Don't be so surprised. I've always pretended
not to like Riesling, which can be true
when I sip a particularly aggressive one
smelling as though it has just been crushed out
from underneath the chassis of your VW,
but when it tastes of lemonade and peaches,
and the alternative is Pimm's, forgive me
for not being quite what you had expected.
If it's surprise that makes good wine great,
let us not always be able to read each other
like summer bestsellers to be remaindered
by the time we share a glass of – I don't know –
Sauvignon Blanc the next hot Oxford summer.
Last summer, I didn't expect you'd feed the ducks
bread dipped in wine, less still that they
would take the bread and wash it in the river
before gulping down their sodden pickings.
You hadn't expected we'd find our restless spirits
growing in communion. But if we now want
to eat our cake and have it, and in so trying
embed sorrow, should it bring you to blink
that I now pull the cork on a thin green bottle
and produce, as if by an undeserved magic,
two impractically tall, tulip-shaped glasses?

Hsien Min Toh's poem 'Riesling' was originally published in his third poetry collection, Means to an End *(2008), which was shortlisted for the Singapore Literature Prize.*

'The mark of objectivity in wine judgement is perhaps best thought of in terms such as appropriateness rather than truth.'

THE PHILOSOPHY OF BLIND WINE TASTING, OBJECTIVELY

by CAIN TODD

TRINITY COLLEGE, CAMBRIDGE, m.1998

Dr Cain Todd lectures in philosophy at Lancaster University, is researching 'Imagination, Emotion, and Value' at the University of Fribourg, Switzerland, and is also affiliated to an interdisciplinary research group on emotions at the University of Geneva.

'Recently there has been a flowering of interest among philosophers, psychologists and neuroscientists in the nature of our perception and appreciation of tastes and smells and in the complex human artefact constituted of them: wine. There is good reason for this. In significant and striking ways, wine raises important philosophical issues concerning the cognitive penetration of perceptual experience, the epistemological and metaphysical status of taste and smell, the role of metaphor in value judgement, the nature of aesthetic and artistic value and intoxication. In *The Philosophy of Wine: A Case of Truth, Beauty and Intoxication*, I explore these issues, but the heart of the book is a defence of the objectivity of wine judgements. I argue that it is true, for example, that a particular Bonnes-Mares really does have notes of chocolate and truffle, that wines genuinely can be brooding, elegant, charming or sexy, and that Château L'Eglise-Clinet 1989 really is a better wine than a cheap Côtes de Bourg.

'A main obstacle confronting such a view is that, in a haste to discharge accusations of elitism, obfuscation and snobbery, even the best wine experts often lurch into proclamations of subjectivity directly at odds with their own beliefs and practices. Indeed, a moment's reflection on practices of wine production, drinking, conversation, criticism and appreciation reveals that they heavily presuppose some level of objectivity. If taste were wholly subjective, there would be little point in trying to talk about wine with others, putting tasting notes on labels, judging wines or communicating one's experiences in hopes of sharing them. It would be pointless to attempt to cultivate, educate or improve one's palate, or to think one could learn about or come to a better understanding of wines.

'An important distinction is that between personal preference and evaluation. Individual preferences for different tastes and styles of wine may be subjective without this trivial fact impugning the objectivity of judgements about wines' characteristics. Whether a wine has crisp acidity and a cut-grass aroma is one thing; whether this is to your taste is another. Expert critics may help you determine the former without offering criticisms of the latter. Of course, a presupposition of objectivity doesn't establish it. Yet objectivity is relatively easy to secure for a large range of descriptive, literal judgements about wine. For example, the judgement that this Chablis has a citrus aroma, or that this Chianti has harsh tannins, will be true insofar as it is based on direct, and in large part empirically testable, correlations between the wines' physical properties and the tastes and smells we perceive them as having.

'It may take a great deal of practice and skill to discern these properties. It is inevitable that expertise plays a fundamental role in determining the meaning and application of terms to wines. This is particularly so in the more complex cases employing metaphorical and evaluative concepts like "cheeky", "bold", "feminine" or "good". Where metaphors are used to describe wine, they will be true or appropriate either if they can be fully paraphrased in terms of non-metaphorical physical attributes of the wine, or if they are at least grounded in certain conventions that are commonly understood, accepted and used among experts whose agreement in part supports and constitutes the convention. "Flabby", for example, is primarily used to describe wines lacking in the acidity necessary to give them balance and body. If someone were to judge a highly acidic Rheingau Riesling as "flabby" or "flat", or a young, powerfully concentrated, tannic Hermitage as "feminine" or "delicate", they would be straightforwardly wrong, either in misperceiving the wines' properties or misusing the vocabulary.

'Is there expertise in wine tasting? MRI brain scans comparing tasting experiences of sommeliers with subjects lacking specific wine-tasting knowledge or abilities have shown significant differences between the way in which experts and non-experts analyse and perceive wine. Only in sommeliers did areas of the brain associated with motivation, memory and cognition light up, suggesting they were expecting rewards and pleasure from tasting and were following specific analytic strategies while tasting, including linguistic ones in putting names to flavours. In other words, people familiar with wine tasting seem to experience the tastes and smells of wine differently from those who aren't. As such, scientific research doesn't so much undermine the possibility of expertise as to some extent reinforce it, insofar as it suggests that people with the same background experience, expectations and knowledge may have the same kinds of experiences when confronted by the same wine, and some people may well be better at perceiving tastes and smells than others.

'Indeed, it also reinforces one of the key practices of wine expertise: blind tasting, designed specifically to negate the adverse affect that knowledge (and personal preferences and prejudices) can have on expectation and perception. For example, knowing in advance that a wine comes from a famous producer might incline one to misjudge what is actually an overripe, rough, relatively poor-quality wine in an unduly positive light. Yet, if successful, it allows accurate judgements of wine to be formed without direct knowledge of what the wine is, where discerning the character of a wine in this way necessarily presupposes a great deal of implicit knowledge in order to make sense of one's otherwise more or less inchoate perceptual experience. Those with sufficient experience of blind tasting can be in no doubt about the way background knowledge and experience structure their tasting, influencing perceptions and judgements in ways that provide *prima facie* evidence for the cognitive penetrability of wine tasting.

'In addition to expertise, the key element in this process is the role in wine judging played by categories: grape variety, geography, winemaking intentions, style and quality. What properties a wine appears to have depend on the category in which it is judged. For example, in the varietal category "Chardonnay", a drinker familiar only with old-style Australian Chardonnays – big, intense, very alcoholic, fruit-driven wines – is likely to assess a white Meursault from Burgundy as "austere" or "reserved". However, compared to a flinty, acidic, minerally Chablis (also Chardonnay) the Meursault will not appear austere at all.

'There are correct categories governing the appreciation and understanding of wine. The establishment of these categories isn't arbitrary or mere convention, but depends ultimately on the existence of certain physical properties of grape and terroir that give rise to valuable experiences in us. Moreover, such categories govern the evaluation of wine. What ultimately grounds the categories of quality is the ability of the best wines to manifest to the highest degree those intrinsic values of which wine *qua* wine is capable, including complexity, intensity, depth, balance, terroir and expressivity.

'Some disagreements, however, seem more intractable. These may signify a difference in the categories and standards against which competing judgements are made, as witnessed in recent clashes over the merits of the 2009 vintage of Right Bank Bordeaux. Some experts have lauded these wines for their expressive power and enormous, concentrated flavours, while others have derided them as clichéd, sacrificing the austere virtues of traditional terroirs. The choice about how to taste these wines, about which categories are the right ones to invoke – e.g. Old Style or New Style Bordeaux – will itself be partly an ineliminable evaluative choice involving decisions about whether the wine is more rewarding tasted in some new light, or whether that way of categorizing its qualities undermines some important value or other. In such cases, it isn't at all obvious that there is simply one true, correct view.

'This doesn't mean anything goes. In the face of marked evaluative disagreements, one must recognize the reasons given as justifying (or not) the appropriateness of an opponent's view. One must be able to "see the point" of the judgement, even where this may involve, in cases of extreme disagreement, an explanation appealing to differences in "taste" or background, categorial standards and norms. In this way, the door is open to a limited relativism for some evaluative disputes about wine quality. For these reasons the mark of objectivity in wine judgement is perhaps best thought of in terms such as appropriateness rather than truth.'

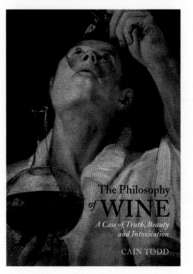

LEFT *The Philisophy of Wine* offers a defence of the objectivity of wine tasting, as well as an account of its value, including the controversial thesis that wine is capable of being expressive of emotion in a way analagous to music.

TOASTING THE AULD ALLIANCE: EDINBURGH VS ST ANDREWS

by WILL LYONS

Will Lyons is wine columnist for the Wall Street Journal *and a past president of The Edinburgh University Wine Society.*

'The imposing vaulted entrance to the University of Edinburgh's principal building, Old College, with its sandstone Doric columns and emerald-green dome, acts as a powerful counterpoint to the chaotic nature of the city's labyrinthine, medieval Old Town. From here, amid the tranquil terraces and immaculate lawn of its quadrangle, it is a short walk to the National Museum of Scotland, where undergraduates from two of Scotland's ancient universities came together on a chilly spring day in 2006 for the second Pol Roger inter-university blind-tasting competition.

'Given the history of the two universities – St Andrews was founded in 1413, before Columbus arrived in the Americas; and Edinburgh, which could boast of introducing modern medicine into China, in 1583 – their formal entry into this competition, more than 40 years after it was created, was perhaps a little late.

'More pertinently, the ports of Edinburgh and Fife had been receiving shipments of wine from Bordeaux since the 12th century, making the country one of the oldest claret-drinking nations on earth. The varsity competition may have been running since 1953, but in those early matches at least, there was a distinct feeling among the tasters in Scotland that when it came to wine tasting, there was life outside of Oxbridge.

'As Pol Roger's two Masters of Wine, Bill Gunn and James Simpson, busily pulled corks, the dozen tasters who had gathered in an oval-shaped room above the great hall of the National Museum of Scotland cracked jokes, outwardly showing no sign of nerves. They probably should have. Blind wine tasting cannot in any way be described as a jovial affair. Anyone who has tasted wine professionally will quickly tell you that attempting to ascertain the grape variety, geographical provenance and vintage of a wine in a blind tasting is one of the most terrifying, challenging and humbling experiences any wine enthusiast can put himself through.

'The competent blind wine taster relies on having a startlingly good palate memory or an encyclopaedic knowledge of the world's wine-growing regions. It is very rare to find anyone with both. More often than not blind wine tasting is a humiliation waiting to happen. The broader your experience, the more confusing and difficult the exercise becomes. If there isn't instant recognition, a laborious process of elimination is carried out, which, for many people, myself included, leaves the taster hopelessly confused.

'Sitting down to the 12 unknown wines, Edinburgh's sextet had the advantage of home turf. Their wine society gathered barely a fairway away in the cellars of the university's legal faculty, Old College. The St Andrews team had left the wind-lashed links of West Sands beach and the medieval cloisters of St Salvator's quadrangle to make the journey south across the Forth's iconic cantilever rail bridge. Their pride was at stake, having lost the inaugural match by the decisive margin of 468 points to 347 just a year earlier when the two teams competed at the Byre Theatre in St Andrews.

'In that second match, scores were judged by two representatives of Scotland's independent wine sector: Adrian Laird Craig, then a director for Berkmann Wine Cellars, and Alan McMillan, who worked with Peebles-based wine merchant Villeneuve Fine Wines. It was close. After the whites had been served there were only 16 points in it, as Edinburgh led by 316 to 300. The reds were even closer, as St Andrews clawed back six points, but the deficit was still ten, at 251 to Edinburgh and 241 to St Andrews. In the end the victory was clear: Edinburgh had snatched another title by ten points.

'"The standard was very high," said Mr Laird Craig. "And there was a pretty fierce competitive edge between the two teams. Having lectured both societies in the weeks leading up to the match, I remember noting the difference between the home team's methodical and sober approach to tasting compared with St Andrews' more cavalier attitude, but in the end the scores were fairly close."

'Although a layman might assume that any blind-tasting match between two Scottish institutions would involve not wine, but rather the soft, amber liquid of that country's most famous exported beverage, Scotch whisky, social historians will tell of a different story. The crenellated walls of Edinburgh Castle and the damp Lomond hills of Fife may seem an age away from the expansive, undulating slopes of the Médoc or the chalky brilliance of the Marne Valley, but wine appreciation in Scotland, particularly those wines emanating from the vineyards of France, can boast a lineage dating back more than 700 years.

'It was the Scottish *makar* (poet-bard) Alan Ramsay who wrote in the 18th century:

> *Guid claret best keeps out the cauld*
> *an drives awa the winter soon*
> *It makes a man baith gash an bauld*
> *An heaves his saul ayont the mune.*

'Ramsay was referring to Bordeaux's dark, brooding ruby-coloured red wine which in youth can smell of blackcurrant, red berries and damson, but with age evolves into an evocative brick-red colour with notes of cedar, old tobacco, roasted meats gloriously rounded off by a silky, soft texture. It was this wine, although not in its present form, that Scottish historian Billy Kay reminds us was "the bloodstream of the Auld Alliance".

'Edinburgh's port of Leith was regularly receiving shipments of claret, which, Kay points out, was not like the heavy red wine we are familiar with today. Then it was an altogether lighter wine, thinner in texture and not unlike a contemporary rosé. This wine came from the lands of Eleanor of Aquitaine, who in 1152 married King Henry II of England, thus bequeathing the area around Bordeaux to the English Crown and opening up a lucrative export market for the region's *vignerons*.

'A couple of centuries later Scotland's wine merchants received another fillip when, during the Hundred Years War, they fought alongside the French to remove the English from southwest France. The reward for their efforts was the granting of favourable privileges. As Kay observes: "While the English had to surrender their arms when entering the Gironde, apply for passports and be subject to curfews, the Scots sailed blithely upriver to get the pick of the new vintage at reduced rates, and head for home in time for Hogmanay!"

'In his memoirs of the 18th century, the Scottish judge and literary figure Lord Cockburn describes how when a cargo of claret arrived at Leith, a hogshead of it would be carried through the town in a cart with a horn. Anyone who wanted to sample the drink could stop the cart and fill up their jug for sixpence.

'Scotland's privileges may have been removed in the 1660s by Jean-Baptiste Colbert, finance minister to France's King Louis XIV, but the country continued its love affair with claret. Indeed, the present national drink, Scotch whisky, "the water of life", or *usquebaugh*, to give its Gaelic name, is, according to Kay, a "rather uncouth Highland *arriviste*". (References to exotic fruit and wild

flowers, other perfumes and potions that make up the modern vocabulary of a contemporary wine taster are far removed from the honest terminology found in whisky writing. Wine is primarily judged by its aroma and palate; whisky, primarily by its nose, with terms such as "hessian", "cereal", "old rope" and "linseed".) In the 17th century it was the families of the Jacobite dissenters, loyal to the House of Stuart and opposed to the Union with England, who drank claret in solidarity with their cousins exiled in France. By the time Napoleon Bonaparte was marching across Europe, Scotland's judiciary would have developed an appreciative taste for claret. And, as Scotland's wine trade continued to flourish, so did the practice of buying barrels direct from the châteaux and bottling in Edinburgh. Based at the nearby port of Leith, Cockburn's of Leith earned a reputation of some repute with its Leith-bottled claret.

'Of course, Scotland's influence didn't stop at Bordeaux. A quick glance through the lodges and *quintas* of northern Portugal and southern Spain reveals their legacy in the Port, Sherry and Madeira trade. Names such as Graham's, Dow's, Cockburn and Sandeman hail from the rugged mountains and heather-strewn glens of the Highlands and Lowlands of Scotland.

'Five years before Pol Roger emulated the varsity match north of the Border, it was a glass of Port that decided the very first blind-tasting competition between Edinburgh and St Andrews universities (St Andrews triumphed). That match took place in the boardroom of fine-wine merchant Justerini & Brooks in Edinburgh's George Street. As a recent Edinburgh graduate and a past president of the Edinburgh University Wine Society, now plying my hand as a wine merchant with Justerini & Brooks, the organization of that event fell to me.

'Edinburgh's Wine Society vowed to get their own back. Addressed by notable speakers from Scotland's flourishing independent wine sector, it was perhaps the pool of talent on Edinburgh's doorstep that enabled its undergraduates to master the art of blind tasting, for they have dominated the competitions held by Pol Roger since, winning eight competitions to one so far.'

ABOVE Silhouette of the Edinburgh skyline. Pol Roger now sponsors the Oxford–Cambridge (since 1992), Edinburgh–St Andrews (since 2005) and Bristol–Bath (since 2013) blind wine-tasting competitions.

An interview with
JANET SCOTT

WORCESTER COLLEGE, OXFORD, m.2002

Dr Janet Scott is a clinical lecturer in Pharmacology and Infectious Disease at the University of Liverpool.

LEFT Bill Gunn MW with Janet Scott at the 2006 match.

'There is something about having to be openly wrong such a lot of the time when training that allows you to get to know and trust one another.'

'I first tasted fine wine in the early 1990s, as a result of a walking accident in the hills above the Margaret River in Western Australia. I had cut myself on vegetation, and wandered into a vineyard looking for a place to wash my leg. I tended to drink Jacobs Creek then, even in the Margaret River, but in this vineyard I had the most amazing taste of a 1990 Leeuwin Estate Art Series Chardonnay, and was shown around a collection of modern art. In Belgium some years later, I attended my first wine tasting in the British Embassy: a "blindfolded" competition (red, white or rosé), in aid of Comic Relief. The wine tasted quite revolting, so I put down rosé – was right and thus randomly won my first wine competition. By the time I applied to study medicine at Oxford, I had developed an interest in wine, and tried the local wine wherever I travelled (which was widely).

'Being new to Oxford and in the insular world of medicine, it was difficult to know which societies to join. The freshers' fair happened six weeks into our course, so medics basically couldn't go. However, having moved my wine rack into the graduate house, a flat mate suggested I join the Oxford University Wine Circle (OUWC). I wanted a hobby that would not detract too much from my studies. Since I had a tendency to run things and be competitive, I thought the OUWC was a) already running itself nicely, so I needn't get involved and b) couldn't possibly be competitive. But in the winter of 2006 I found myself captain of the blind-tasting team, with a competition within weeks of my finals!

'During my membership from 2002 to 2008, the OUWC ran blind tasting, although I assisted in splitting up the two societies (the Oxford Blind-Tasting Society now takes its membership from the whole of the university) which I hope has strengthened both. When I first competed in 2004, blind tasting was open to OUWC members, but not known about or open to others. Despite how much of a beginner I was, I was initially chosen for

the team simply because there was nobody else. When I took over from Yohan Graham (St Benet's) as co-captain for 2006 (with Rob Hayward, Brasenose), I made a conscious effort to broaden participation.

'I was also a member of Bacchus from 2004 to 2008. OUWC was more expensive to join and restricted its number of members, but all members could potentially attend all events. Bacchus did not restrict its membership, but its tastings were often booked out, and membership did not guarantee a place. Bacchus was the younger of the two societies, and rumoured to have been set up by disgruntled students who felt the Wine Circle was elitist. I was a member of both, and enjoyed both.

'I made a big effort during freshers' week in 2005–06. As we were not allowed to give away wine inside the freshers' fair, we hired a table inside the Oxford Union and had a stall instead, next to the queue for Oxford Union membership. Jancis Robinson MW gave me over a case of assorted wines she'd been tasting and finished with – all of it open with one glass out of it. It was mostly Riesling. The stall attracted a good few people who later became members – one of whom was Sarah Knowles (Regent's). Sarah claimed to drink principally Bacardi Breezers at the time, but tried some Riesling since it was free. It was apparently pretty good. Sarah got top score for Oxford (second overall in the competition) four months later, and top taster at Pol Roger in the summer competition against the French – at which point she conceded to herself that she might be quite good at it. She is now working as a wine buyer and writing her MW dissertation. In freshers' week, we also held a free beginners wine tasting – with a huge attendance – with wine donated from Pol Roger. And we revamped the rules for competing – not only to open up the team to those outside of the OUWC, but to ensure that eligibility to compete be based on Blues rules, regarding official and active student status in a recognized course at a university college.

'I was the only woman competing for Oxford in 2004, and in 2006 there were two of us. I never felt discriminated against – it was simply that more men came along to training; I do not know why. When I competed in France in summer 2006 against the Université Paris Dauphine, only three of us had to compete – and the by then appointed 2007 captain Piers Barclay (Queen's) chose me and Sarah Knowles to join him. The (all-male) French team members were surprised that "les filles" were the ones competing. And it was the same in a follow up competition held in the Médoc at Château Lafite. It seems that French women, despite an honorable history of female French winemakers, may suffer from more discrimination than we do in the UK.

'As captain, I actively encouraged anybody interested to come to blind-tasting sessions. Wines were paid for through tickets (£5 a head) – which could be a struggle for students – and donated by wine merchants who were former blind tasters: James Simpson MW (Pol Roger), Jasper Morris MW (Berry Bros. & Rudd), and Mark Savage MW (Savage Selection). Theo Sloot of the Oxford Wine Company was great, and we practised by participating in the Summertown Wine Café regular tastings – as blind as possible. We met at least once a week with a "tutor" – an ex-member or prior captain, wine merchant, and often our coach (and source of encouragement and inspiration) Hanneke Wilson.

'We used a regularly updated crib sheet – on what different wines are supposed to taste like – and exercises from Jancis Robinson's *Wine-Tasting Workbook*. Hugh Johnson's *World Atlas of Wine* was also helpful for beginners. We tasted anything we could get our hands on, but college cellars were largely closed to us: Old World, New World – Odd World (Tenerife, anyone?!). I used a technique that Jasper Morris favoured, which we called "to Jasper the wines" – i.e., look at them all, smell them all, take notes; reorder the wine in lightest to darkest before tasting, re-smell, and taste. Try not to jump to conclusions.

'In 2003 Britain joined the USA in the second Iraq war; then there was "Make Poverty History". There was also a permanent protest against the animal research house that was being built in Oxford at the time. However, compared to the University of Glasgow, where I'd been previously, politically Oxford seemed a bit tame. Maybe I had mellowed. From Glasgow (where I lived upstairs from a member of the PLO), I remember the street party when Thatcher resigned, pro-Cuban revolution ceilidhs, the Iranian opposition in exile, poll tax marches and sitting on the Glasgow flight at Heathrow while the IRA threatened to mortar attack the runway singing "I belong to Glasgow" and drinking something alcoholic from a rugby trophy that was being passed round.

'The amount I spend on wine has gone up a lot as a result of blind tasting, and I am more specific in the wine I want to drink and the age at which I want to drink it. I have grown to like Alsace Riesling, in particular, and also Gewurztraminer. I like classic French wines. I still drink Leeuwin Estate, and like Hamilton Russell Pinot Noir and Chardonnay, which is less hit or miss than Burgundy and the higher end South African Vergelegen. I have been utterly spoiled for sweet wines, too. Oddly the one wine which has really stuck with me from my university years is Sherry from Javier Hidalgo, not a blind-tasting wine

admittedly, but I always have the Oloroso, Amontillado and PX in the house – it has its own rack.

'Solid friendships were made during blind tasting. There is something about having to be openly wrong such a lot of the time when training that allows you to get to know and trust one another.'

TOP American oak barrels discovered in Bordeaux by Will Pearce.
CENTRE A close match in 2006. Oxford won 557 to 542.
BELOW Co-captains Janet Scott and Rob Hayward (right).

An interview with DAVID BEALL

FITZWILLIAM COLLEGE, CAMBRIDGE, m.2010

David Beall is from Missoula, Montana, USA. He graduated from the University of Montana and was commissioned as a second lieutenant in the US Army in 2002. He is currently a serving US Army officer, with over ten years of service, including deployments to Iraq and Afghanistan. He has been awarded the Bronze Star three times and received the Purple Heart for combat wounds.

'Previously I had been surrounded by soldiers dedicated to the service of their nation and the protection of a way of life. Now I was among a dedicated group devoted to the celebration and appreciation of wine, one of the true, great joys of that way of life.'

'I've spent more than three years of my life deployed to Iraq and Afghanistan as an officer in the US Army, during which time it was forbidden for soldiers to consume alcohol. I have always enjoyed wine, but it was after returning from my second deployment to Iraq when I really started to develop a love for it. A group of fellow army officers and I would get together every other week and go out to dinner at one of the finer restaurants in Anchorage, Alaska (often Orso, Saks Café or the Southside Bistro), where we were based. For the previous 15 months we had been living in a camp besieged by mortars and rockets, going out on missions where our vehicles were hit by roadside bombs, and losing friends in combat. What kept us going was a dedication to our mission, but, more importantly, a comradeship and dedication to one another – a refusal to let each other down.

'Once we came back to America, the distractions of everyday life returned and we saw less of each other, but our biweekly dinners served as the continuity of our comradeship. The food was great, but the centrepiece of the table was always the wine. We would endlessly debate the merits of one bottle versus another, quite happy to embrace this new form of combat around the dinner table where there were no losers. Our favourites then were the wines of Tenuta dell'Ornellaia of Tuscany and Justin Winery of Paso Robles, California. Lively correspondence on the differences between the merits of Justin's Left Bank Bordeaux-style blend, Isoceles, and its Right Bank Bordeaux-style blend, Justification, still continue to this day, via Facebook and email.

'Following my deployment to Afghanistan, I arrived in Cambridge in the autumn of 2010, this time to face academics to read for a master of philosophy in the Department of Politics and International Studies, instead of facing al-Qaeda or the Taliban. In some respects my life was more spartan in Cambridge than Afghanistan: the bed in my college

ABOVE A bonnie bunch at Bonhams: Cambridge tasters from the 2005-2013 teams at the 60th anniversary reunion party in 2013. Kneeling: David Beall, James Hutchinson. Standing front row, left to right: Claire Novorol, Lionel Nierop, Lucy Yang, Jennifer Yen, Ellie Kim, Katherine Smith, Natasha Redcliffe, Gareth Powell, Rosalynne Watt and Mark Barber. Standing back row, left to right: Carlos del Cueto, Eric Denton, Vaiva Imbrasaite, Felix Nissen and John (Jack) Rose.

room was much smaller and the food made me reconsider the talents of military cooks forward-deployed to the far-flung reaches of the global war on terror. However, the variety and éclat of opportunity that Cambridge had to offer outshone any possible complaints. The most rewarding of all these opportunities was the Cambridge University Blind Wine-Tasting Society (CUBWTS).

'I first learned of the blind-tasting team from my friend Susi Varga Nagl (Brasenose). Susi was involved with blind tasting at Oxford in the early 1990s and told me about the match against Cambridge. Once in Cambridge I sought out CUBWTS and was determined to make the 2011 team. In addition to attending weekly society meetings, I trained on my own with a military discipline, studying material and drilling my tasting skills on every glass I encountered. Friends would deliver random glasses of wine when we went to pubs, and I would try to work out what they were. To my friends it was a party trick, but to me it was training.

'I found that my fellow teammates comprised a group not unlike the military units of my other life. Previously I had been surrounded by soldiers dedicated to the service of their nation and the protection of a way of life. Now I was among a dedicated group devoted to the celebration and appreciation of wine, one of the true, great joys of that way of life. Regardless, I was a part of a team of zealous individuals connected through a common exercise of a honed and disciplined passion.

'Following the completion of my degree, I stayed in Cambridge for both the army and wine. I work at RAF Molesworth for US Africa Command and have been the Cambridge University Wine Society president and trained the blind-tasting team in the evening since 2012. Team members frequently remark that my military side comes out during training; I don't tolerate many excuses, am methodical in training approaches and even sometimes (jokingly!) threaten push-ups for incorrect responses. The team is chosen by conducting two mock-varsity matches, and selecting the seven highest cumulative scorers as its members. So far, the Cambridge teams of the 2010

decade are typically comprised mostly of graduate students with roughly equal numbers of men and women. The team always exhibits a wide range of colleges and disciplines; for example, in 2011, each team member was from a different Cambridge college, and the disparate disciplines included genetics, physics, medieval history, conducting (music), theology and international relations.

'While my fatigues remain camouflaged in Cambridge, my progression from teetotal combat soldier to wine-tasting connoisseur is near complete. Perhaps the pour is mightier than the sword!'

JANCIS ROBINSON CALLED 2011
'The Trickiest Blind Tasting Ever'

Off-piste and obscure, the 2011 competition wines (from Lea & Sandeman) were chosen by Pol Roger's Cassidy Dart. Cambridge capped a three-year winning streak, 669 to 611.

Whites
Domaine Le Fay d'Homme 2008, Muscadet

Domaine Paul et Marie Jacqueson 2009
Bourgogne Aligoté

Château de Roquefort Clairette 2009
IGP Bouches du Rhône

Dönnhoff QbA Riesling 2009, Nahe

Rustenberg Roussanne 2010, Stellenbosch

Dom de l'Aujardière, Fié Gris 2009,
Vin de Pays de Loire

Reds
Cantina San Donaci Anticaia Primitivo 2009,
Salento

Domaine Rochette 2009, Regnié

Bodegas Docampo Mencía 2009, Ribeiro

Nittnaus, Kalk und Schiefer Blaufränkisch 2007,
Burgenland

Château des Tours 2007, Côtes du Rhône

Dom Joël Remy, Aux Fourneaux 2005
Savigny-lès-Beaune

ABOVE The 2011 match. Centre: David Beall and, on his left, Oxford captain, James Flewellen, top taster for 2011 and 2010.

JUDGES AND VIPS

O ft A-team judges, Hugh Johnson and Jancis Robinson MW (right), and special guest stars o'er the ages: David Orr (Château Latour), Bill Baker, Charles Metcalfe, Neal Martin (Wine-Journal.com), Anthony Hanson MW (Christie's) and Sebastian Payne MW (The Wine Society), John Harvey, and Jasper Morris MW. From Pol Roger, Hubert de Billy, Bill Gunn MW and James Simpson MW preside. Since 1992, judges have also included Lisa Barnard, John Avery MW, Nancy Gilchrist MW and Professor Stephen Elliott.

2013 VARSITY MATCH

ABOVE 2013 featured a Wine Press versus Trade tasting match [names page 256]. The trade team won – but journalist Anthony Rose collected the prize for top taster. From Pol Roger, Cassidy Dart organized, while Laurent d'Harcourt presented the trophy.

BLIND TASTING TODAY:
From Buenos Aires to Beijing

by EDWARD RAGG

SELWYN COLLEGE, CAMBRIDGE m.1999 and

FONGYEE WALKER

THE QUEENS' COLLEGE, CAMBRIDGE m.1999

Dr Edward Ragg and his wife, Fongyee Walker,
both former presidents of CUBWTS, are co-authors
of the CUBWTS Guide to Blind Wine Tasting.
In 2007, they co-founded Dragon Phoenix Wine
Consulting in Beijing, a pioneer in WSET education
in mainland China. Edward is also an associate
professor at Tsinghua University and a poet. Fongyee
is mainland China's most qualified wine educator
and a Mandarin-English wine translation specialist.

'The *Cambridge University Guide to Blind Wine Tasting* was first compiled in 2004 (with revisions in 2006, 2010 and 2012). The year 2004 was a pivotal one in the recent history of the varsity blind wine-tasting match because it saw the return of Cambridge to victory, from the relative doldrums of consistent losses against Oxford over a number of years. The competition in the late 1990s and early 2000s often saw Cambridge neck-and-neck with Oxford at the half-way stage (after the white wine tasting); but, crucially, the light Blues would then lose by up to a 100 points on the red wines (20 possible points are allotted to each wine). Clearly, something had to be done to reverse the tide of Cambridge defeats, other than merely reiterating the mantra of 'more practice on reds, more practice on reds'. The Guide was thus born as a reference tool, although the real impetus for winning the varsity match came from those individuals who committed themselves to intensive and regular blind-tasting training.

'Since 2004, the varsity match has been much more of a closely contested "match", with standards in blind tasting higher than ever before. It is not necessarily that the match has attracted better tasters, but that a broader group of individuals, from both genders, are having a go at blind tasting, often with a degree of systematic rigour that has stemmed from the general rise in wine education, most certainly influenced by the WSET. Importantly, these tasters also come from a wider range of socio-economic and ethnic backgrounds than ever before, bringing fresh vocabularies and perspectives to the business of discussing wine blind.

'On writing this introduction, the sun is just bathing the recently built high-rises and shopping malls of Beijing's new urban landscape; and we will shortly witness yet another bunch of eager Chinese students clamouring at our doors for WSET training (our primary focus being WSET Levels 1, 2, and 3) – 2012 was the first year in which a WSET Level 4 diploma course was offered in mainland China, via WSET London in conjunction with Dragon Phoenix Wine Consulting. The rise in demand for formal wine education – not only in China, but across the globe – has run parallel with changes in the wine industry over the last decade and a half. It is no surprise that interest in wine has grown so rapidly in so many places when, due to advances in modern winemaking, the quality and consistency of wines has improved all over the world; resulting in a dizzying array of expressions and styles. Undoubtedly, this makes the practice of blind tasting all the more demanding. As any MW or WSET diploma student will tell you, assessing a wine's origin in particular is now harder than it's ever been.

'Thus, as new generations come to the art of blind-tasting, from Buenos Aires to Beijing – a good number of them Oxbridge-educated – the time is nigh to throw out some of the preoccupations that used to apply to a British, or at least more "traditional", context for assessing wine. When we first began teaching blind-tasting techniques in the late 1990s and early 2000s at Cambridge, distinguishing between specific Old World wines versus their New World counterparts was comparatively easy: Cabernet blends, for example, from Western Australia – typified by distinct herbaceousness, even an excess of that green bell-pepper character – were plainly distinguishable from the 'mint' of Cabernets from South Australia's Coonawarra, the less fruity and more savoury character of Bordeaux's Cabernet blends or the rich, voluptuous bodies and extraction of many Californian Cabernets. This made it possible for us to circulate a clear-cut list of "Bankers"; that is, of relatively easy-to-recognize wines that any card-carrying blind taster would "learn" and practise spotting.

'Today, with certain oaked Chardonnays from the Mornington Peninsula or Yarra Valley, both in Victoria, Australia, being much closer in style to some oaked Chardonnays from Burgundy's Côte de Beaune, the distinctions between these wines are much harder to detect (note also the 'Chablis-style' wines now coming out of Victoria).

'To work the other way, consider, also, just how "New World" in character have become many of the wines of the South of France, central and southern Italy, the central and southern parts of the Iberian Peninsula, Greece and elsewhere in the Mediterranean (and even, much to the chagrin of some, in more "traditional" regions such as Bordeaux). European winemakers have responded to consumer demand, offering wines with fruitier profiles and the kind of near instant drinkability that was initially only delivered by Australia and Chile.

'Indeed, gone are the days when one could confidently say that a Marlborough Sauvignon Blanc would definitely be packed with passion fruit, guava and grass, with a plumper, less acidic body and a more generous lashing of alcohol than would ever be found on "Old World" examples (say, from Sancerre). New Zealand "Savvy" is now produced in a bewildering range of styles: with lees-stirring, experimentation with new and old oak and differential grape-picking times all contributing to wider expressions of the varietal.

Bankers

'Thankfully, though, there are still "Bankers" out there: reliable, benchmark wines that can help the blind-taster orient herself, from Alsace Gewurztraminer to Barossa Valley Shiraz to generic Beaujolais. "Bankers" studied in the context of the varsity match have traditionally been the kinds of wines that appear regularly in the competition, with only a handful of the 12 wines in the contest being considered more "unusual". But the "Bankers" are evolving. Consider how distinctive and more widely drunk Argentinean Torrontes is now or how widely recognized are the signature dried-fruit notes of Californian Zinfandel (notwithstanding the range of styles that exists with the likes of Zin).

'What may help today's blind taster is to think less in terms of an "Old World" versus "New World" paradigm and to focus more on the types of climate and the latitudes of grape-growing regions in the northern and southern hemispheres (and how these relate to wine styles). A cool-climate Australian Riesling from Tasmania, for example, expresses more in common with a cool-climate Mosel Riesling from Germany than a medium-bodied, much fruitier Clare Valley Riesling from South Australia. Likewise, Cabernet Sauvignon from the maritime vineyards of Uruguay has more in common with Médoc Cabernet blends than with the Cabernet-based wines of Argentina's Mendoza, and so forth.

'But, if it has never been more difficult to blind taste wine with a view to detecting origin, it must also be said that this is one of the less important reasons why one might blind taste wine in the first place. Certainly,

FACING PAGE Edward Ragg and Fongyee Walker at the CUDOS Annual Dinner, 2002. ABOVE The winning Cambridge team 2005. From left to right: Ainsley Mayhew Seers, Robert Fenster, Fongyee Walker, Patrice Noyelle of Pol Roger, Benjamin Drew (captain), Lionel Nierop, Aidan Craig and James Kirkbride (reserve).

identifying a wine and its origin builds confidence in putting together a mental map of the classic wines of the world and how these taste (in theory and in practice for the individual blind taster). But it is the discipline of – and lessons learned from – blind tasting that really count. All of us, however experienced, have made the mistake of taking a quick swirl, sniff and preliminary taste, prematurely mentally pronouncing what we think a wine to be, then fitting our analysis and tasting notes to the particular wine we have in mind. This is a road to disaster in blind tasting effectively.

'Knowing your grape varietals, wine regions and what to expect of specific styles as they are affected by climate, viticulture and winemaking are all-important; as is tasting systematically in the right environment and with those with enough humility and experience to keep blind tasting both informative and fun! Wines give us all sorts of clues as to where they come from, how they have been made and what their current condition and drinkability are. Indeed, it is only perhaps by tasting blind – without the influences of scores, labels, prices and opinions – that we can hone our tasting skills and achieve some degree of objectivity in assessing a wine's characteristics and quality.

'As Michael Broadbent MW deftly put it: "Tasting completely blind, without any hint of what it might be, is the most useful and salutary discipline that any self-respecting taster can be given. It is not infrequently the most humiliating". Without taking the plunge of blind tasting, one risks only ever floating on the sea of wine without discovering the remarkable topographies of colour, aroma and flavour that rise to the surface to delight us, in some cases for years to come; irrespective of where we come from.'

Overleaf is an abbreviated list of classic "Bankers". When blind tasting a wine consider the balance of all its characteristics, and the length and finish of a wine.

GRAPE VARIETY Country, region: sub-regions	APPEARANCE/ COLOUR	NOSE/KEY AROMAS which may translate to flavours on palate	PALATE weight/body, acidity, alcohol, residual sugar; notes leading to identification
RIESLING **Germany** Mosel-Saar-Ruwer; Rhine: Rheingau, Rheinhessen, Pfalz	Often spritz. Pale lemon-green (young); darkens to deep gold with age.	**Highly aromatic, fruity and floral:** harvested in cooler climates green apple and grape aromas lead, while in more moderate climates white peach may become dominant; floral: honey, petrol/kerosene (with developing/older examples); mineral/flinty. Unoaked.	Light bodied (if dry or off-dry) with crisp, high acidity. Low to medium alcohol (Mosel 7–9%, Rheingau 10–12% abv, depending on style). Residual sugar often present, enhancing body, but high acidity moderates body (dry/'Trocken' examples also exist, and fine sweet wines from grapes with noble rot/botrytis, e.g. Beerenauslese).
France Alsace: Bas-Rhin, Haut-Rhin	Pale straw/lemon-green to green-gold; more golden with age or late harvest/SGN.	Green/red apple, lemon citrus, stone fruits; honey, petrol/kerosene (with developing/older examples). Unoaked.	Light to medium bodied with crisp, high acidity. Medium (sometimes high) alcohol (12–13.5% abv). Bone-dry or with residual sugar (styles vary). Fruitier, with more body than Mosel Rieslings.
Australia South Australia: Clare Valley, Eden Valley	Can have spritz. Pale to medium lemon-green (gold with age).	**Citrus, but more exotic:** lime, lemon freshener, tangerine, grapefruit; sherbet, mineral and petrol/kerosene (smoky, petrol note can even develop in younger examples). Unoaked.	More often medium bodied with racy, high acidity. Medium to high alcohol (can be 13%+ abv). Often totally dry. Fruit-forward wines, often with great ageing potential. Some off-dry examples now appearing!
SAUVIGNON BLANC **France**, Loire: Sancerre, Pouilly-Fumé (30–50° N latitude)	Very pale green.	**Highly aromatic, herbaceous cool climate character** (note: 'cat's pee' [Jancis Robinson]): light gooseberry or green apple fruit with grass, blackcurrant leaf, asparagus, nettle; flint, mineral. Usually unoaked (some Pouilly-Fumé wines may be lightly oaked).	Light to medium bodied with crisp, high acidity. Medium alcohol (12% abv). Very dry.
New Zealand South Island: Marlborough (30–50° S latitude)	Pale to medium green. Can have spritz.	**Fruit forward (typically less herbaceous than from the Loire):** Pungent with ripe guava, gooseberry, lime citrus, passion fruit and other tropical fruits; tomato leaves. Classic style is unoaked.	Light to medium bodied with crisp, medium to high acidity. Medium to high alcohol (13%+ abv). Effectively dry. Fruity. New styles can be leaner (Loire style); with lees (dead or residual yeast) influence; or even oak matured.
CHARDONNAY **France**, Burgundy (north to south): Chablis (cool climate) Côte de Beaune, Côte Chalonnaise and the Mâconnais (moderate climate)	Pale straw through to deep lemon, or gold (with oak and age).	**If unoaked (Chablis):** green apple and pear, cucumber, lemon citrus and mineral/stone/flint (sucking on a 'wet pebble' [Hugh Johnson] from a stream); (moderate climate) some white stone fruit (peach) and melon (Mâconnais). **If oaked (Côte de Beaune, Côte Chalonnaise):** savoury, cedar, clove spice, toast (French oak). With malolactic fermentation: cream/butter notes.	Light to full bodied (depending on style: use of oak and winemaking techniques – e.g. stirring in/ageing on lees adds creamy texture – enhances body). Generally medium acidity (but Chablis high acidity). Medium to high alcohol (12.5–14% abv). Dry.
Australia, Western Australia: Margaret River; South Australia: Adelaide Hills; New South Wales: Hunter Valley; **USA**, California: Napa Valley, Sonoma (Carneros, Russian River); **Chile**, Central Valley: Casablanca Valley	Deep lemon or gold.	Often ripe, tropical fruit – banana and pineapple in warmer climates – with vanilla, coconut, buttery oak (especially noticeable with American oak on California wines). French and/or American oak may be used; 'buttered popcorn' notes with malolactic fermentation.	Full bodied, medium-to-thick texture with medium acidity. High alcohol (can be 14% abv). Can smell sweet, but taste dry. Australia and other New World countries (particularly USA) now also produce more restrained styles with little to no oak, less malolactic and higher acidity; these Chardonnays are closer to white Burgundy styles.
VIOGNIER **France**, Northern Rhône (Condrieu); Languedoc-Roussillon (Pays d'Oc); **Australia**, South Australia; **Chile**, Central Valley	Medium to deep lemon or gold.	**Aromatic, peachy and floral:** fresh, tinned or dried peaches and apricots. Mostly unoaked or only lightly oaked. Sometimes floral (white flowers), perfumed. Condrieu may express minerality.	Medium to full bodied, 'fat' or oily texture, with usually low to medium acidity. Can have high alcohol (14%+ abv) with 'bitter almond' finish. Often confused with Gewurztraminer, but fruit characteristics are different and wines may also be oaked.
GEWURZTRAMINER **France** Alsace: Bas-Rhin, Haut-Rhin	Medium to deep gold; may have pinkish hue.	**Highly aromatic, perfumed:** lychee, roses/rosewater, orange blossom, orange peel, gingerbread, Turkish delight. Typically unoaked. Best drunk young, but some meat/ honey/nut aromas may develop with age.	Medium to full bodied: 'fat', at times syrupy texture; often distinct bitterness on finish. Low to medium acidity. Usually medium to high alcohol (13%+ abv). Smells sweet but tastes dry (apart from some with residual sugar, e.g. late harvest/Vendange Tardive and Sélection des Grains Nobles/SGN).

GRAPE VARIETY Country, region; sub-regions	APPEARANCE/ COLOUR	NOSE/KEY AROMAS which may translate to flavours on palate	PALATE weight/body, acidity, alcohol, residual sugar, tannins; notes leading to identification
GAMAY France Burgundy: Beaujolais	Bright purple or ruby; may have blue tinge.	Strawberry, raspberry, cherry; bubblegum or artificial fruit smell, e.g. bananas, if carbonic maceration (whole grape fermentation in CO2-rich environment prior to crushing). Basic Beaujolais style is unoaked, often chapralized (sugar added to unfermented grape must to increase alcohol).	Light (usually) to medium bodied. Medium to high acidity. Medium alcohol (12–13% abv). Dry. Low level of smooth tannins (in 'Cru' Beaujolais – select vineyards/villages – tannins may be higher; good for ageing, these wines, e.g. Morgon, Moulin-à-Vent, typically made without carbonic maceration). Fruit driven: generally drunk fresh and young.
PINOT NOIR France Burgundy: Côte de Nuits, Côte de Beaune	Pale to medium (can be deep) ruby.	Cool red fruits: raspberry (Beaune), strawberry, cherry (Nuits) (black fruits in ripe vintages). Can be gamey or metallic, red cabbage. Often perfumed, floral: violets. 'Barnyard' nose with oxidation/age: mushroom, leather, sous bois (undergrowth). Savoury French oak (cedar, spice).	Light (Beaune) to medium (Nuits) bodied. Medium to high acidity. Medium to high alcohol (grape can routinely produce 13.5% abv, especially with chaptalization). Dry. Low to medium silky tannins (some villages known for more overt tannin, e.g. Pommard).
PINOT NOIR New Zealand. NI: Martinborough; SI: Marlborough, Central Otago; USA, Oregon; California	Pale to medium (can be deep) ruby.	Exaggerated red fruit; may have vegetal characteristics, but seldom gamey; less delicate than Burgundy, can become jammy. Typically matured in French oak, thus spice.	Fuller bodied than Burgundy (but for cooler climate Oregon which produces Burgundy-style wines). Medium acidity (lower than Burgundy). High alcohol. Dry/off dry. Moderate tannins.
PINOTAGE South Africa, Stellenbosch	Purple.	Pungent: sharp vintage Cheddar, tar/burnt rubber; baked bananas/jammy fruit aromas; can be oaked (usually French).	Typically full bodied with high acidity. High alcohol. Dry. Moderate tannins. Generally drunk young; some oaked wines suitable for ageing.
TEMPRANILLO Spain Rioja: Rioja Alta, Rioja Alavesa, Rioja Baja	Medium ruby; with age, bricking at rim to garnet (e.g. Reservas, Gran Reservas).	Ripe/warm red fruits: strawberry, cranberry, redcurrant; chocolate, tobacco leaf, white pepper. Sweet vanilla and coconut notes from American oak in traditional examples: overall 'sweet spice oak' nose.	Medium bodied with medium acidity. Medium to high alcohol (can be 13.5%+ abv). Perception of 'sweetness' of flavour, but dry. Low to medium, smooth tannins, but can be bitter (may pick up further wood tannins in cases of prolonged maturation in cask).
NEBBIOLO (Barolo and Barbaresco) Italy, Piemonte	Medium red; brick rim with barrel age.	Tar and violets (also roses); may be aged in old or new (more pronounced aroma) oak; liquorice; vegetal notes with age.	Full bodied with high acidity. High alcohol. Dry. Moderate to high, coarse, tannins.
CABERNET SAUVIGNON France, Bordeaux, Left Bank: Médoc; Haut-Médoc; Graves (Péssac-Léognan).	Medium to dark purple or ruby (with age, garnet).	In youth: blackcurrant/cassis and other black fruits; savoury French oak, wood and pencil shavings, cedar. With age: expresses less primary black fruit; complex with cigar box, leather, game, vegetal qualities.	Full bodied. High acidity (with tannin, provides backbone for significant ageing). Typically medium alcohol (12.5–13% abv). Dry. Can be very tannic in youth with angular/spiky/grainy tannins (tannins soften with age). Blended with Merlot to soften harsh acidity/tannins.
SYRAH Australia, WA: Margaret River; SA: Coonawarra; New Zealand, NI: Hawke's Bay; USA, California: Napa Valley, Sonoma	Dark purple or ruby.	Mint/eucalyptus, blackcurrant leaf, herb aromas/flavours accompany black fruit (cherry, blackcurrant). In the US, green bell-pepper character in cooler regions. Oak.	Full bodied. Lower/medium acidity. Medium to high alcohol. Dry. High levels of soft, ripe tannins.
MERLOT France, Bordeaux, Right Bank: St-Emilion, Pomerol; USA, California; Chile, Central Maipo Valley	Medium to dark purple; garnet with age.	Cool climate: red fruit/plum, mint; warm/very ripe vintages: black fruit/plum, fruitcake, spice, chocolate; green stalks (young tannins). Cigar box, cedar notes with age. Typically aged in new French oak.	Full bodied with lower (warmer climate) to medium (cooler climate) acidity. Medium to high alcohol. Moderate, gentle, inky, smooth tannins. Dry. 'Softer' than Left Bank Bordeaux wines. Blended with Cabernet Sauvignon to add acidity/tannins for structure.
SYRAH France, Northern Rhône: Côte-Rôtie, St-Joseph, Hermitage, Crozes-Hermitage, Cornas	Medium to dark purple or ruby.	Soft, or dried (Hermitage), black fruits: blackberry, black cherry. Cracked black pepper (Cornas)! May be leathery or vegetal notes; rubber; 'salty bacon'. Côte-Rôtie often shows floral aromas.	Medium to full bodied with medium to high acidity. Medium to high alcohol. Dry. Medium to high, supple, tannins. Can be very peppery on the palate. May be oaked (new or old French oak) or unoaked depending on appellation, producer and price.
SHIRAZ (same grape as Syrah) Australia, South Australia: Clare Valley, Barossa Valley, McLaren Vale	Very dark in colour; inky purple to black.	Very ripe, often cooked/dried, black fruits: also blueberry. Sweet, powerful smell. Some spice, e.g. cinnamon, liquorice (not peppery like Northern Rhône Syrah). Chocolate/mocha. Eucalyptus/menthol may be present. Sweet vanilla oak (American); French oak also used.	Full bodied. Lower/medium acidity. High alcohol (may exceed 15%+ abv). Intense 'sweetness' of ripe fruit, but dry on palate. Medium to high chunky, velvety, tannins. Barossa Shiraz displays more dried fruit aromas and a 'beefier' style than McLaren Vale which has sweeter/ripe fruit notes. Clare Valley wines have less bright fruit than McLaren Vale.
ZINFANDEL (same grape as Primitivo) USA, California: Sonoma (Dry Creek and Alexander Valleys – the 'Zin Zone')	Deep purple or ruby.	Dried black, bramble fruits: prune, cherry, blackberry, mulberry, damson; vanilla/toasted American oak and/or French oak (cinnamon/clove); also chocolate/mocha notes.	Full bodied. Lower/medium acidity. Can be very high alcohol (15.5%+ abv). Dry, with rounded, medium to high tannins. Top wines have intense dried 'sweet' black fruits, with plenty of oak and extract.

INDEX

Page numbers in *italics* denotes an illustration

PICTURE CREDITS

The publishers would like to thank all the individuals and the various Oxford and Cambridge colleges and societies with help with sourcing images for this book. Every effort has been made to trace the rights holders to obtain the necessary permissions. We would be pleased to insert the appropriate acknowledgment in subsequent editions.

Acumen Publishing 239
Frederika Adam 4 above, 6 below, 89 left, 227, 228, 229, 230 below, 256
Advertising Archives 65 all
Alamy/Alex Segre 187 above
All Souls College, Oxford, By Permission of the Warden and Fellows, 23 below both, 156 above
Anova Books 68, 69 above
Mimi Avery 83 above, 84 both, 85 right, 85 below right
The Barbarians Rugby Football Club 25 below
Fiona Barlow MW 167 all
Lisa Barnard 176
Pascal Bates 193 both, 197, 199 both, 201, 204
David Beall 210 centre
Greg Bennett 181, 183, 184

Bern's Steak House, Tampa, Florida/Amy Pezzicara 9, 11, 12
Bristol Record Office, Harveys of Bristol Archives 15 above, 27, 31, 64 above, 92, 146 below
Rupert Britton 208, 210 above left and right
Caius College, Cambridge, By Permission of the Master and Fellows 63 (photographer Anthony Barrington-Brown)
Cambridge Evening News 128, 139 below
Cambridge University Wine & Food Society (CUWFS) 44
Cambridge University Débouché Oenological Society (CUDOS) 248
Champagne Bollinger 54 both
Christie's Images/The Bridgeman Art Library/Private Collection 18 below, 54 left
Christ Church, Oxford, By Kind Permission of the Governing Body, 47

Christ's College, Cambridge, By Permission of the Master and Fellows, 22 both, 30 above
Oz Clarke 108 left
Robert Clement-Jones 127 below
Cloudy Bay 178
Andrew Comrie-Picard 220
Corbis 42 right (Hulton-Deutsch Collection), 134 (Bettmann)
Lord Crathorne KCVO 7 above, 68 above, 69 below, 72, 73 both, 74 all, 75 both, 76 both, 77 both
Sir James Cropper KCVO 66 above, 70
The Daily Telegraph 145 above right, 224 top right, 243 below (Eleanor Bentall)
Viscount Davidson 44, 49 right, 200 top
Ronnie Davidson-Houston 61

Tony Doggart 62 above
The Elizabeth Restaurant/Frederika Adam 89 left
Penny Elliott 103 above, 105 above, 127 above, 131 left,
    135, 159 both, 174
Emmanuel College, Cambridge, By Permission of the
    Master and Fellows, 45 below
Coralie Evison 205
Evening Standard/JAK 109
Sir Ewen Fergusson 29 left
Financial Times 199 above
Christopher FitzGerald 7 below, 85 below left, 86, 87
The Fitzwilliam Museum, Cambridge 105 below
Tim Forse 128, 151
Friends of Wine 13
Château Gruaud-Larose 162 below
James Hardy 211 (tie)
Harveys Cellars/Sian Tudor Photography 15 below
Hedonism Wines, Mayfair 67 right
Andrew Holroyd 154, 156 below, 157
Luke Hughes 103 below left and right, 132, 143
The Institute of Masters of Wine 169
International Wine & Food Society (IWFS) 16, 21, 30
    below, 32 both, 33 both, 36, 50, 53, 56 centre, 66
    below, 83 below
The Rt Hon the Lord King of Bridgwater 45 above
King's College, Cambridge, By Permission of the Master
    and Fellows, 60 (photographer Edward Leigh)
Gavin Knight 67 left
Simon Kverndal 14, 19, 161, 162 above, 163, 164
    both, 166, 180
Château Lafite 62 below
Robin Lane 142
Albert Lee 248
Kingsley Liu 94, 144, 145 above left and right
O W Loeb 56 above and below, 57
James Long 42 left
Will Lyons 240, 241
Rosie MacGregor 64 below, 107, 108 right, 111 both, 113
    all, 114, 117 above, 119 right, 125, 126 below
Magnum Images (Bruce Davidson) 51

Château Margaux 26
Lord Marks QC 136 both
John Marks 139 below
Christie Marrian 130, 131 above right and below right,
    133 right
Mark Martin 235
Dr Robert Mather 139 above
Charles Metcalfe 110
Moët et Chandon 120
Charles Moore 99 both, 100, 101
Sarah Morphew Stephen MW 98 left
Jasper Morris MW 148
National Portrait Gallery 24
    (Anne-Katrin Purkiss); 46 (Hay Wrightson Ltd)
The New York Times/Michael Klein 188
Newark Advertiser 102
Antony Northrop 119 left, 123, 126 above, 137
The Oxford Mail 94, 139 above
Oxford University Blind Tasting Society 223
Oxfordshire County Council/Thomas Photos 58 both,
    80, 91 right
Peter Palmer 206, 211 above, 211 (tie), 214
Victor and Hazel Patterson 38
David Peake 52
Charles Pendred 149
Claudia Pendred 93 below, 152, 153
David Peppercorn MW 18, 78
Peterhouse, Cambridge, By Permission of the Master
    and Fellows, 23 above
Pol Roger 43 (all), 71, 200 (newsletter), 202, 203, 224 top
    left, 243 below, 246 4th row right;
    /Eleonore de Bonneval 244 both; / Will Clarkson 224
    centre and below, 246 3rd row left and right; /John
    Deehan 4 below, 91 left, 177, 187 both, 198, 200 below
    right, 209, 212, 213 both, 215, 221, 222, 226, 230
    left, 232, 236, 238, 242, 243 centre, 246 top, 2nd row
    all, 3rd row left and right below, 4th row left, 249; /
    Sebastien Dehesdin 5, 210 below left and right, 246 3rd
    row right above; / Michael Heath 1, 82;
Christopher Purvis 117 below, 121, 122, 149

Private Eye 97 left
Jonathan Ray 157 centre right
Domaines Barons de Rothschild 129
Nicholas de Rothschild 124 both
David Rutherford 20 (all)
The Rt Hon Sir Timothy Sainsbury 39
St Anne's College Oxford, By Permission of the Master and
    Fellows, 90
St Catharine's College, Cambridge 105 below
Mark Savage MW 115
Janet Scott 243
Scottish Rugby Union 25 above
Jennifer Segal 6 above left and right, 234, 245
Jeremy Seysses 211 (tie), 216, 217, 218, 219 both
Robin Scott-Martin 179
Scottish Rugby Union 25 above
Michael Shires 116
James Simpson MW 170 both, 171, 172, 211 (tie)
Sotheby's 79
Stacey International 49 left
Sarah Stewart-Brown 96, 97 right, 98 right, 106 both
Tessa Strickland 158 all, 160
The Sunday Times 98 right
Serena Sutcliffe MW 233
The Times 144
Trinity College, Cambridge, By permission of the Master
    and Fellows, 70, 133 left, 175
Ed Tulley 211 (tie)
Lynne Turner Stokes 141
Prue Waugh 2 (photo John Chillingworth), 10
Paul White 186, 195 both
Anthony Whittaker 211 (tie)
Jeremy Williams 190, 191 all, 192
Dr Hanneke Wilson 231
Arabella Woodrow MW 93 above, 145 below, 146 above,
    147
Worcester College, Oxford, By Permission of the Master and
    Fellows, 40
Yapp Brothers 140

ACKNOWLEDGEMENTS

It has been a privilege to meet everyone involved with this project. Although I had a grandfather in the wine trade, I became aware of blind tasting in 2005 as a member of the Oxford University Wine Circle, through which I first met James Simpson MW at a tasting of Pol Roger Champagne. This book has come about through his tremendous support, and that of everyone at Pol Roger: Cassidy Dart, Freya Miller, James Clark, Paul Graham, Bill Gunn MW, Elizabeth Vaughan, Nick James, Patrice Noyelle, Laurent d'Harcourt and Hubert de Billy and family; as well as from the enthusiasm of its contributors, some of whom feature more or less overtly throughout, all of whom deserve special thanks (not least, for some exceptional bottles shared along the way). A very big thank you to Jancis Robinson OBE MW for her elegant essay, leads and introductions, to Hugh Johnson OBE for his stylish contributions, and to Oz Clarke (with whom we shared a 1948 Château Mouton-d'Armailhacq – his last bottle from his first case of wine) for his enormous spirit and animated entry. Thank you to Prue, Jamie and Harriet Waugh; and to everyone at Anova Books: Robin Wood, Polly Powell, David Proffit, Charlotte Selby, Dicken Goodwin, Georgina Hewitt, Welmoet Wartena, Jamie Ambrose and especially Fiona Holman. David Peppercorn MW noted, 'Wine can be a great social cement. It brings people together and it keeps people together.' Thank you to everyone in the Oxford and Cambridge varsity blind wine-tasting match community.

Additional acknowledgements to those who have been helpful in the making of this book: Andrea Warren (IWFS); Mimi Avery (Averys of Bristol); Berry Bros. & Rudd: Simon Berry, Rebecca Lamont and Ann McHale MW; Lutyens Restaurant; Edward Ragg, Fongyee Walker (Cantab) and Frederika Adam (Oxon.) for input on the blind wine-tasting 'Bankers'; Wine & Spirit Trade Association (WSTA); International Wine & Spirit Research (IWSR); from Cambridge alumni offices/publications: Nathalie Walker, Morven Knowles, Eloise Hays, Jacqueline Cox, Rachel Gardner and Anna Kay. From Oxford Today alumni magazine: Dr Richard Lofthouse and Janet Avison; Dr Richard Wayne (Christ Church); Andrew Thomas (St Peter's College); James Flewellen (Oxon.); Natasha Redcliffe (Cantab); Bern's Steak House; Jonathan Kelly; Gavin Knight; Neil Beckett (The World of Fine Wine magazine); Robert M Parker Jr.

For further resources on blind wine tasting we suggest the many books, websites/blogs, courses and programmes produced by members of the varsity match community whose names appear throughout the book, including members of the 2013 Wine Press and Trade teams; photos on page 247: (Press, left to right) Matthew Jukes, Anthony Rose, Will Lyons, Joe Wadsack, Oz Clarke, Peter Richards MW, Michael Schuster (and Patrice Noyelle of Pol Roger); (Trade, left to right) Christopher Delalonde MS, (Patrice Noyelle of Pol Roger), George Scratcherd, Arabella Morris MW, Jasper Morris MW, Gearoid Devaney MS and Jon Pedley MW.

The lists of team names by decade may not be comprehensive. If you have been part of the varsity blind wine-tasting match extended family and your name does not appear in the book, please write to us at varsitybook@polroger.co.uk.

EDITOR'S BIOGRAPHY

Jennifer Segal, a former member of the Oxford University Wine Circle, has worked in publishing, film and media with established companies and entrepreneurial ventures, across print and digital formats and platforms. She shares time between New York and London where she directed the development and sale of a digital media application and business on behalf of BBC Worldwide. She has an MBA from the University of Oxford and in 2006 was awarded seed funding and a fellowship to the Royal Society for the encouragement of Arts, Manufactures and Commerce (RSA) for first-place in the Oxford Entrepreneurs university-wide business pitch and plan competition. Prior to the UK she began her career in New York working with editor Tina Brown, Miramax and Hearst Corporation, and with hotelier André Balazs. She now develops and markets content via her boutique agency JSNewMedia.

First published in 2013 by PAVILION BOOKS
10 Southcombe Street, London W14 ORA

An imprint of Anova Books Company Ltd
www.anovabooks.com

Design and layout copyright © 2013 Anova Books
    Company Ltd
Text copyright © 2013 Pol Roger UK Ltd and Jennifer
Segal/JSNewMedia

All rights reserved. No part of this work may be reproduced or utilized in any form or by any means, electronic or mechanical, including photocopying, recording, or by any information storage and retrieval system, without the prior permission of the publishers.

ISBN: 9781909108288

A CIP catalogue record for this book is available from
the British Library

10 9 8 7 6 5 4 3 2 1

Reproduction by Dot Gradations Ltd, UK
Printed by G. Canale & C. SpA, Italy

Commissioning editor: Jennifer Segal
Managing editor: Fiona Holman
Designer: Welmoet Wartena